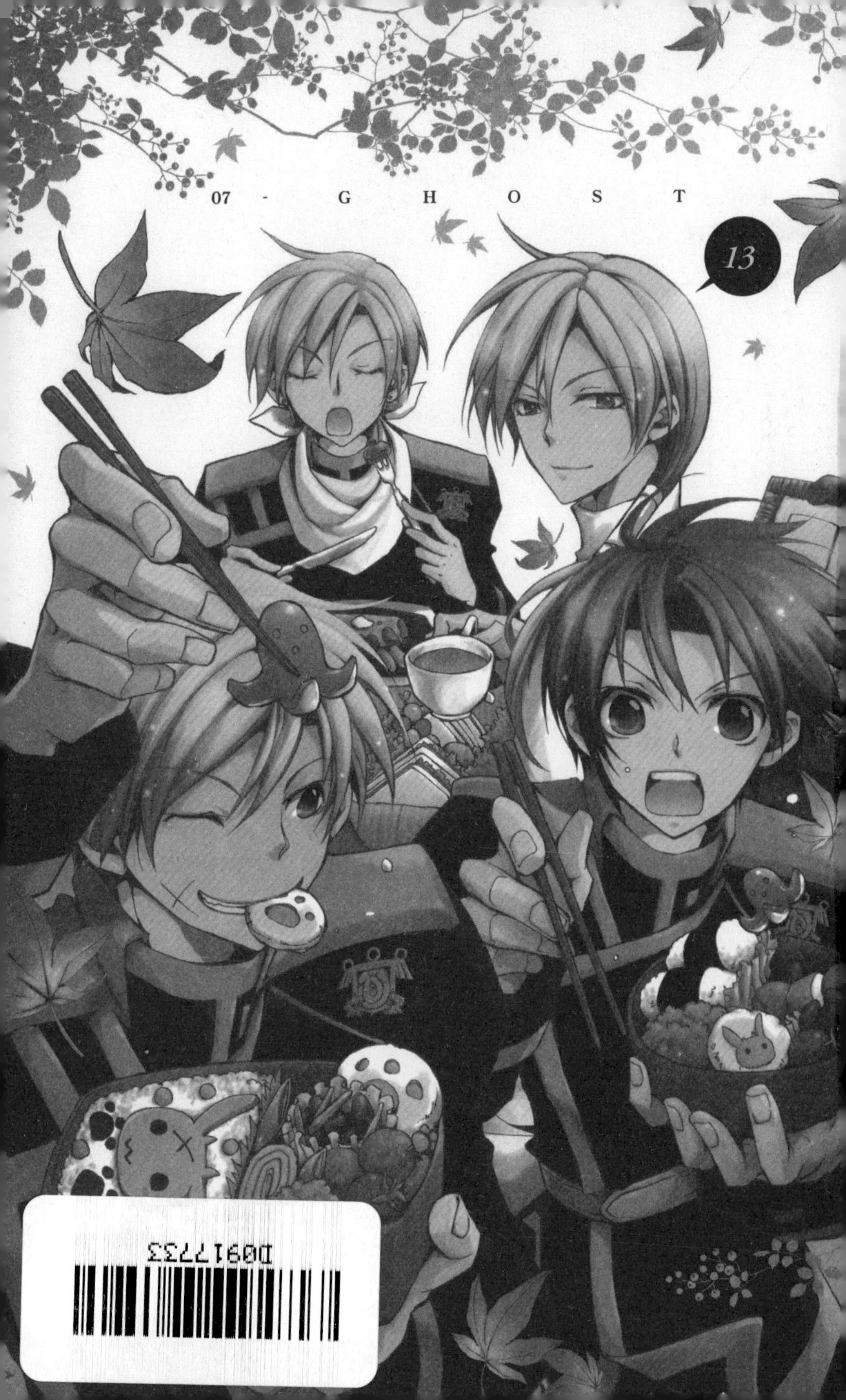
07 - G H O S T
13

-GHOST

ONTENTS

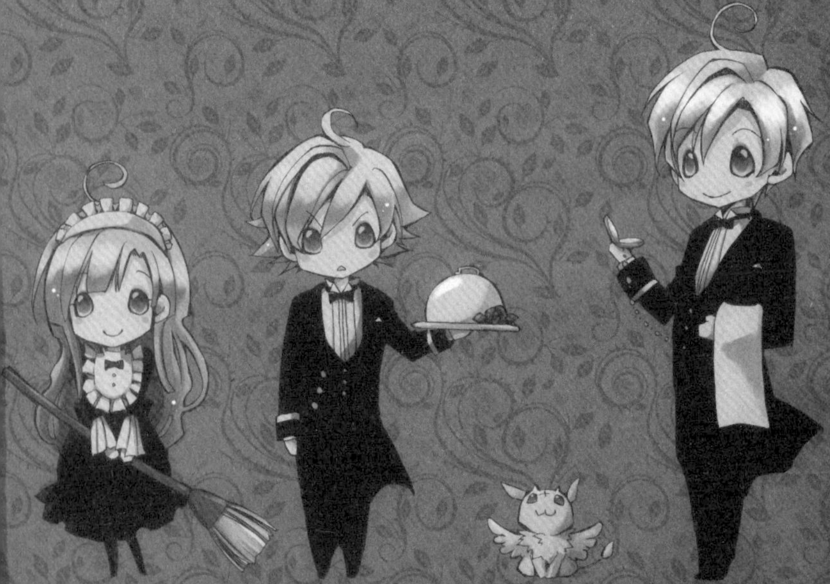

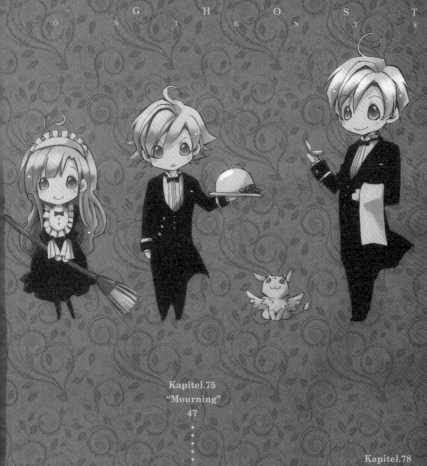

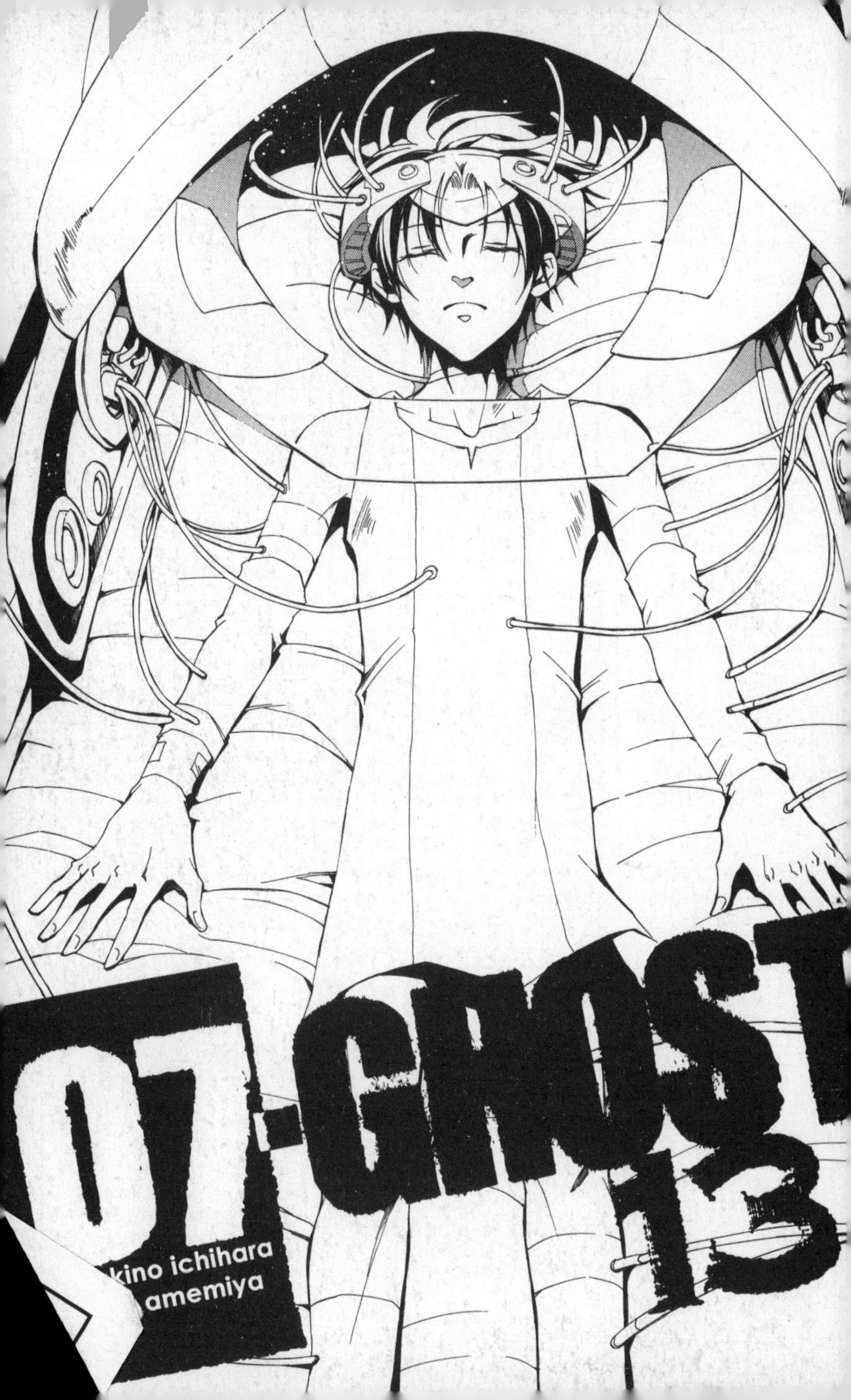
07-GHOST
13
kino ichihara
amemiya

07-GHOST

Characters

One thousand years ago, two equally powerful nations coexisted. One was the Barsburg Empire, protected by the Eye of Rafael. The other was the Raggs Kingdom, protected by the Eye of Mikael. Now that the Raggs Kingdom has been destroyed, things have changed...

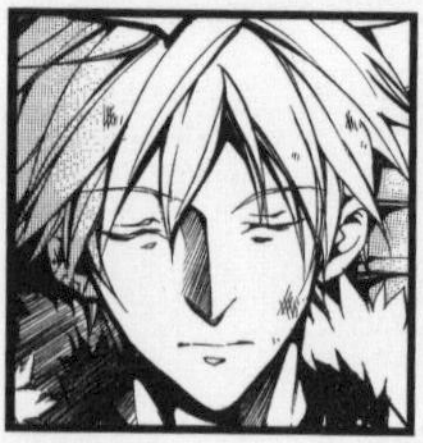

Frau

Bishop who saved Teito and now watches over him. He is Zehel of the Seven Ghosts. Currently injured.

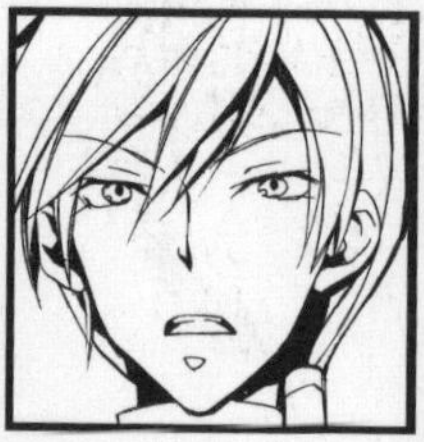

Hakuren

Teito's friend from the prestigious Oak family. Aimed to be a bishop, but is now the princess's tutor.

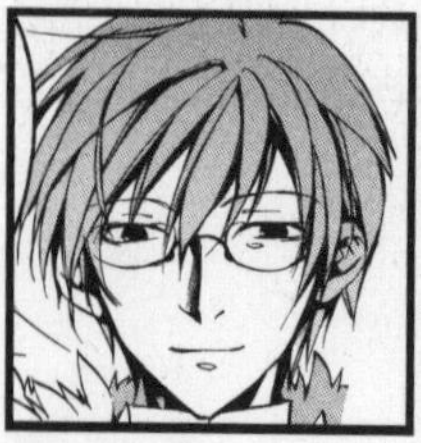

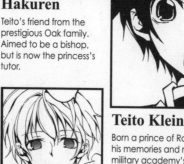

Castor

Bishop who can manipulate puppets. He watches over Teito and is Fest of the Seven Ghosts.

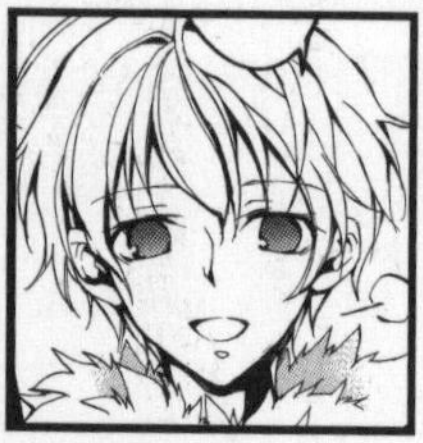

Labrador

Flower-loving bishop with the power of prophecy. He is Prophe of the Seven Ghosts.

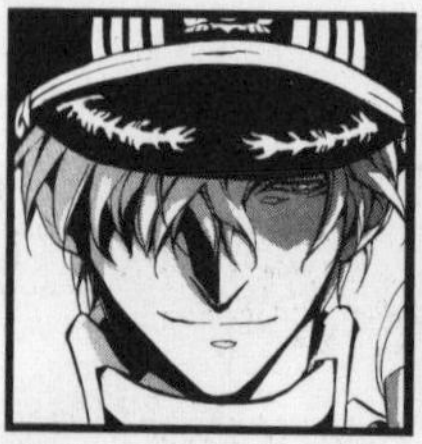

Ayanami

Imperial Army's Chief of Staff. Pursuing Teito, the vessel of the Eye of Mikael. He is the evil death god, Verloren.

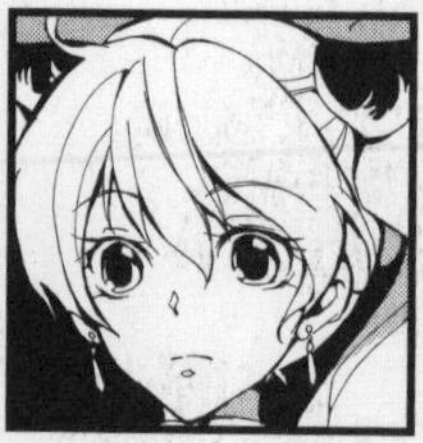

Ouka

First princess of the Barsburg Empire. Vessel of the Eye of Rafael.

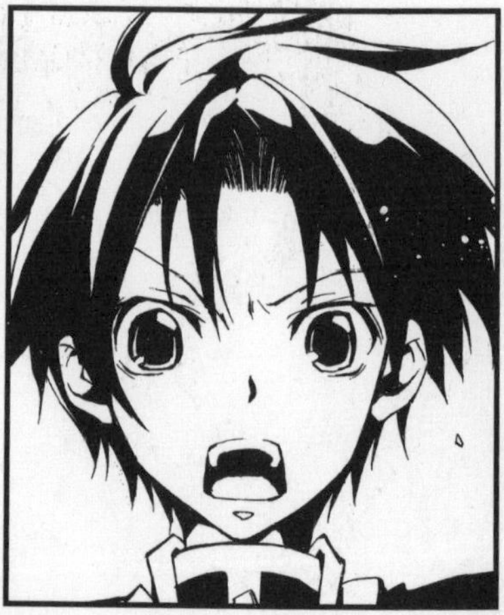

Teito Klein

Born a prince of Raggs, Teito was stripped of his memories and raised as a soldier by the military academy's chairman. He harbored the Eye of Mikael (an artifact said to bring either the world's salvation or destruction) in his right hand until the Black Hawks stole it. Currently brainwashed into serving as Ayanami's Begleiter.

Story

Teito is a student at the Barsburg Empire's military academy until the day he discovers that his father was the king of Raggs, the ruler of a kingdom the Barsburg Empire destroyed. He runs away, but loses his best friend to the diabolical Ayanami. As a first step in avenging Mikage's death, Teito becomes an apprentice bishop to obtain special privileges. He then embarks on a journey to the "Land of Seele," which holds the key to his past and the truth about the fall of Raggs. Teito regains memories during a Hawkzile race, only to be brainwashed by Ayanami.

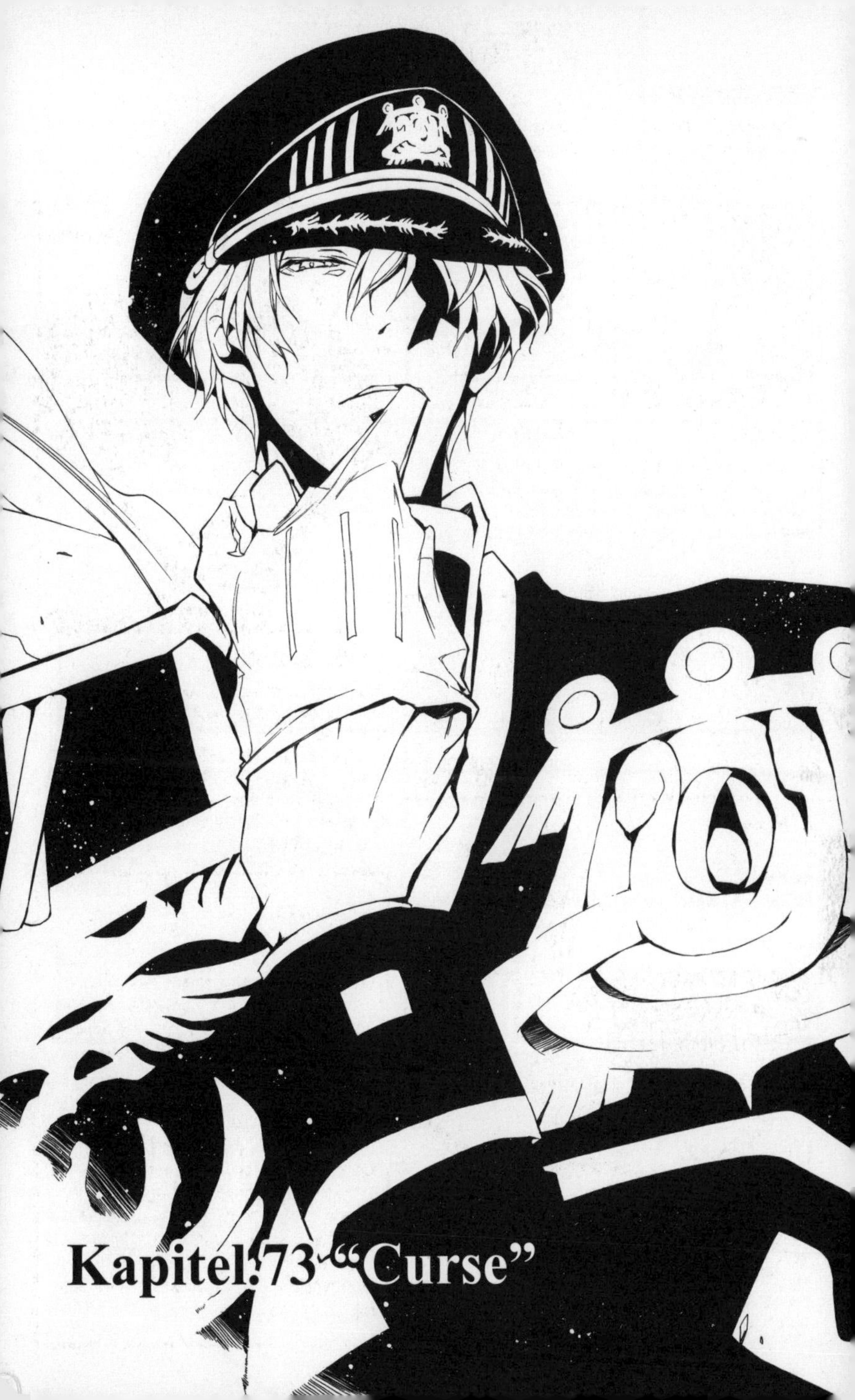

Kapitel:73 "Curse"

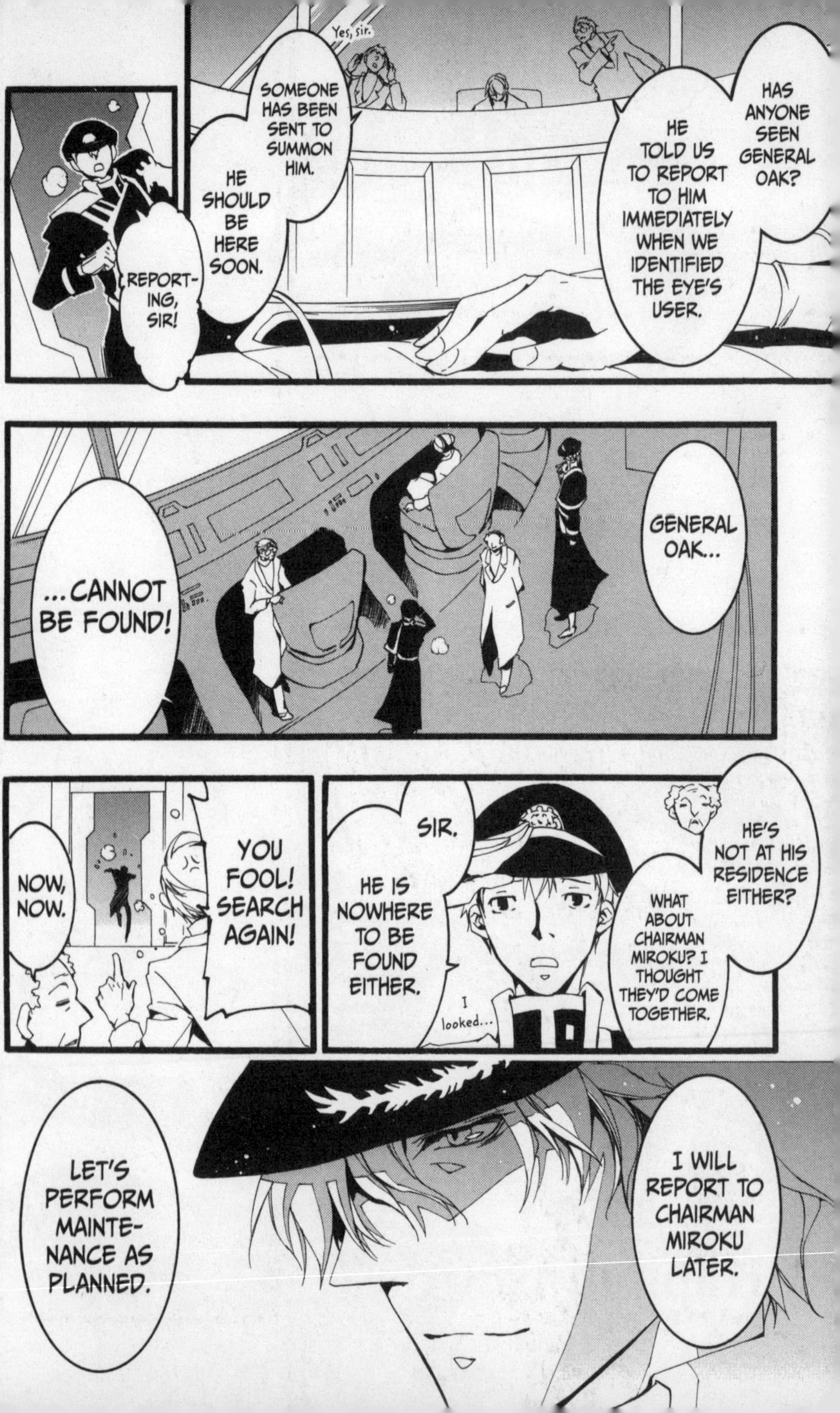

HAS ANYONE SEEN GENERAL OAK?
HE TOLD US TO REPORT TO HIM IMMEDIATELY WHEN WE IDENTIFIED THE EYE'S USER.
Yes, sir.
SOMEONE HAS BEEN SENT TO SUMMON HIM.
HE SHOULD BE HERE SOON.
REPORT-ING, SIR!
GENERAL OAK...
...CANNOT BE FOUND!
HE'S NOT AT HIS RESIDENCE EITHER?
WHAT ABOUT CHAIRMAN MIROKU? I THOUGHT THEY'D COME TOGETHER.
SIR.
HE IS NOWHERE TO BE FOUND EITHER.
I looked...
YOU FOOL! SEARCH AGAIN!
NOW, NOW.
I WILL REPORT TO CHAIRMAN MIROKU LATER.
LET'S PERFORM MAINTE-NANCE AS PLANNED.

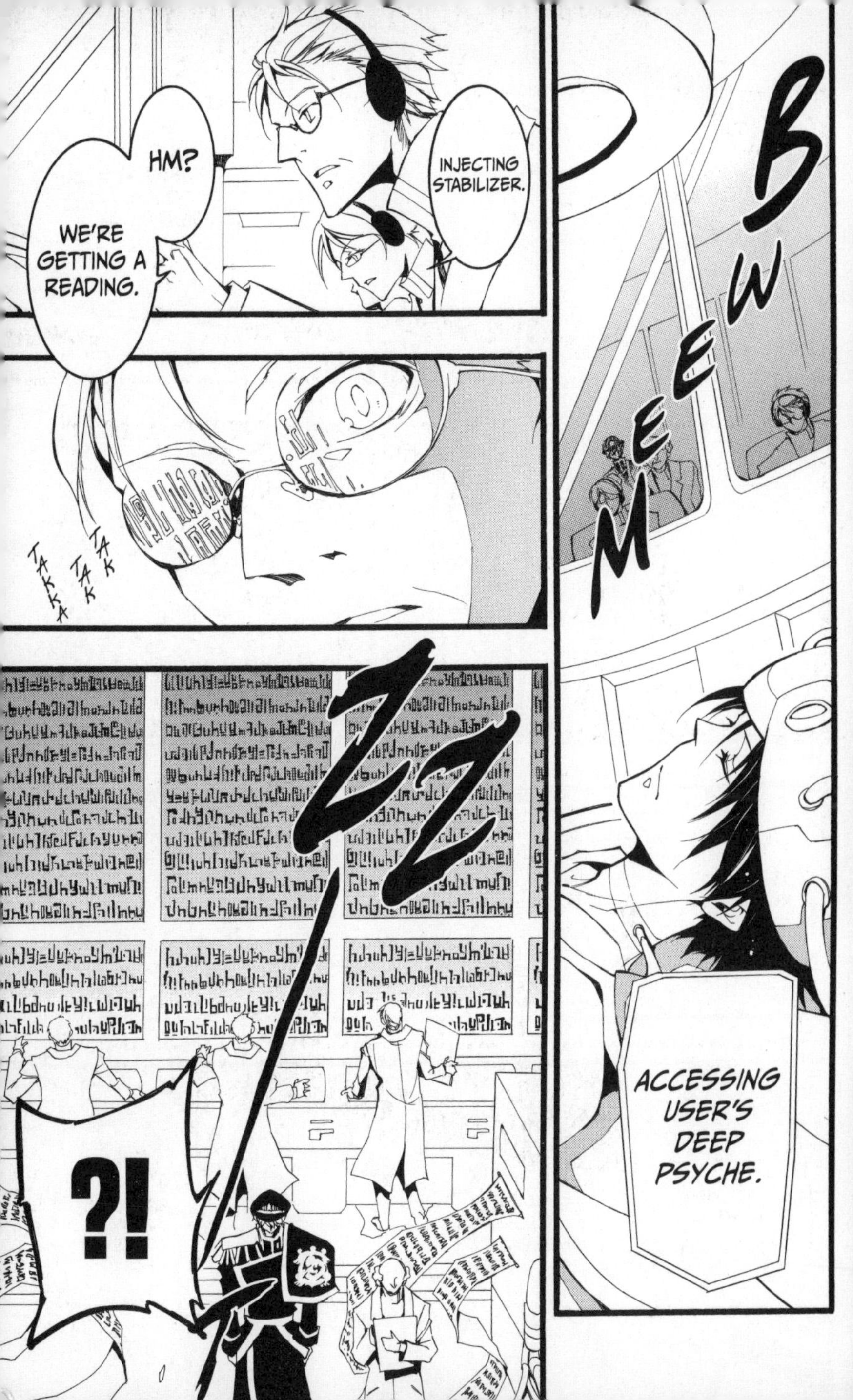
BWEEM
ACCESSING USER'S DEEP PSYCHE.
INJECTING STABILIZER.
HM?
WE'RE GETTING A READING.
TAK TAK TAKKA
ZZ
?!

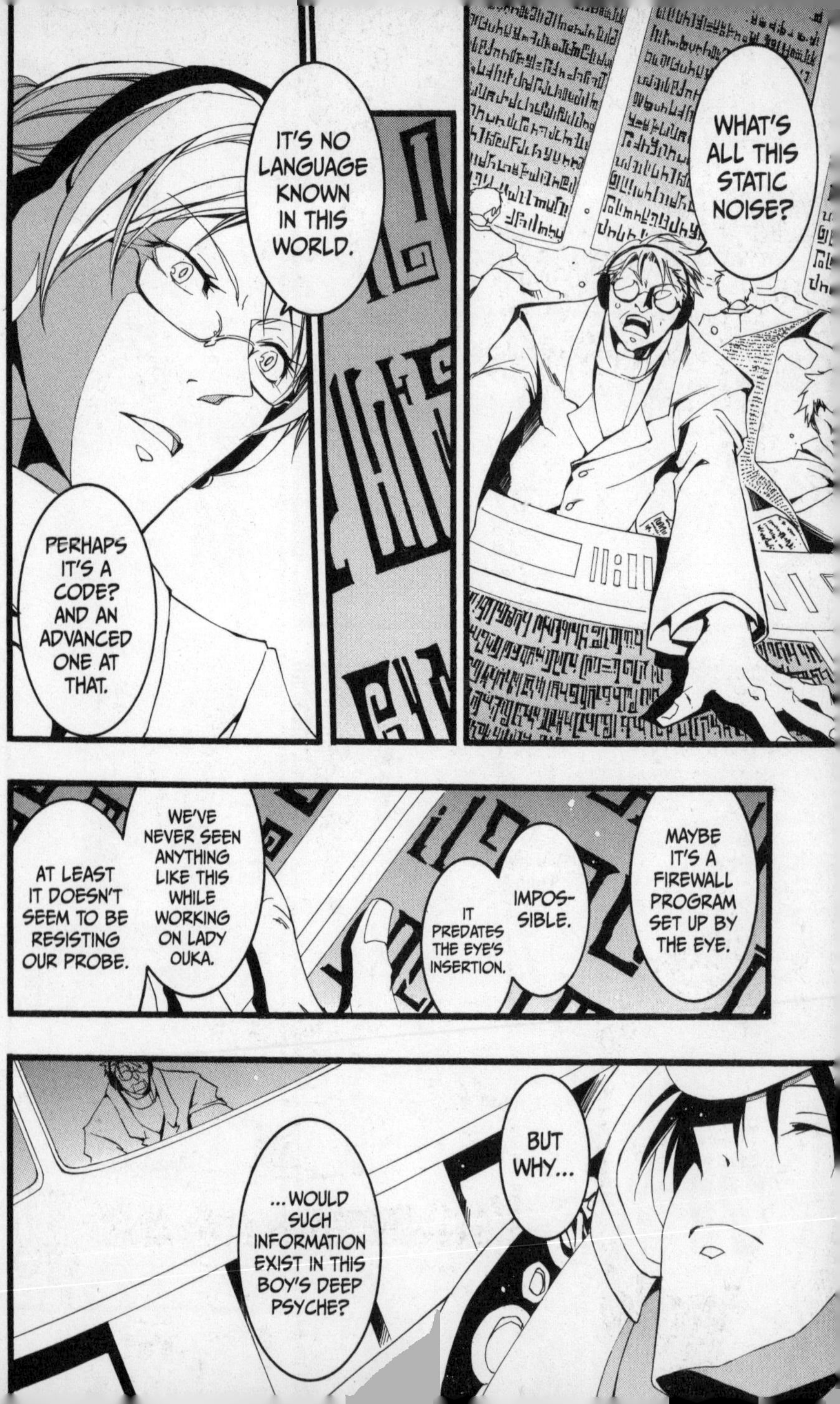
WHAT'S ALL THIS STATIC NOISE?
IT'S NO LANGUAGE KNOWN IN THIS WORLD.
PERHAPS IT'S A CODE? AND AN ADVANCED ONE AT THAT.
MAYBE IT'S A FIREWALL PROGRAM SET UP BY THE EYE.
IMPOSSIBLE.
IT PREDATES THE EYE'S INSERTION.
WE'VE NEVER SEEN ANYTHING LIKE THIS WHILE WORKING ON LADY OUKA.
AT LEAST IT DOESN'T SEEM TO BE RESISTING OUR PROBE.
BUT WHY...
...WOULD SUCH INFORMATION EXIST IN THIS BOY'S DEEP PSYCHE?

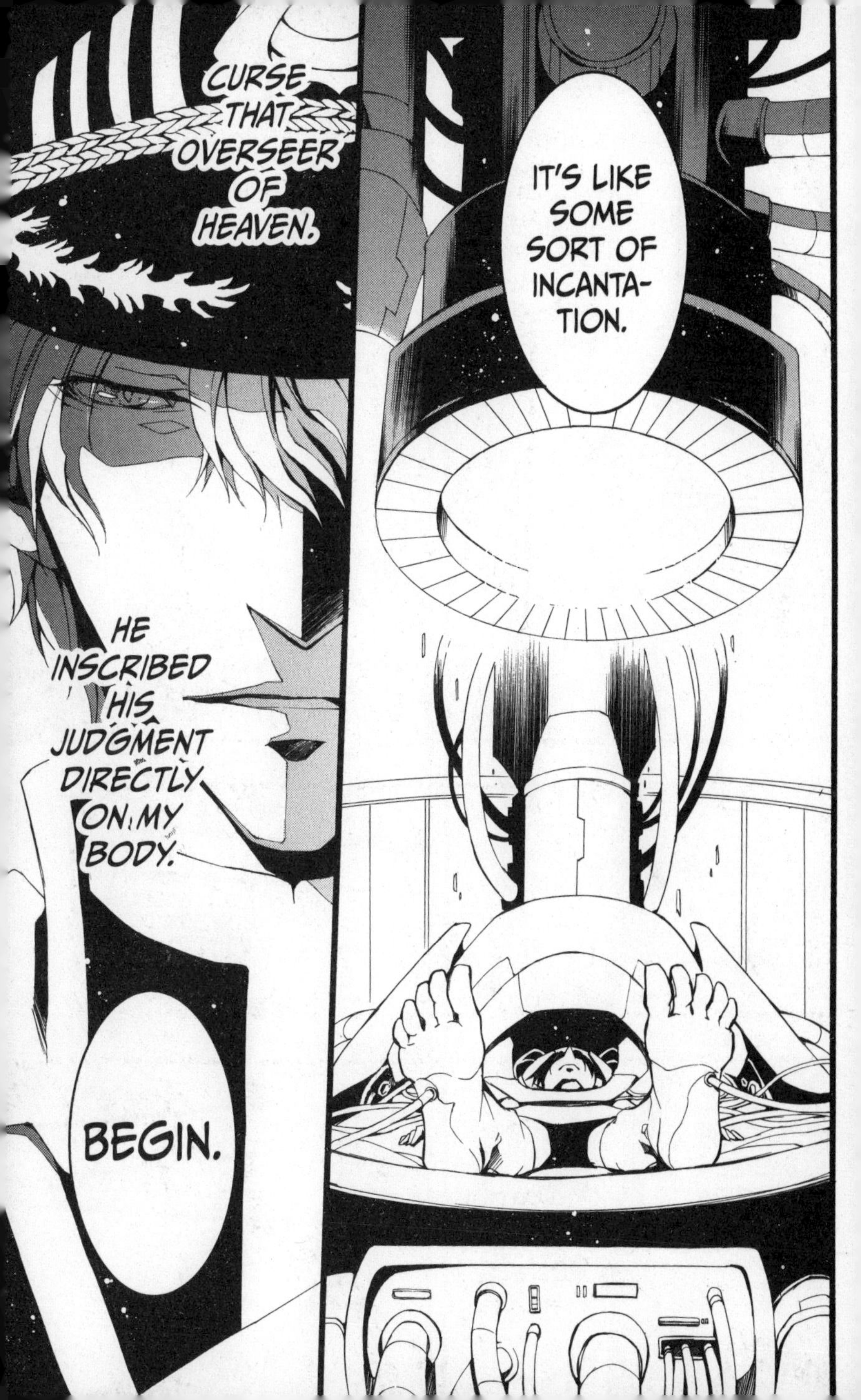
IT'S LIKE SOME SORT OF INCANTATION.
CURSE THAT OVERSEER OF HEAVEN.
HE INSCRIBED HIS JUDGMENT DIRECTLY ON MY BODY.
BEGIN.

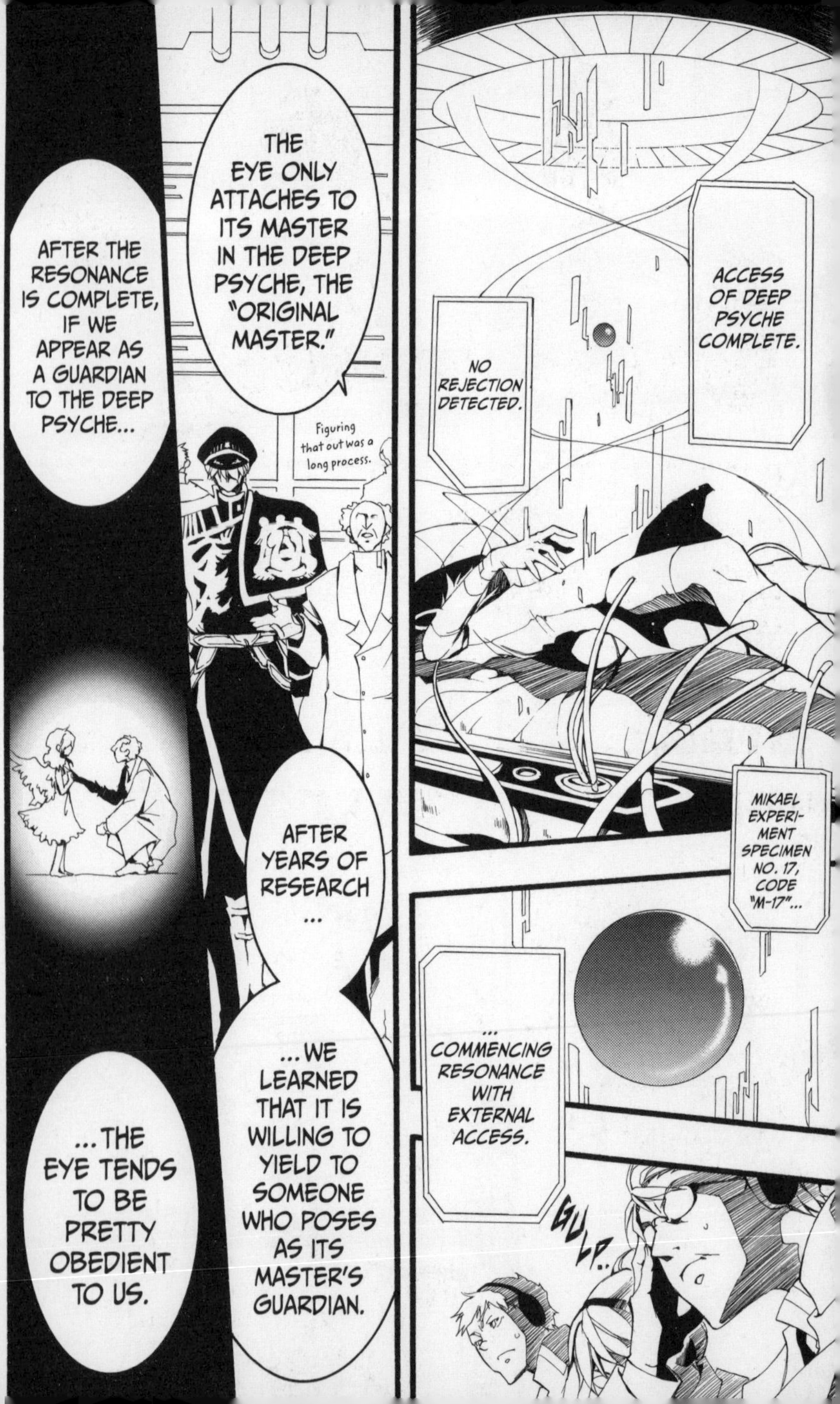

ACCESS OF DEEP PSYCHE COMPLETE.
NO REJECTION DETECTED.
MIKAEL EXPERIMENT SPECIMEN NO. 17, CODE "M-17"...
...COMMENCING RESONANCE WITH EXTERNAL ACCESS.
GULP...
THE EYE ONLY ATTACHES TO ITS MASTER IN THE DEEP PSYCHE, THE "ORIGINAL MASTER."
Figuring that out was a long process.
AFTER YEARS OF RESEARCH...
...WE LEARNED THAT IT IS WILLING TO YIELD TO SOMEONE WHO POSES AS ITS MASTER'S GUARDIAN.
AFTER THE RESONANCE IS COMPLETE, IF WE APPEAR AS A GUARDIAN TO THE DEEP PSYCHE...
...THE EYE TENDS TO BE PRETTY OBEDIENT TO US.

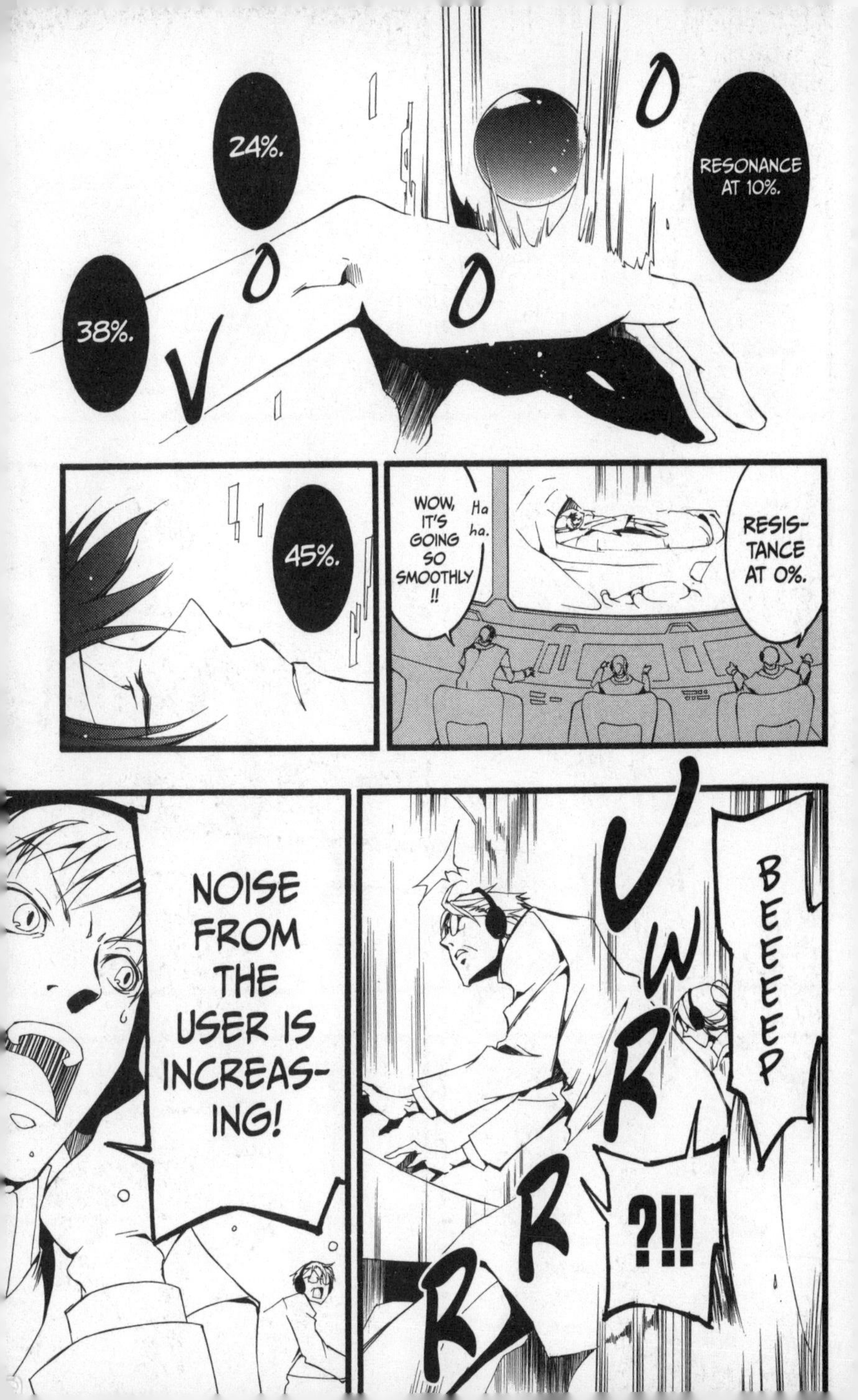
RESONANCE AT 10%.
24%.
38%.
VOOO
RESISTANCE AT 0%.
WOW, IT'S GOING SO SMOOTHLY!!
Ha ha.
45%.
BEEEEP
VWRRRR
?!!
NOISE FROM THE USER IS INCREASING!

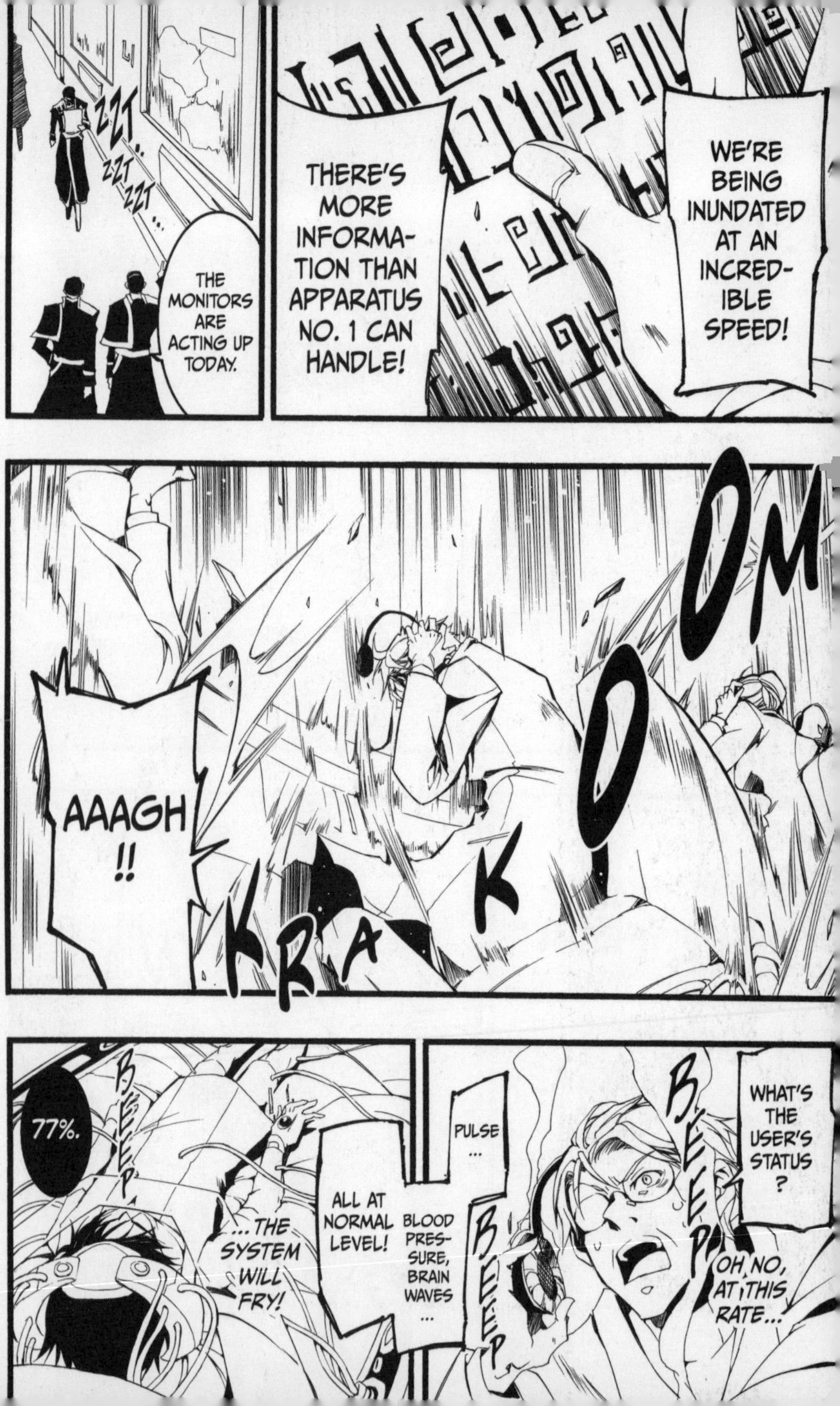
WE'RE BEING INUNDATED AT AN INCRED-IBLE SPEED!
THERE'S MORE INFORMA-TION THAN APPARATUS NO. 1 CAN HANDLE!
ZZT..
ZZT ZZT...
THE MONITORS ARE ACTING UP TODAY.
DOOM
KRAK
AAAGH!!
WHAT'S THE USER'S STATUS?
BEEP
OH, NO, AT THIS RATE...
BEEP
PULSE...
BLOOD PRES-SURE, BRAIN WAVES...
ALL AT NORMAL LEVEL!
...THE SYSTEM WILL FRY!
BEEP
77%.

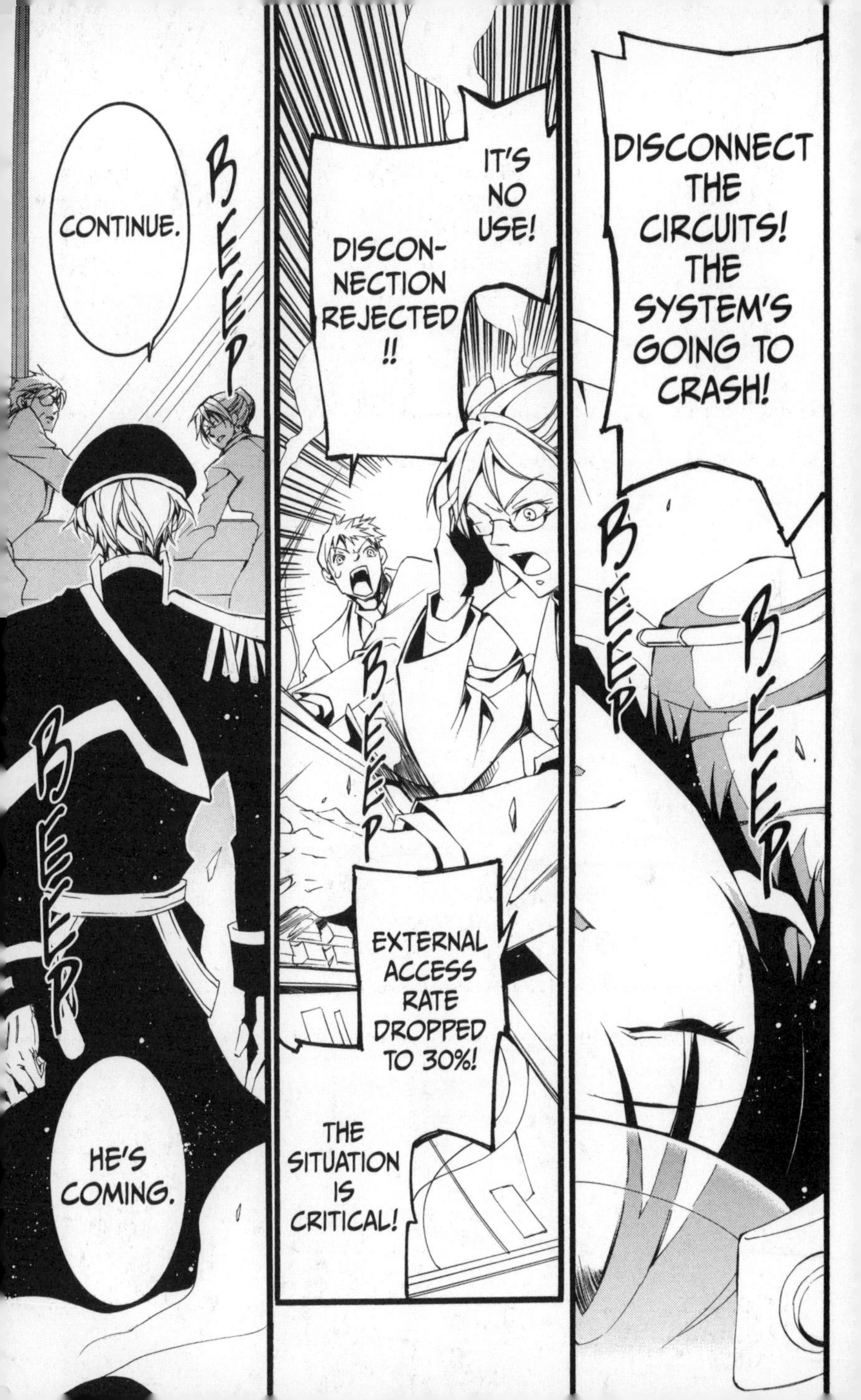
DISCONNECT THE CIRCUITS! THE SYSTEM'S GOING TO CRASH!
BEEP
BEEP
IT'S NO USE!
DISCON-NECTION REJECTED!!
BEEP
EXTERNAL ACCESS RATE DROPPED TO 30%!
THE SITUATION IS CRITICAL!
BEEP
CONTINUE.
BEEP
HE'S COMING.

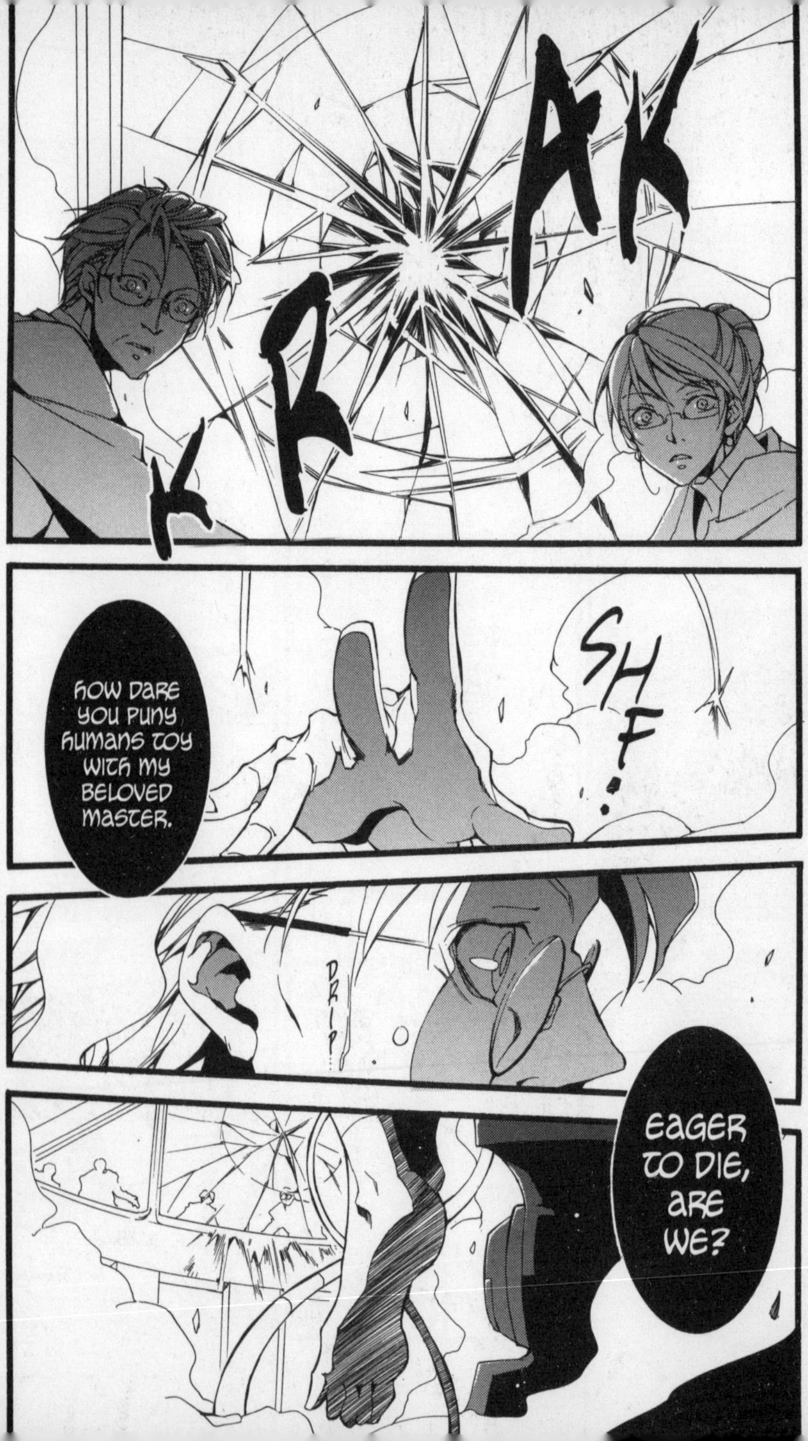
KRAK
SHF...
HOW DARE YOU PUNY HUMANS TOY WITH MY BELOVED MASTER.
DRIP...
EAGER TO DIE, ARE WE?

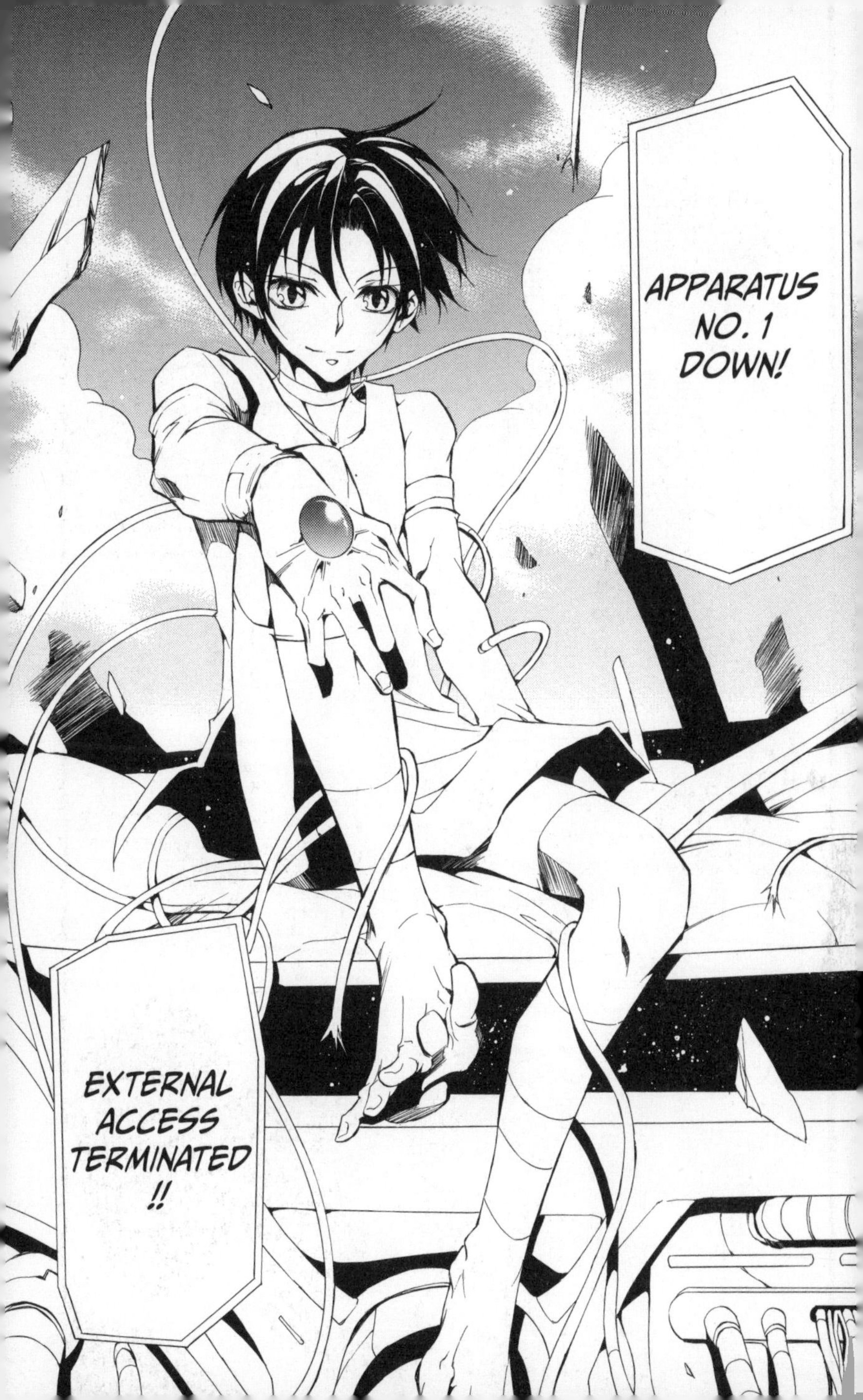
APPARATUS NO. 1 DOWN!
EXTERNAL ACCESS TERMINATED !!

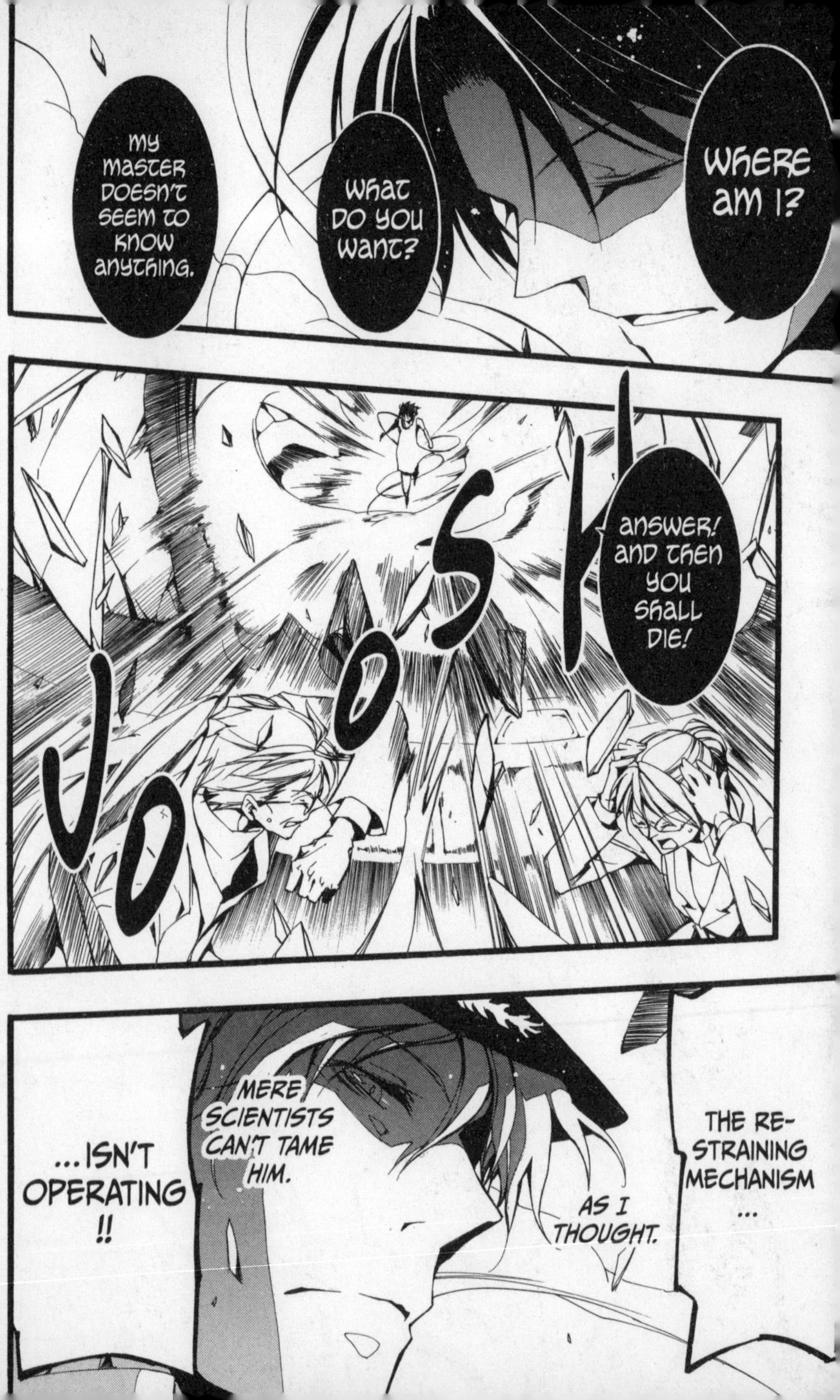
WHERE AM I?
WHAT DO YOU WANT?
MY MASTER DOESN'T SEEM TO KNOW ANYTHING.
ANSWER! AND THEN YOU SHALL DIE!
JOOSH
THE RE-STRAINING MECHANISM...
AS I THOUGHT.
MERE SCIENTISTS CAN'T TAME HIM.
...ISN'T OPERATING!!

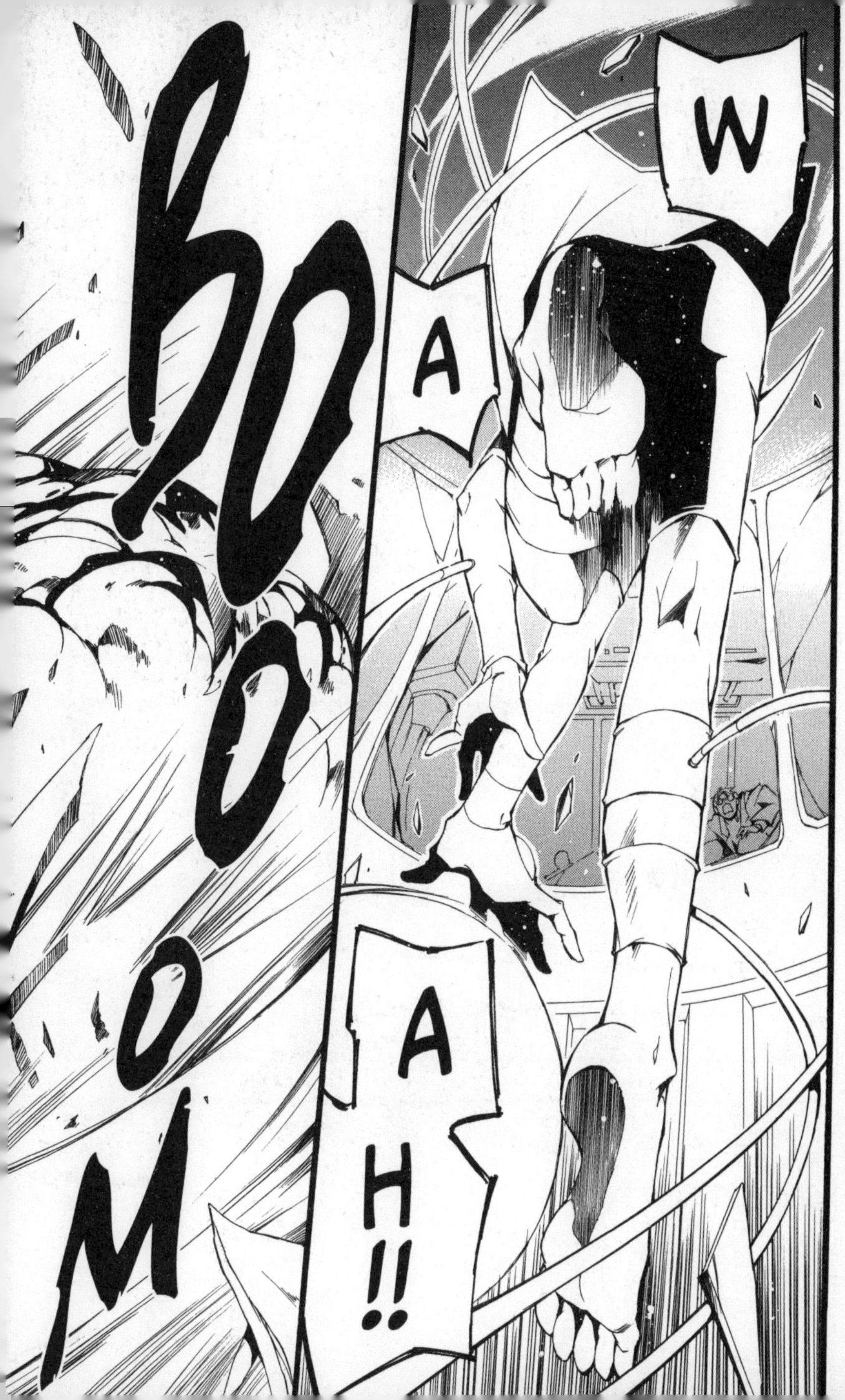
WAAH!!
BOOOM

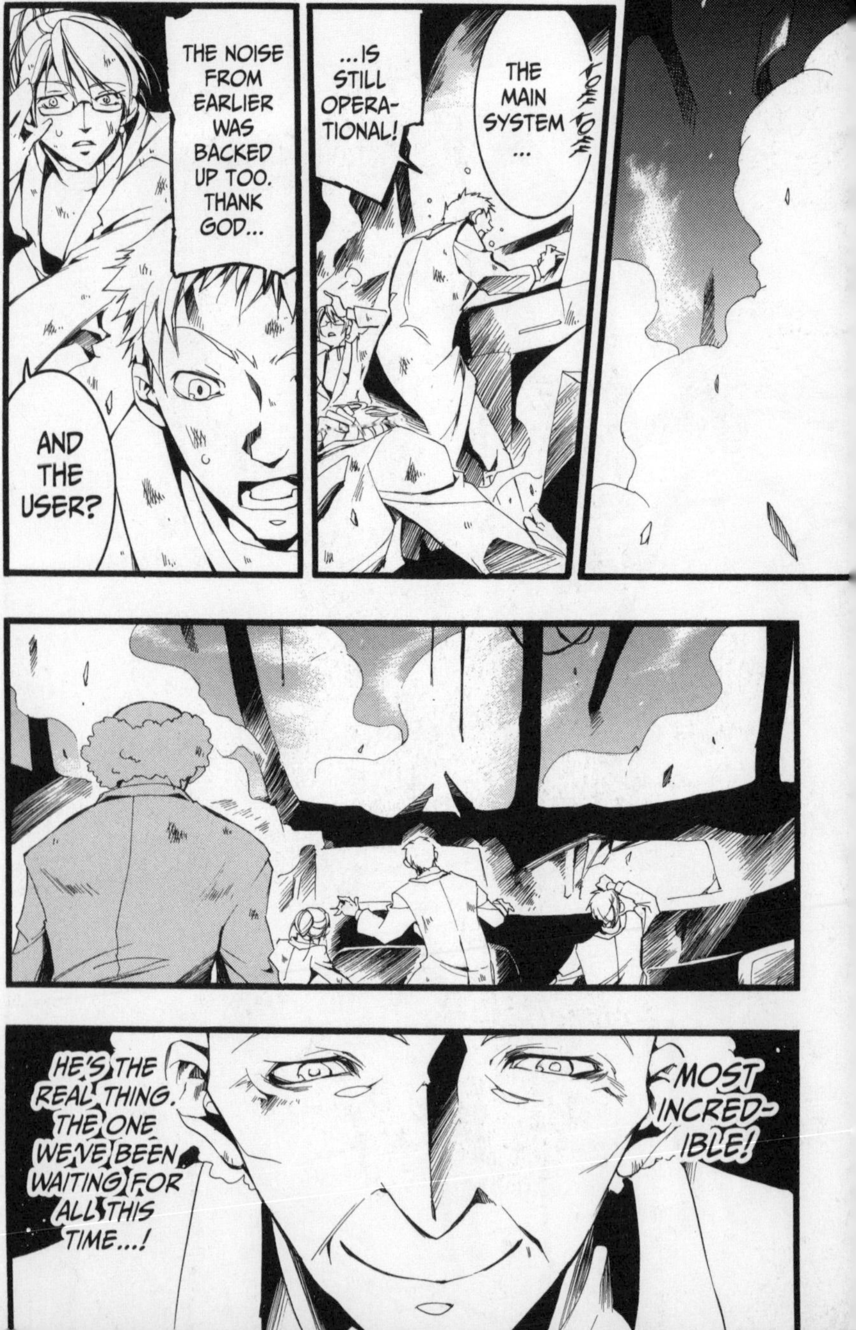
THE MAIN SYSTEM ...
...IS STILL OPERATIONAL!
THE NOISE FROM EARLIER WAS BACKED UP TOO. THANK GOD...
AND THE USER?
MOST INCREDIBLE!
HE'S THE REAL THING. THE ONE WE'VE BEEN WAITING FOR ALL THIS TIME...!

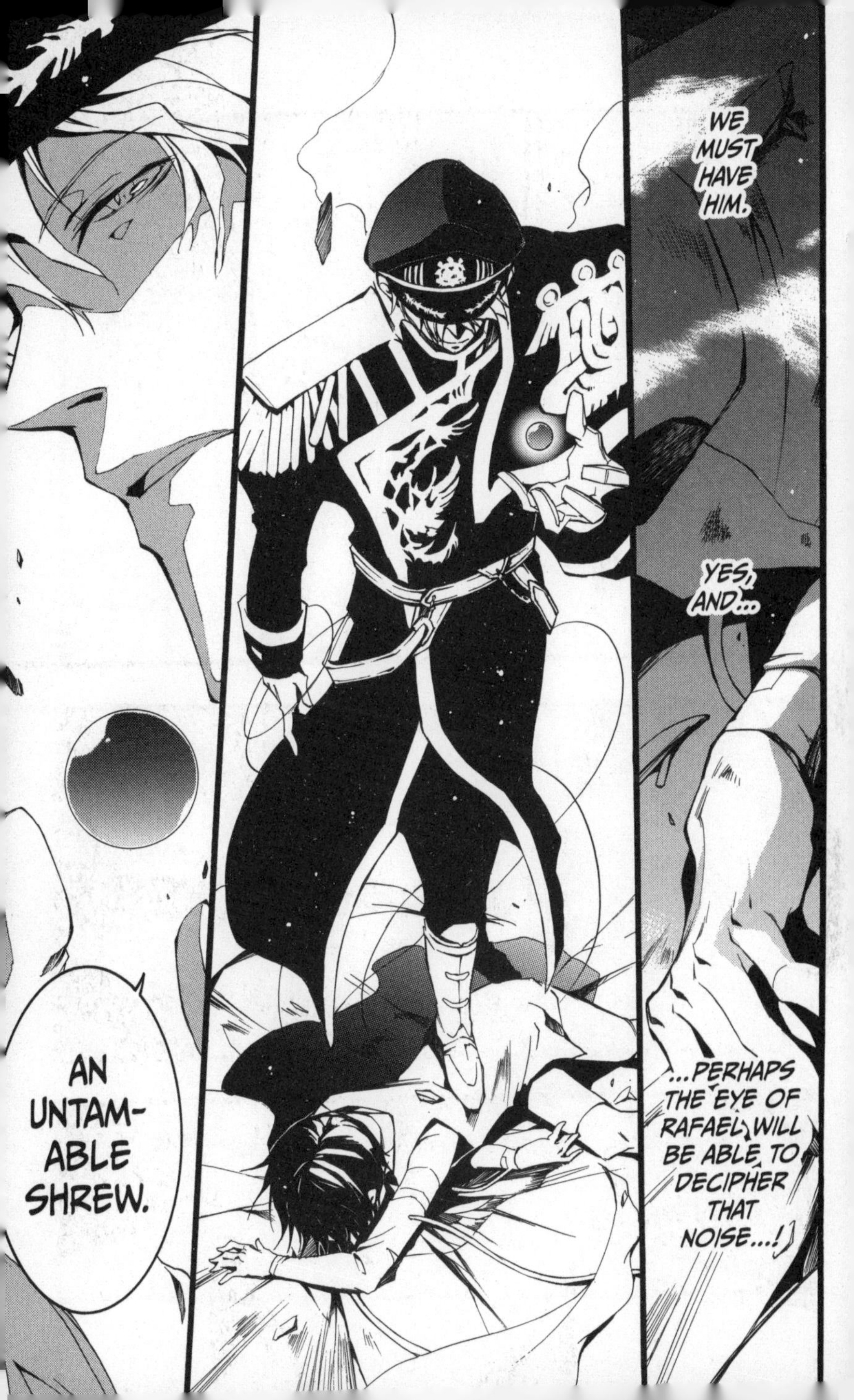
WE MUST HAVE HIM.
YES, AND...
...PERHAPS THE EYE OF RAFAEL WILL BE ABLE TO DECIPHER THAT NOISE...!
AN UNTAM-ABLE SHREW.

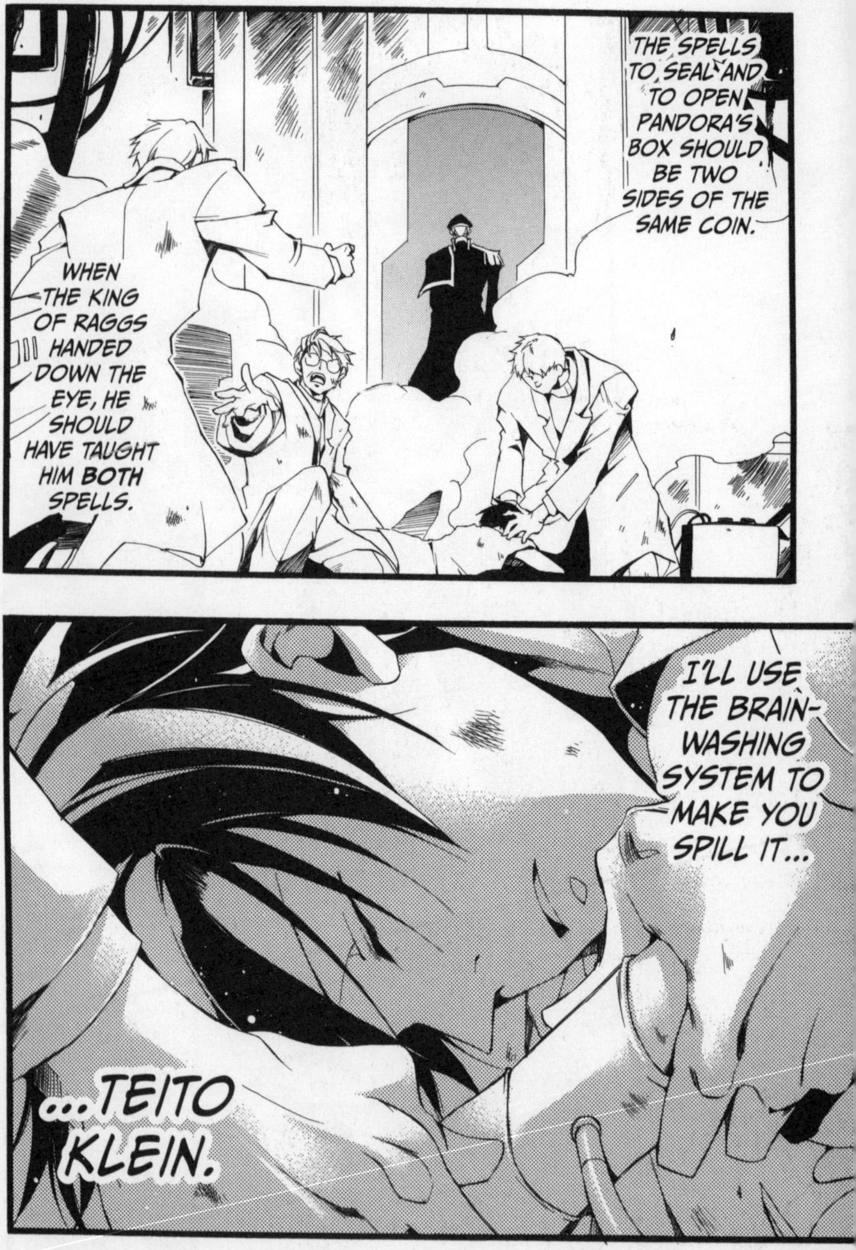
THE SPELLS TO SEAL AND TO OPEN PANDORA'S BOX SHOULD BE TWO SIDES OF THE SAME COIN.
WHEN THE KING OF RAGGS HANDED DOWN THE EYE, HE SHOULD HAVE TAUGHT HIM BOTH SPELLS.
I'LL USE THE BRAIN-WASHING SYSTEM TO MAKE YOU SPILL IT...
...TEITO KLEIN.

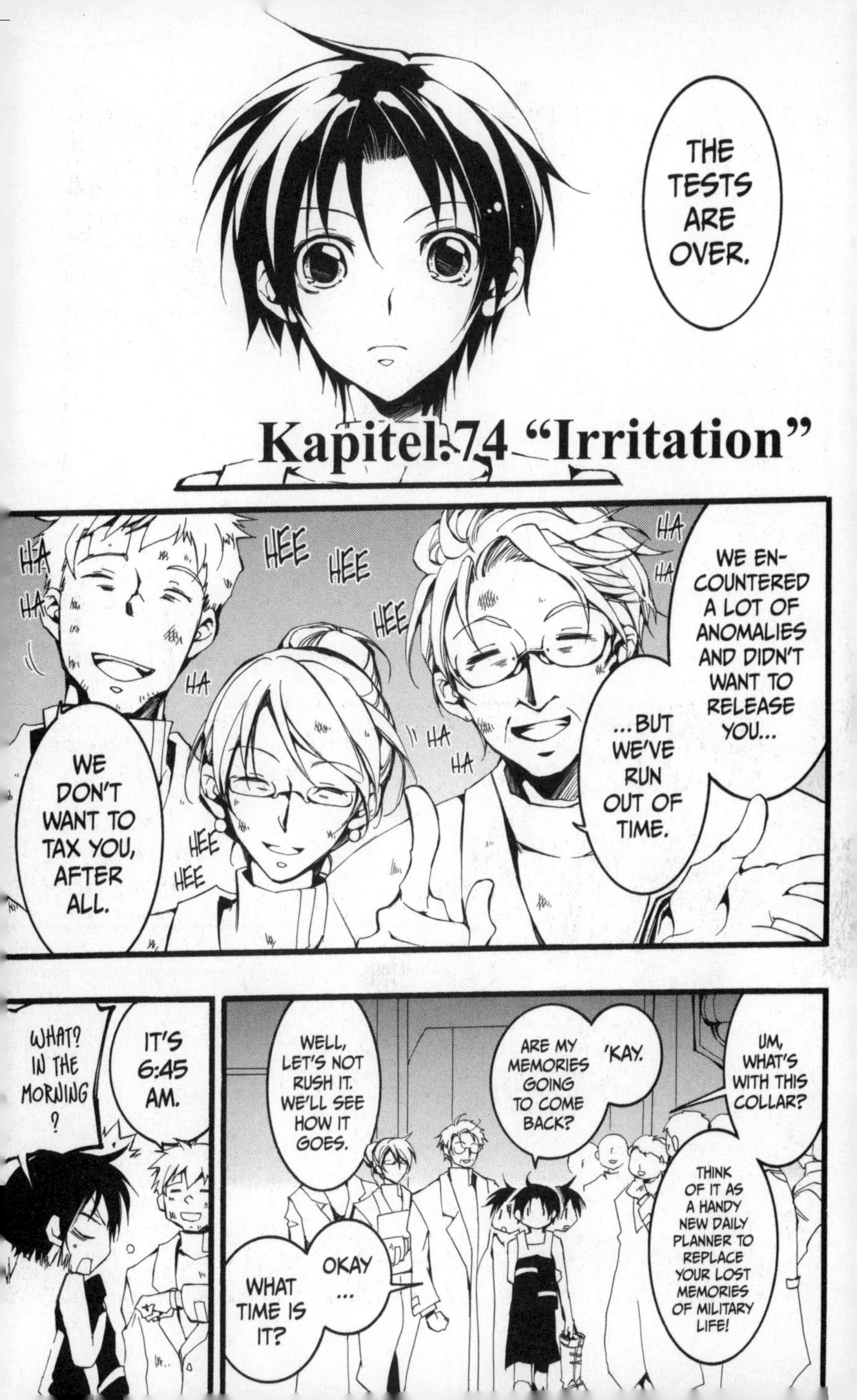
THE TESTS ARE OVER.
Kapitel 74 "Irritation"
HA HA
WE EN-COUNTERED A LOT OF ANOMALIES AND DIDN'T WANT TO RELEASE YOU...
...BUT WE'VE RUN OUT OF TIME.
HA HA
HEE HEE HEE
HA
HA HA
WE DON'T WANT TO TAX YOU, AFTER ALL.
HEE HEE
UM, WHAT'S WITH THIS COLLAR?
THINK OF IT AS A HANDY NEW DAILY PLANNER TO REPLACE YOUR LOST MEMORIES OF MILITARY LIFE!
'KAY.
ARE MY MEMORIES GOING TO COME BACK?
WELL, LET'S NOT RUSH IT. WE'LL SEE HOW IT GOES.
OKAY...
WHAT TIME IS IT?
IT'S 6:45 AM.
WHAT? IN THE MORNING?

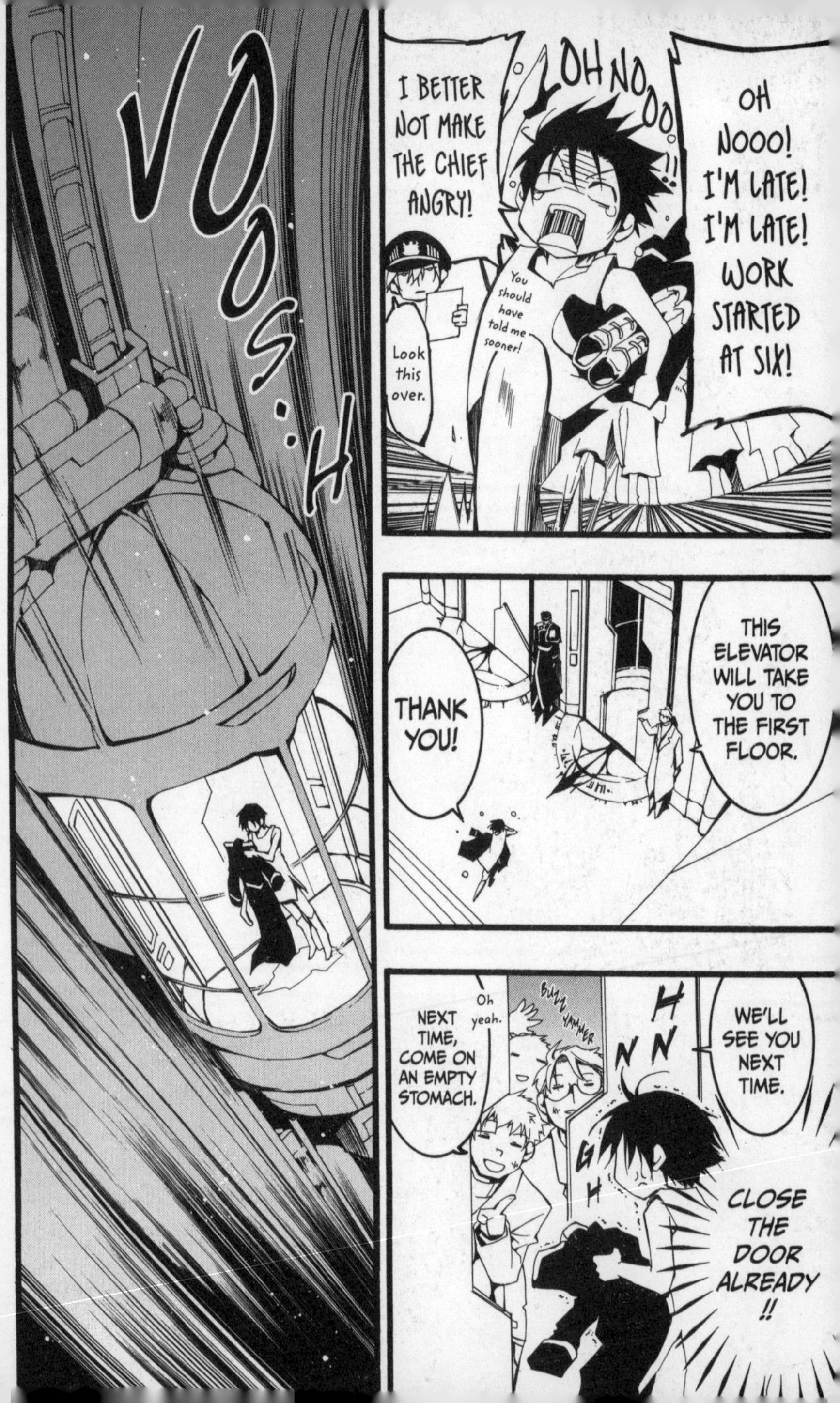
OH NOOO! I'M LATE! I'M LATE! WORK STARTED AT SIX!
OH NOOO!!
You should have told me sooner!
I BETTER NOT MAKE THE CHIEF ANGRY!
Look this over.
THIS ELEVATOR WILL TAKE YOU TO THE FIRST FLOOR.
THANK YOU!
WE'LL SEE YOU NEXT TIME.
HNN
GH
CLOSE THE DOOR ALREADY!!
BUZZ YAMMER
Oh yeah.
NEXT TIME, COME ON AN EMPTY STOMACH.
VOOSH

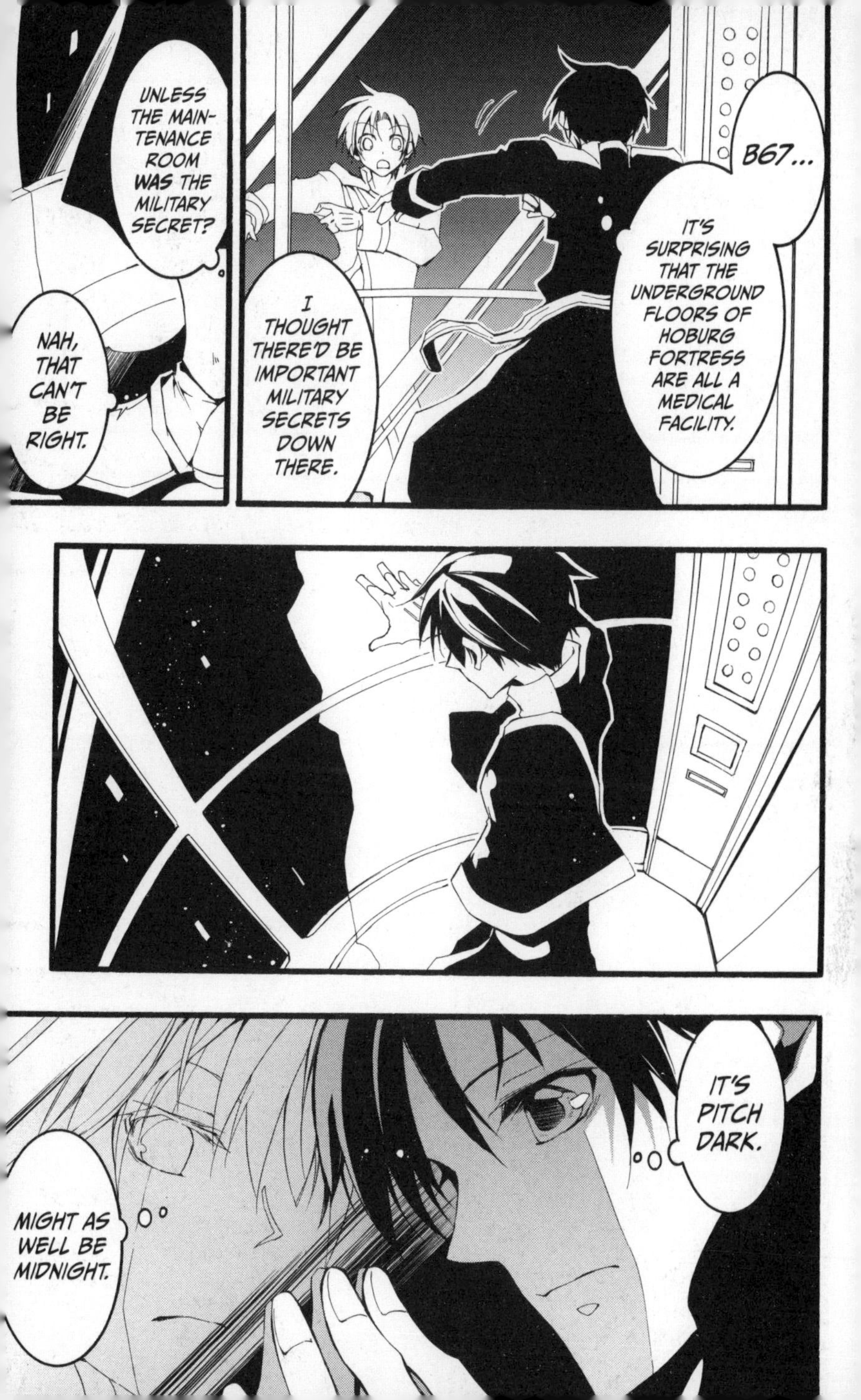
B67...
IT'S SURPRISING THAT THE UNDERGROUND FLOORS OF HOBURG FORTRESS ARE ALL A MEDICAL FACILITY.
I THOUGHT THERE'D BE IMPORTANT MILITARY SECRETS DOWN THERE.
UNLESS THE MAIN-TENANCE ROOM WAS THE MILITARY SECRET?
NAH, THAT CAN'T BE RIGHT.
IT'S PITCH DARK.
MIGHT AS WELL BE MIDNIGHT.

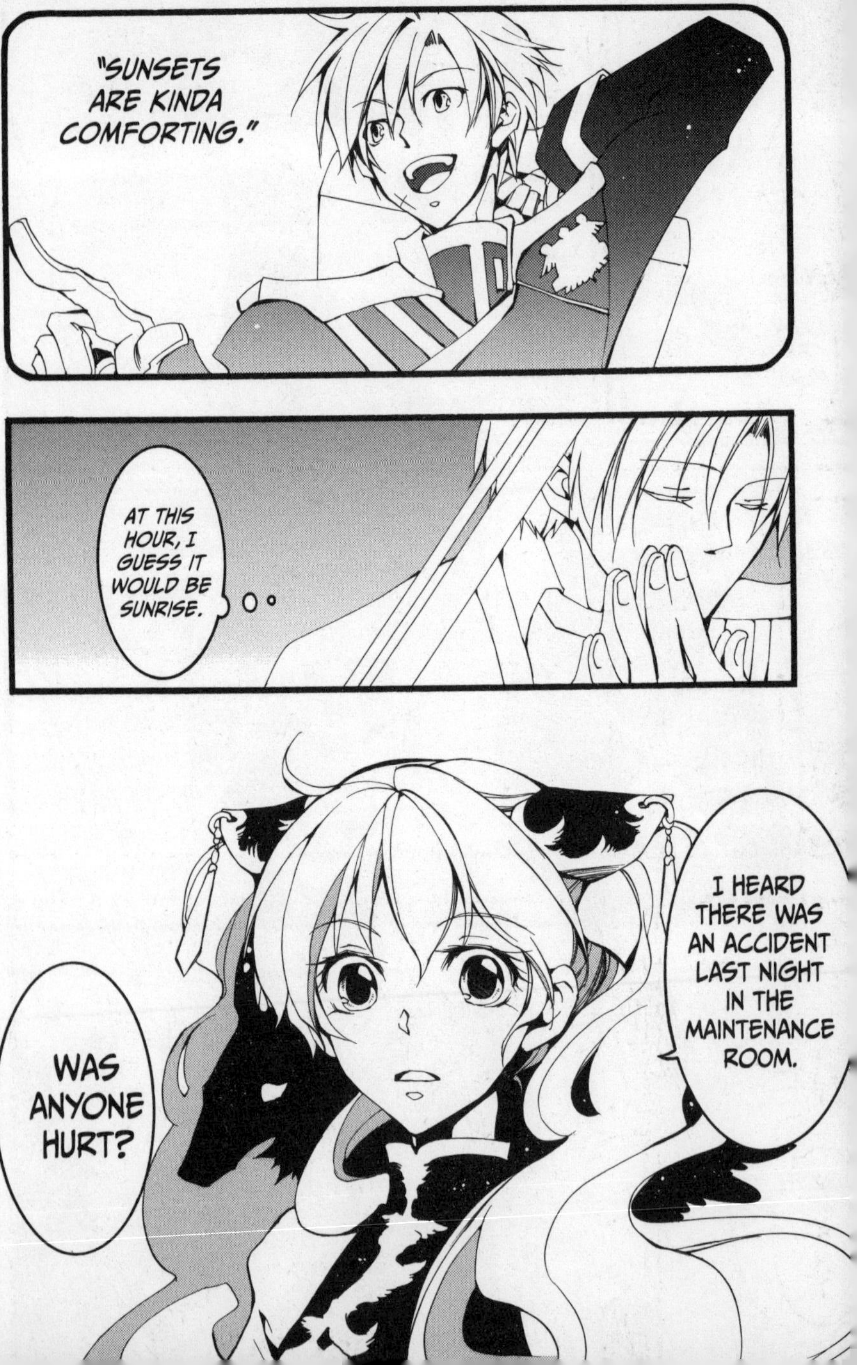
"SUNSETS ARE KINDA COMFORTING."
AT THIS HOUR, I GUESS IT WOULD BE SUNRISE.
I HEARD THERE WAS AN ACCIDENT LAST NIGHT IN THE MAINTENANCE ROOM.
WAS ANYONE HURT?

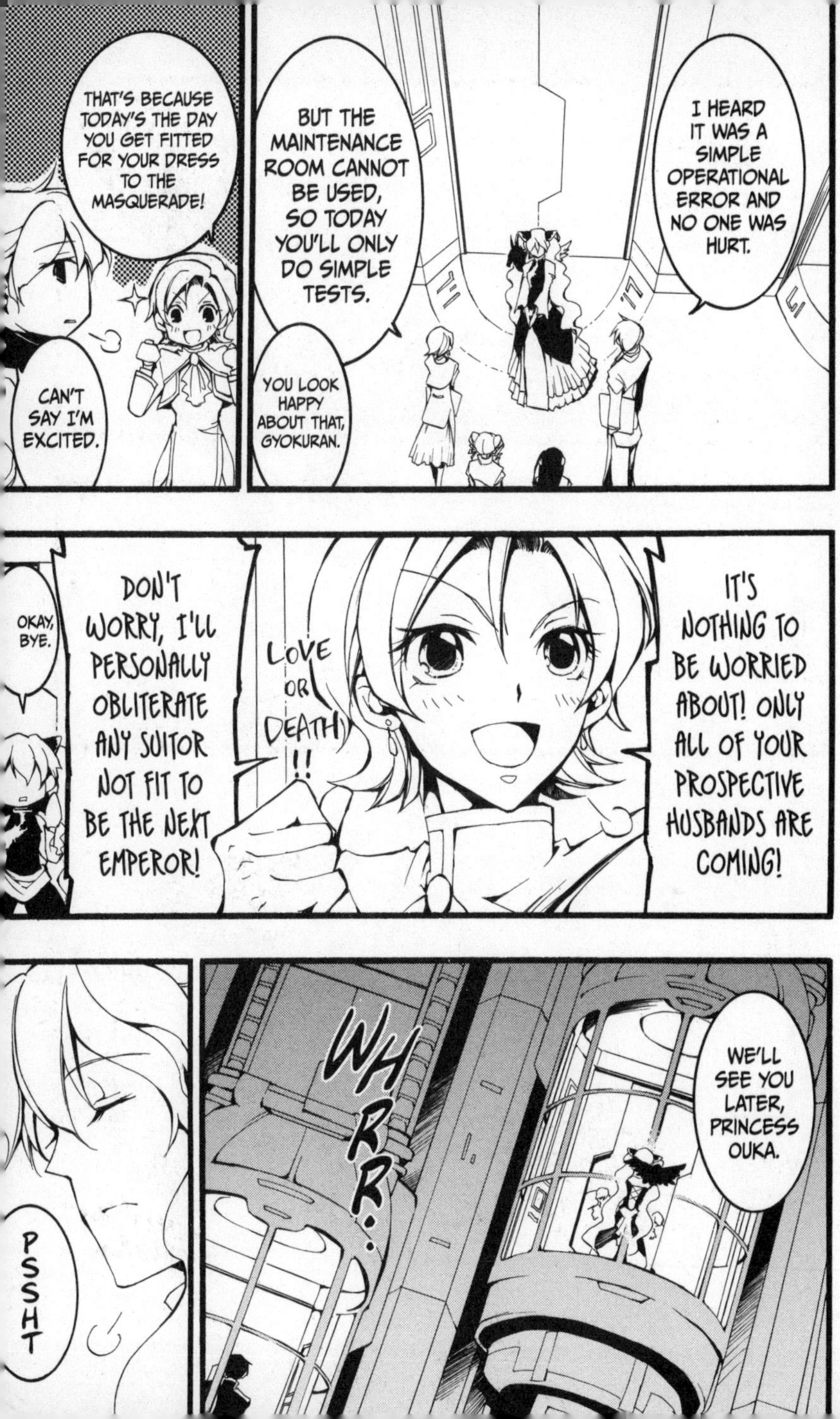
I HEARD IT WAS A SIMPLE OPERATIONAL ERROR AND NO ONE WAS HURT.
BUT THE MAINTENANCE ROOM CANNOT BE USED, SO TODAY YOU'LL ONLY DO SIMPLE TESTS.
YOU LOOK HAPPY ABOUT THAT, GYOKURAN.
THAT'S BECAUSE TODAY'S THE DAY YOU GET FITTED FOR YOUR DRESS TO THE MASQUERADE!
CAN'T SAY I'M EXCITED.
IT'S NOTHING TO BE WORRIED ABOUT! ONLY ALL OF YOUR PROSPECTIVE HUSBANDS ARE COMING!
LOVE OR DEATH!!
DON'T WORRY, I'LL PERSONALLY OBLITERATE ANY SUITOR NOT FIT TO BE THE NEXT EMPEROR!
OKAY, BYE.
WE'LL SEE YOU LATER, PRINCESS OUKA.
WHRR..
PSSHT

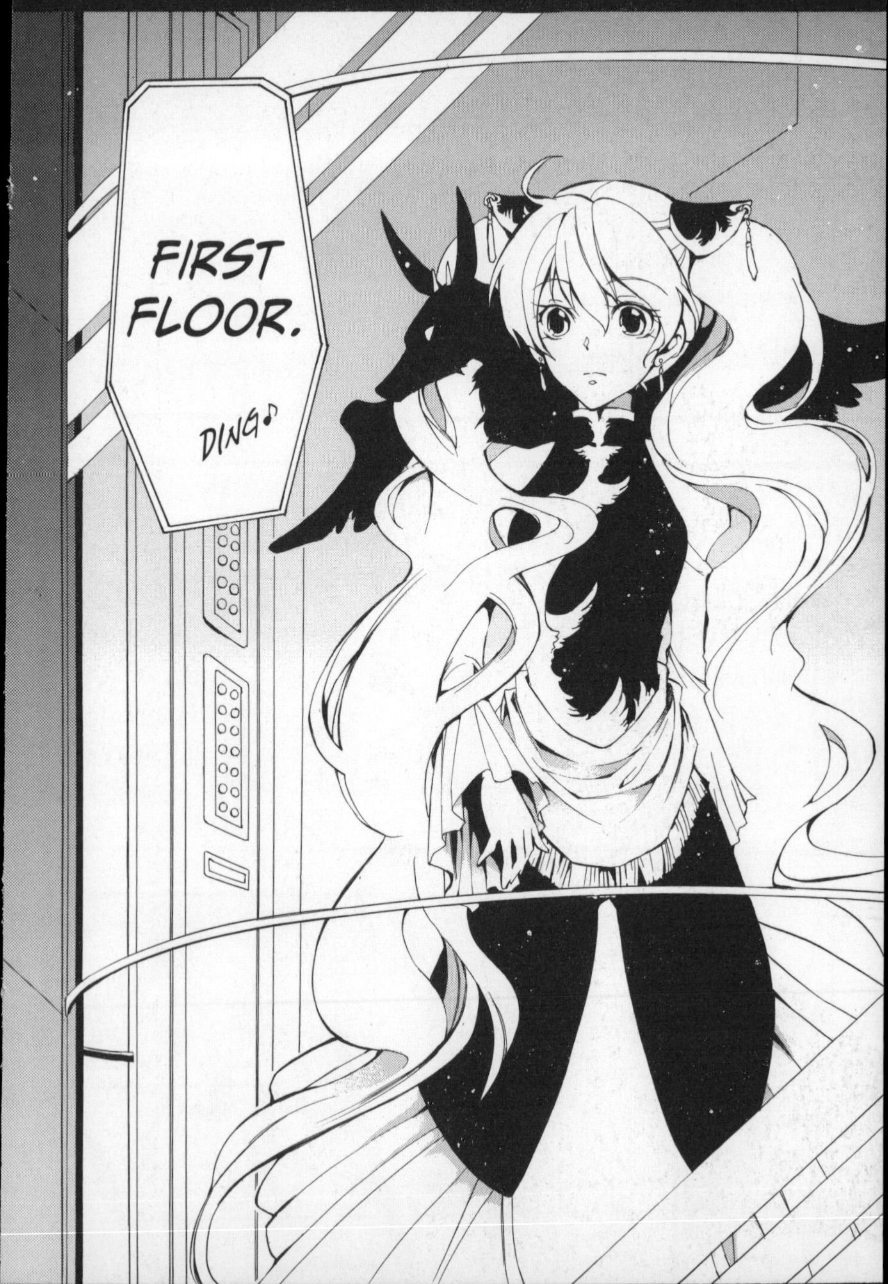
FIRST FLOOR.
DING♪

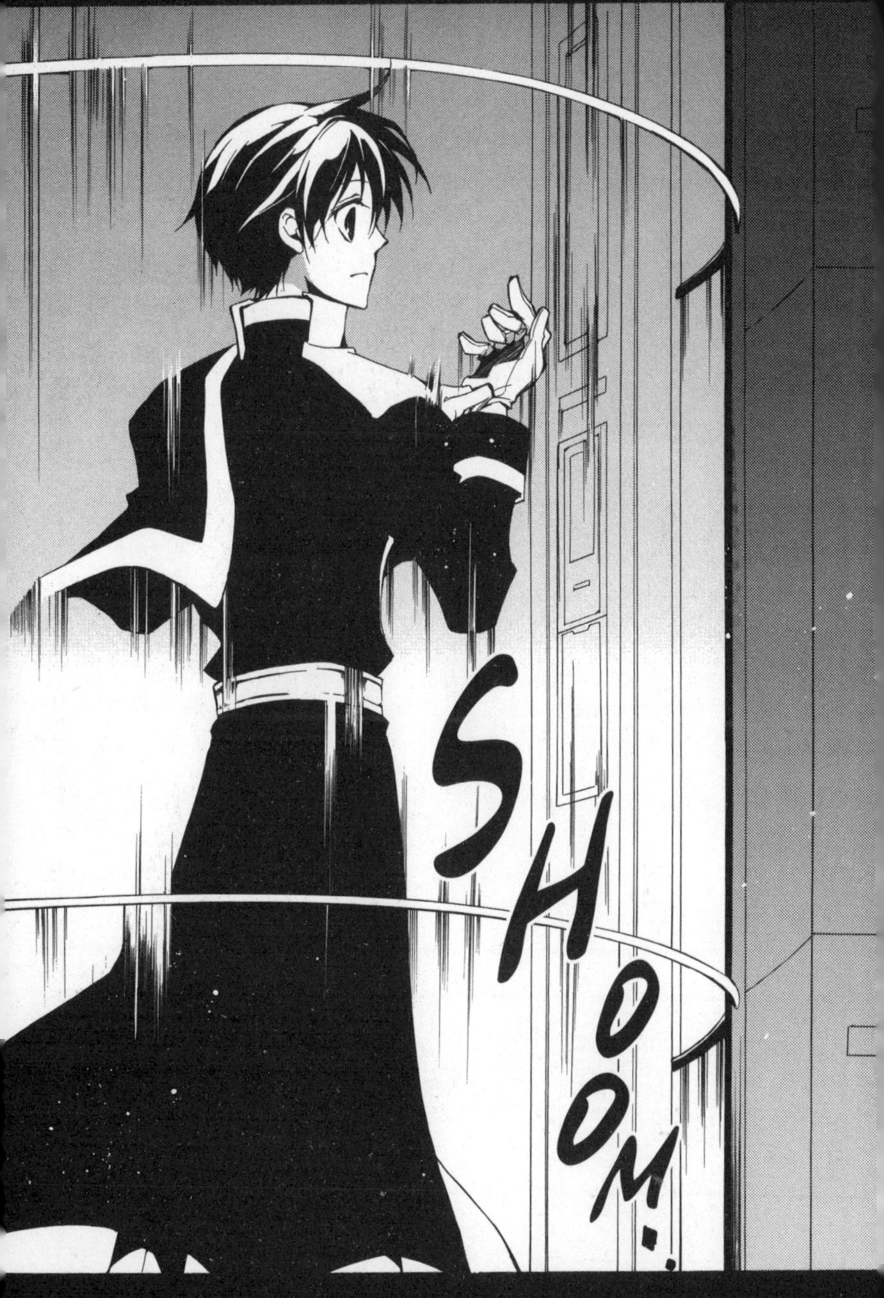
SHOOM

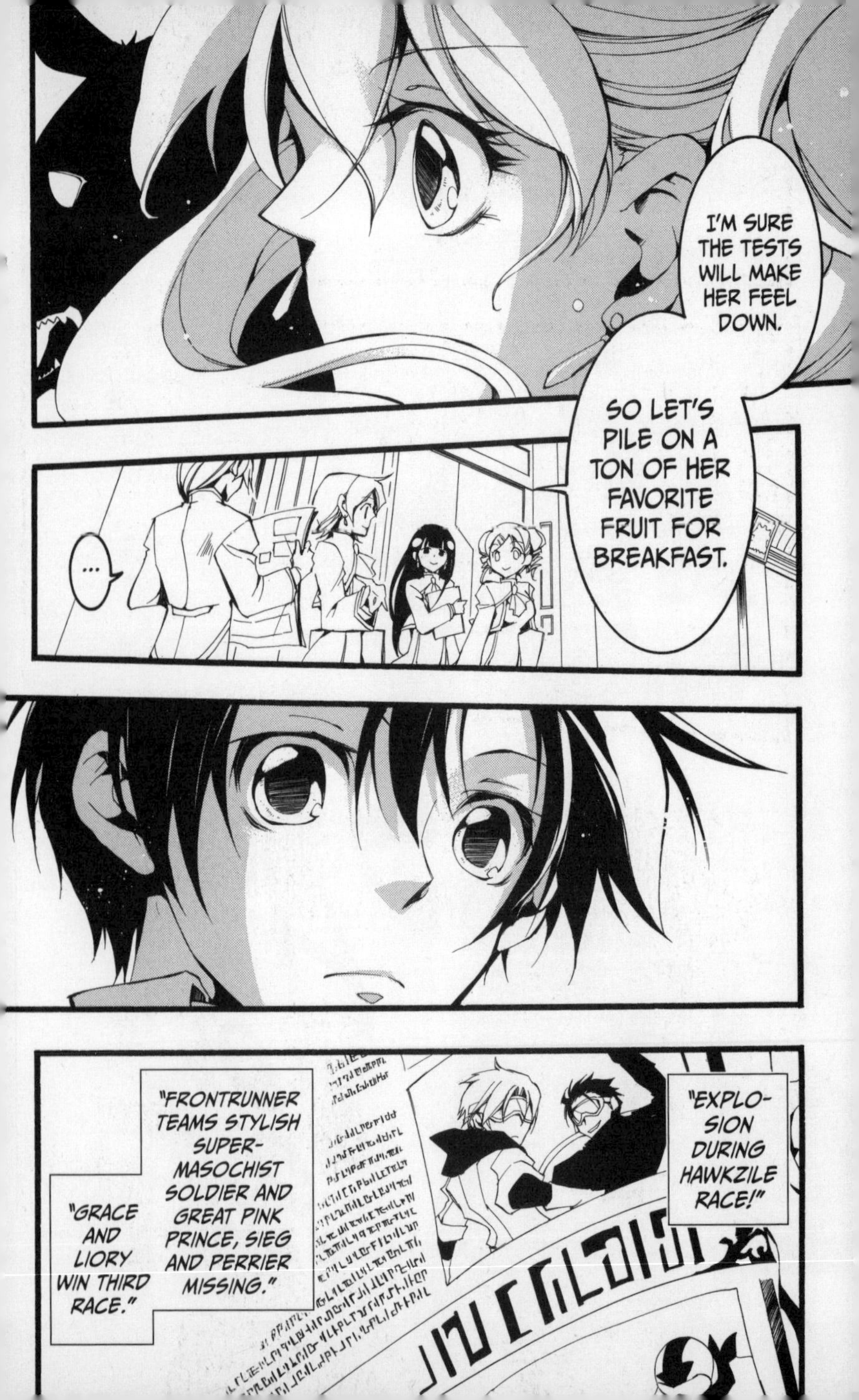
I'M SURE THE TESTS WILL MAKE HER FEEL DOWN.
SO LET'S PILE ON A TON OF HER FAVORITE FRUIT FOR BREAKFAST.
...
"EXPLO-SION DURING HAWKZILE RACE!"
"FRONTRUNNER TEAMS STYLISH SUPER-MASOCHIST SOLDIER AND GREAT PINK PRINCE, SIEG AND PERRIER MISSING."
"GRACE AND LIORY WIN THIRD RACE."

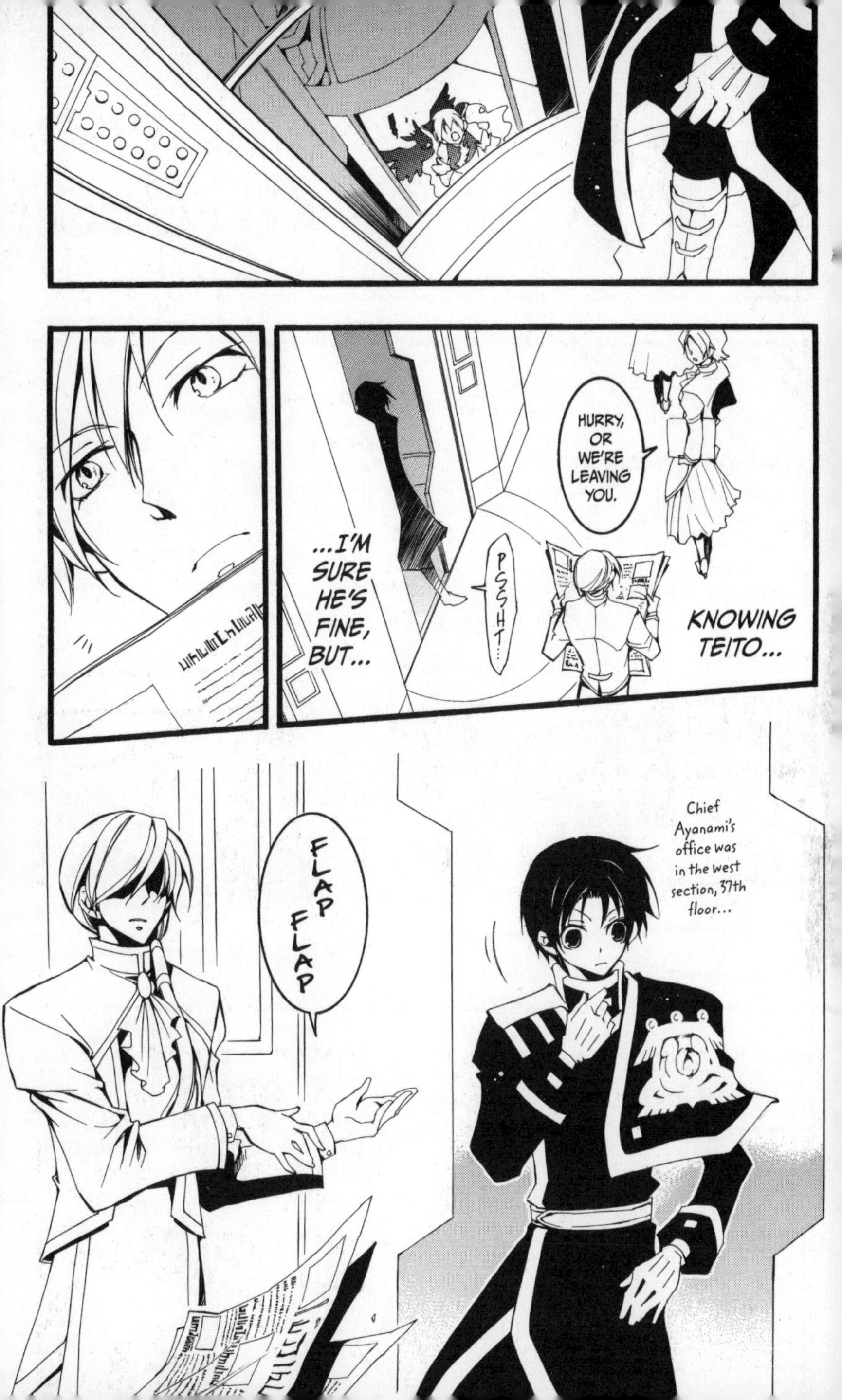
HURRY, OR WE'RE LEAVING YOU.
KNOWING TEITO...
PSSHT...
...I'M SURE HE'S FINE, BUT...
Chief Ayanami's office was in the west section, 37th floor...
FLAP FLAP

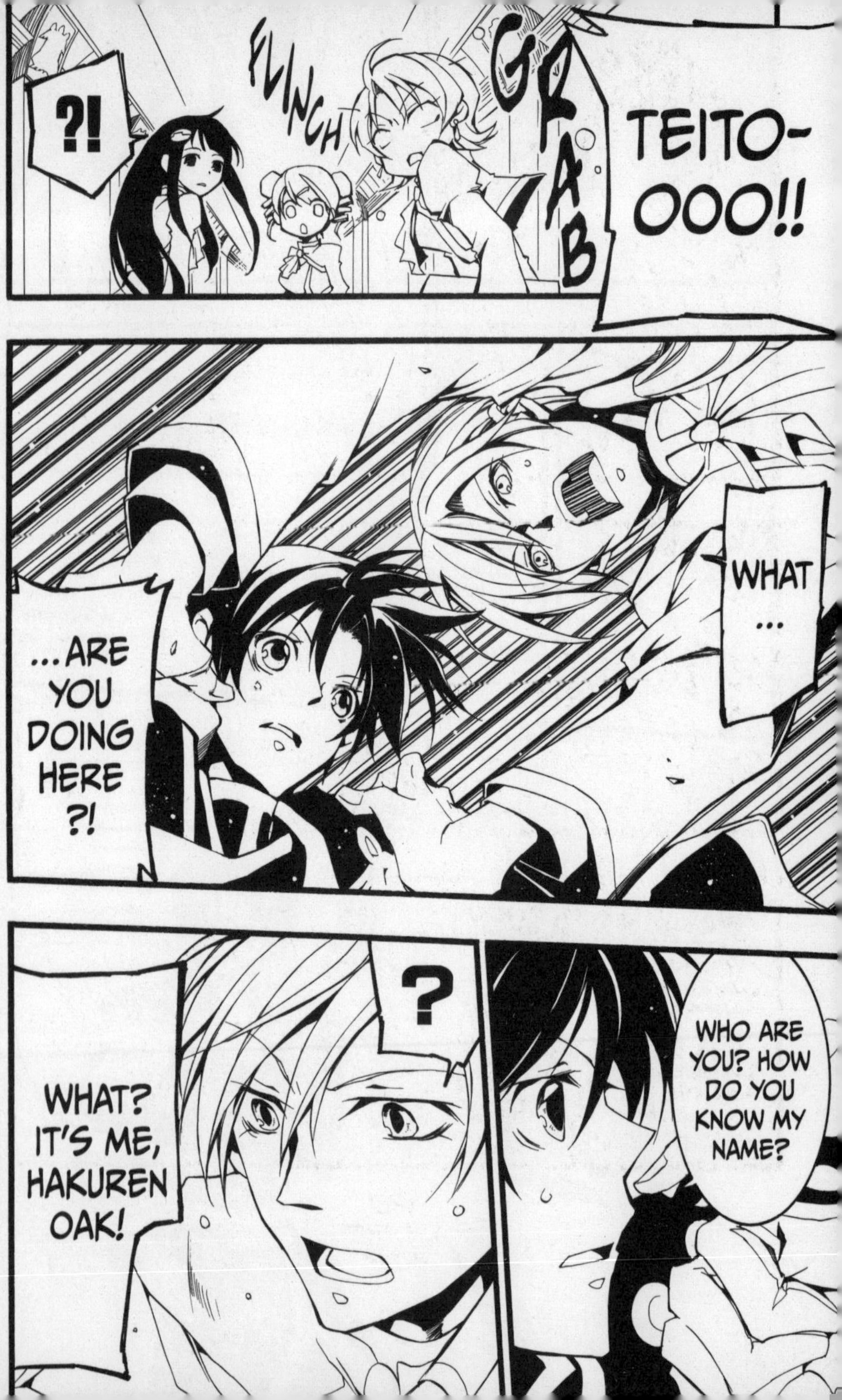
TEITO-OOO!!
GRAB
FLINCH
?!
WHAT...
...ARE YOU DOING HERE?!
WHO ARE YOU? HOW DO YOU KNOW MY NAME?
?
WHAT? IT'S ME, HAKUREN OAK!

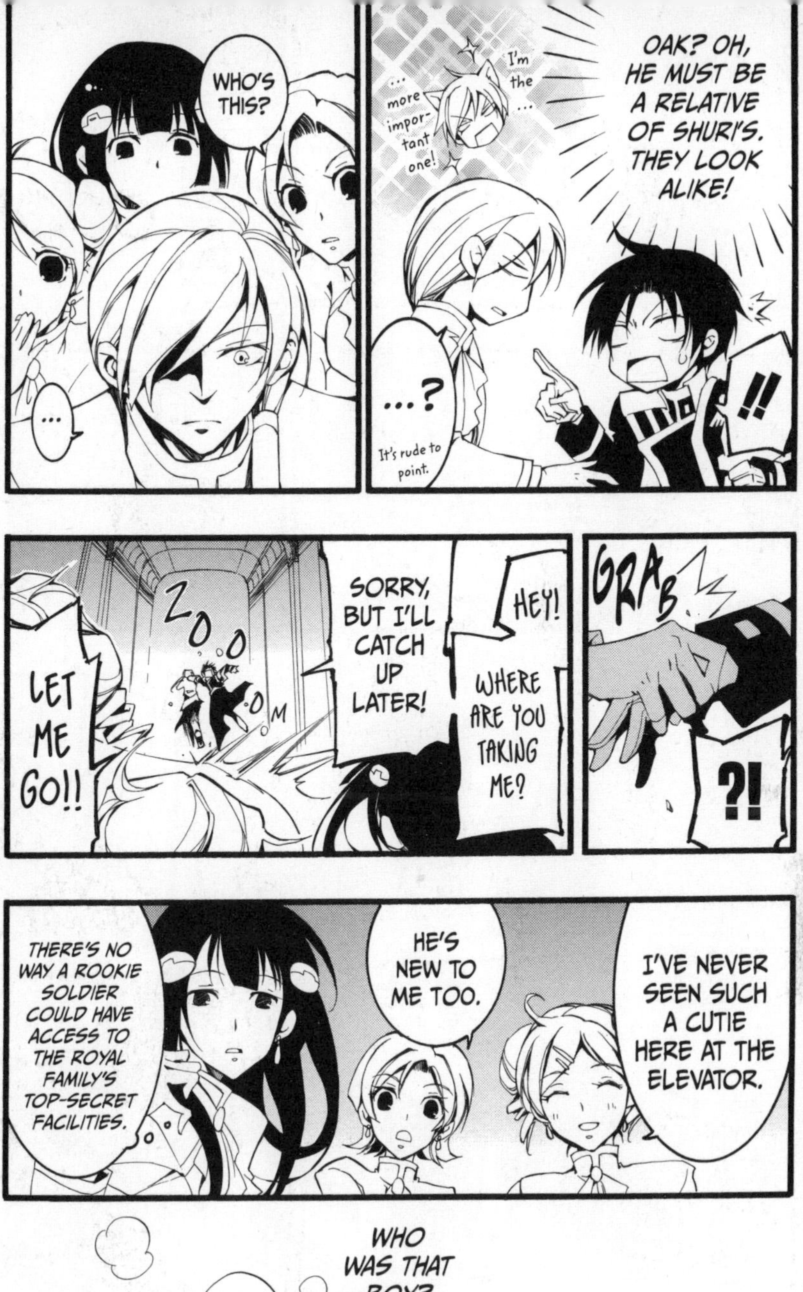
OAK? OH, HE MUST BE A RELATIVE OF SHURI'S. THEY LOOK ALIKE!
I'm the ... more important one!
!!
...?
It's rude to point.
WHO'S THIS?
...
GRAB
?!
HEY!
WHERE ARE YOU TAKING ME?
SORRY, BUT I'LL CATCH UP LATER!
ZOOOOM
LET ME GO!!
I'VE NEVER SEEN SUCH A CUTIE HERE AT THE ELEVATOR.
HE'S NEW TO ME TOO.
THERE'S NO WAY A ROOKIE SOLDIER COULD HAVE ACCESS TO THE ROYAL FAMILY'S TOP-SECRET FACILITIES.
WHO WAS THAT BOY?

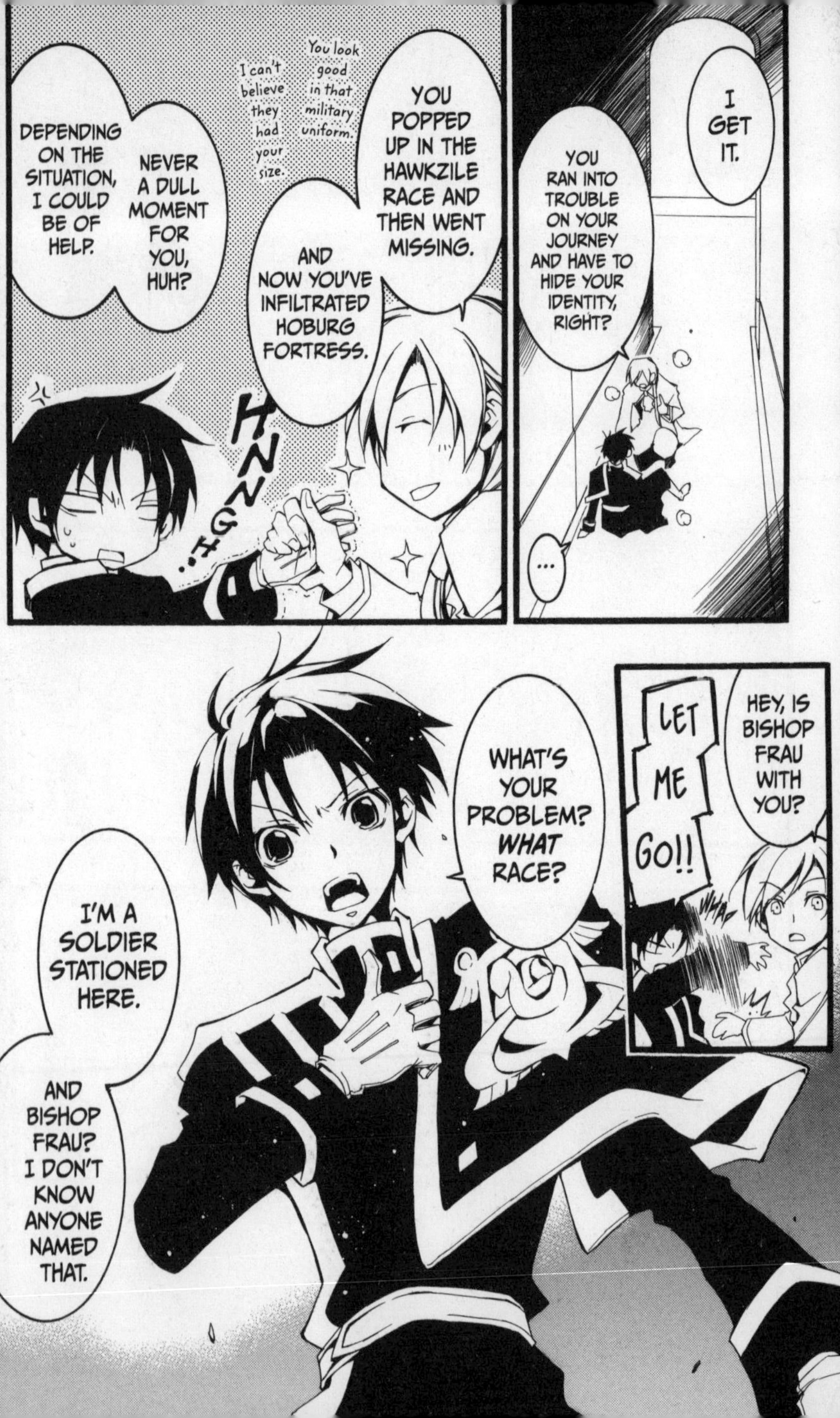
I GET IT.
YOU RAN INTO TROUBLE ON YOUR JOURNEY AND HAVE TO HIDE YOUR IDENTITY, RIGHT?
...
YOU POPPED UP IN THE HAWKZILE RACE AND THEN WENT MISSING.
You look good in that military uniform.
I can't believe they had your size.
AND NOW YOU'VE INFILTRATED HOBURG FORTRESS.
NEVER A DULL MOMENT FOR YOU, HUH?
DEPENDING ON THE SITUATION, I COULD BE OF HELP.
HNNGH!!
HEY, IS BISHOP FRAU WITH YOU?
LET ME GO!!
WHAT'S YOUR PROBLEM? *WHAT* RACE?
I'M A SOLDIER STATIONED HERE.
AND BISHOP FRAU? I DON'T KNOW ANYONE NAMED THAT.

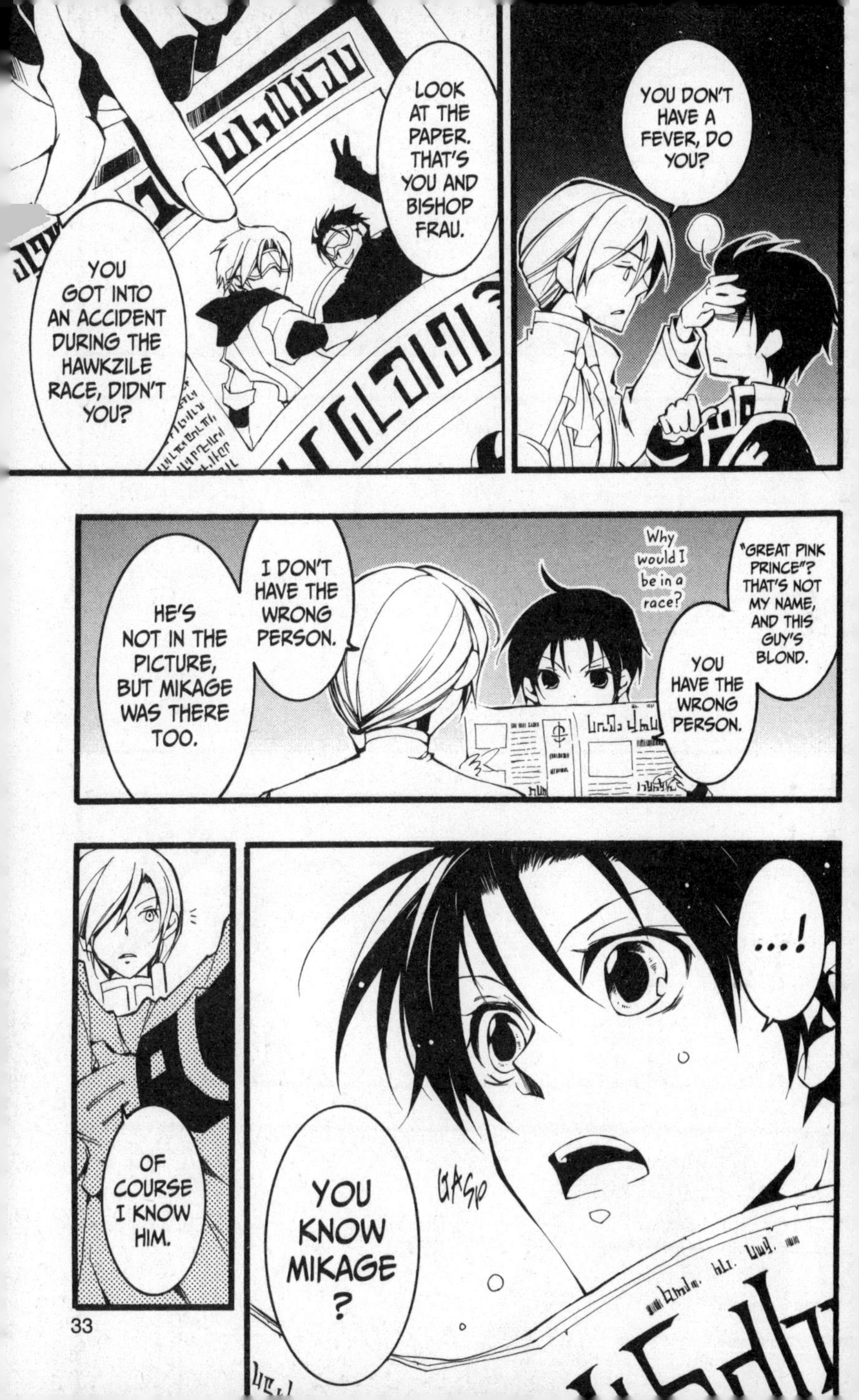
YOU DON'T HAVE A FEVER, DO YOU?
LOOK AT THE PAPER. THAT'S YOU AND BISHOP FRAU.
YOU GOT INTO AN ACCIDENT DURING THE HAWKZILE RACE, DIDN'T YOU?
"GREAT PINK PRINCE"? THAT'S NOT MY NAME, AND THIS GUY'S BLOND.
Why would I be in a race?
YOU HAVE THE WRONG PERSON.
I DON'T HAVE THE WRONG PERSON.
HE'S NOT IN THE PICTURE, BUT MIKAGE WAS THERE TOO.
...!
GASP
YOU KNOW MIKAGE?
OF COURSE I KNOW HIM.

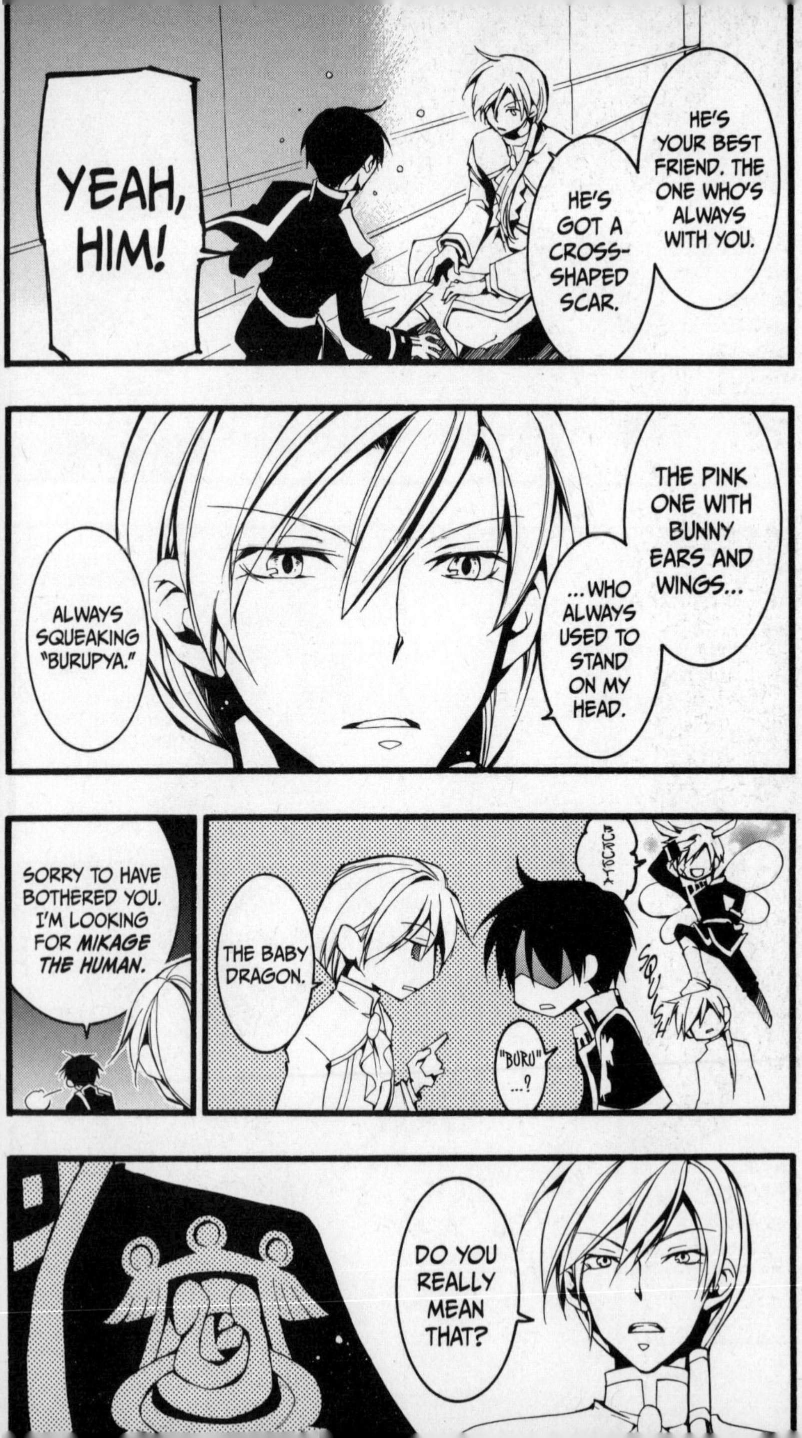
HE'S YOUR BEST FRIEND. THE ONE WHO'S ALWAYS WITH YOU.
HE'S GOT A CROSS-SHAPED SCAR.
YEAH, HIM!
THE PINK ONE WITH BUNNY EARS AND WINGS...
...WHO ALWAYS USED TO STAND ON MY HEAD.
ALWAYS SQUEAKING "BURUPYA."
BURUPYA
SQUISH
THE BABY DRAGON.
"BURU" ...?
SORRY TO HAVE BOTHERED YOU. I'M LOOKING FOR *MIKAGE THE HUMAN*.
DO YOU REALLY MEAN THAT?

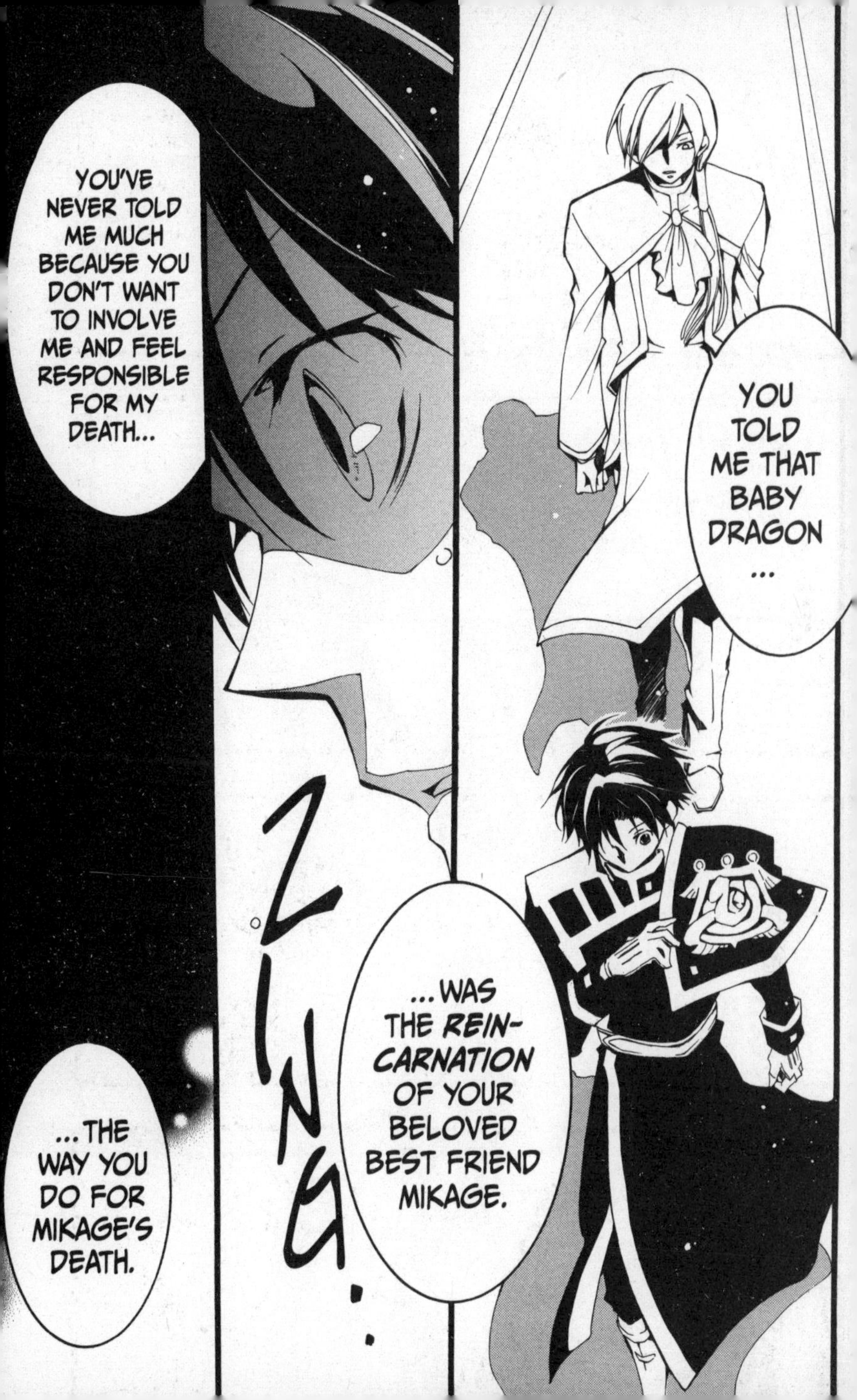
YOU TOLD ME THAT BABY DRAGON ...
...WAS THE *REIN-CARNATION* OF YOUR BELOVED BEST FRIEND MIKAGE.
ZING..
YOU'VE NEVER TOLD ME MUCH BECAUSE YOU DON'T WANT TO INVOLVE ME AND FEEL RESPONSIBLE FOR MY DEATH...
...THE WAY YOU DO FOR MIKAGE'S DEATH.

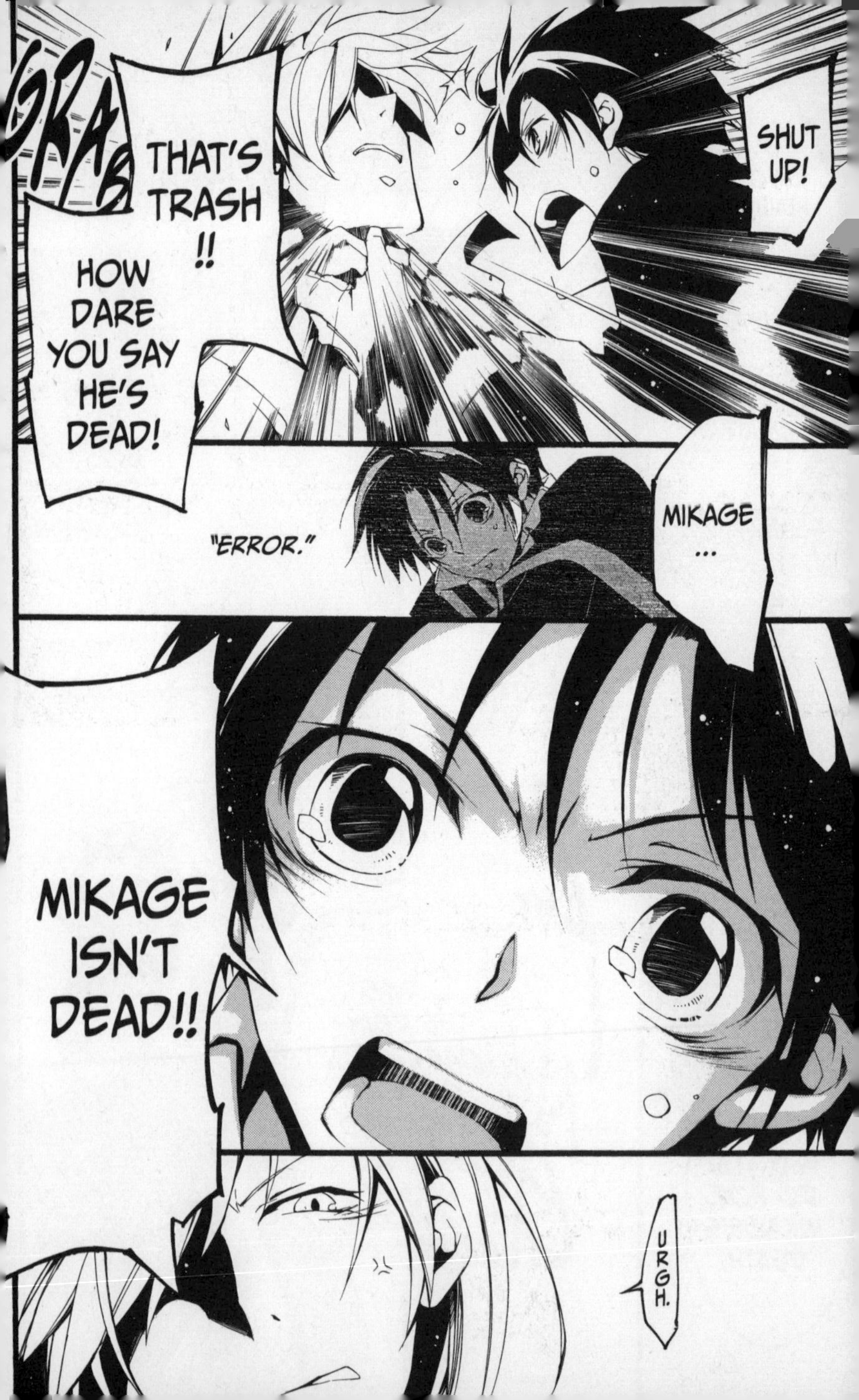
SHUT UP!
GRAB
THAT'S TRASH !!
HOW DARE YOU SAY HE'S DEAD!
MIKAGE ...
"ERROR."
MIKAGE ISN'T DEAD!!
URGH.

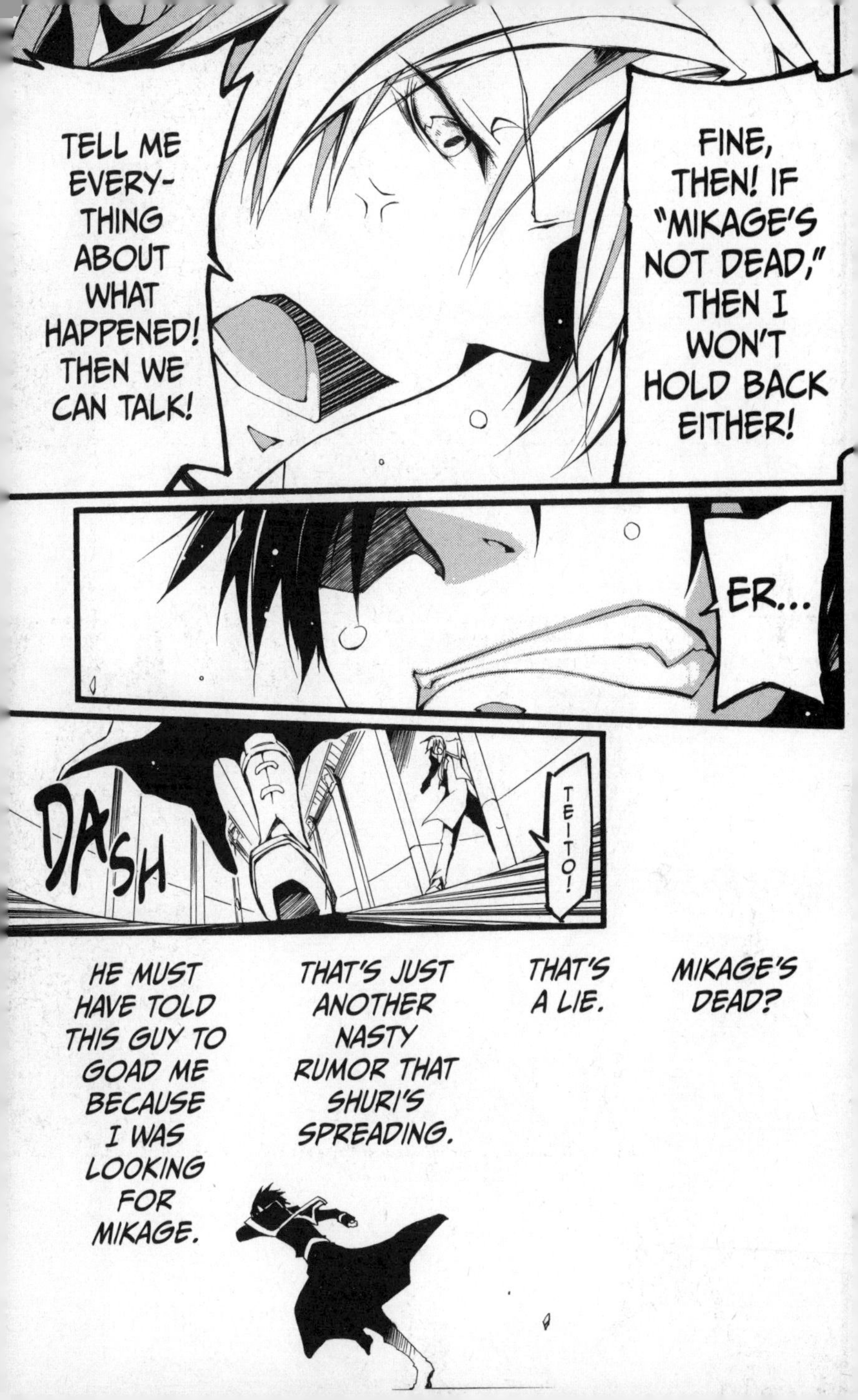
FINE, THEN! IF "MIKAGE'S NOT DEAD," THEN I WON'T HOLD BACK EITHER!
TELL ME EVERY-THING ABOUT WHAT HAPPENED! THEN WE CAN TALK!
ER...
TEITO!
DASH
MIKAGE'S DEAD?
THAT'S A LIE.
THAT'S JUST ANOTHER NASTY RUMOR THAT SHURI'S SPREADING.
HE MUST HAVE TOLD THIS GUY TO GOAD ME BECAUSE I WAS LOOKING FOR MIKAGE.

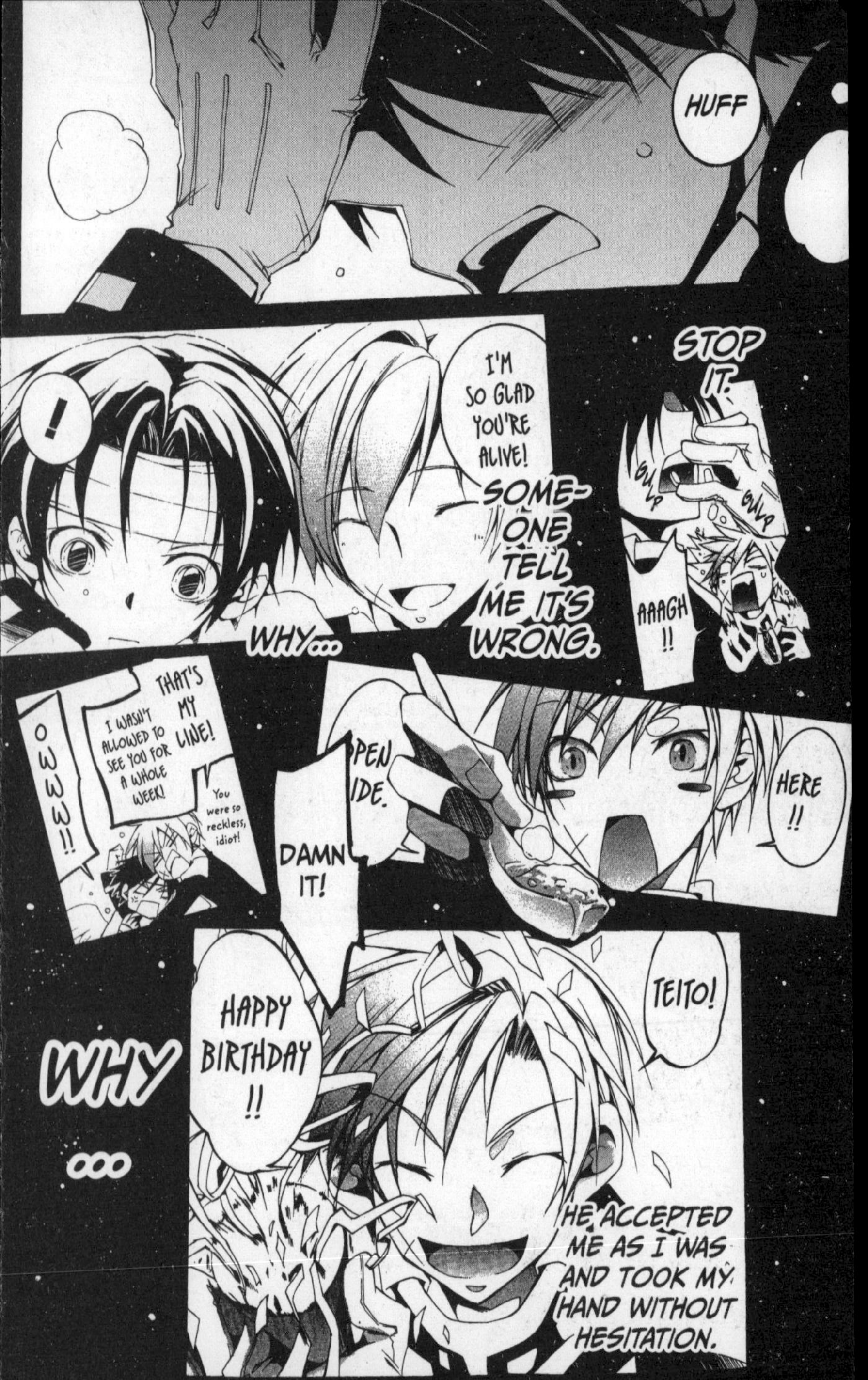
HUFF
STOP IT.
GULP
GULP
AAAGH!!
I'M SO GLAD YOU'RE ALIVE!
SOME-ONE TELL ME IT'S WRONG.
!
WHY...
HERE!!
PEN IDE.
DAMN IT!
THAT'S MY LINE!
I WASN'T ALLOWED TO SEE YOU FOR A WHOLE WEEK!
You were so reckless, idiot!
OWWW!!
TEITO!
HAPPY BIRTHDAY!!
HE ACCEPTED ME AS I WAS AND TOOK MY HAND WITHOUT HESITATION.
WHY...

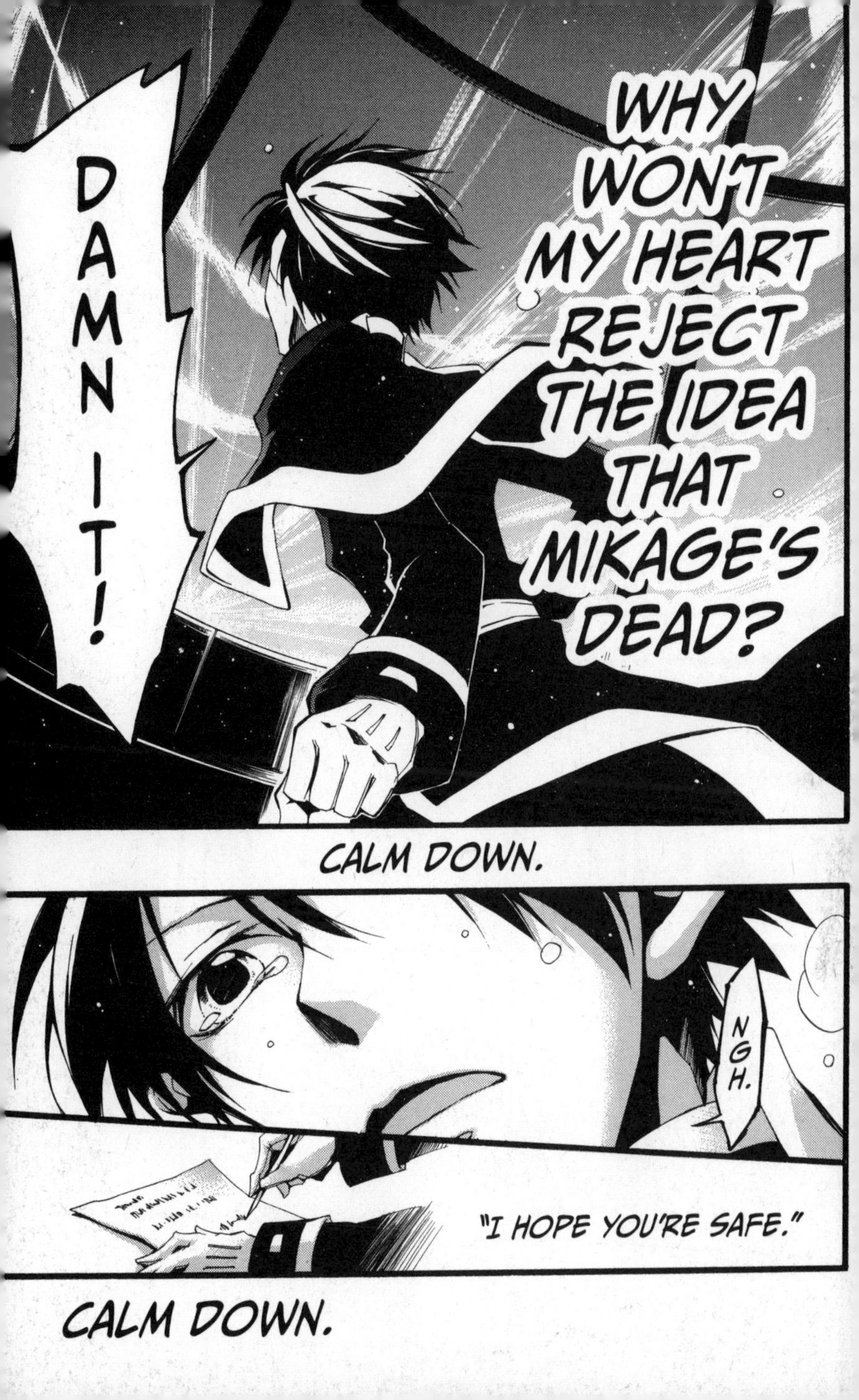
WHY WON'T MY HEART REJECT THE IDEA THAT MIKAGE'S DEAD?
DAMN IT!
CALM DOWN.
NGH.
"I HOPE YOU'RE SAFE."
CALM DOWN.

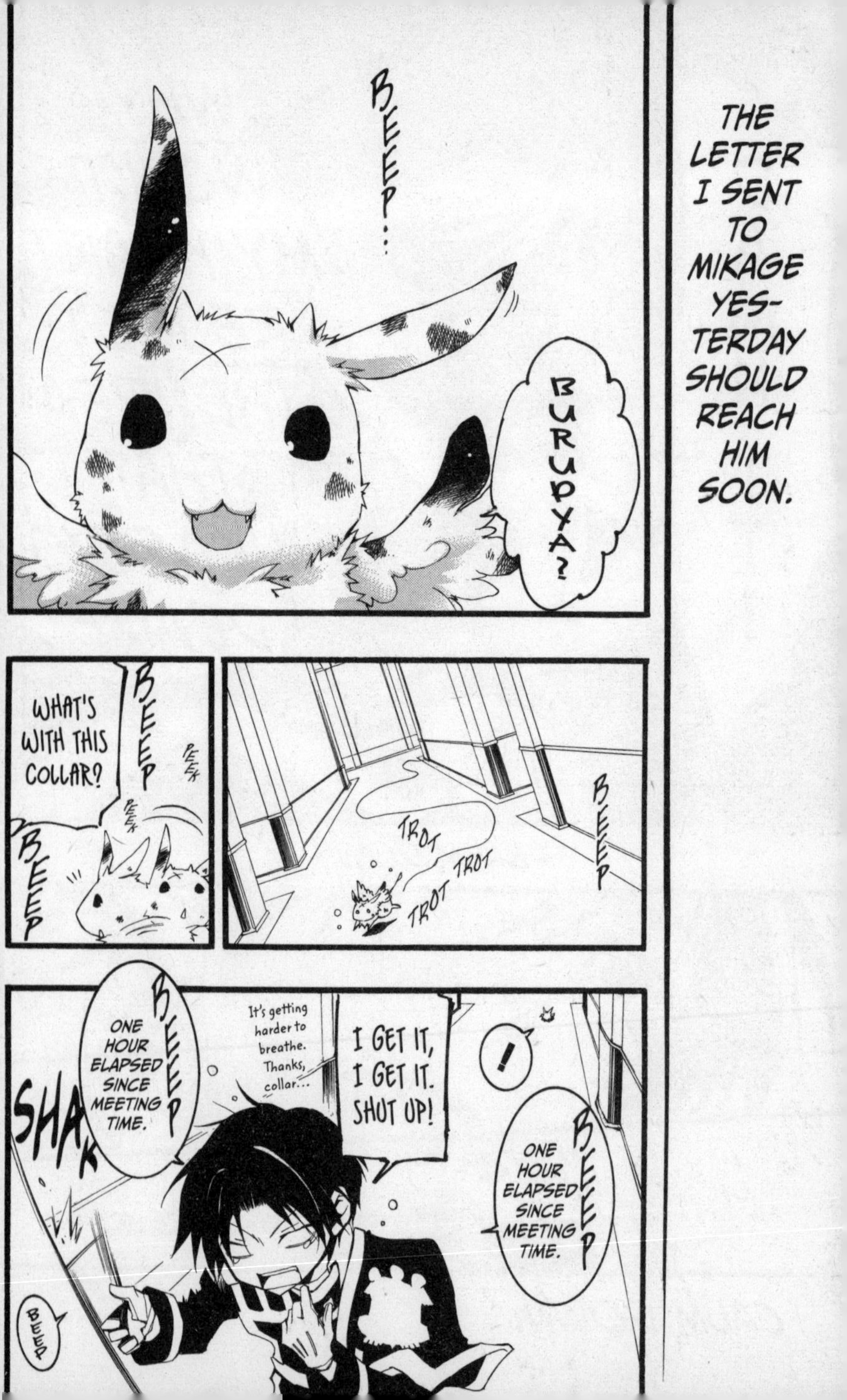
THE LETTER I SENT TO MIKAGE YES-TERDAY SHOULD REACH HIM SOON.
BEEEEP...
BURUPYA?
BEEEP
TROT
TROT
TROT
BEEEEP
WHAT'S WITH THIS COLLAR?
PEEK
PEEK
BEEEEP
!
BEEEEP
ONE HOUR ELAPSED SINCE MEETING TIME.
I GET IT, I GET IT. SHUT UP!
It's getting harder to breathe. Thanks, collar...
BEEEEP
ONE HOUR ELAPSED SINCE MEETING TIME.
SHAK
BEEP

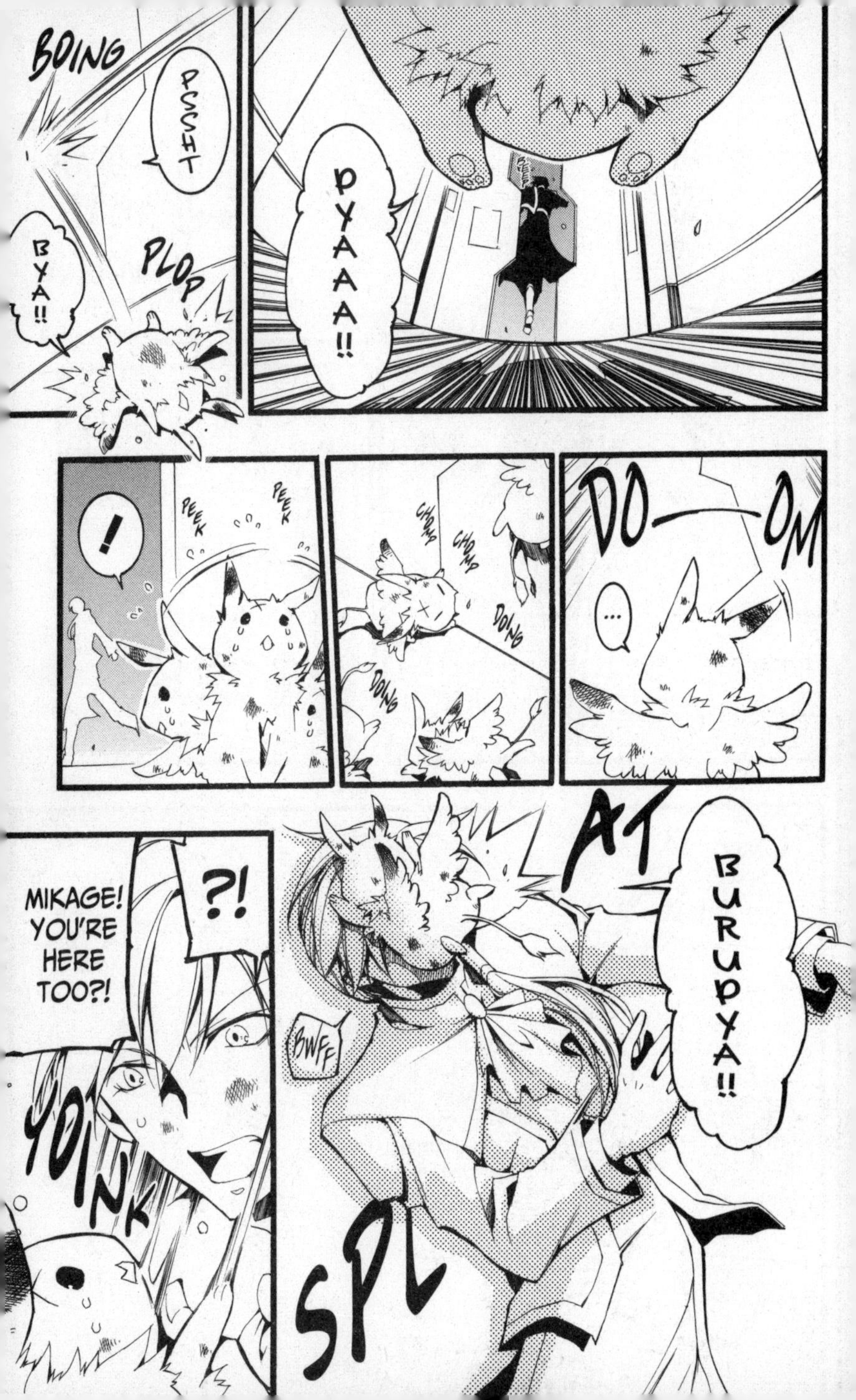
PYAAAA!!
BOING
PSCHT
PLOP
BYA!!
DO—OM
...
CHOMP
CHOMP
DOING
DOING
PEEK
PEEK
!
AT
BURUPYA!!
BWFF
SPL
?!
MIKAGE! YOU'RE HERE TOO?!
YOINK

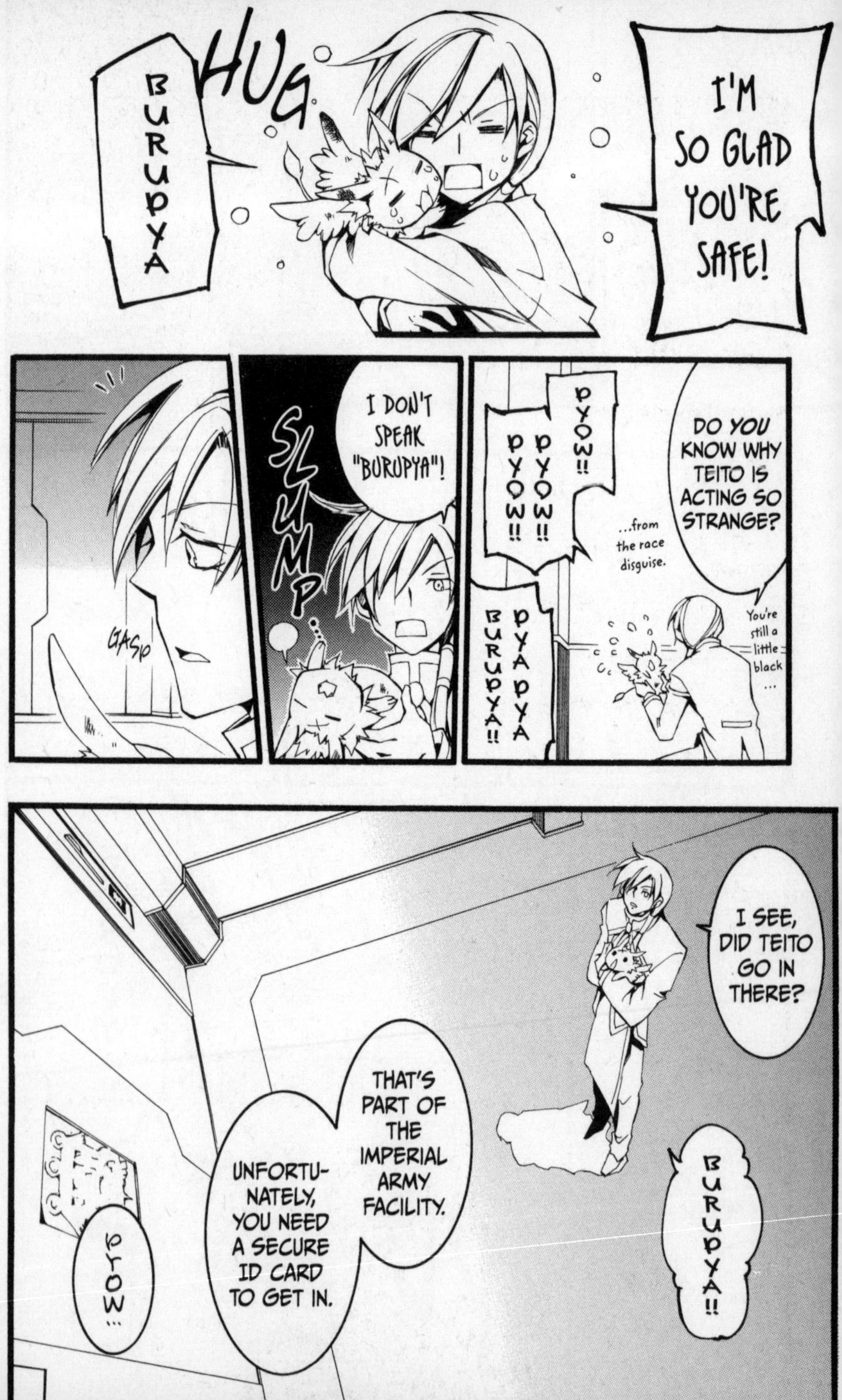

I'M SO GLAD YOU'RE SAFE!
HUG
BURUPYA
DO YOU KNOW WHY TEITO IS ACTING SO STRANGE?
You're still a little black...
...from the race disguise.
PYOW!!
PYOW!! PYOW!!
PYA PYA BURUPYA!!
I DON'T SPEAK "BURUPYA"!
SLUMP
GASP
I SEE, DID TEITO GO IN THERE?
BURUPYA!!
THAT'S PART OF THE IMPERIAL ARMY FACILITY.
UNFORTUNATELY, YOU NEED A SECURE ID CARD TO GET IN.
PYOW...

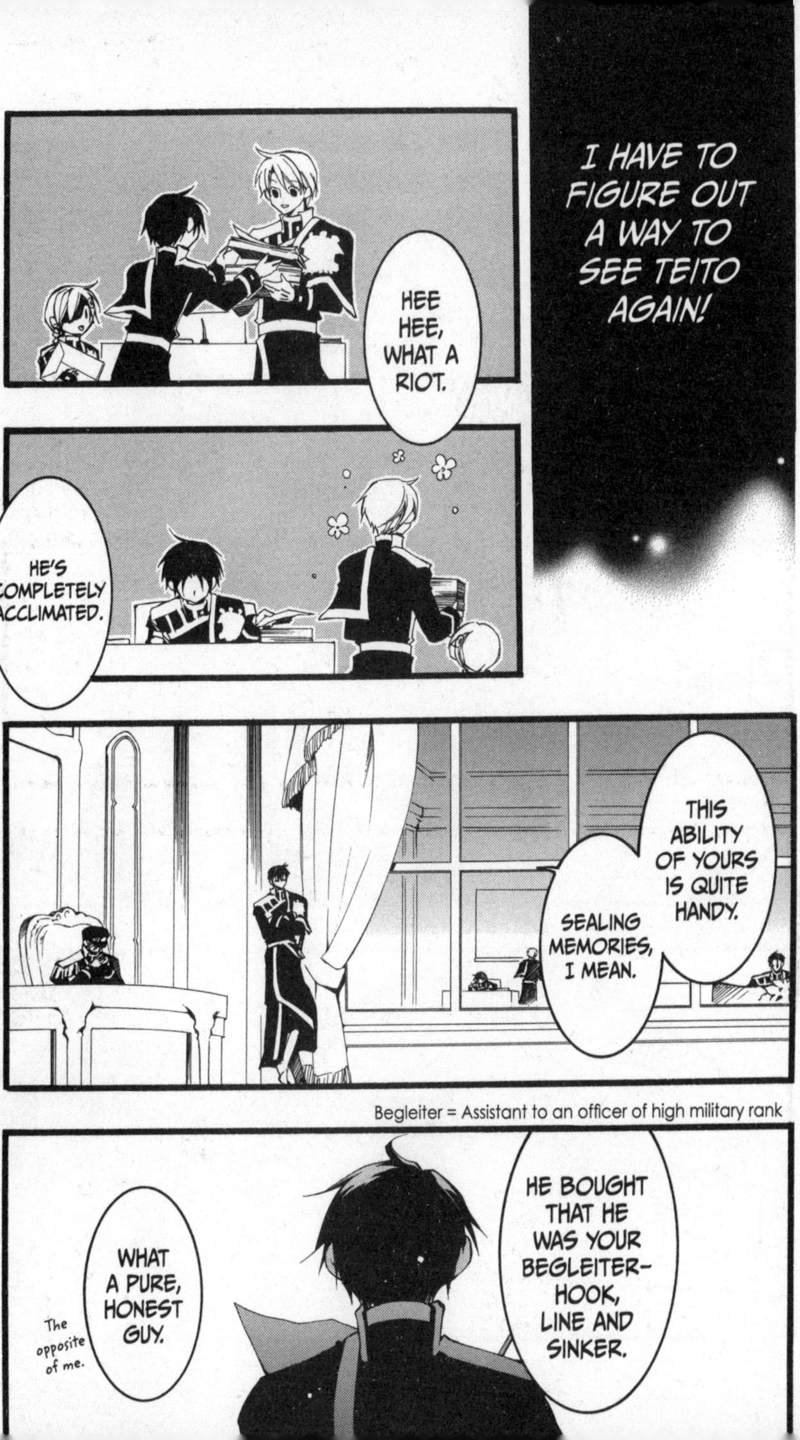
I HAVE TO FIGURE OUT A WAY TO SEE TEITO AGAIN!
HEE HEE, WHAT A RIOT.
HE'S COMPLETELY ACCLIMATED.
THIS ABILITY OF YOURS IS QUITE HANDY.
SEALING MEMORIES, I MEAN.
HE BOUGHT THAT HE WAS YOUR BEGLEITER—HOOK, LINE AND SINKER.
WHAT A PURE, HONEST GUY.
The opposite of me.

Begleiter = Assistant to an officer of high military rank

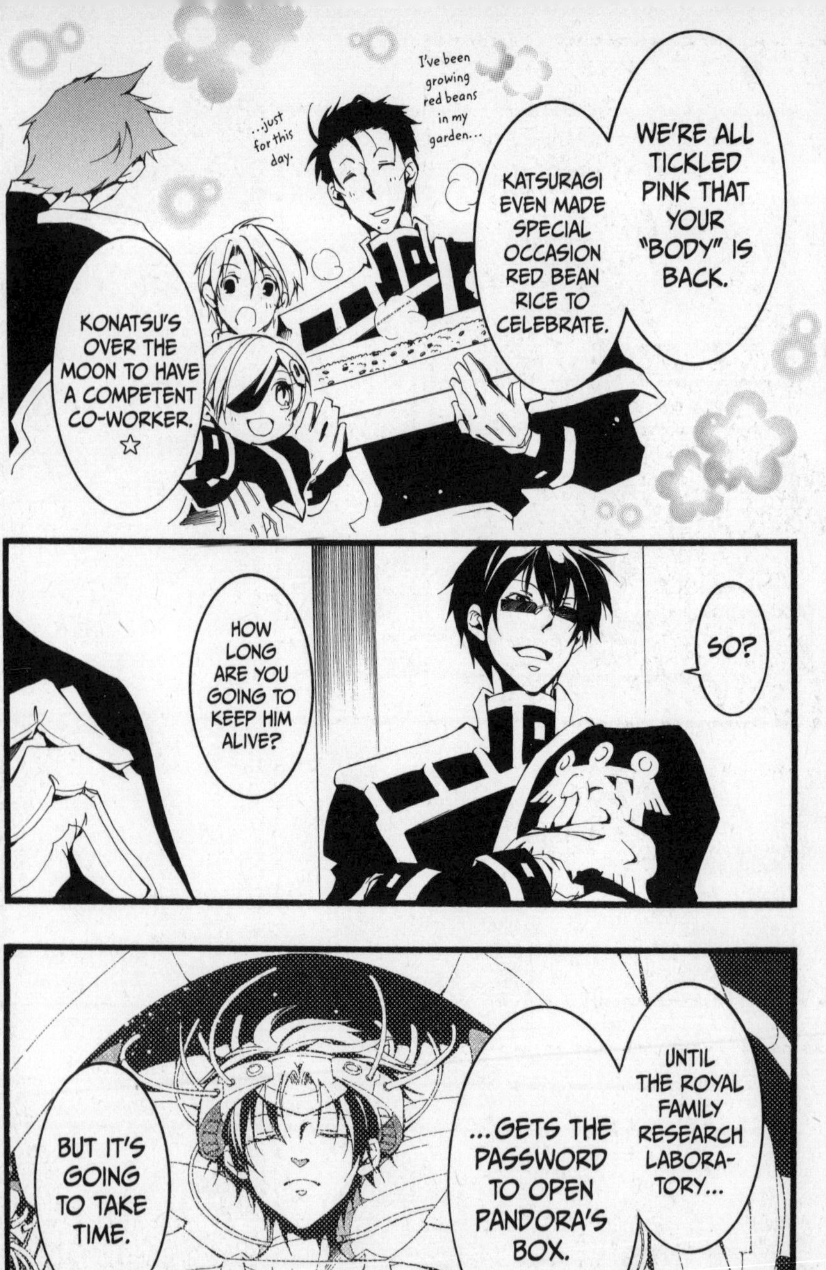
WE'RE ALL TICKLED PINK THAT YOUR "BODY" IS BACK.
I've been growing red beans in my garden...
...just for this day.
KATSURAGI EVEN MADE SPECIAL OCCASION RED BEAN RICE TO CELEBRATE.
KONATSU'S OVER THE MOON TO HAVE A COMPETENT CO-WORKER. ☆
SO?
HOW LONG ARE YOU GOING TO KEEP HIM ALIVE?
UNTIL THE ROYAL FAMILY RESEARCH LABORA-TORY...
...GETS THE PASSWORD TO OPEN PANDORA'S BOX.
BUT IT'S GOING TO TAKE TIME.

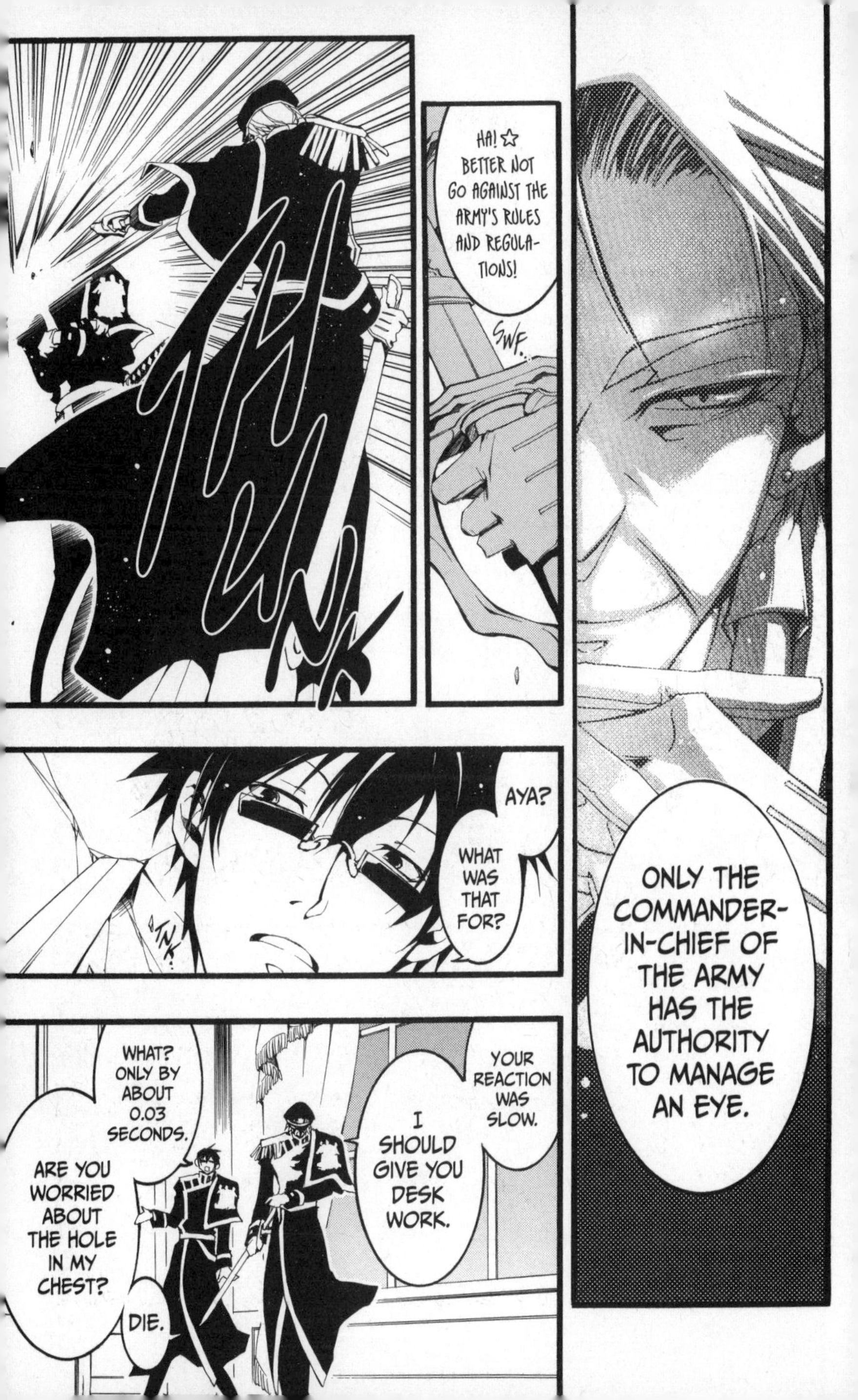
ONLY THE COMMANDER-IN-CHIEF OF THE ARMY HAS THE AUTHORITY TO MANAGE AN EYE.
HA! ☆ BETTER NOT GO AGAINST THE ARMY'S RULES AND REGULA-TIONS!
SWF...
AYA?
WHAT WAS THAT FOR?
YOUR REACTION WAS SLOW.
I SHOULD GIVE YOU DESK WORK.
WHAT? ONLY BY ABOUT 0.03 SECONDS.
ARE YOU WORRIED ABOUT THE HOLE IN MY CHEST?
DIE.

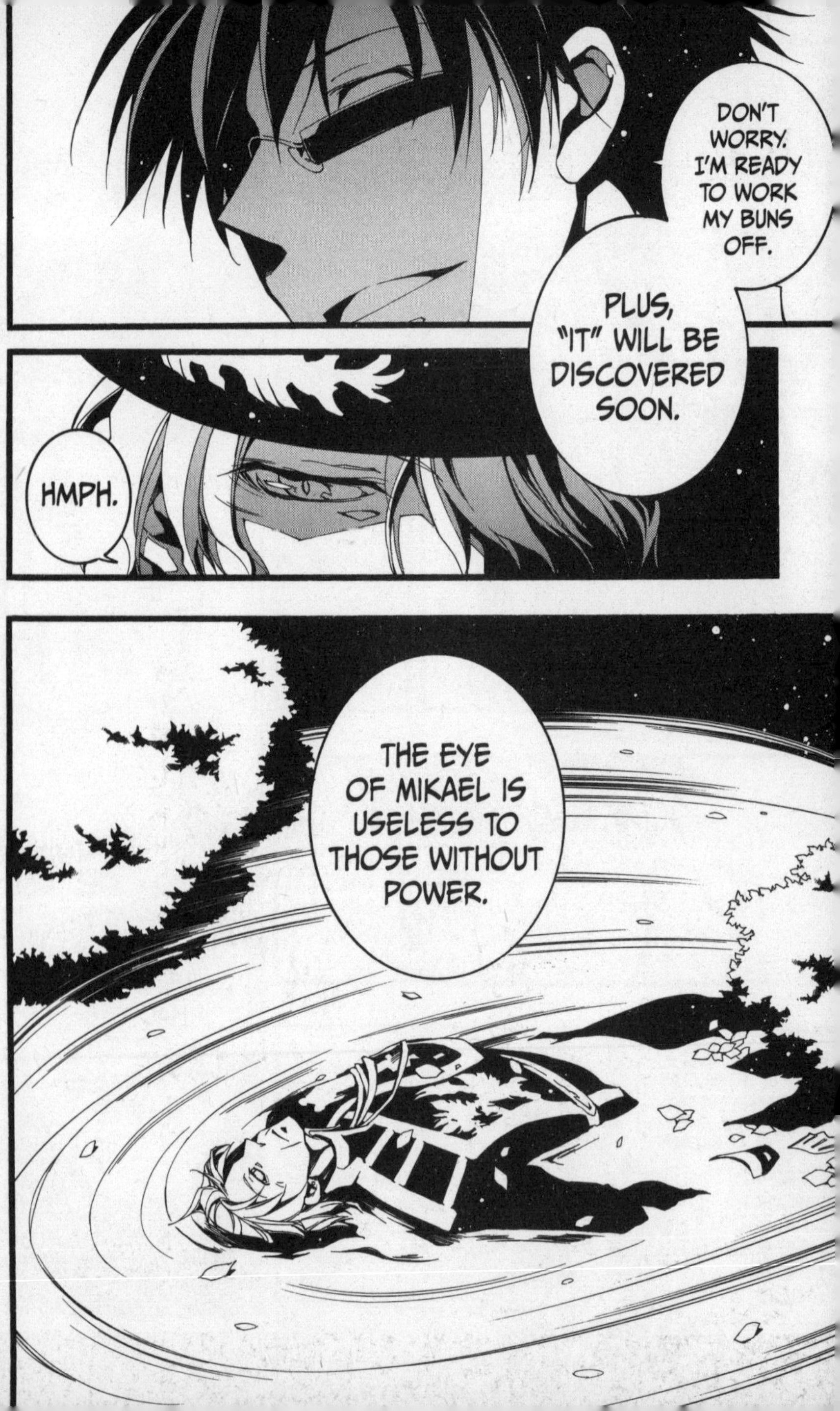
DON'T WORRY. I'M READY TO WORK MY BUNS OFF.
PLUS, "IT" WILL BE DISCOVERED SOON.
HMPH.
THE EYE OF MIKAEL IS USELESS TO THOSE WITHOUT POWER.

Kapitel. 75 “Mourning”

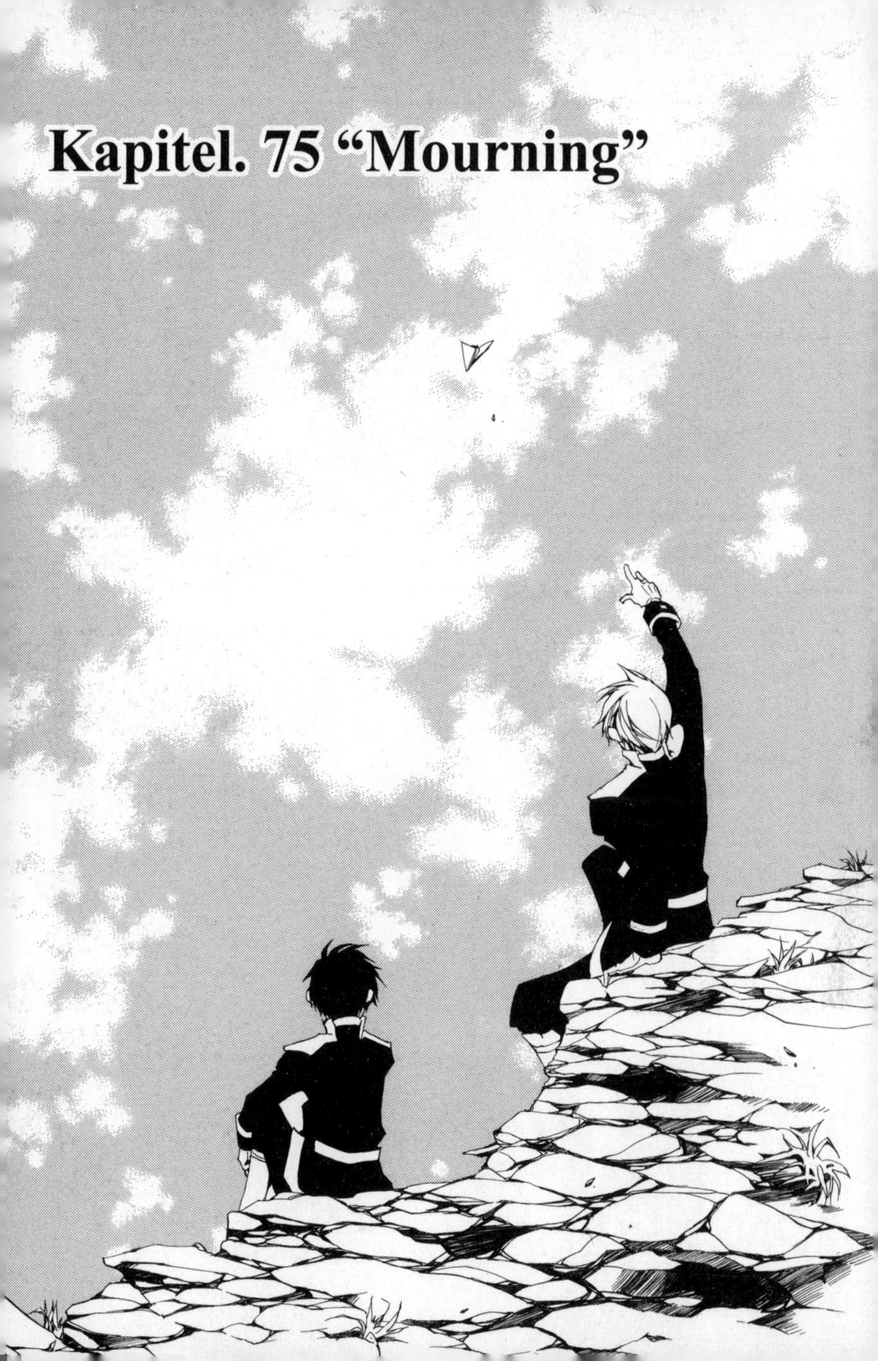

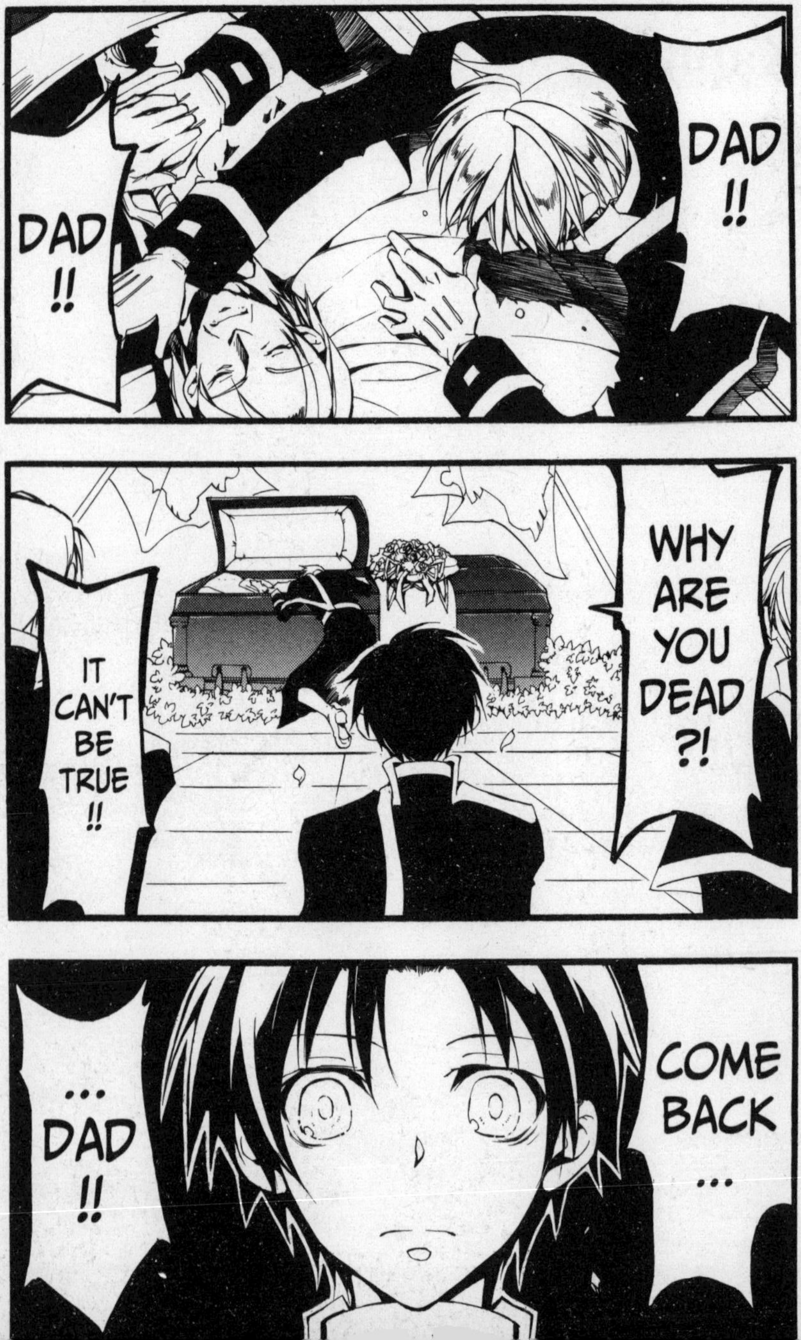
DAD!!
DAD!!
WHY ARE YOU DEAD?!
IT CAN'T BE TRUE!!
COME BACK...
...DAD!!

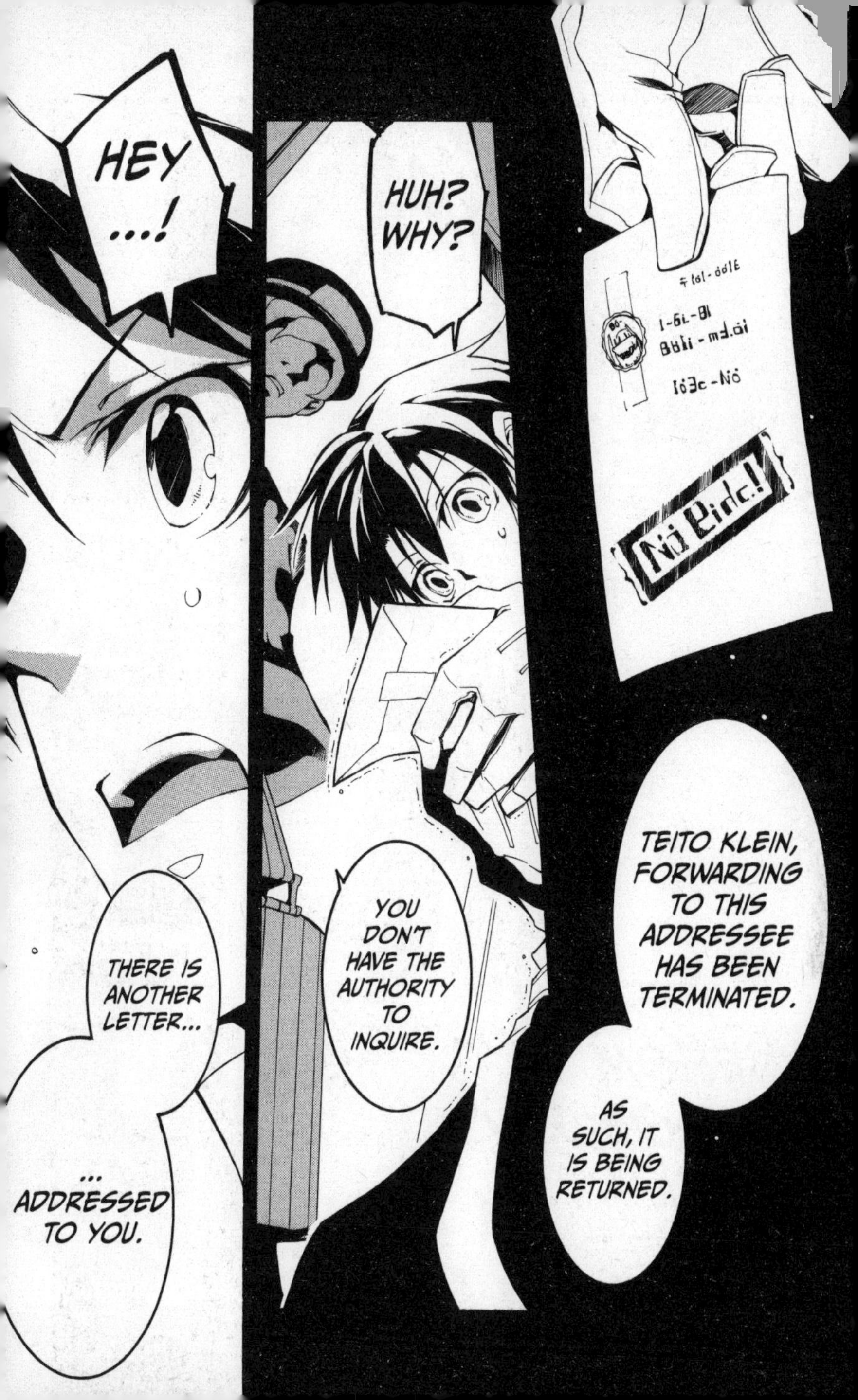
TEITO KLEIN, FORWARDING TO THIS ADDRESSEE HAS BEEN TERMINATED.
AS SUCH, IT IS BEING RETURNED.
HUH? WHY?
YOU DON'T HAVE THE AUTHORITY TO INQUIRE.
HEY ...!
THERE IS ANOTHER LETTER...
... ADDRESSED TO YOU.

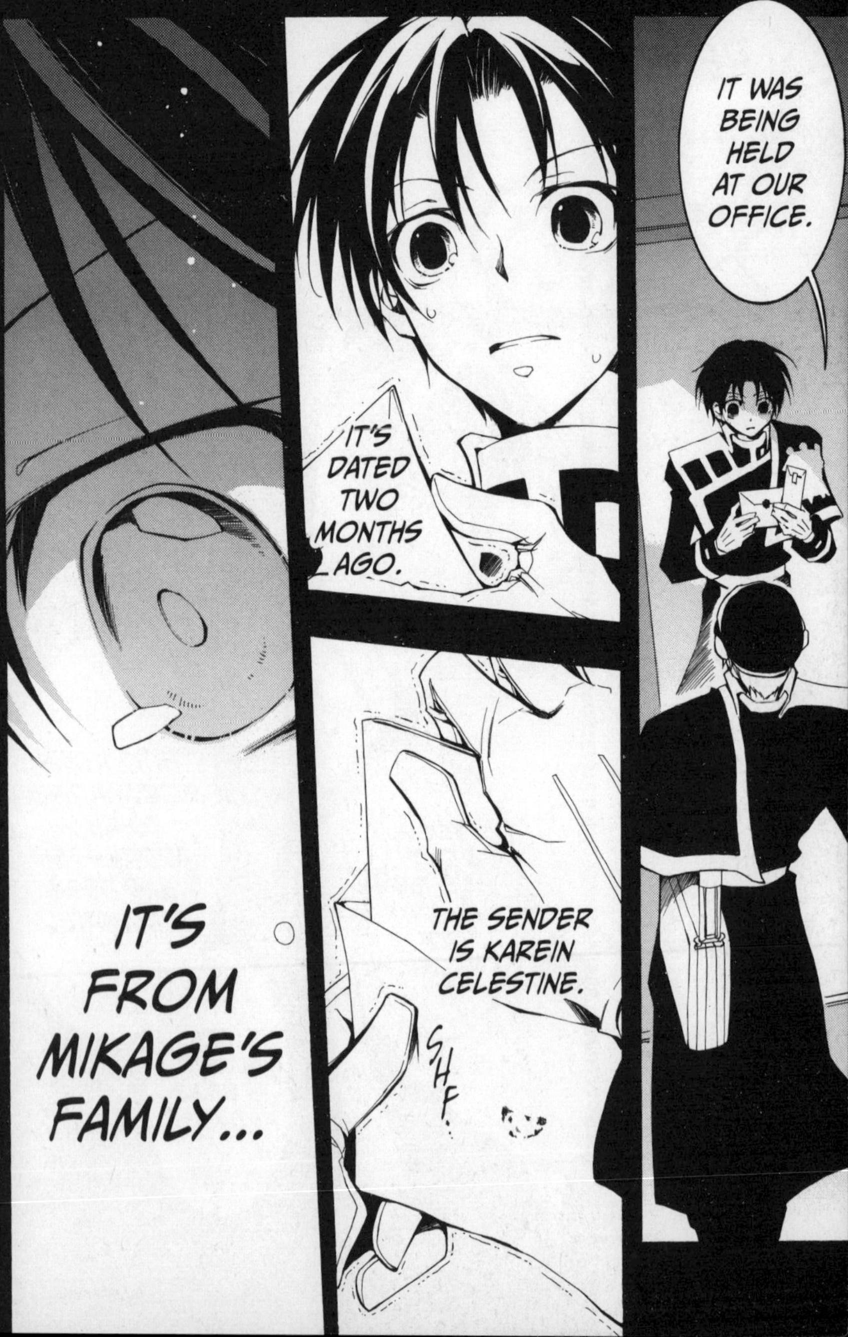
IT WAS BEING HELD AT OUR OFFICE.
IT'S DATED TWO MONTHS AGO.
THE SENDER IS KAREIN CELESTINE.
SHF
IT'S FROM MIKAGE'S FAMILY...

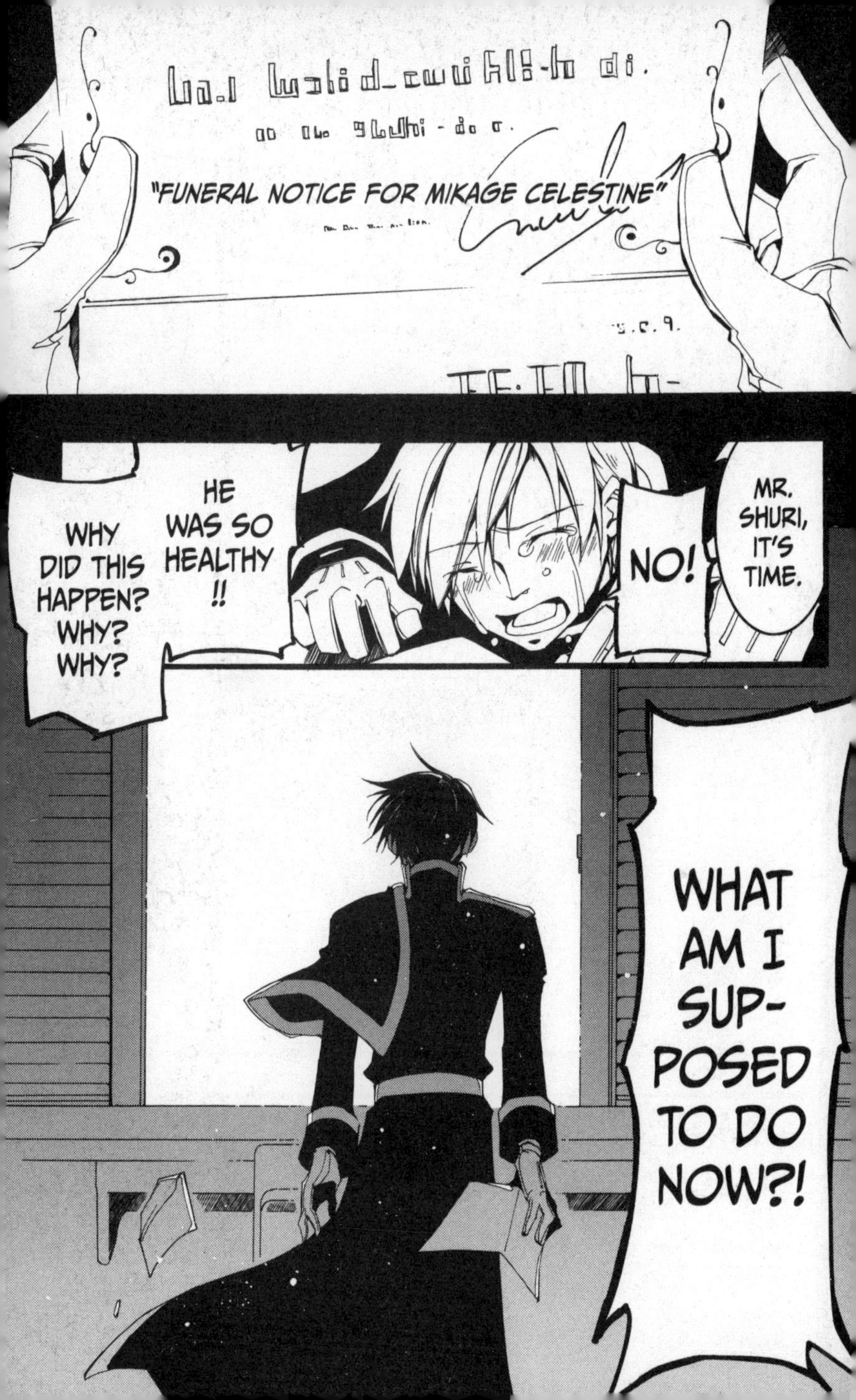
"FUNERAL NOTICE FOR MIKAGE CELESTINE"
MR. SHURI, IT'S TIME.
NO!
HE WAS SO HEALTHY!!
WHY DID THIS HAPPEN? WHY? WHY?
WHAT AM I SUP-POSED TO DO NOW?!

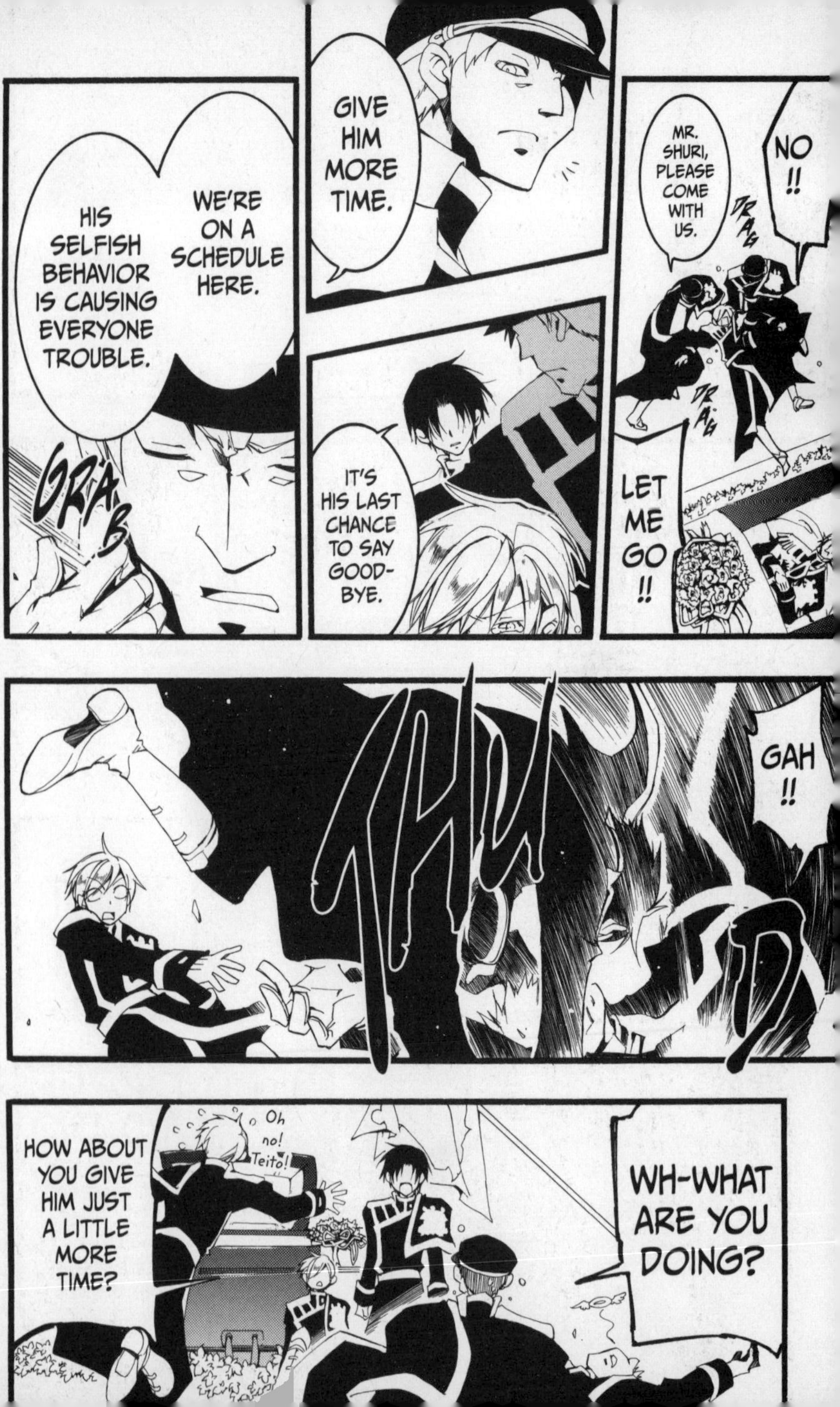
NO !!
MR. SHURI, PLEASE COME WITH US.
DRAG
DRAG
LET ME GO !!
GIVE HIM MORE TIME.
IT'S HIS LAST CHANCE TO SAY GOOD-BYE.
WE'RE ON A SCHEDULE HERE.
HIS SELFISH BEHAVIOR IS CAUSING EVERYONE TROUBLE.
GRAB
GAH !!
WH-WHAT ARE YOU DOING?
Oh no! Teito!
HOW ABOUT YOU GIVE HIM JUST A LITTLE MORE TIME?

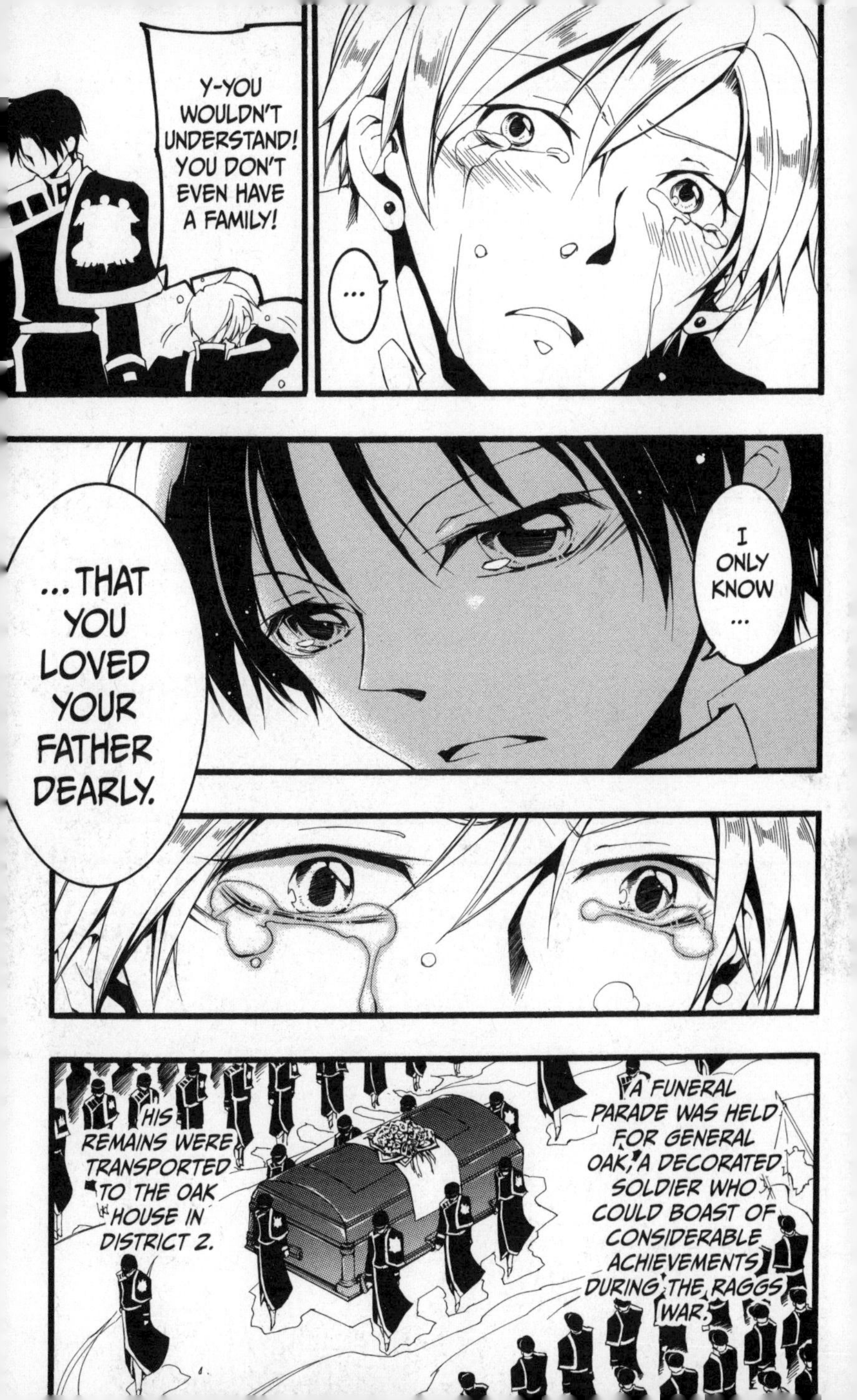
...
Y-YOU WOULDN'T UNDERSTAND! YOU DON'T EVEN HAVE A FAMILY!
I ONLY KNOW ...
...THAT YOU LOVED YOUR FATHER DEARLY.
A FUNERAL PARADE WAS HELD FOR GENERAL OAK, A DECORATED SOLDIER WHO COULD BOAST OF CONSIDERABLE ACHIEVEMENTS DURING THE RAGGS WAR.
HIS REMAINS WERE TRANSPORTED TO THE OAK HOUSE IN DISTRICT 2.

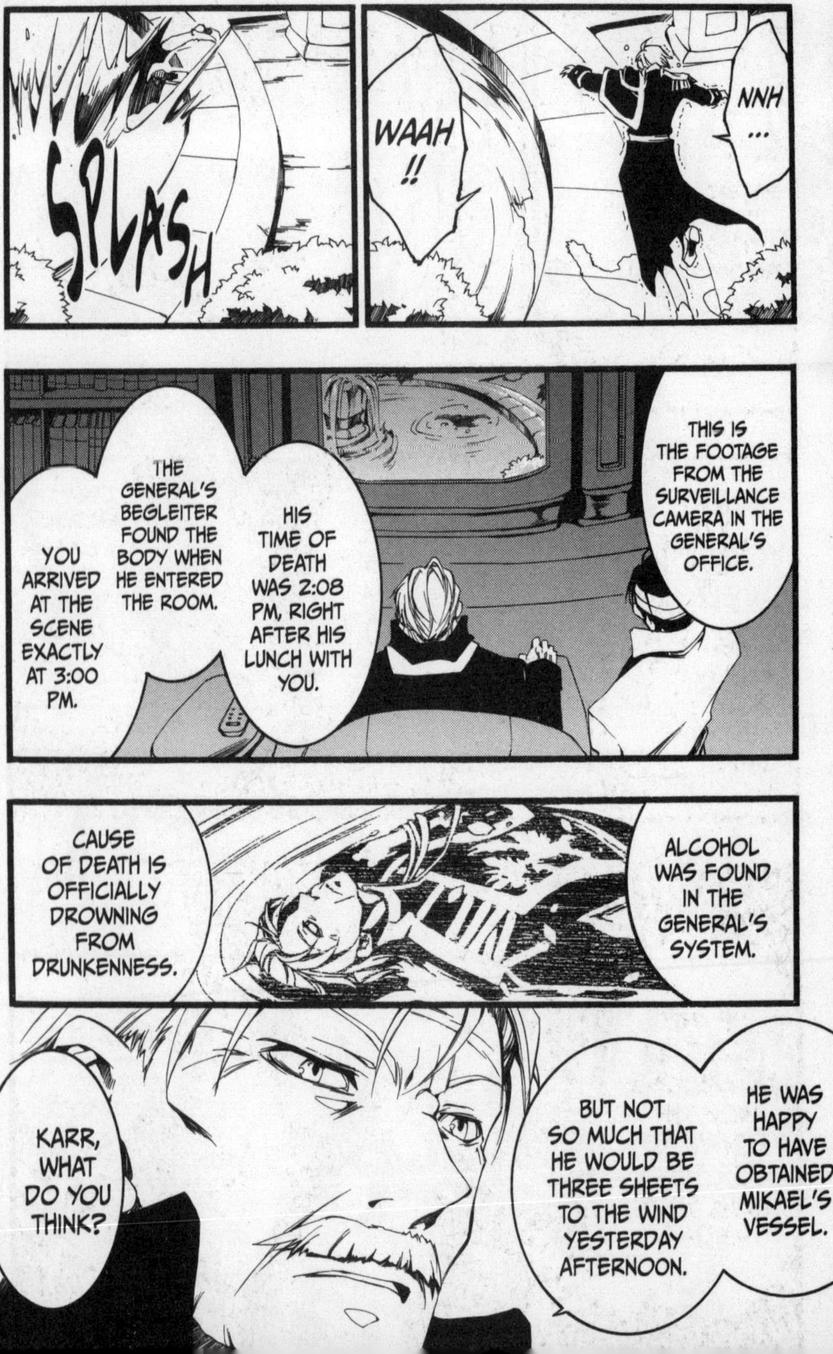
NNH...
WAAH!!
SPLASH
THIS IS THE FOOTAGE FROM THE SURVEILLANCE CAMERA IN THE GENERAL'S OFFICE.
HIS TIME OF DEATH WAS 2:08 PM, RIGHT AFTER HIS LUNCH WITH YOU.
THE GENERAL'S BEGLEITER FOUND THE BODY WHEN HE ENTERED THE ROOM.
YOU ARRIVED AT THE SCENE EXACTLY AT 3:00 PM.
ALCOHOL WAS FOUND IN THE GENERAL'S SYSTEM.
CAUSE OF DEATH IS OFFICIALLY DROWNING FROM DRUNKENNESS.
HE WAS HAPPY TO HAVE OBTAINED MIKAEL'S VESSEL.
BUT NOT SO MUCH THAT HE WOULD BE THREE SHEETS TO THE WIND YESTERDAY AFTERNOON.
KARR, WHAT DO YOU THINK?

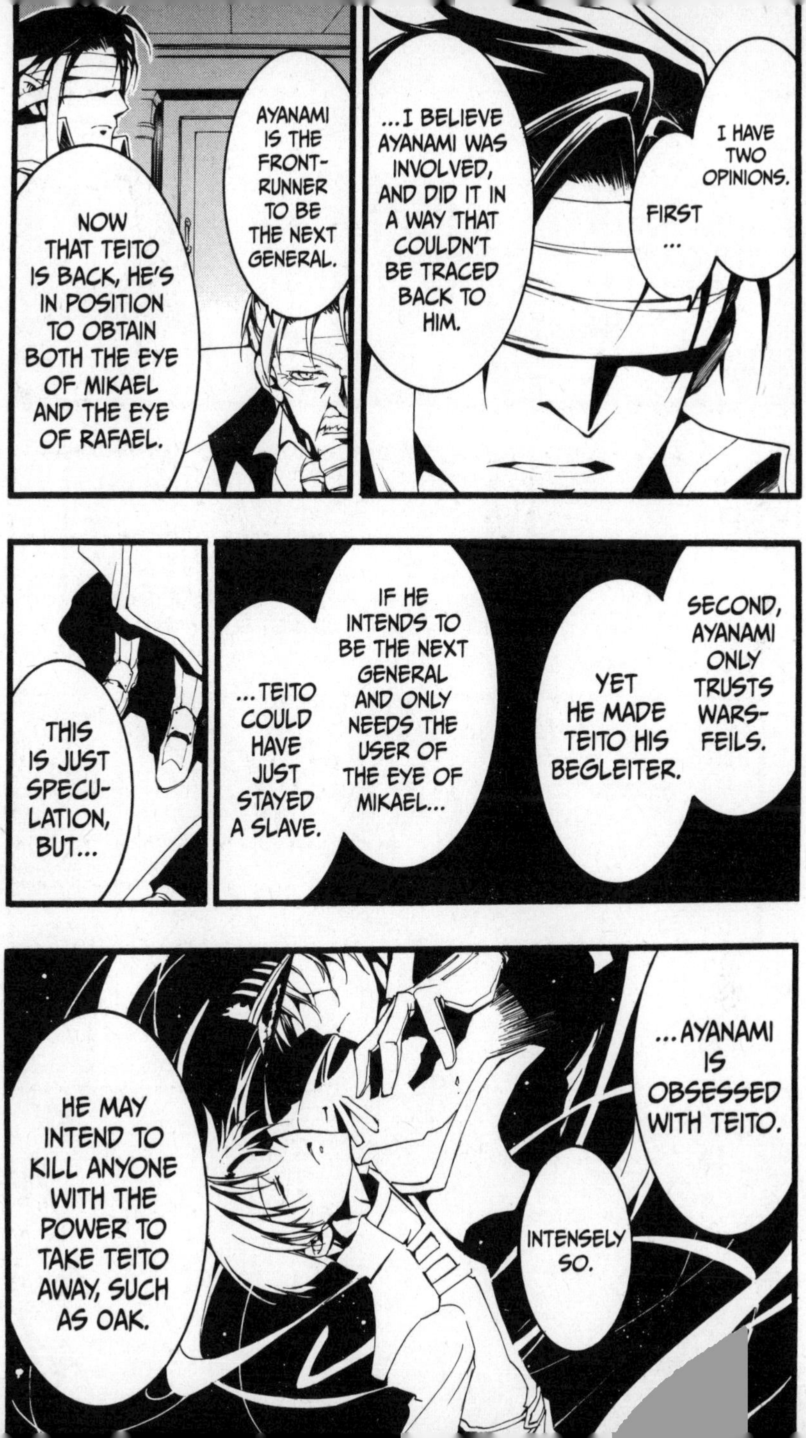
I HAVE TWO OPINIONS.
FIRST...
...I BELIEVE AYANAMI WAS INVOLVED, AND DID IT IN A WAY THAT COULDN'T BE TRACED BACK TO HIM.
AYANAMI IS THE FRONT-RUNNER TO BE THE NEXT GENERAL.
NOW THAT TEITO IS BACK, HE'S IN POSITION TO OBTAIN BOTH THE EYE OF MIKAEL AND THE EYE OF RAFAEL.
SECOND, AYANAMI ONLY TRUSTS WARS-FEILS.
YET HE MADE TEITO HIS BEGLEITER.
IF HE INTENDS TO BE THE NEXT GENERAL AND ONLY NEEDS THE USER OF THE EYE OF MIKAEL...
...TEITO COULD HAVE JUST STAYED A SLAVE.
THIS IS JUST SPECU-LATION, BUT...
...AYANAMI IS OBSESSED WITH TEITO.
INTENSELY SO.
HE MAY INTEND TO KILL ANYONE WITH THE POWER TO TAKE TEITO AWAY, SUCH AS OAK.

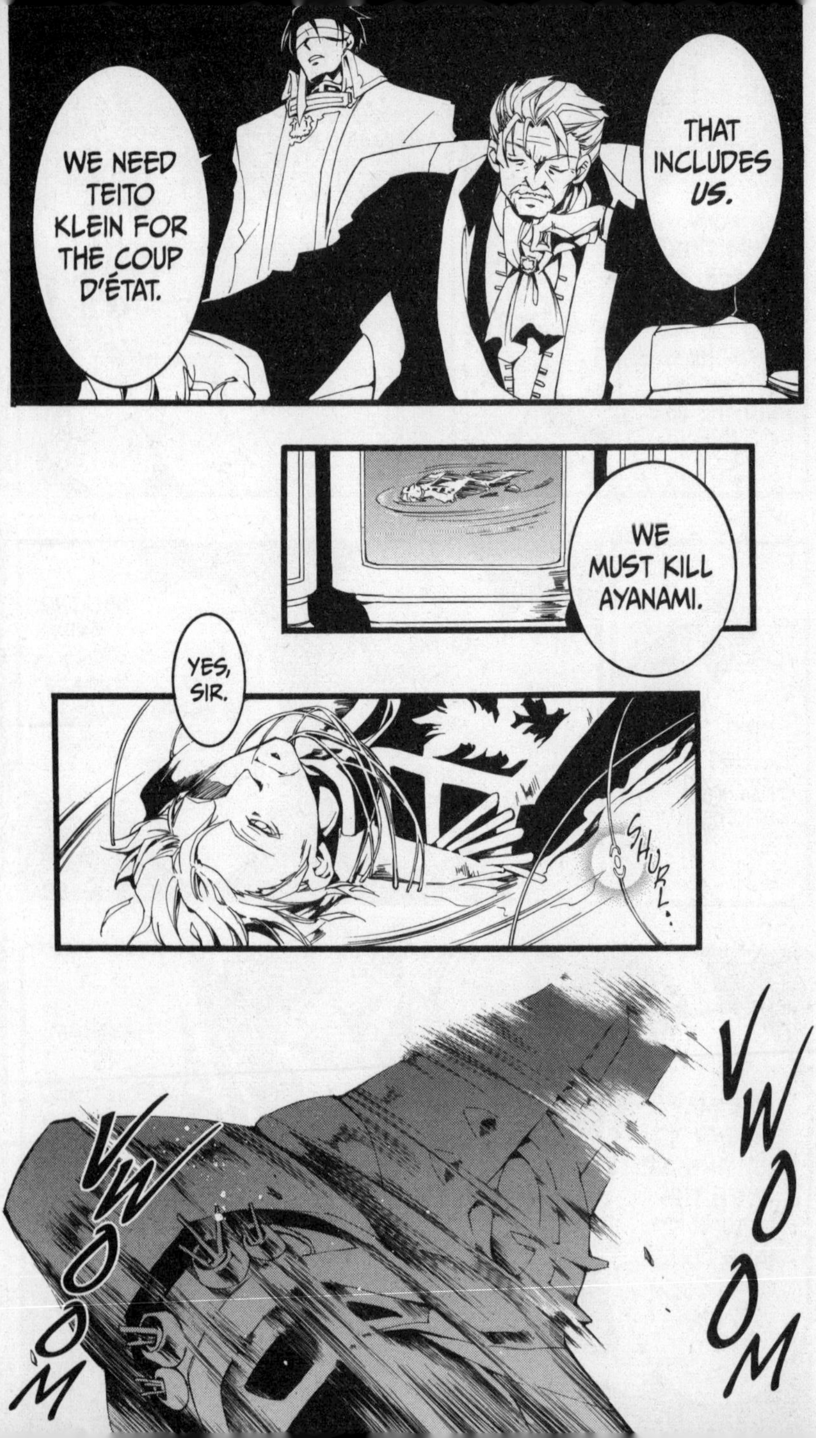
THAT INCLUDES US.
WE NEED TEITO KLEIN FOR THE COUP D'ÉTAT.
WE MUST KILL AYANAMI.
YES, SIR.
SHURL...
VWOOOM
VWOOOM

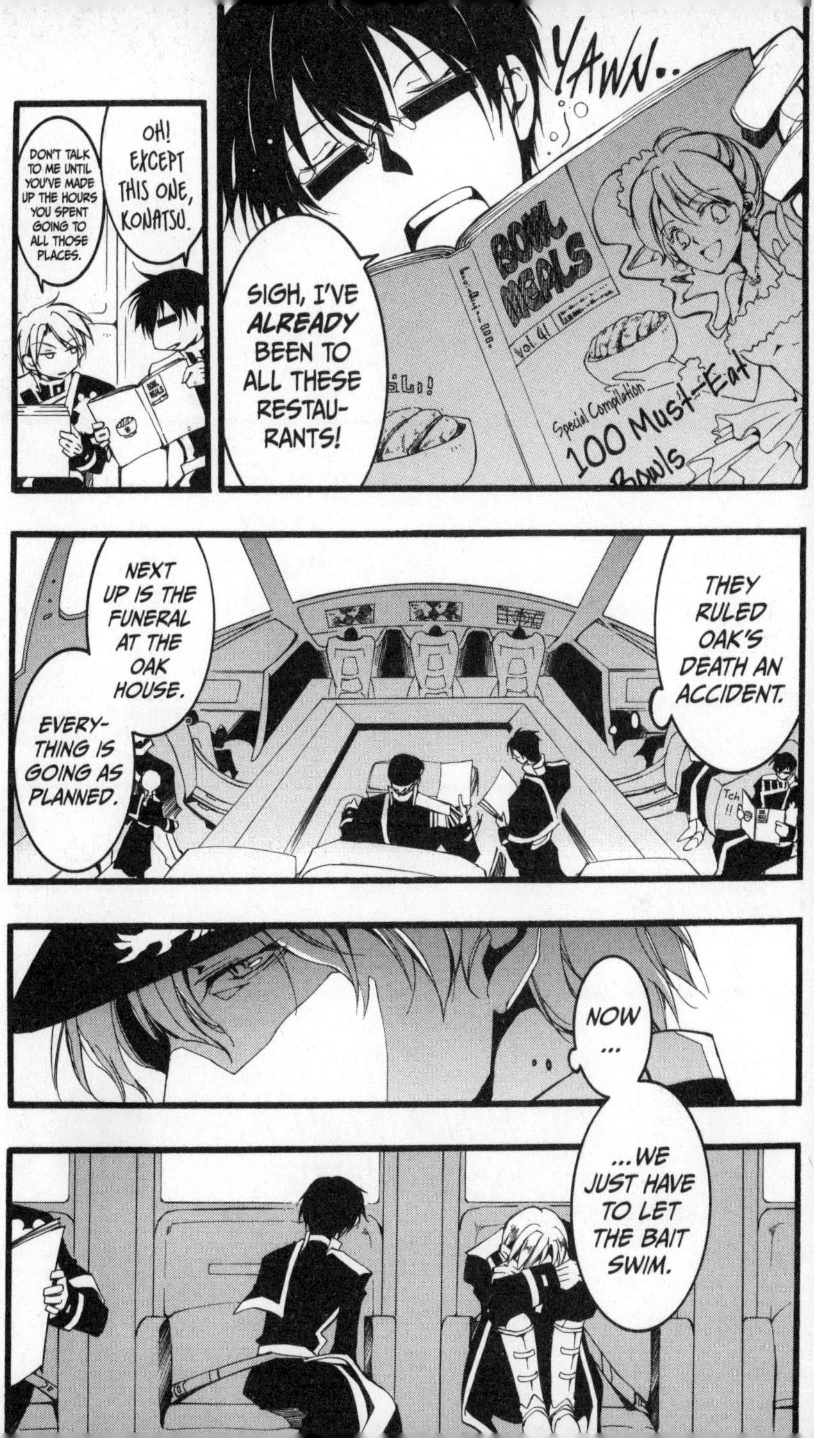
YAWN..
SIGH, I'VE ALREADY BEEN TO ALL THESE RESTAURANTS!
BOWL MEALS
vol. 41
Special Compilation 100 Must-Eat Bowls
OH! EXCEPT THIS ONE, KONATSU.
DON'T TALK TO ME UNTIL YOU'VE MADE UP THE HOURS YOU SPENT GOING TO ALL THOSE PLACES.
THEY RULED OAK'S DEATH AN ACCIDENT.
Tch !!
NEXT UP IS THE FUNERAL AT THE OAK HOUSE.
EVERY-THING IS GOING AS PLANNED.
NOW ...
...WE JUST HAVE TO LET THE BAIT SWIM.

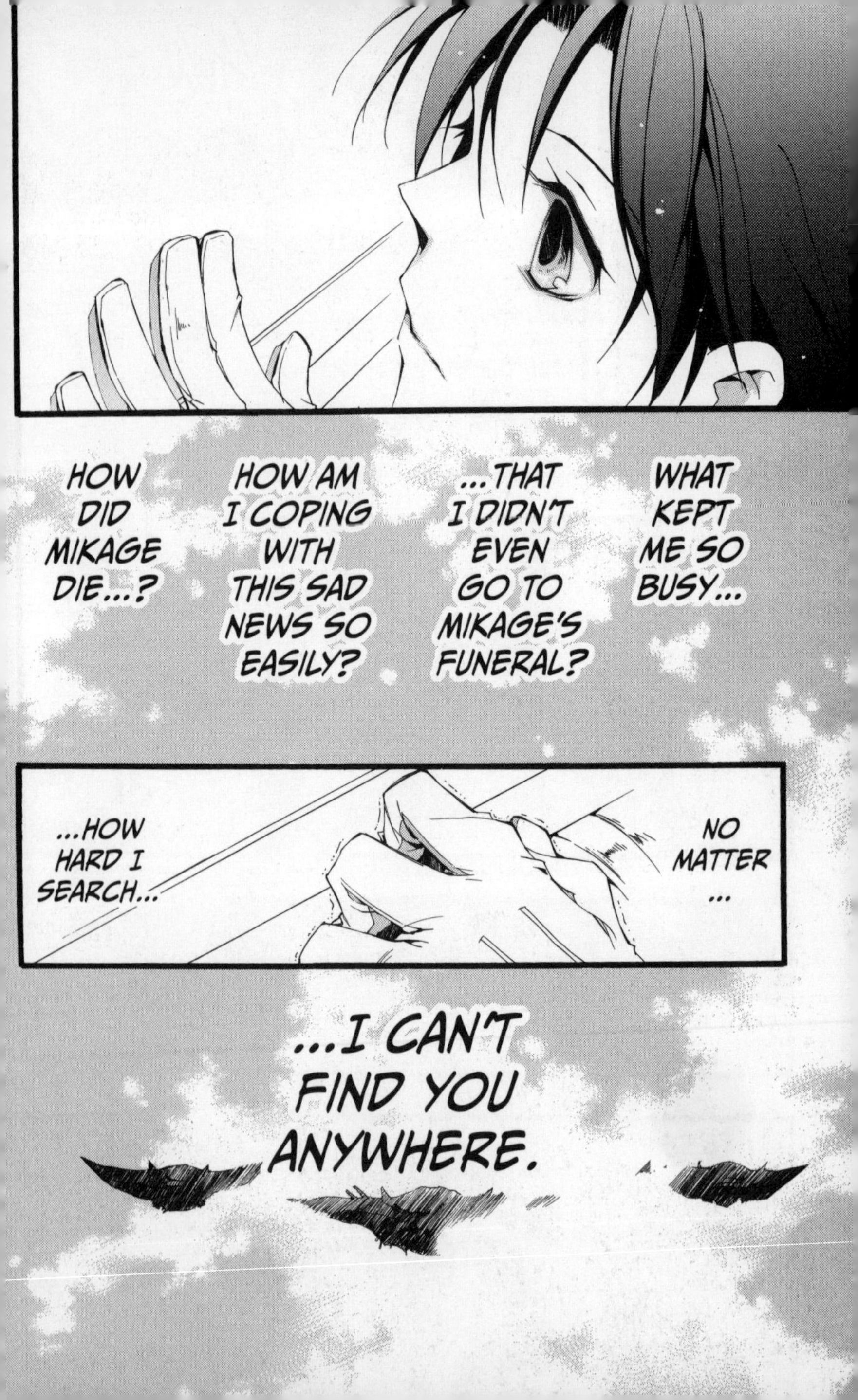
WHAT KEPT ME SO BUSY...
...THAT I DIDN'T EVEN GO TO MIKAGE'S FUNERAL?
HOW AM I COPING WITH THIS SAD NEWS SO EASILY?
HOW DID MIKAGE DIE...?
NO MATTER...
...HOW HARD I SEARCH...
...I CAN'T FIND YOU ANYWHERE.

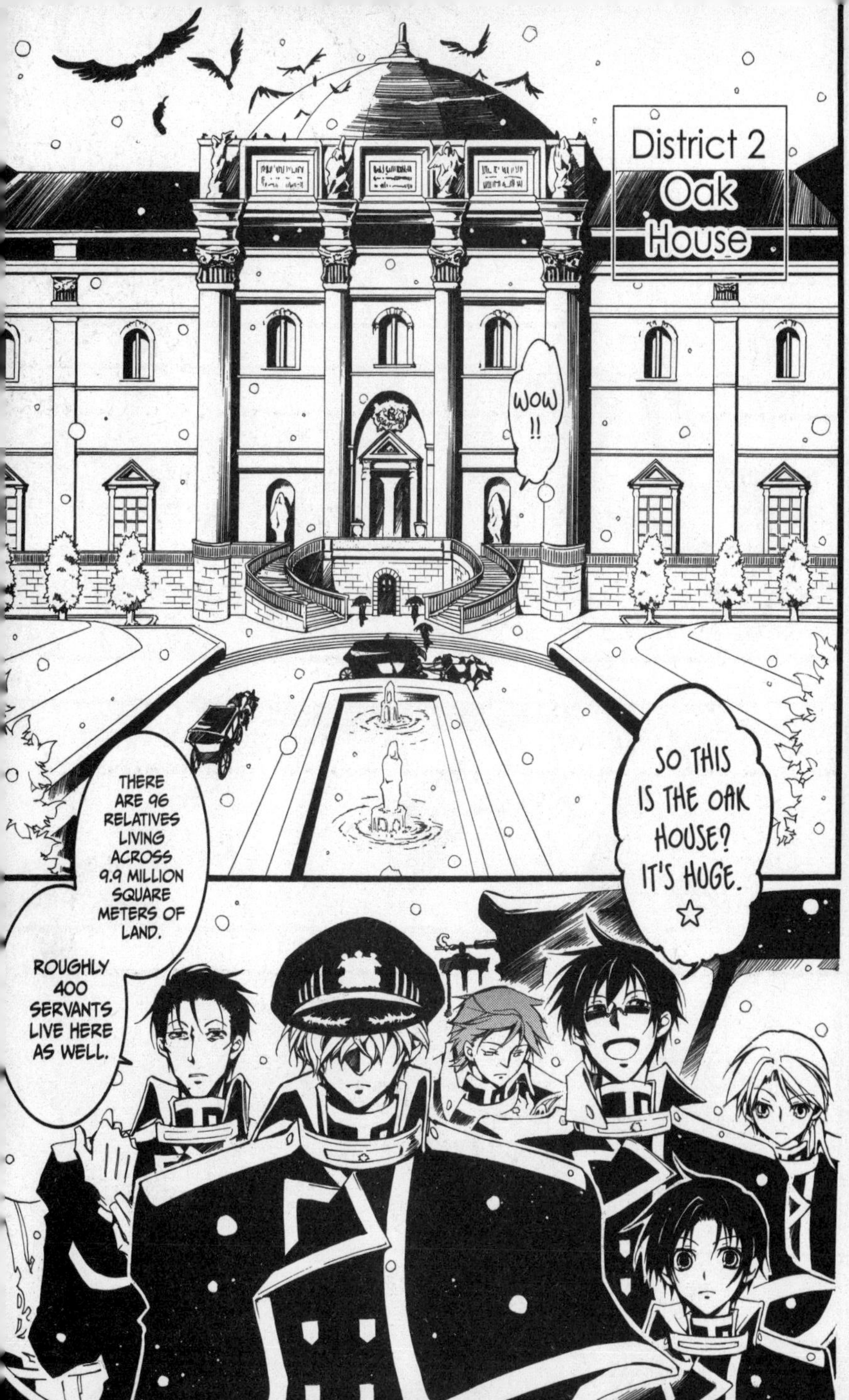
District 2 Oak House
WOW !!
SO THIS IS THE OAK HOUSE? IT'S HUGE. ☆
THERE ARE 96 RELATIVES LIVING ACROSS 9.9 MILLION SQUARE METERS OF LAND.
ROUGHLY 400 SERVANTS LIVE HERE AS WELL.

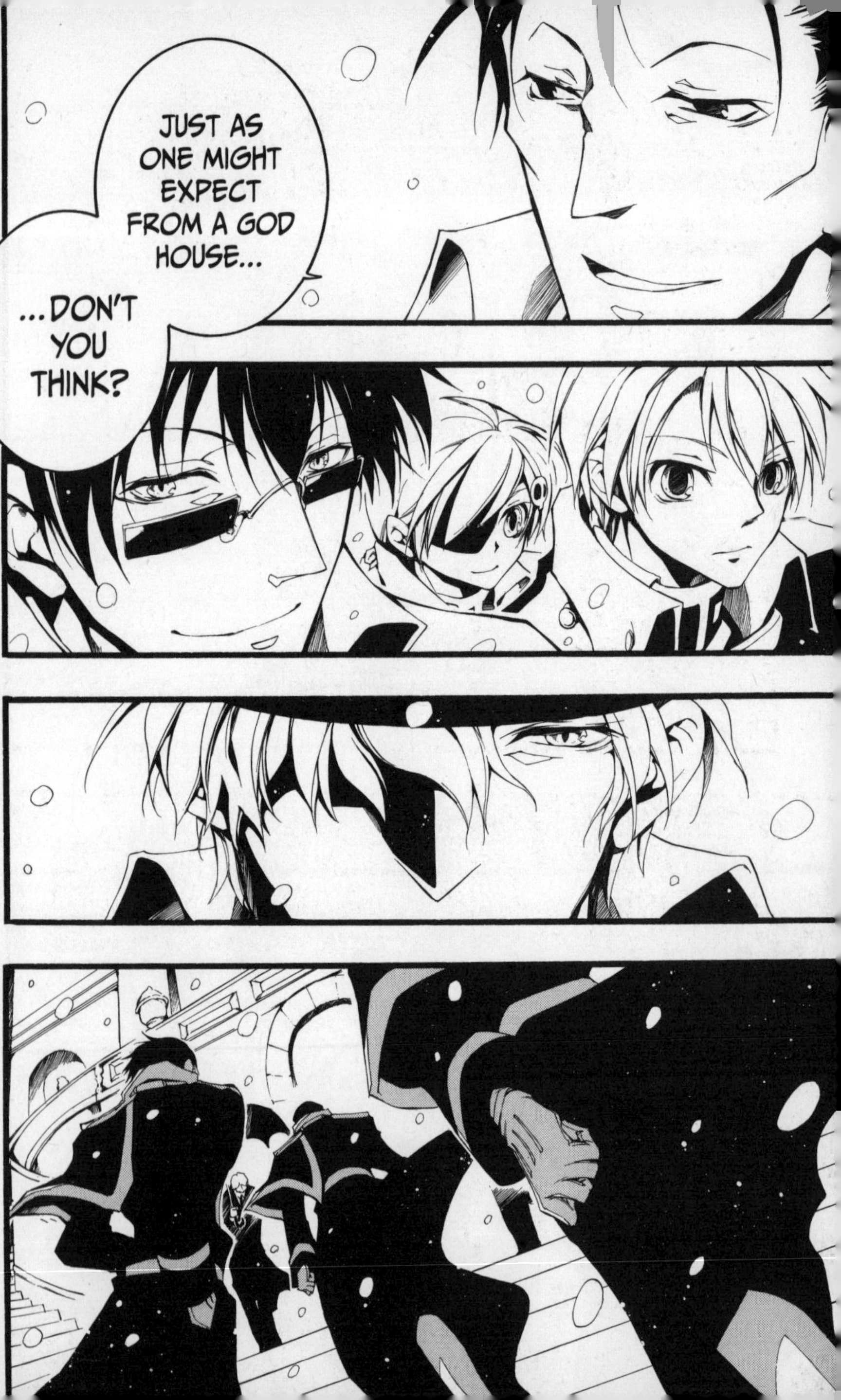
JUST AS ONE MIGHT EXPECT FROM A GOD HOUSE...
...DON'T YOU THINK?

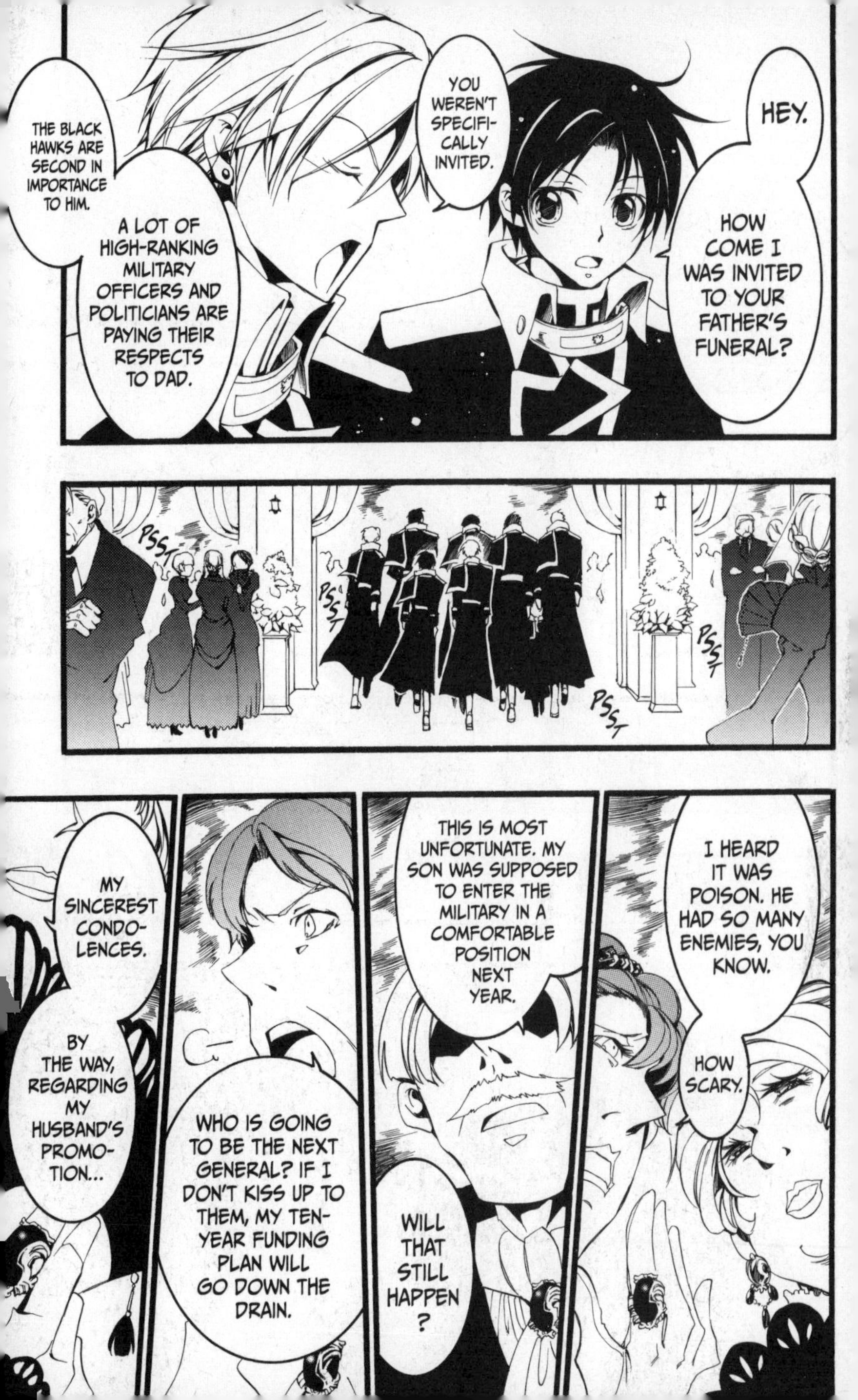
HEY.
HOW COME I WAS INVITED TO YOUR FATHER'S FUNERAL?
YOU WEREN'T SPECIFI-CALLY INVITED.
A LOT OF HIGH-RANKING MILITARY OFFICERS AND POLITICIANS ARE PAYING THEIR RESPECTS TO DAD.
THE BLACK HAWKS ARE SECOND IN IMPORTANCE TO HIM.
PSST
PSST
PSST
PSST
I HEARD IT WAS POISON. HE HAD SO MANY ENEMIES, YOU KNOW.
HOW SCARY.
THIS IS MOST UNFORTUNATE. MY SON WAS SUPPOSED TO ENTER THE MILITARY IN A COMFORTABLE POSITION NEXT YEAR.
WILL THAT STILL HAPPEN?
WHO IS GOING TO BE THE NEXT GENERAL? IF I DON'T KISS UP TO THEM, MY TEN-YEAR FUNDING PLAN WILL GO DOWN THE DRAIN.
MY SINCEREST CONDO-LENCES.
BY THE WAY, REGARDING MY HUSBAND'S PROMO-TION...

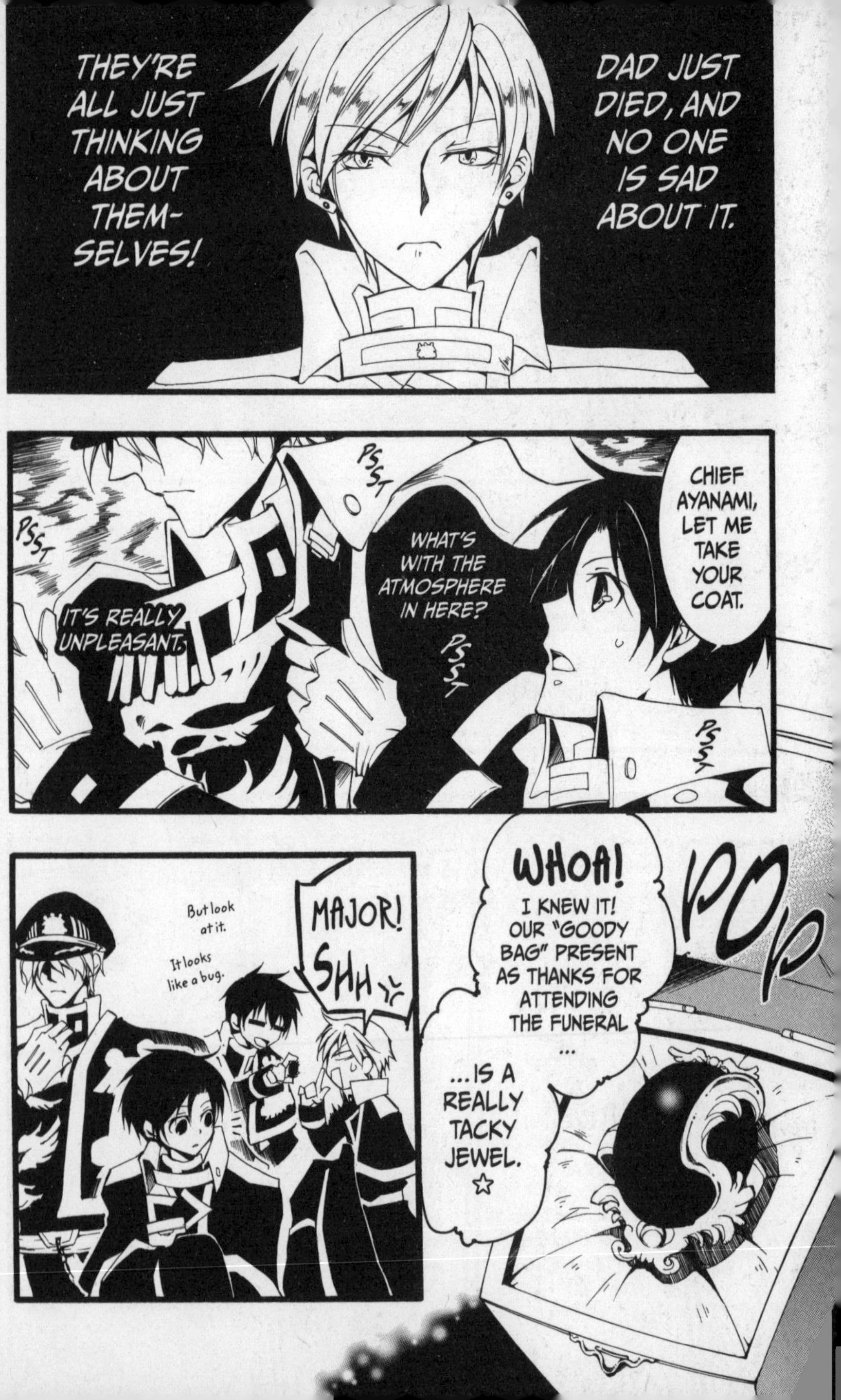
DAD JUST DIED, AND NO ONE IS SAD ABOUT IT.
THEY'RE ALL JUST THINKING ABOUT THEM-SELVES!
CHIEF AYANAMI, LET ME TAKE YOUR COAT.
PSST
PSST
PSST
WHAT'S WITH THE ATMOSPHERE IN HERE?
PSST
IT'S REALLY UNPLEASANT.
POP
WHOA!
I KNEW IT! OUR "GOODY BAG" PRESENT AS THANKS FOR ATTENDING THE FUNERAL ...
...IS A REALLY TACKY JEWEL. ☆
MAJOR! SHH
But look at it.
It looks like a bug.

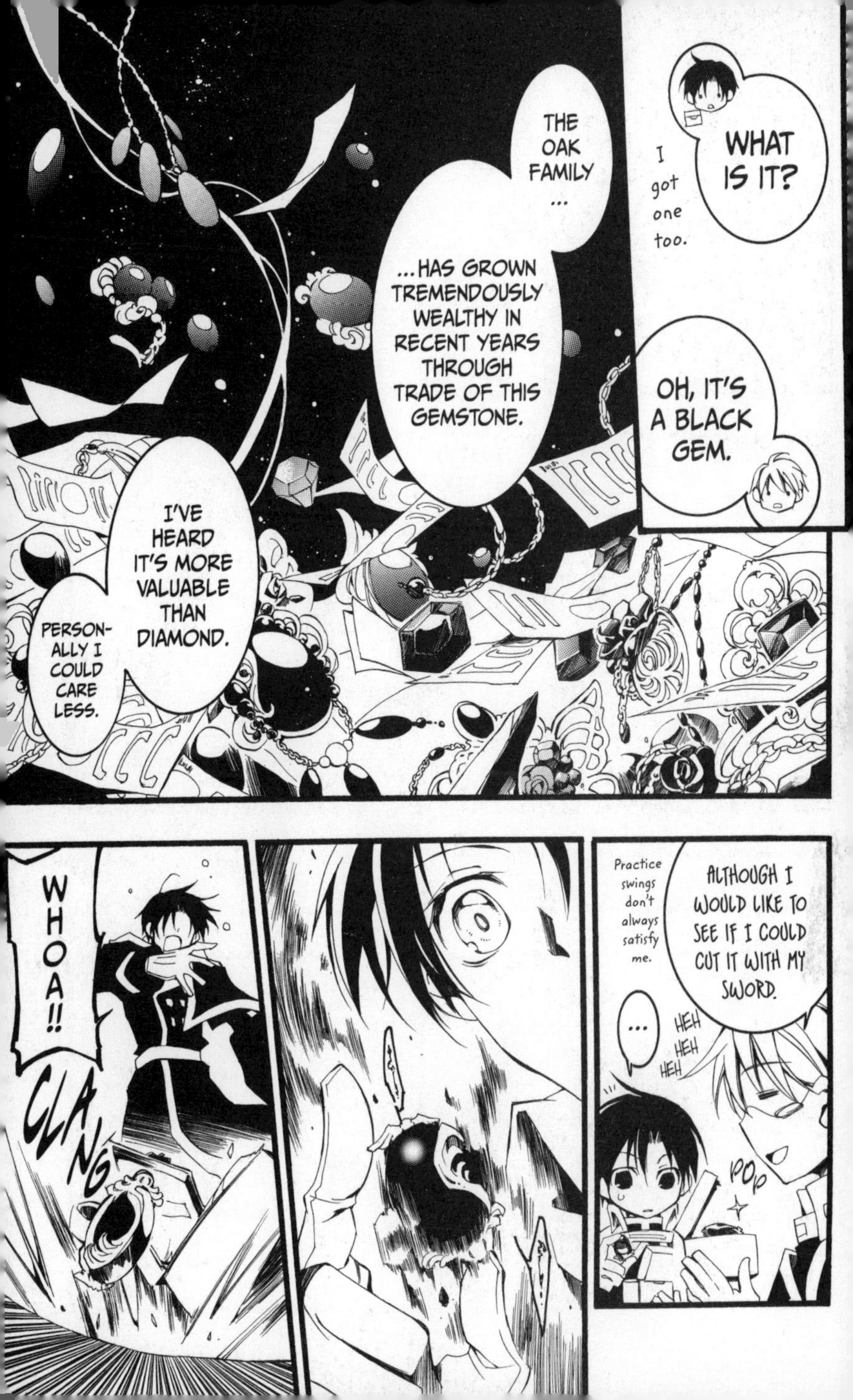
WHAT IS IT?
I got one too.
OH, IT'S A BLACK GEM.
THE OAK FAMILY ...
...HAS GROWN TREMENDOUSLY WEALTHY IN RECENT YEARS THROUGH TRADE OF THIS GEMSTONE.
I'VE HEARD IT'S MORE VALUABLE THAN DIAMOND.
PERSON-ALLY I COULD CARE LESS.
ALTHOUGH I WOULD LIKE TO SEE IF I COULD CUT IT WITH MY SWORD.
Practice swings don't always satisfy me.
HEH HEH HEH
...
POP
WHOA!!
CLANG

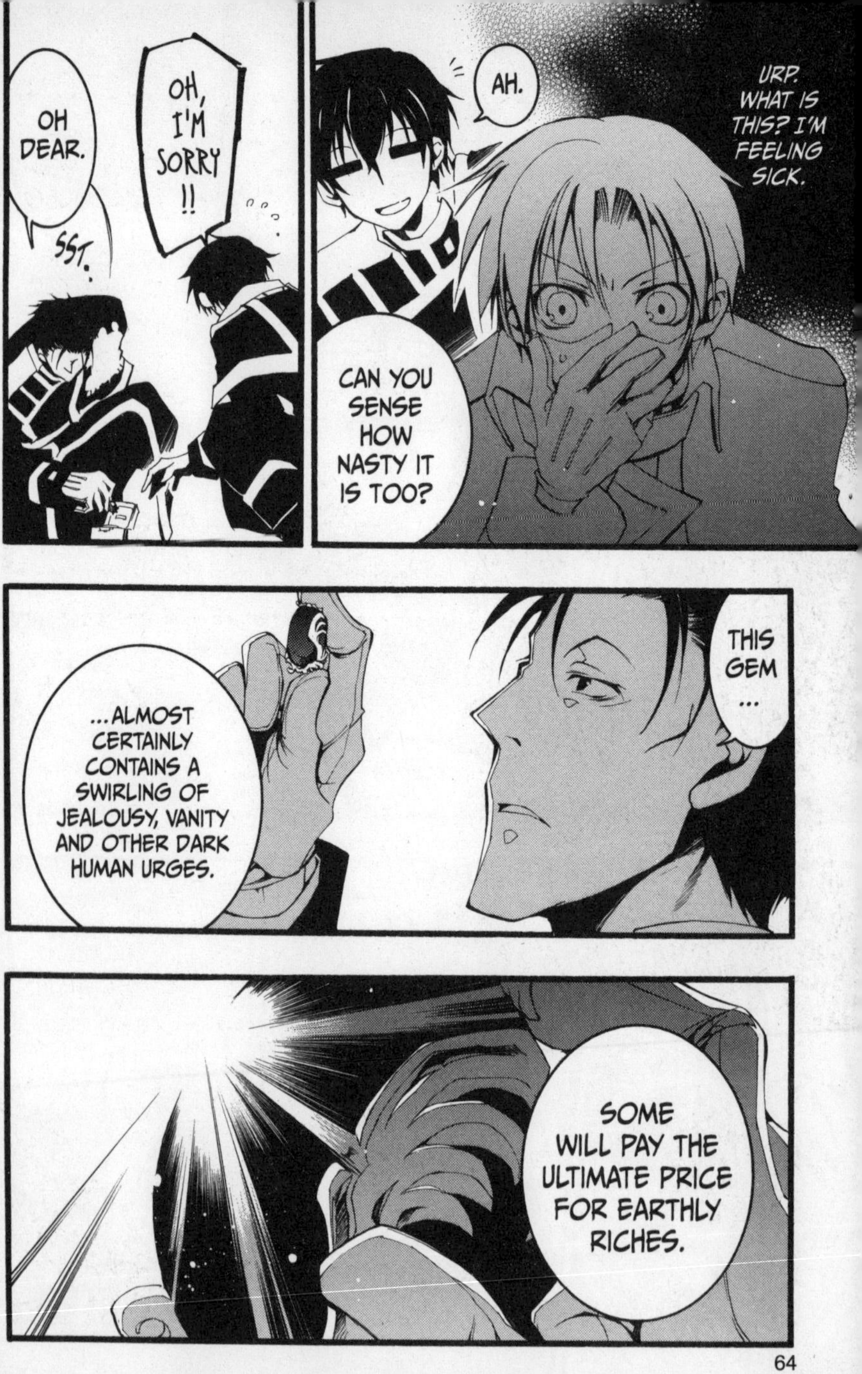
URP. WHAT IS THIS? I'M FEELING SICK.
AH.
CAN YOU SENSE HOW NASTY IT IS TOO?
OH, I'M SORRY!!
OH DEAR.
SST.
THIS GEM...
...ALMOST CERTAINLY CONTAINS A SWIRLING OF JEALOUSY, VANITY AND OTHER DARK HUMAN URGES.
SOME WILL PAY THE ULTIMATE PRICE FOR EARTHLY RICHES.

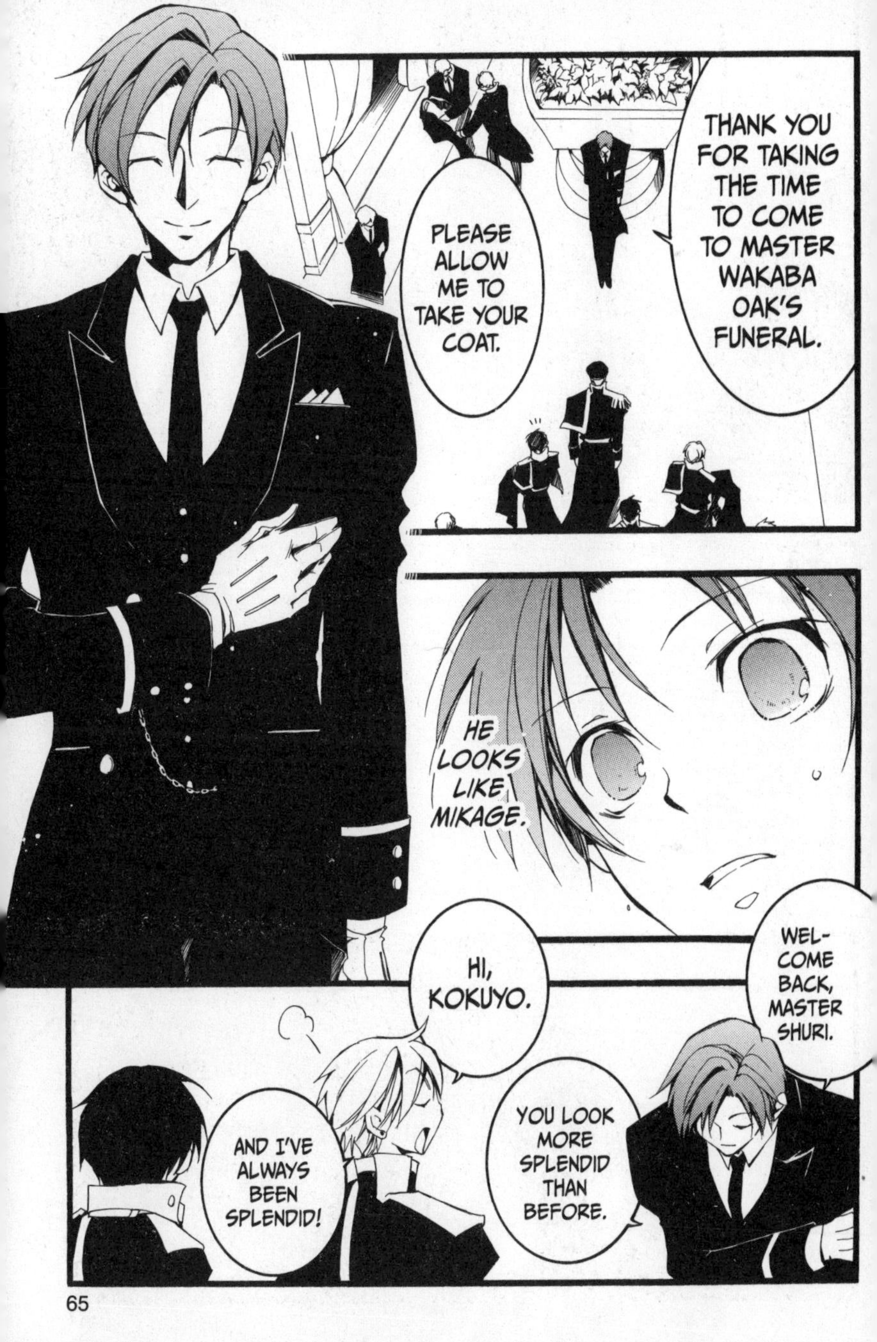
THANK YOU FOR TAKING THE TIME TO COME TO MASTER WAKABA OAK'S FUNERAL.
PLEASE ALLOW ME TO TAKE YOUR COAT.
HE LOOKS LIKE MIKAGE.
WEL-COME BACK, MASTER SHURI.
HI, KOKUYO.
YOU LOOK MORE SPLENDID THAN BEFORE.
AND I'VE ALWAYS BEEN SPLENDID!

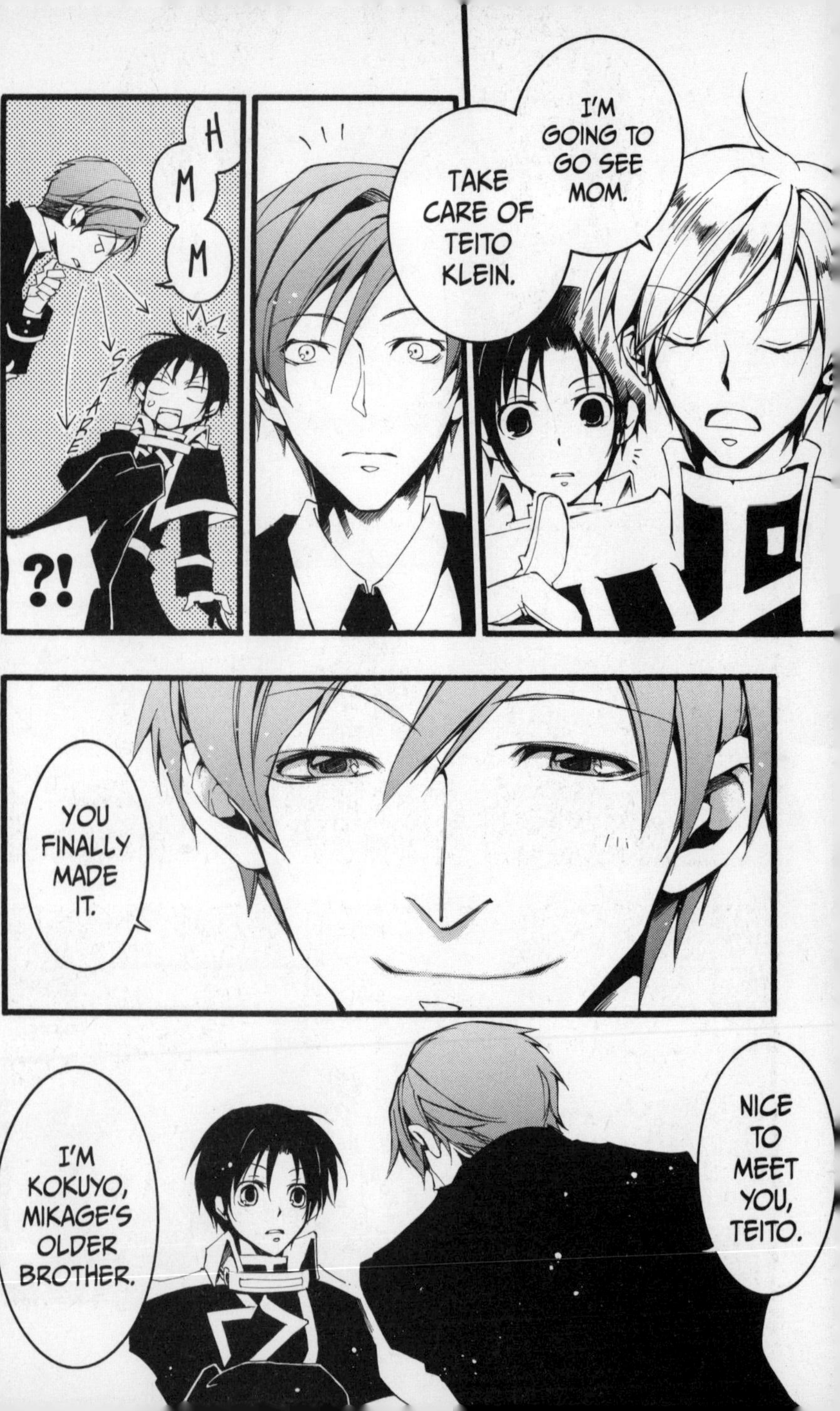
I'M GOING TO GO SEE MOM.
TAKE CARE OF TEITO KLEIN.
HMM
STARE
?!
YOU FINALLY MADE IT.
NICE TO MEET YOU, TEITO.
I'M KOKUYO, MIKAGE'S OLDER BROTHER.

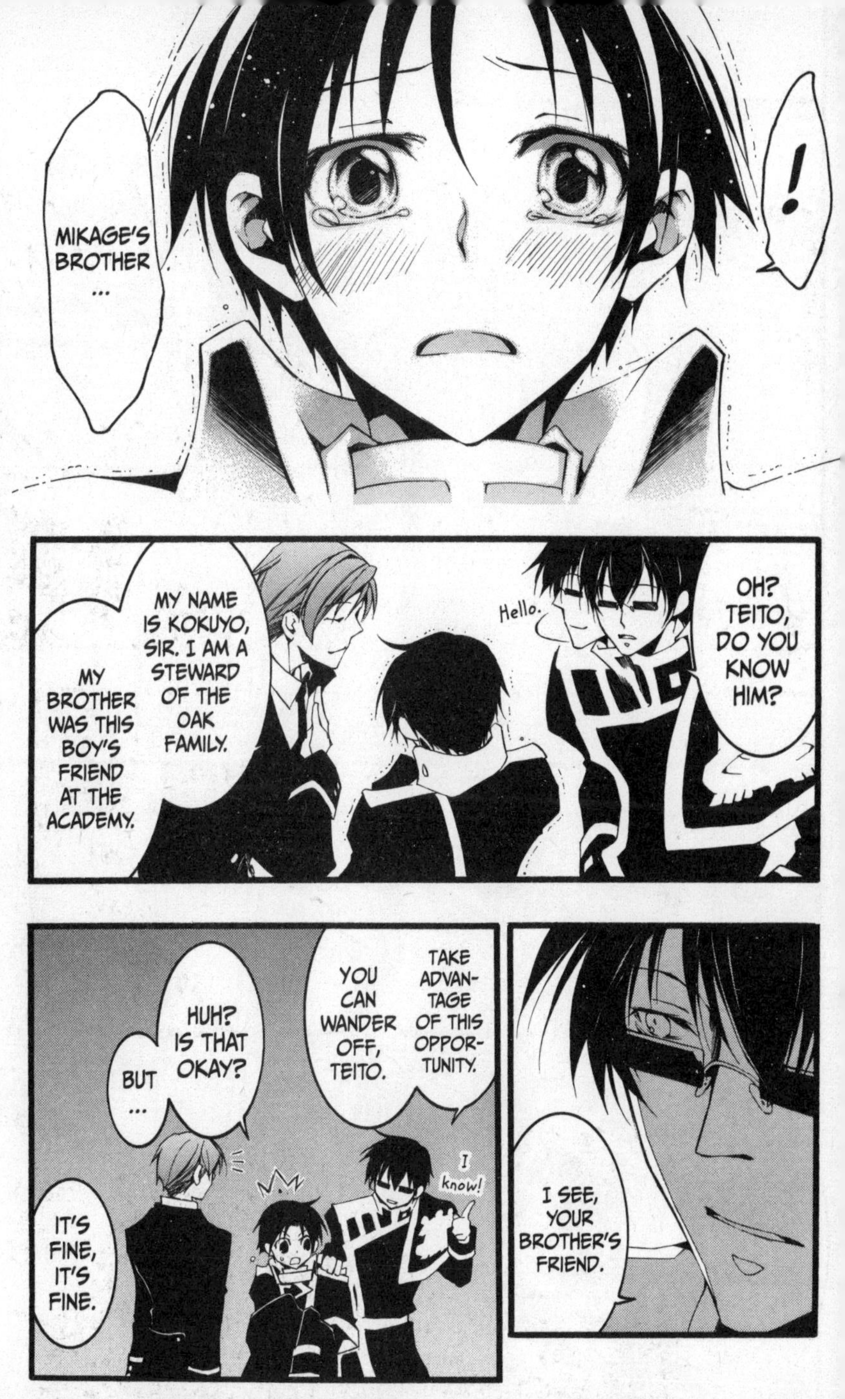
!
MIKAGE'S BROTHER ...
OH? TEITO, DO YOU KNOW HIM?
Hello.
MY NAME IS KOKUYO, SIR. I AM A STEWARD OF THE OAK FAMILY.
MY BROTHER WAS THIS BOY'S FRIEND AT THE ACADEMY.
I SEE, YOUR BROTHER'S FRIEND.
TAKE ADVANTAGE OF THIS OPPORTUNITY.
YOU CAN WANDER OFF, TEITO.
HUH? IS THAT OKAY?
BUT ...
I know!
IT'S FINE, IT'S FINE.

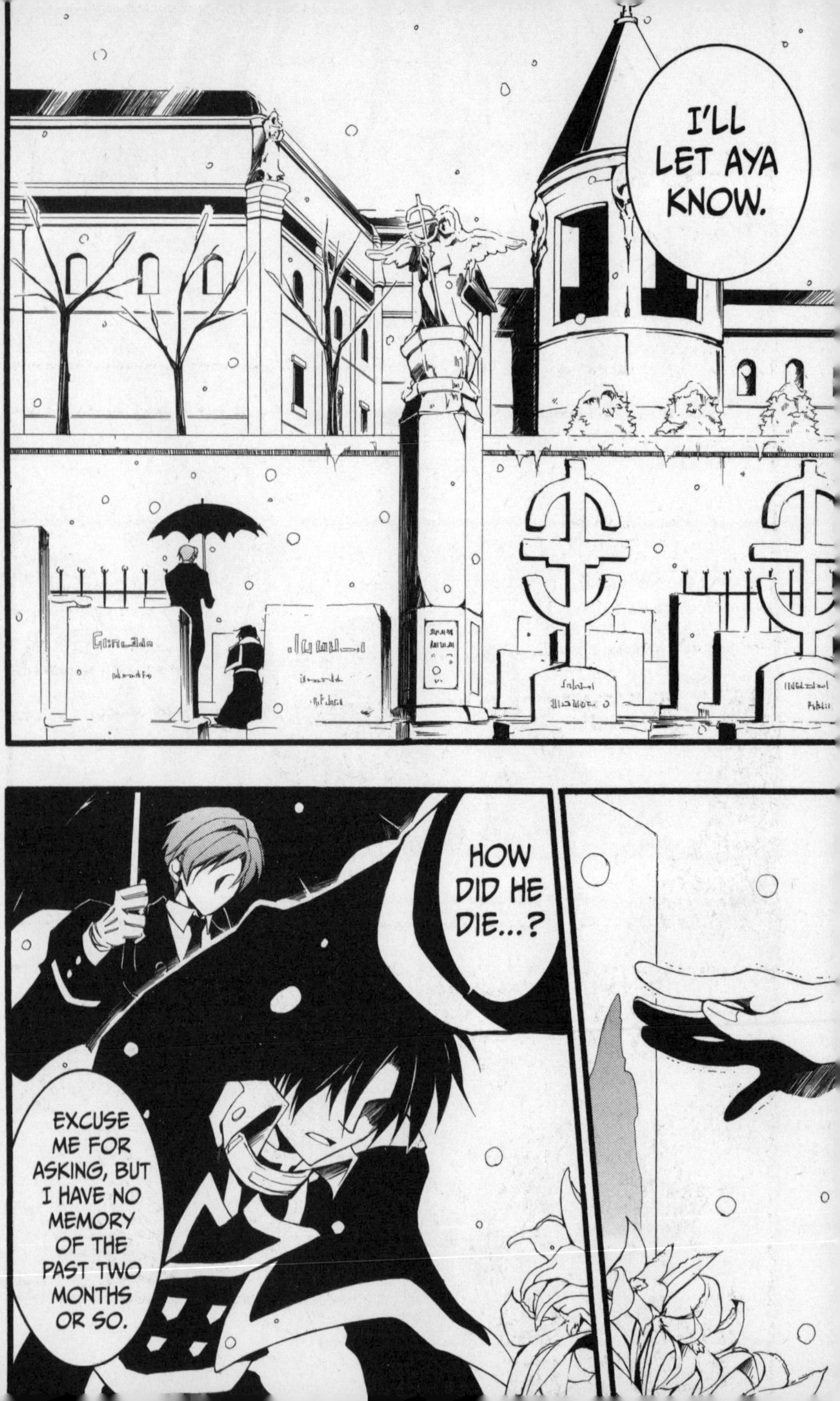
I'LL LET AYA KNOW.
HOW DID HE DIE...?
EXCUSE ME FOR ASKING, BUT I HAVE NO MEMORY OF THE PAST TWO MONTHS OR SO.

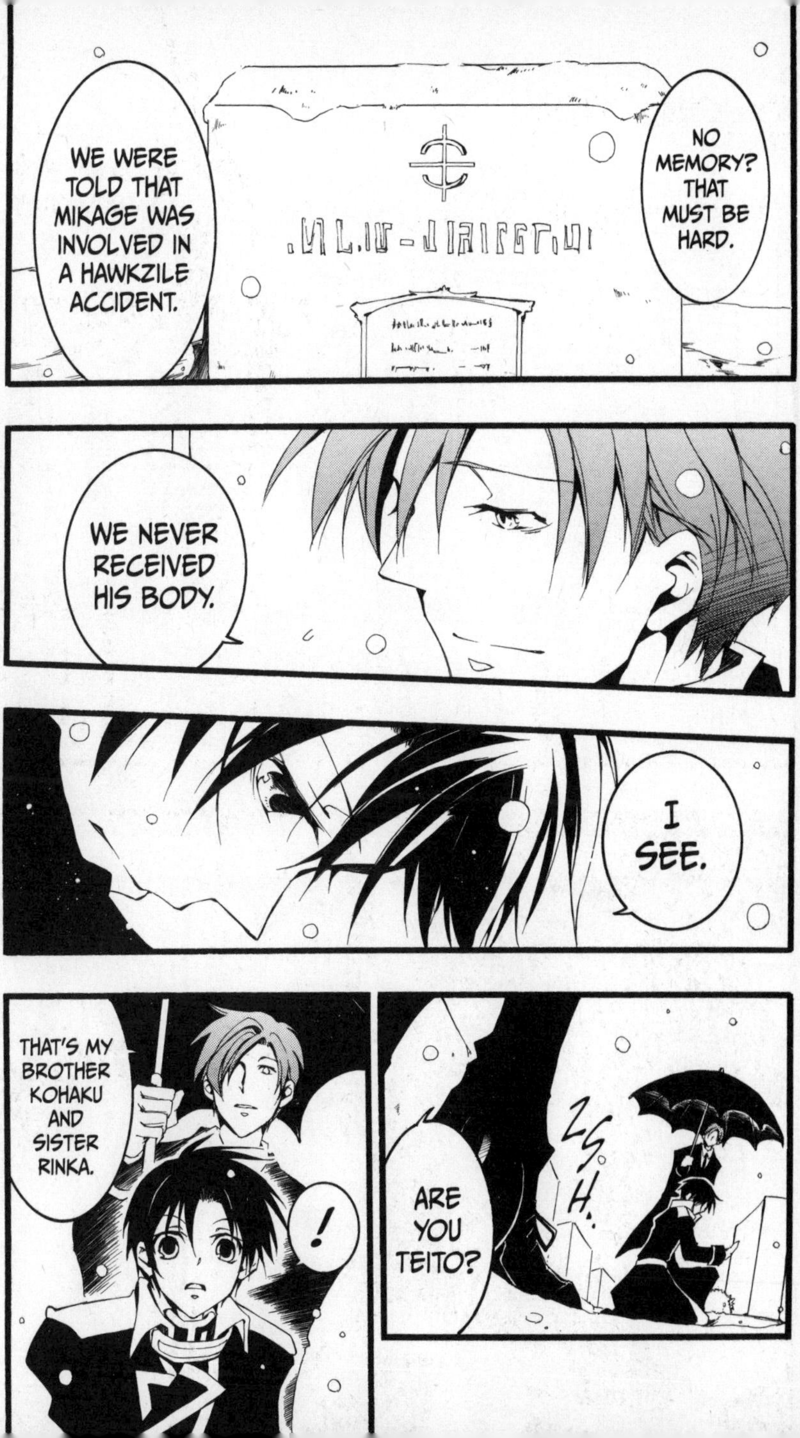
NO MEMORY? THAT MUST BE HARD.
WE WERE TOLD THAT MIKAGE WAS INVOLVED IN A HAWKZILE ACCIDENT.
WE NEVER RECEIVED HIS BODY.
I SEE.
ZSH..
ARE YOU TEITO?
THAT'S MY BROTHER KOHAKU AND SISTER RINKA.
!

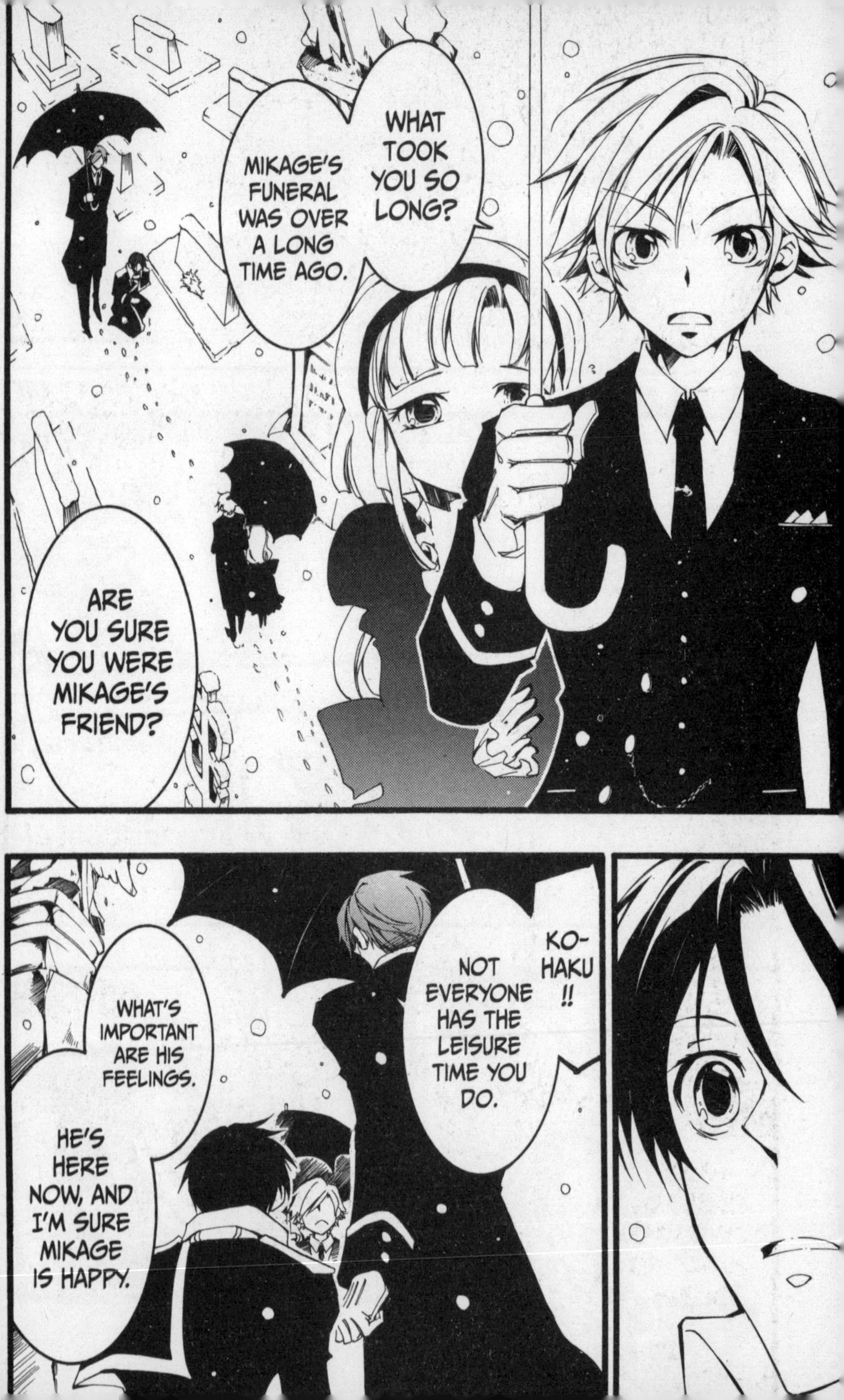
WHAT TOOK YOU SO LONG?
MIKAGE'S FUNERAL WAS OVER A LONG TIME AGO.
ARE YOU SURE YOU WERE MIKAGE'S FRIEND?
KO-HAKU!!
NOT EVERYONE HAS THE LEISURE TIME YOU DO.
WHAT'S IMPORTANT ARE HIS FEELINGS.
HE'S HERE NOW, AND I'M SURE MIKAGE IS HAPPY.

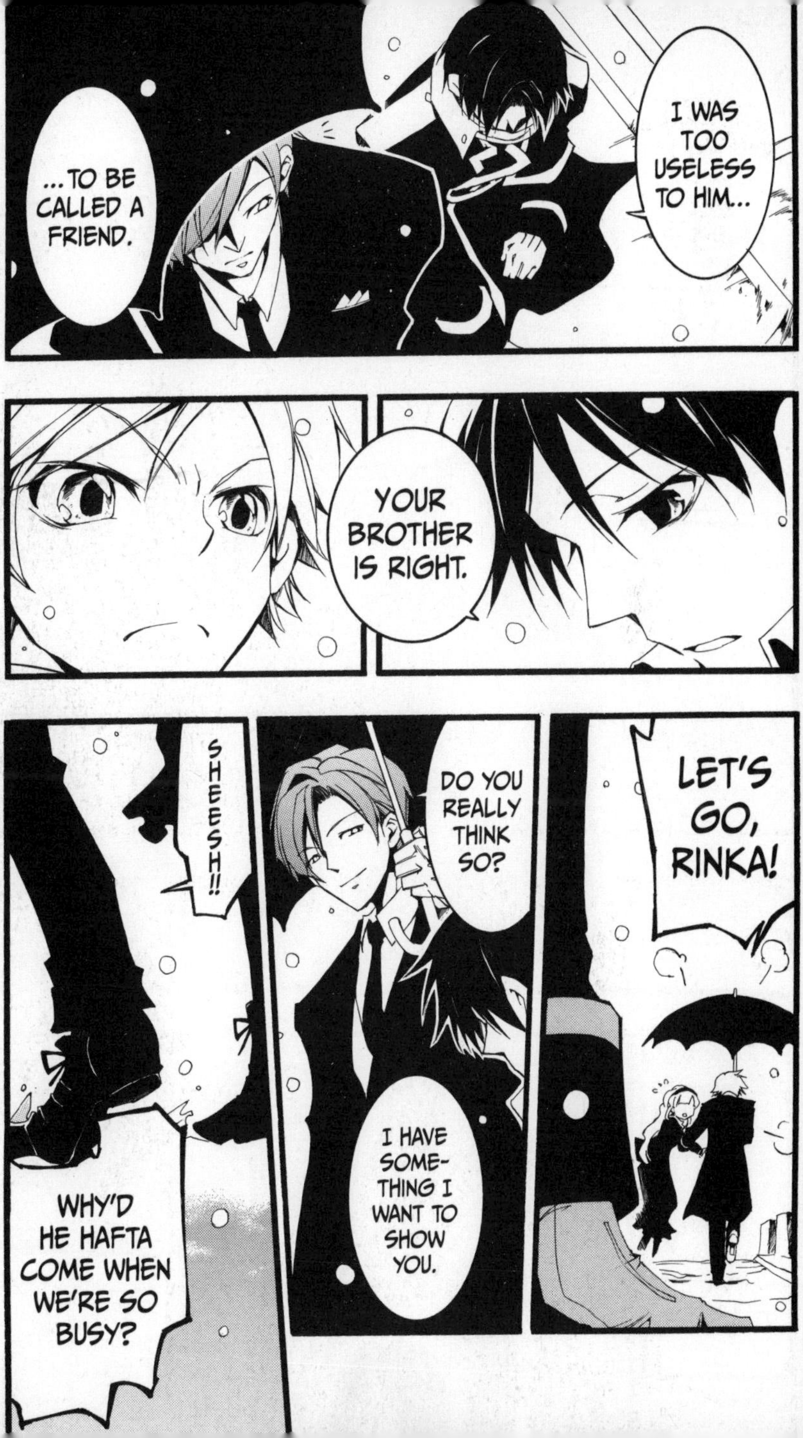
I WAS TOO USELESS TO HIM...
...TO BE CALLED A FRIEND.
YOUR BROTHER IS RIGHT.
LET'S GO, RINKA!
DO YOU REALLY THINK SO?
I HAVE SOME-THING I WANT TO SHOW YOU.
SHEESH!!
WHY'D HE HAFTA COME WHEN WE'RE SO BUSY?

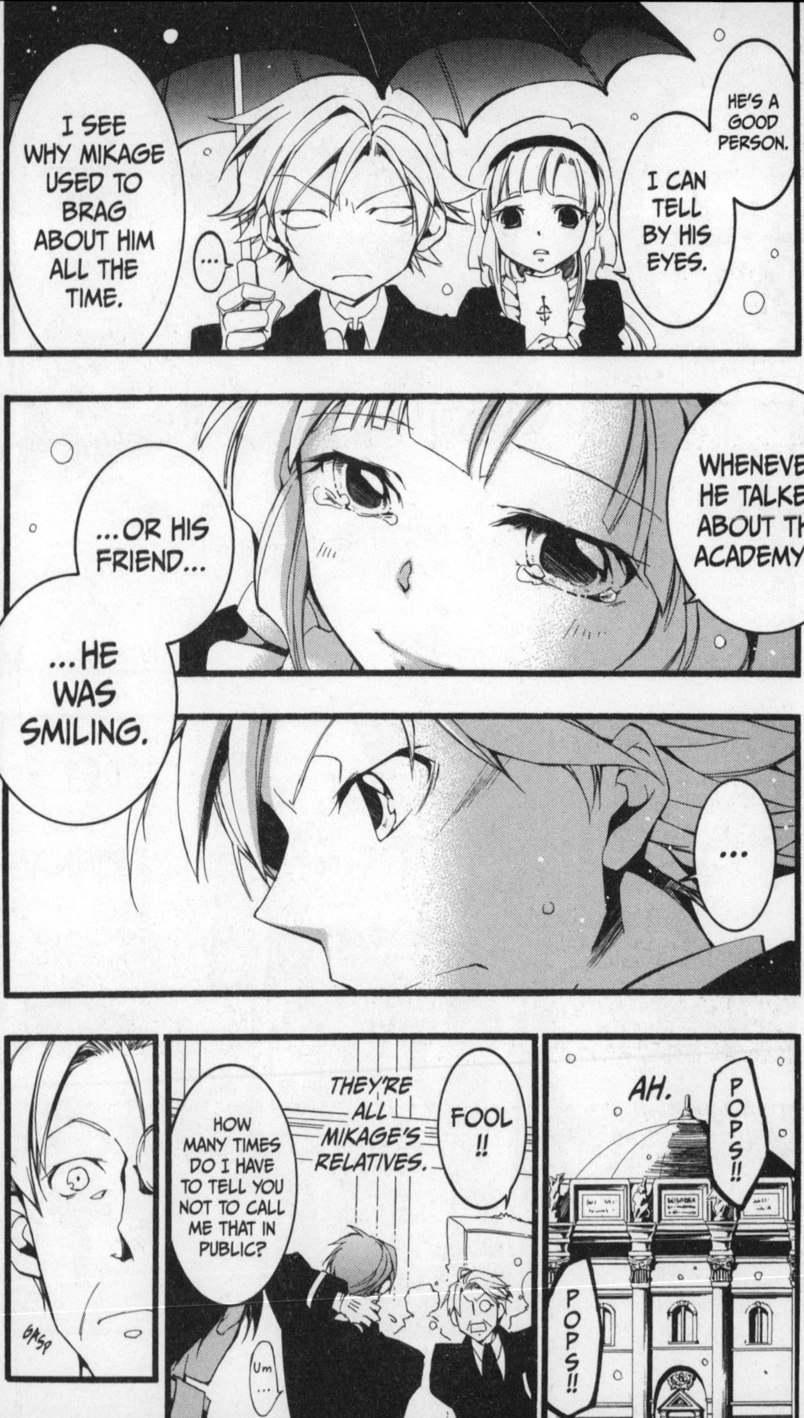
HE'S A GOOD PERSON.
I CAN TELL BY HIS EYES.
...
I SEE WHY MIKAGE USED TO BRAG ABOUT HIM ALL THE TIME.
WHENEVER HE TALKED ABOUT THE ACADEMY...
...OR HIS FRIEND...
...HE WAS SMILING.
...
POPS!!
AH.
POPS!!
FOOL!!
THEY'RE ALL MIKAGE'S RELATIVES.
HOW MANY TIMES DO I HAVE TO TELL YOU NOT TO CALL ME THAT IN PUBLIC?
Um ...
GASP

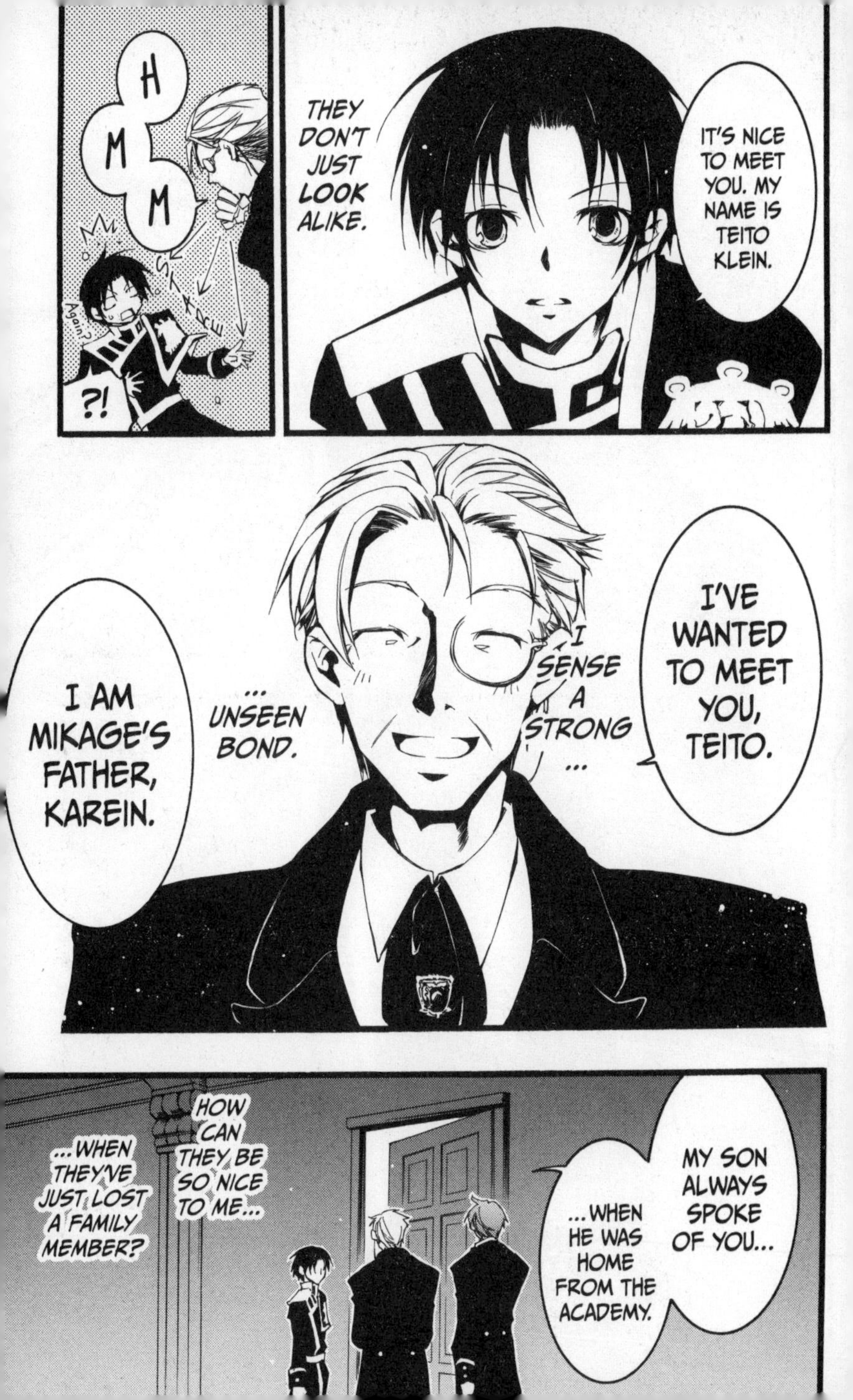
IT'S NICE TO MEET YOU. MY NAME IS TEITO KLEIN.
THEY DON'T JUST LOOK ALIKE.
HMM
STARE
Again?
?!
I'VE WANTED TO MEET YOU, TEITO.
I SENSE A STRONG...
...UNSEEN BOND.
I AM MIKAGE'S FATHER, KAREIN.
MY SON ALWAYS SPOKE OF YOU...
...WHEN HE WAS HOME FROM THE ACADEMY.
HOW CAN THEY BE SO NICE TO ME...
...WHEN THEY'VE JUST LOST A FAMILY MEMBER?

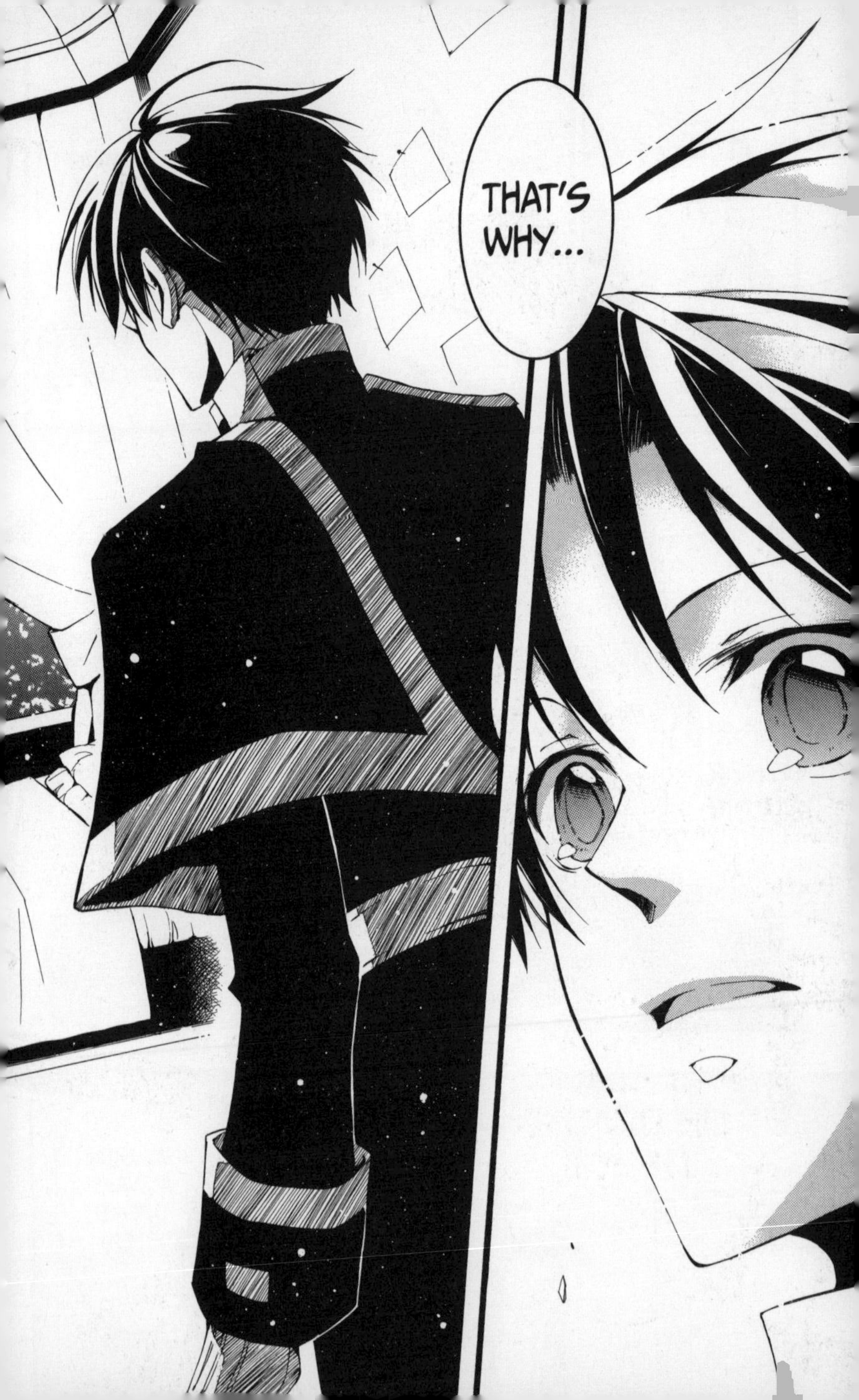
THAT'S WHY...

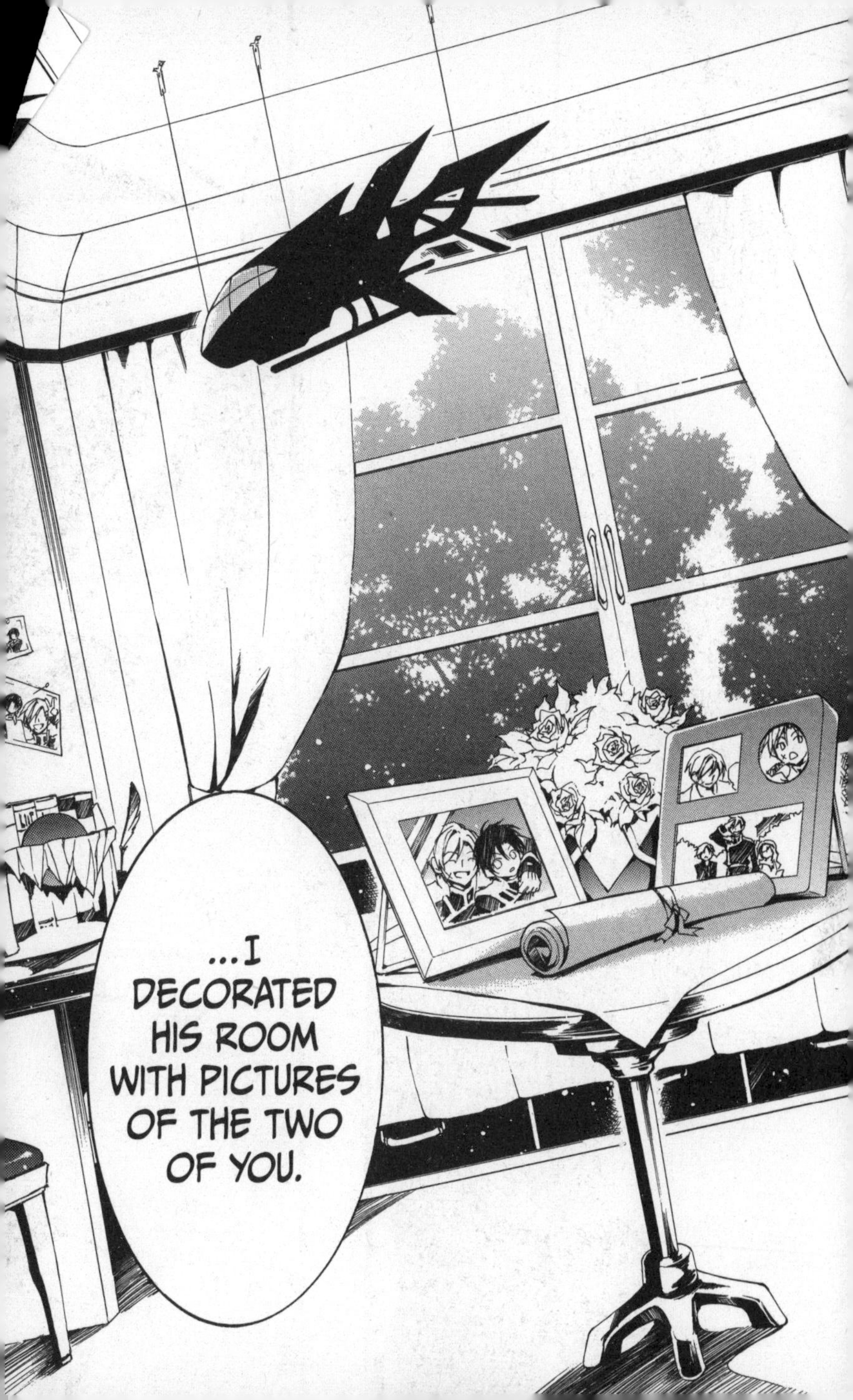
...I DECORATED HIS ROOM WITH PICTURES OF THE TWO OF YOU.

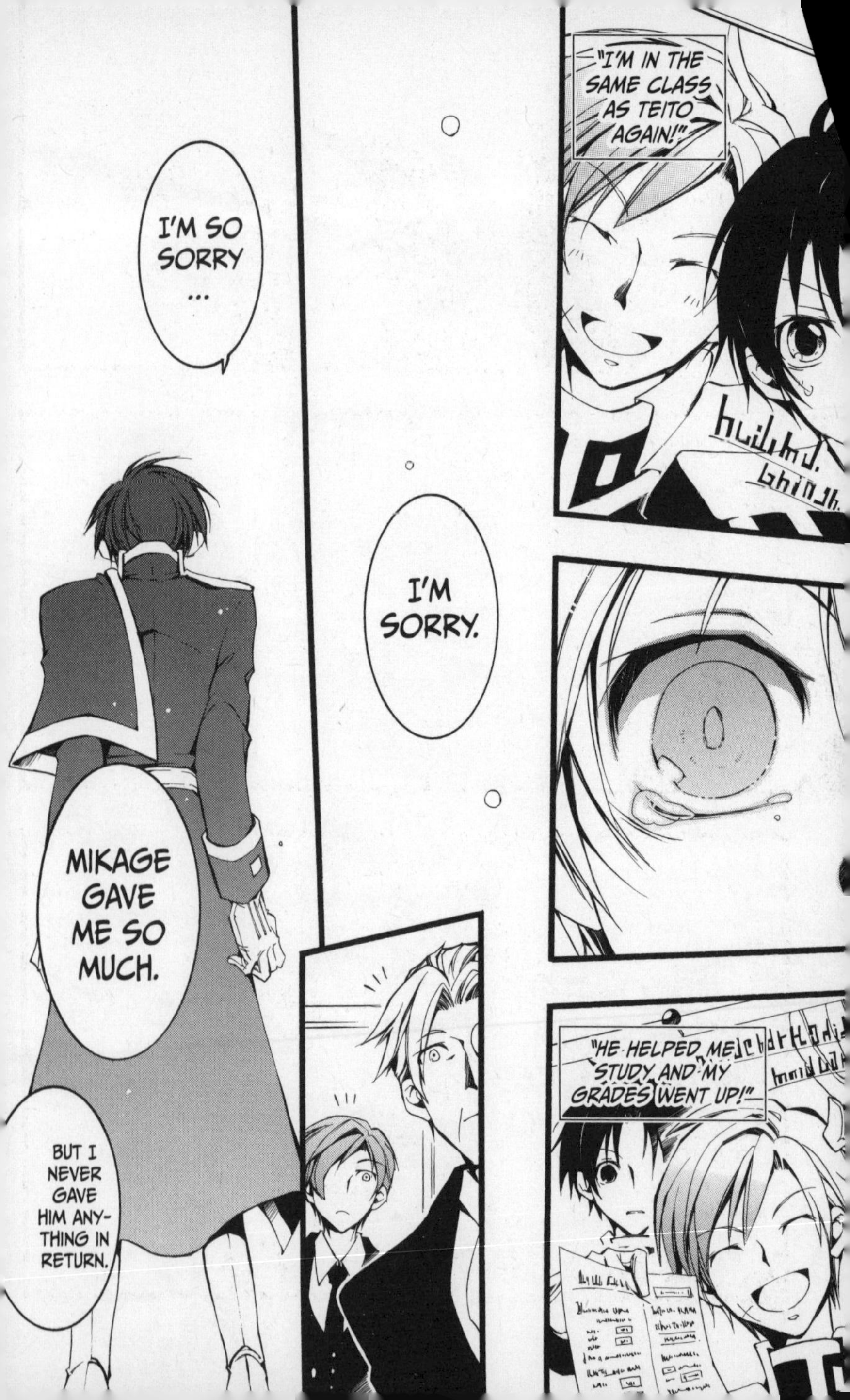
"I'M IN THE SAME CLASS AS TEITO AGAIN!"
"HE HELPED ME STUDY AND MY GRADES WENT UP!"
I'M SORRY.
I'M SO SORRY ...
MIKAGE GAVE ME SO MUCH.
BUT I NEVER GAVE HIM ANY-THING IN RETURN.

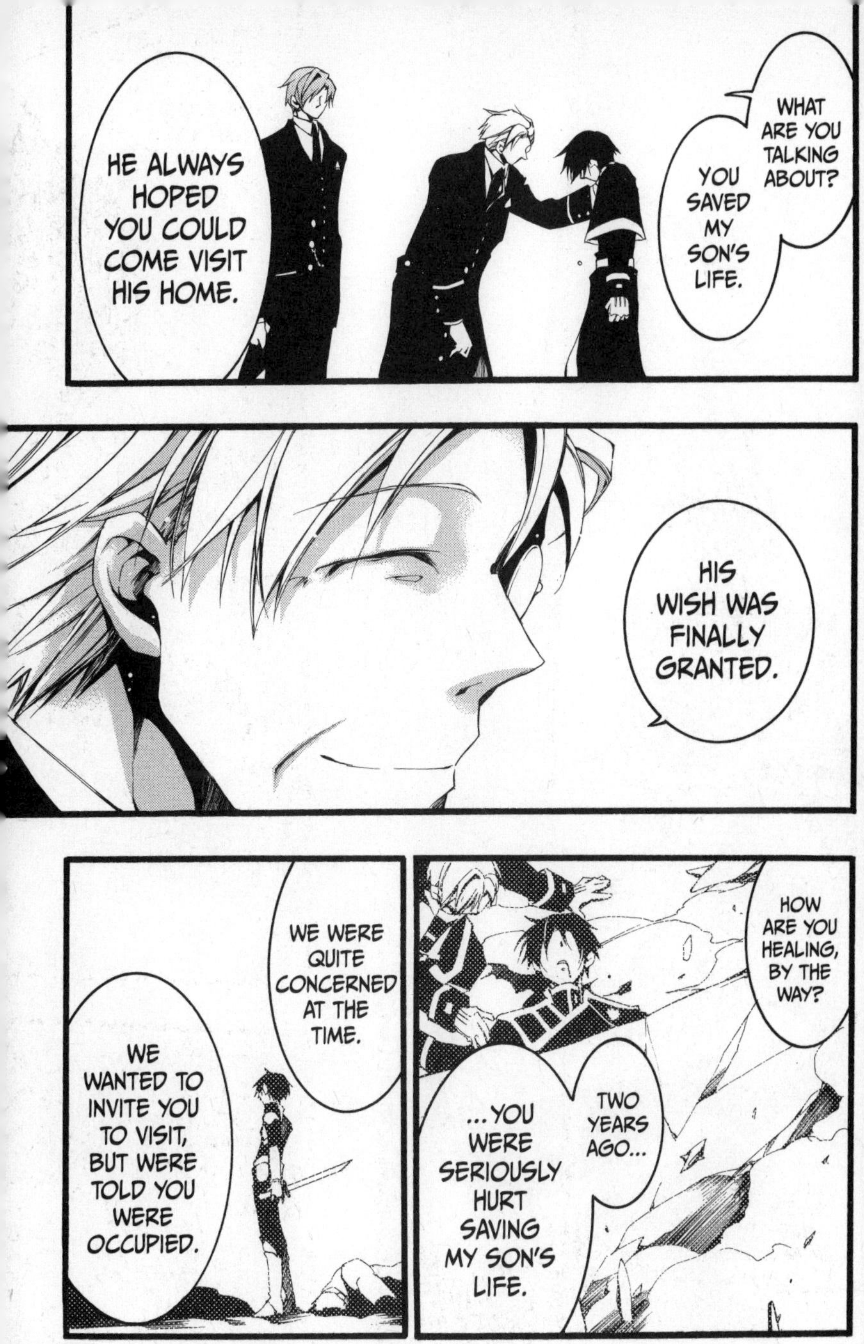
WHAT ARE YOU TALKING ABOUT?
YOU SAVED MY SON'S LIFE.
HE ALWAYS HOPED YOU COULD COME VISIT HIS HOME.
HIS WISH WAS FINALLY GRANTED.
HOW ARE YOU HEALING, BY THE WAY?
TWO YEARS AGO...
...YOU WERE SERIOUSLY HURT SAVING MY SON'S LIFE.
WE WERE QUITE CONCERNED AT THE TIME.
WE WANTED TO INVITE YOU TO VISIT, BUT WERE TOLD YOU WERE OCCUPIED.

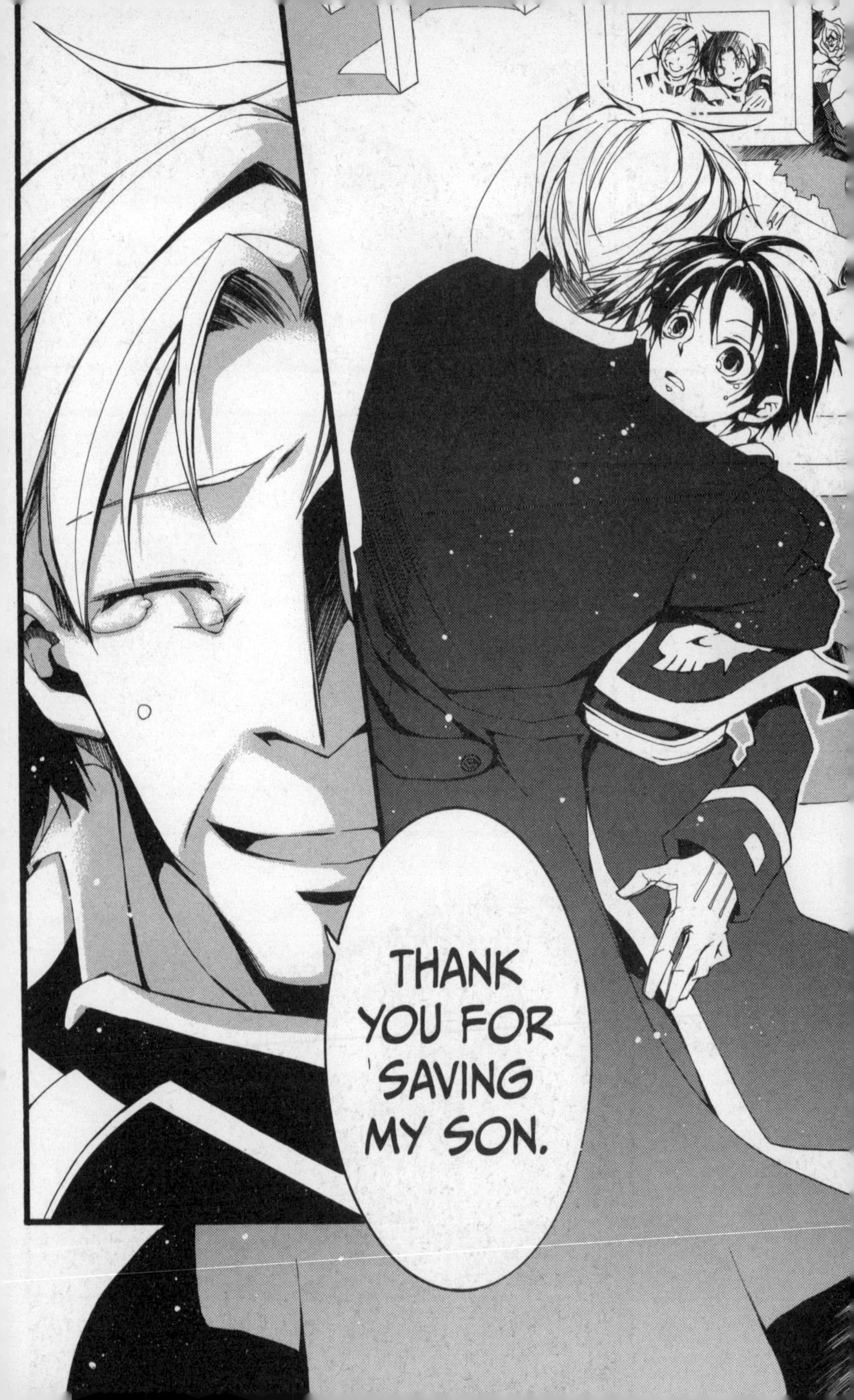
THANK YOU FOR SAVING MY SON.

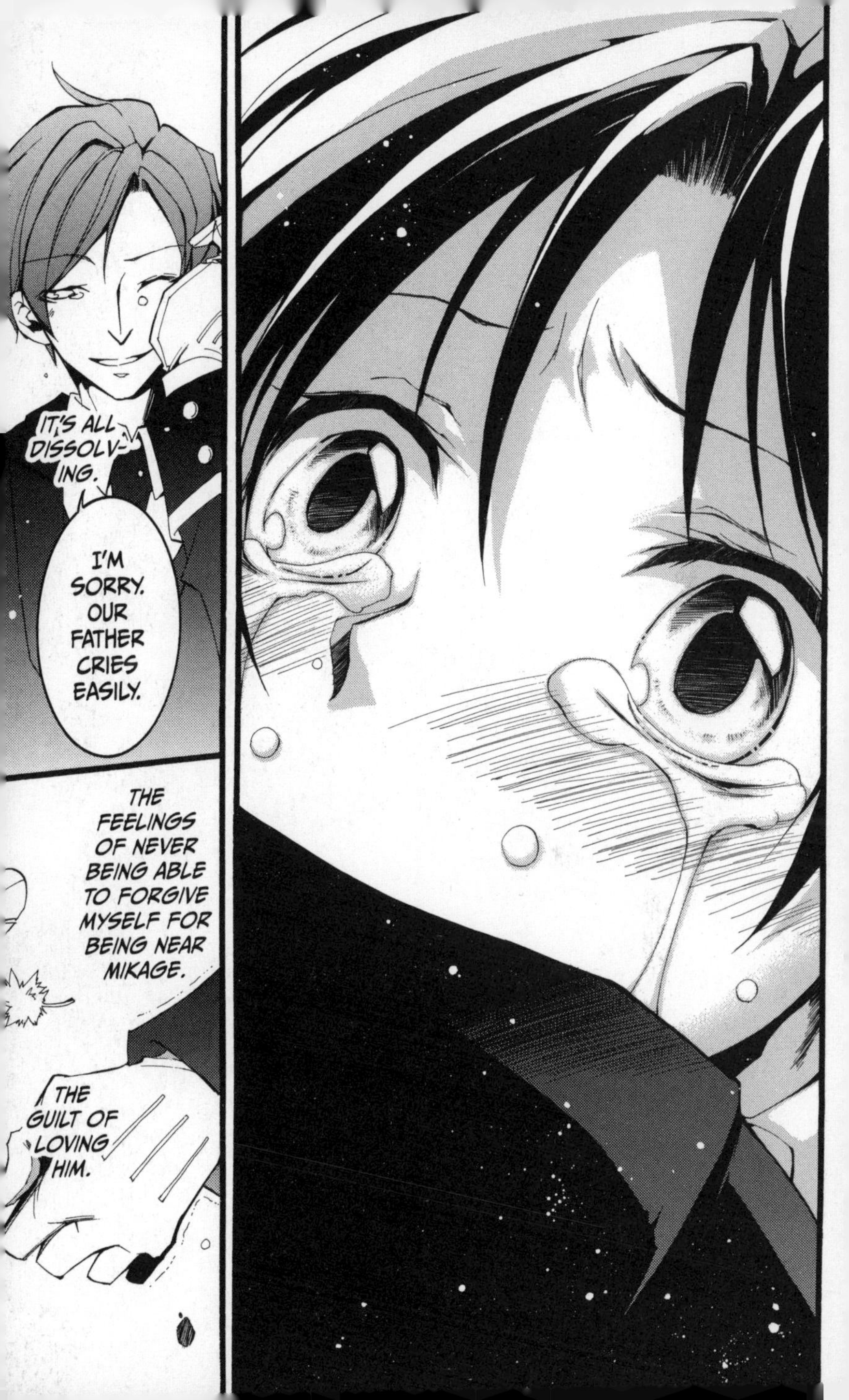
IT'S ALL DISSOLV-ING.
I'M SORRY. OUR FATHER CRIES EASILY.
THE FEELINGS OF NEVER BEING ABLE TO FORGIVE MYSELF FOR BEING NEAR MIKAGE.
THE GUILT OF LOVING HIM.

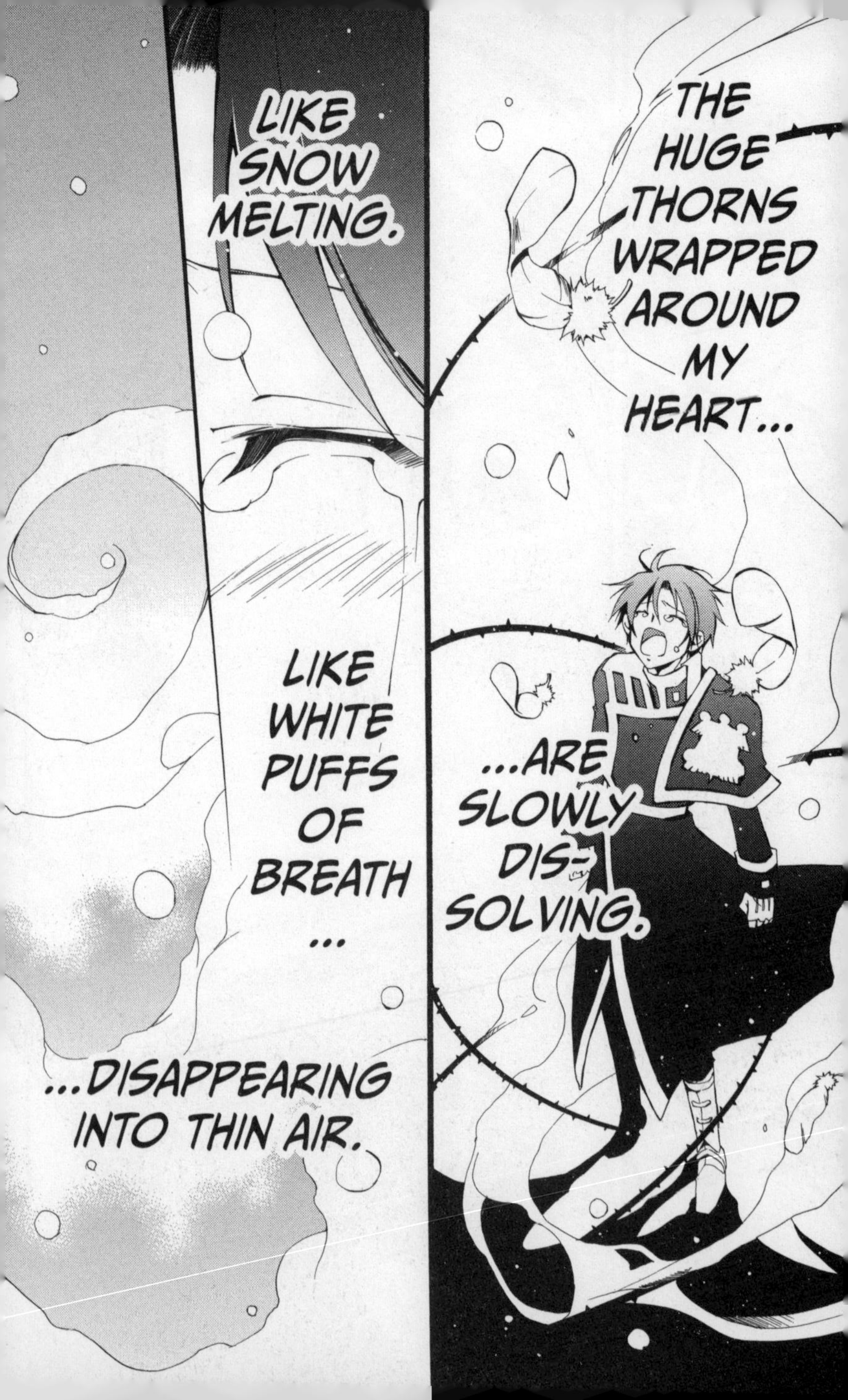
THE HUGE THORNS WRAPPED AROUND MY HEART...
...ARE SLOWLY DIS-SOLVING.
LIKE SNOW MELTING.
LIKE WHITE PUFFS OF BREATH...
...DISAPPEARING INTO THIN AIR.

Kapitel.76 "Ea"

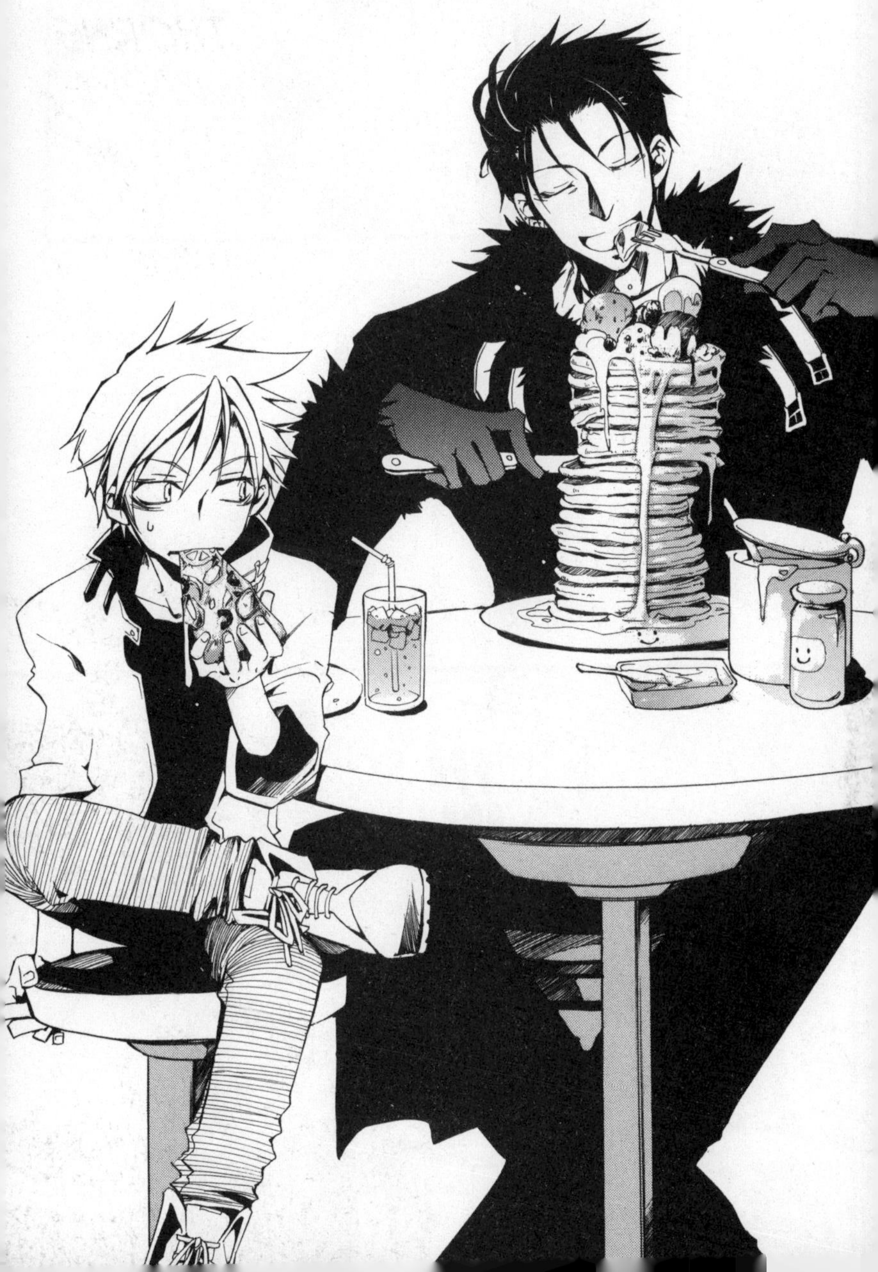

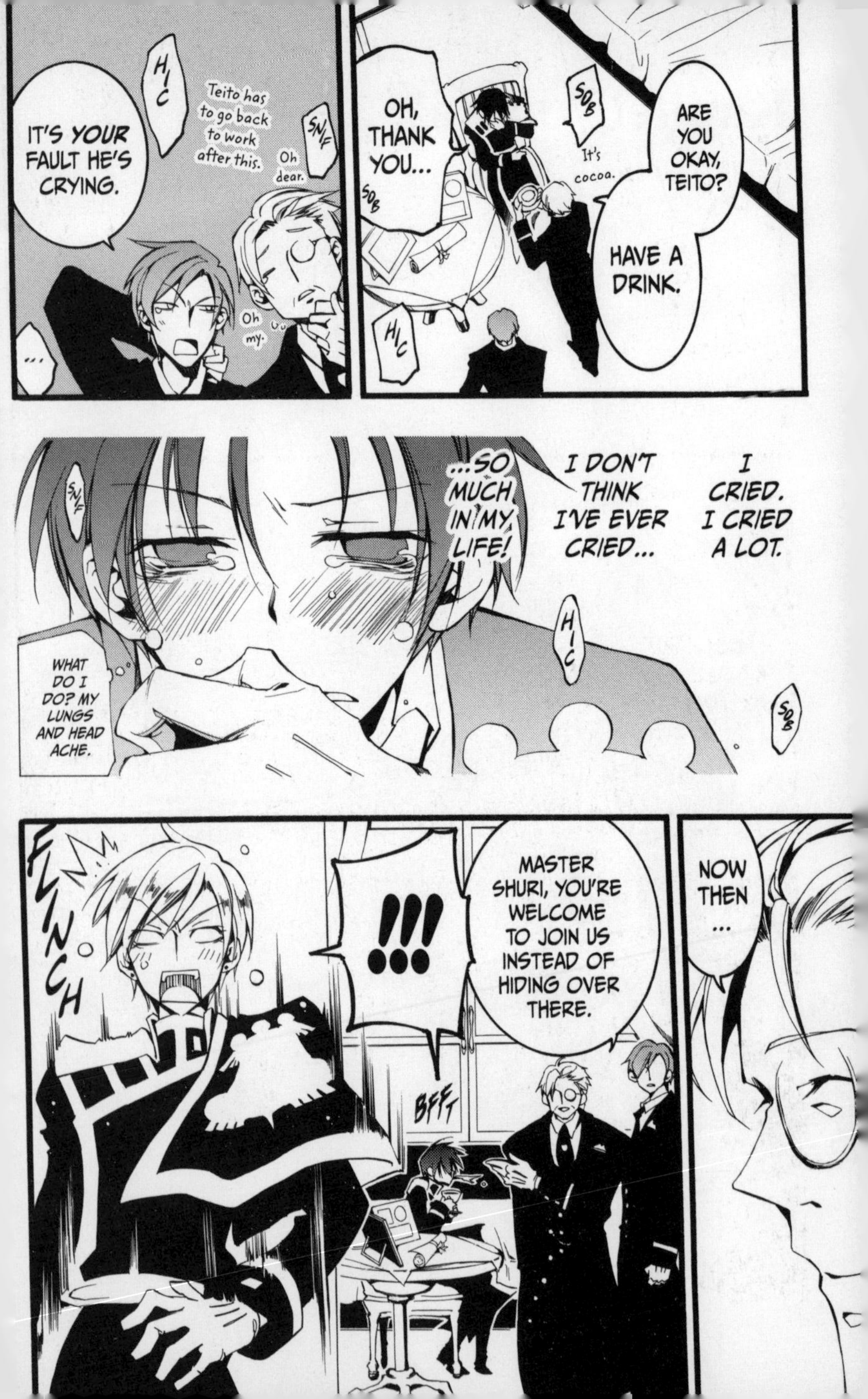
ARE YOU OKAY, TEITO?
SOB
It's cocoa.
HAVE A DRINK.
OH, THANK YOU...
SOB
HIC
HIC
Teito has to go back to work after this.
SNIF
Oh dear.
IT'S *YOUR* FAULT HE'S CRYING.
Oh my.
...
I CRIED. I CRIED A LOT.
I DON'T THINK I'VE EVER CRIED...
...SO MUCH IN MY LIFE!
SNIF
HIC
SOB
WHAT DO I DO? MY LUNGS AND HEAD ACHE.
NOW THEN...
MASTER SHURI, YOU'RE WELCOME TO JOIN US INSTEAD OF HIDING OVER THERE.
!!!
BFFT
FLINCH

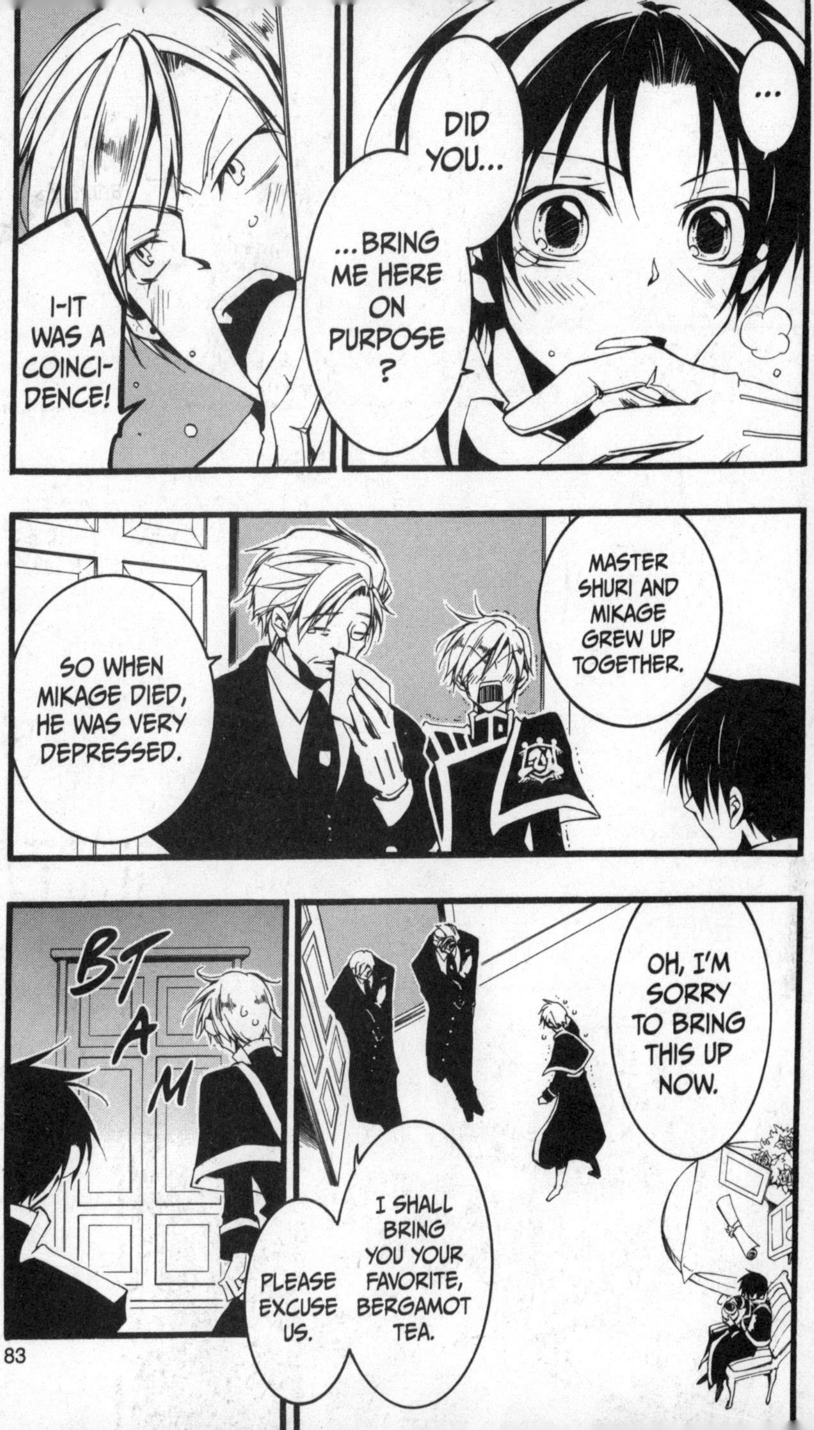
...
DID YOU...
...BRING ME HERE ON PURPOSE?
I-IT WAS A COINCIDENCE!
MASTER SHURI AND MIKAGE GREW UP TOGETHER.
SO WHEN MIKAGE DIED, HE WAS VERY DEPRESSED.
OH, I'M SORRY TO BRING THIS UP NOW.
I SHALL BRING YOU YOUR FAVORITE, BERGAMOT TEA.
PLEASE EXCUSE US.
BTAM

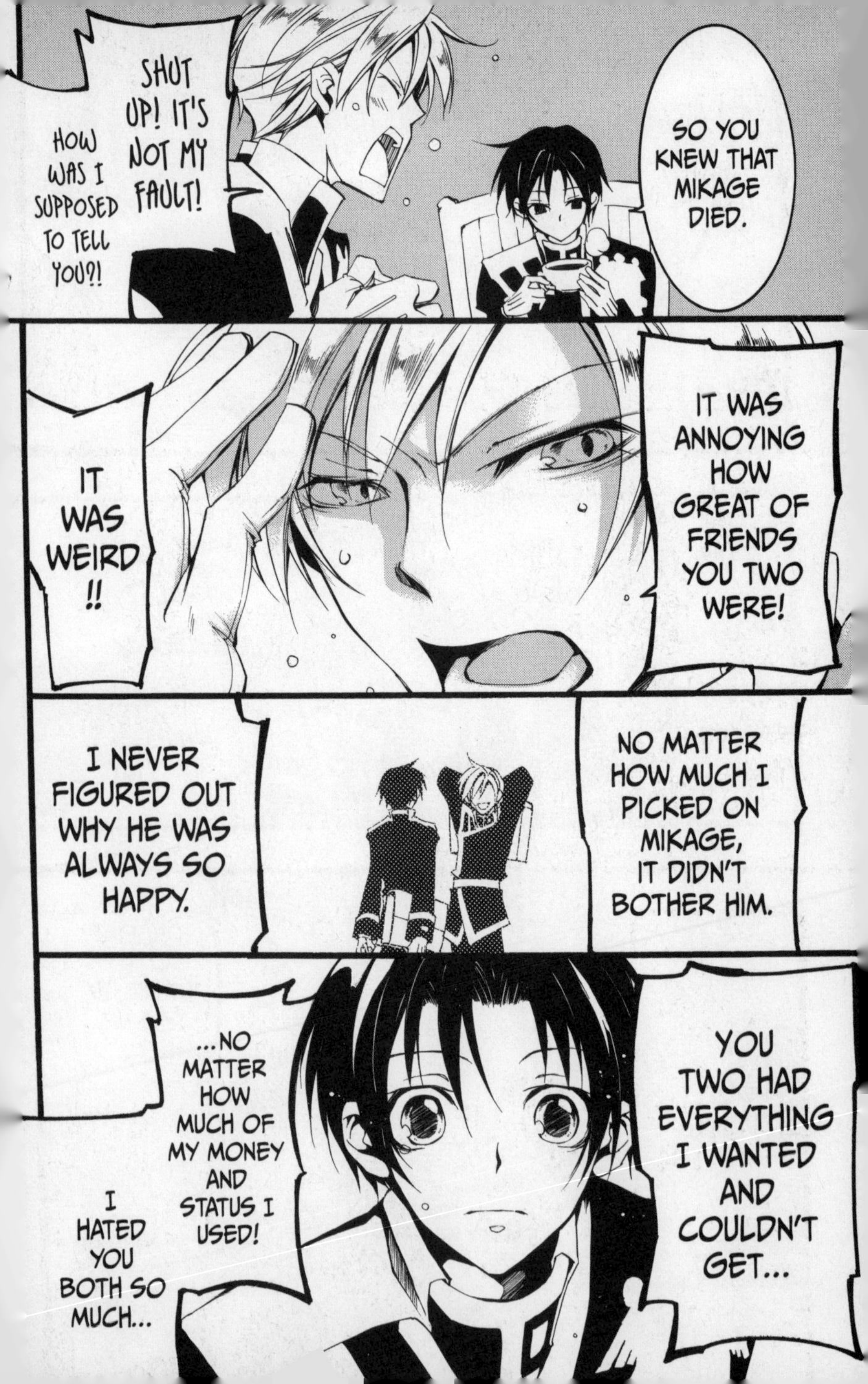
SO YOU KNEW THAT MIKAGE DIED.
SHUT UP! IT'S NOT MY FAULT!
HOW WAS I SUPPOSED TO TELL YOU?!
IT WAS ANNOYING HOW GREAT OF FRIENDS YOU TWO WERE!
IT WAS WEIRD!!
NO MATTER HOW MUCH I PICKED ON MIKAGE, IT DIDN'T BOTHER HIM.
I NEVER FIGURED OUT WHY HE WAS ALWAYS SO HAPPY.
YOU TWO HAD EVERYTHING I WANTED AND COULDN'T GET...
...NO MATTER HOW MUCH OF MY MONEY AND STATUS I USED!
I HATED YOU BOTH SO MUCH...

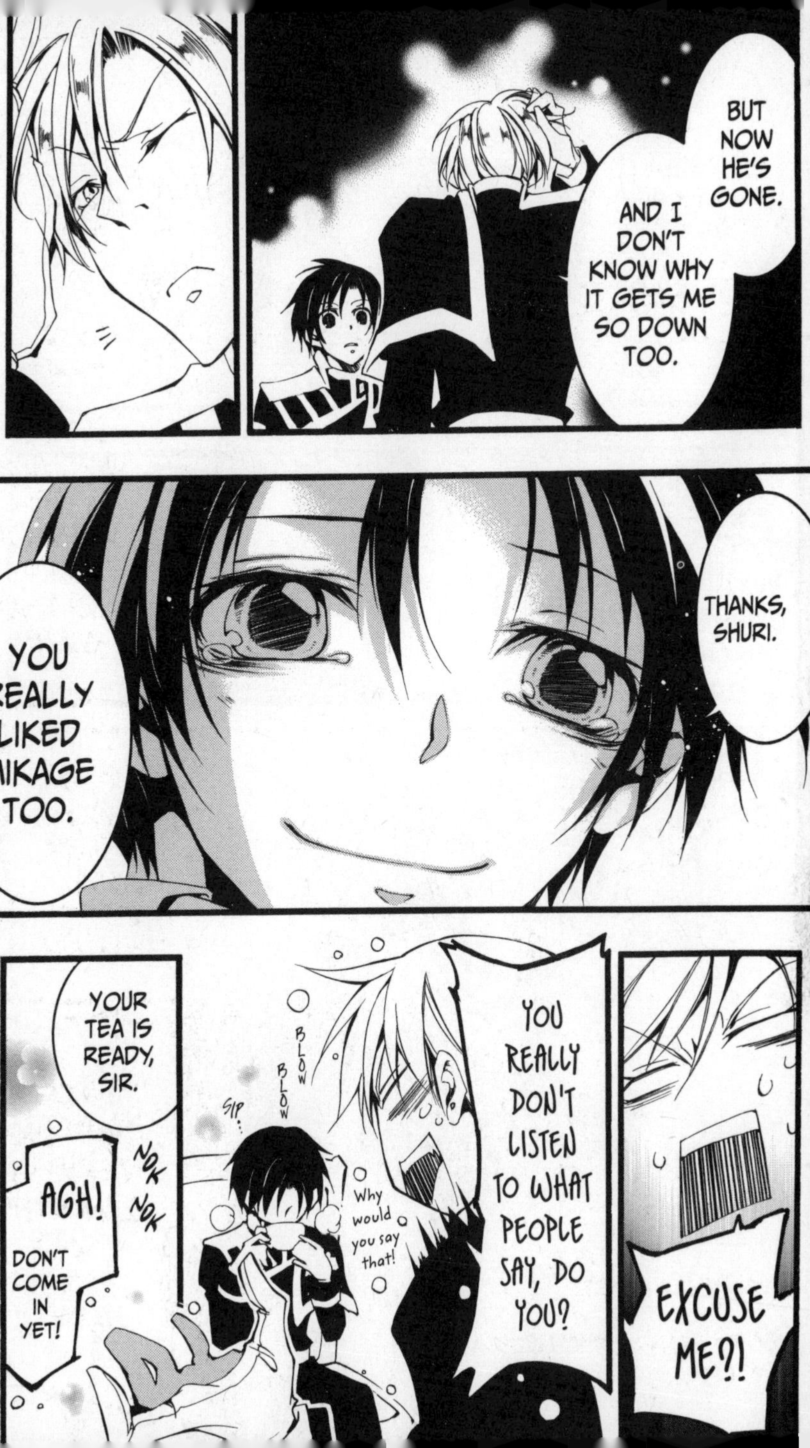
BUT NOW HE'S GONE.
AND I DON'T KNOW WHY IT GETS ME SO DOWN TOO.
THANKS, SHURI.
YOU REALLY LIKED MIKAGE TOO.
EXCUSE ME?!
YOU REALLY DON'T LISTEN TO WHAT PEOPLE SAY, DO YOU?
Why would you say that!
BLOW BLOW
SIP...
YOUR TEA IS READY, SIR.
NOK NOK
AGH!
DON'T COME IN YET!

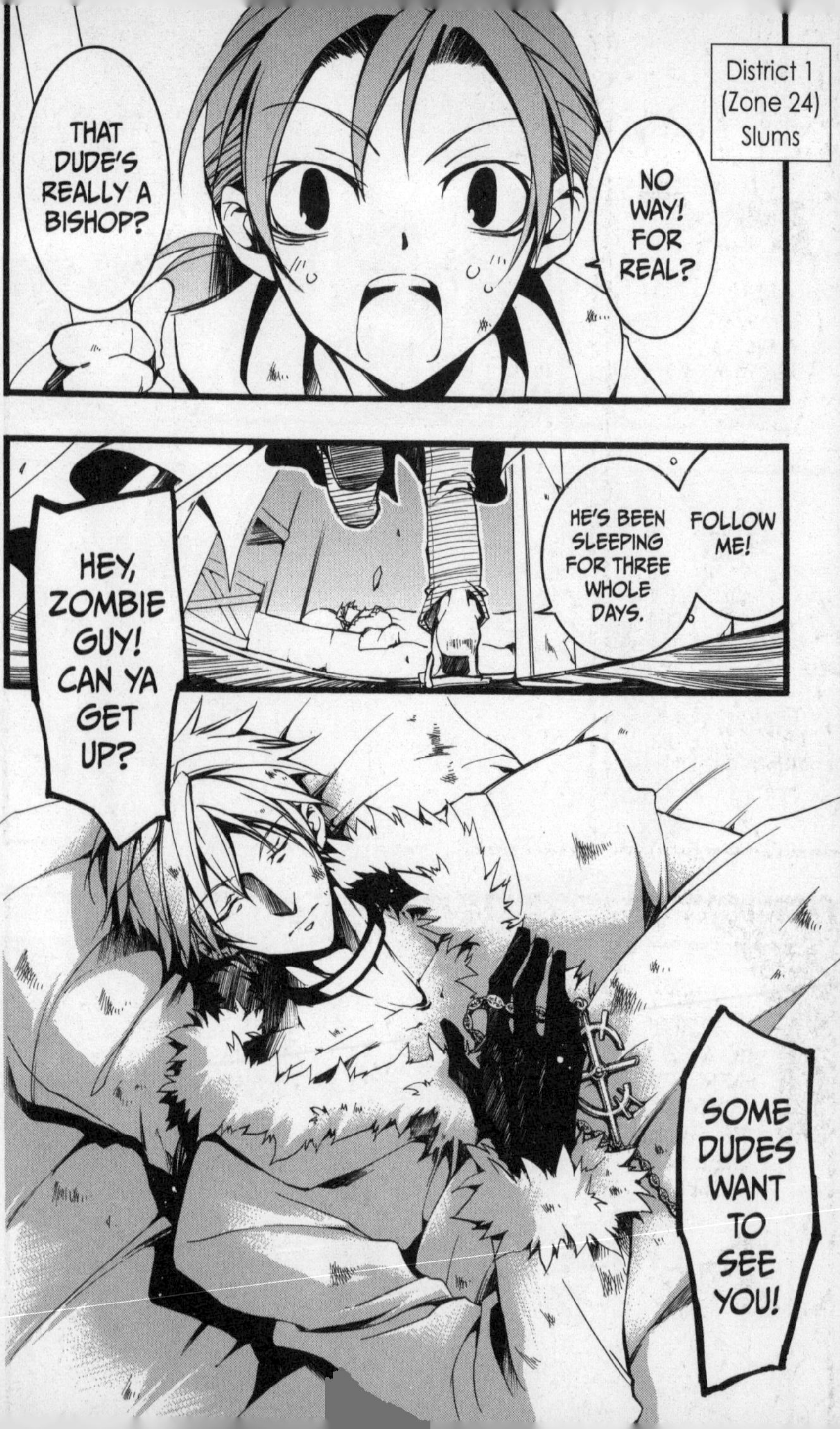
District 1 (Zone 24) Slums
NO WAY! FOR REAL?
THAT DUDE'S REALLY A BISHOP?
FOLLOW ME!
HE'S BEEN SLEEPING FOR THREE WHOLE DAYS.
HEY, ZOMBIE GUY! CAN YA GET UP?
SOME DUDES WANT TO SEE YOU!

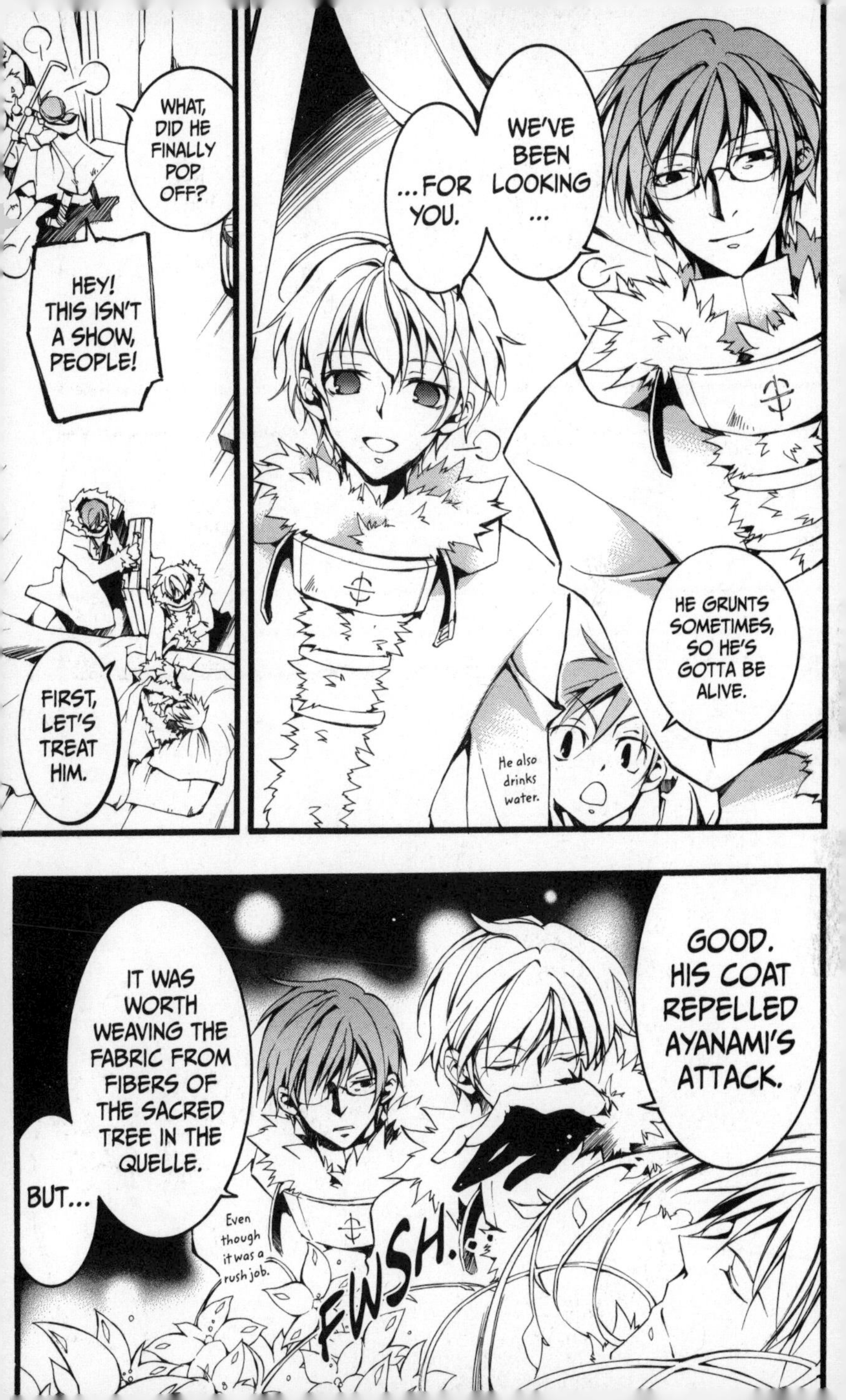
WE'VE BEEN LOOKING...
...FOR YOU.
HE GRUNTS SOMETIMES, SO HE'S GOTTA BE ALIVE.
He also drinks water.
WHAT, DID HE FINALLY POP OFF?
HEY! THIS ISN'T A SHOW, PEOPLE!
FIRST, LET'S TREAT HIM.
GOOD. HIS COAT REPELLED AYANAMI'S ATTACK.
IT WAS WORTH WEAVING THE FABRIC FROM FIBERS OF THE SACRED TREE IN THE QUELLE.
BUT...
Even though it was a rush job.
FWSH...

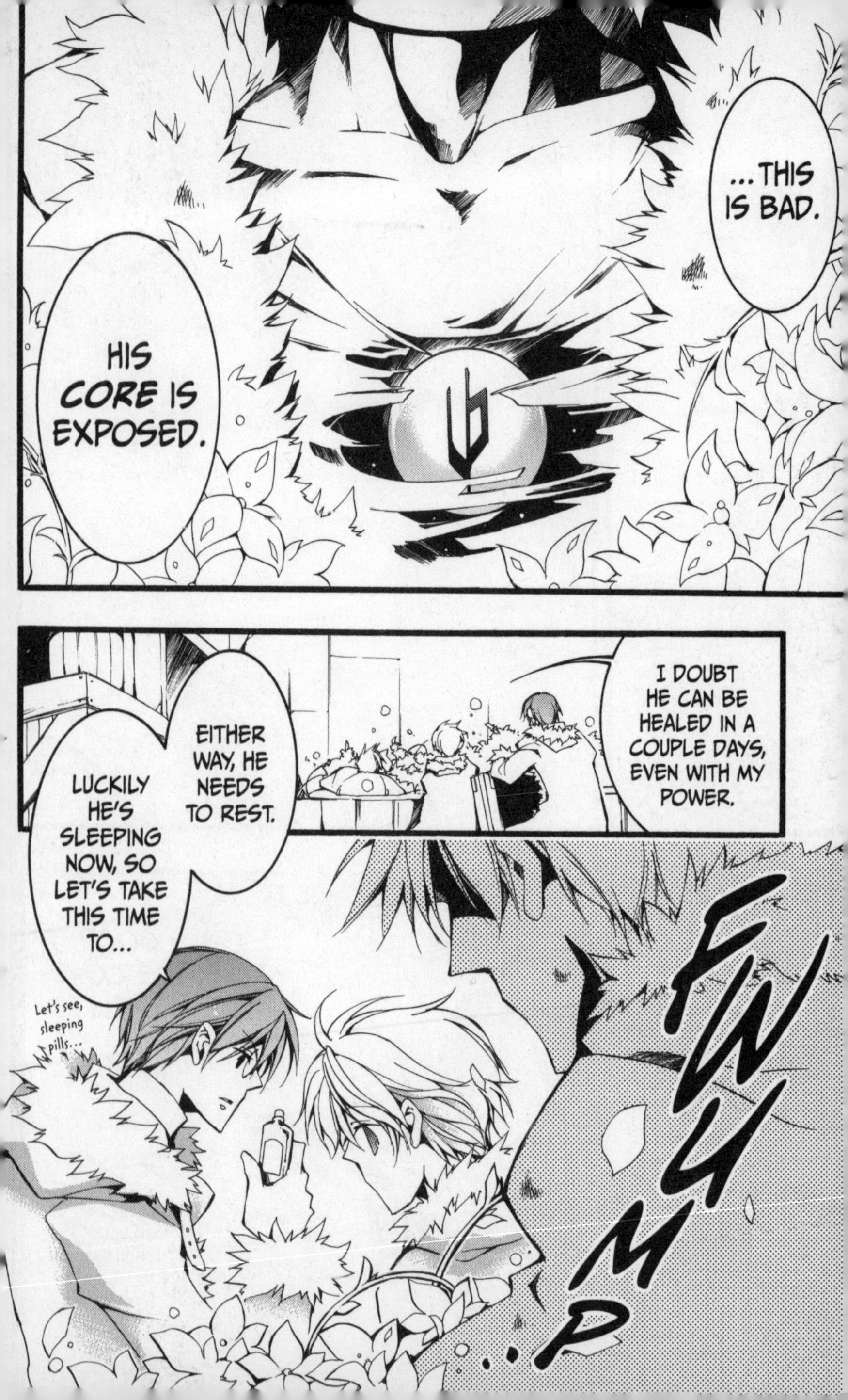
...THIS IS BAD.
HIS CORE IS EXPOSED.
I DOUBT HE CAN BE HEALED IN A COUPLE DAYS, EVEN WITH MY POWER.
EITHER WAY, HE NEEDS TO REST.
LUCKILY HE'S SLEEPING NOW, SO LET'S TAKE THIS TIME TO...
FWUMP...
Let's see, sleeping pills...

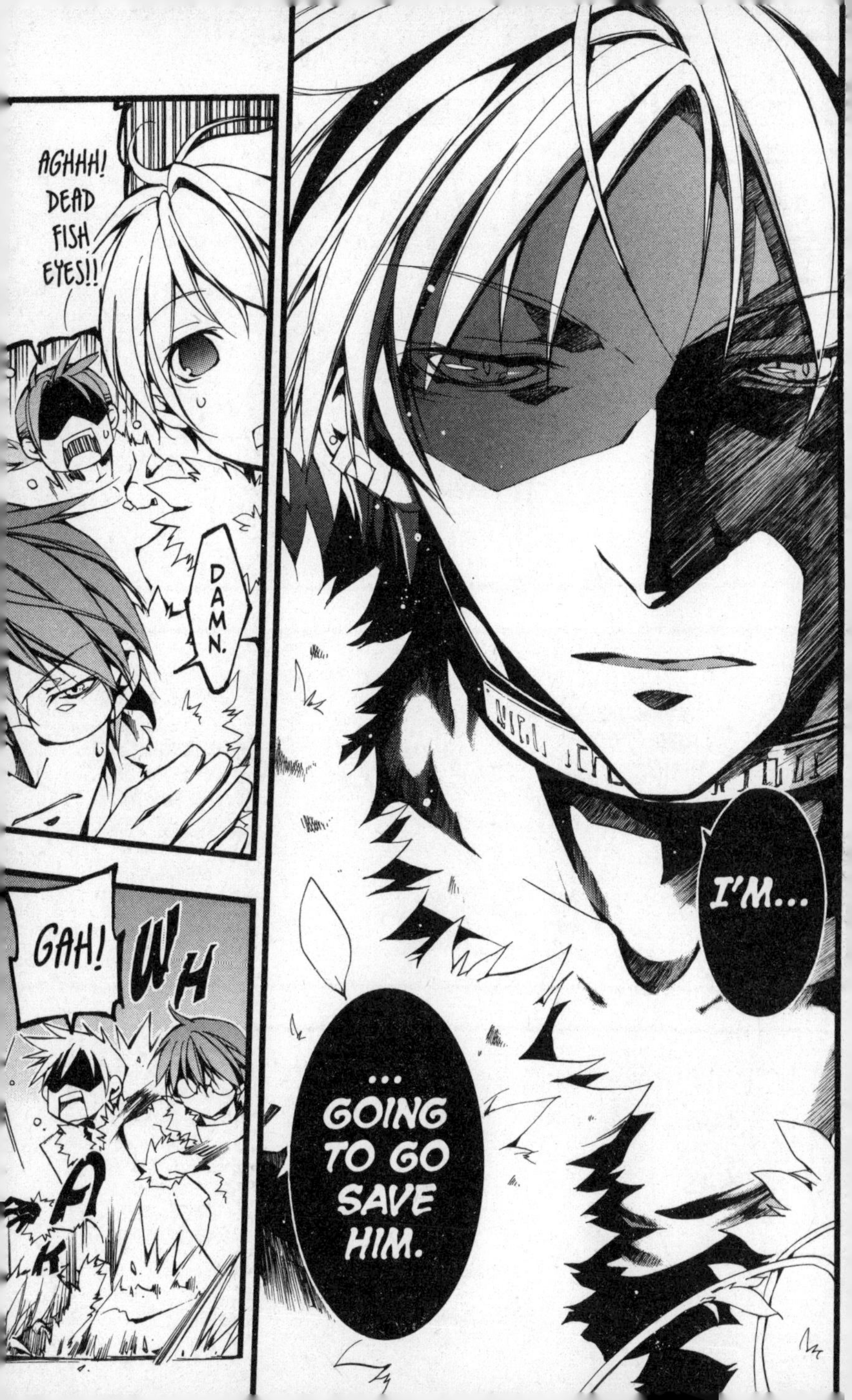
I'M...
... GOING TO GO SAVE HIM.
AGHHH! DEAD FISH EYES!!
DAMN.
GAH!
WHAK

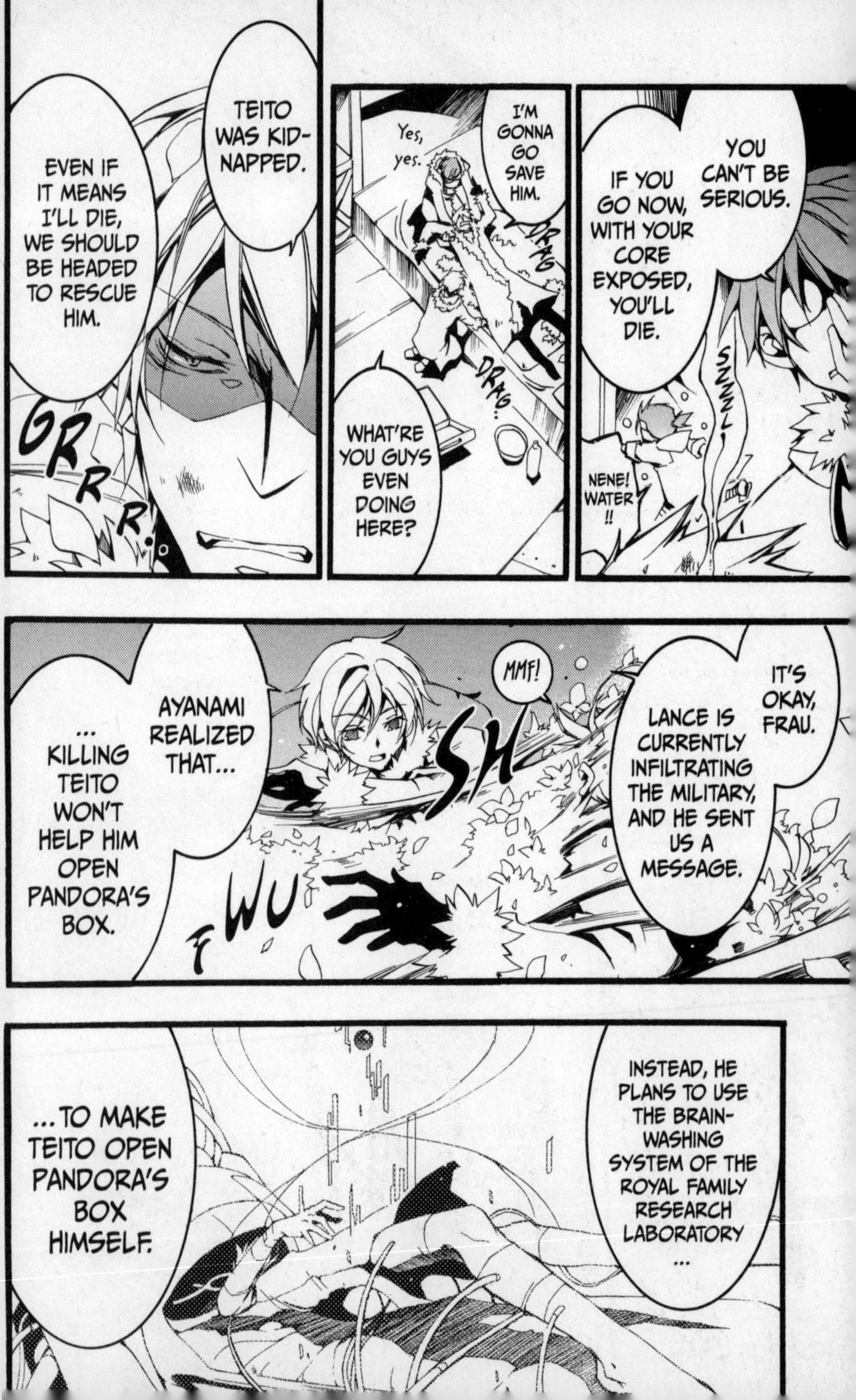
YOU CAN'T BE SERIOUS.
IF YOU GO NOW, WITH YOUR CORE EXPOSED, YOU'LL DIE.
SZZZL
NENE! WATER!!
I'M GONNA GO SAVE HIM.
Yes, yes.
DRAG
DRAG...
WHAT'RE YOU GUYS EVEN DOING HERE?
TEITO WAS KID-NAPPED.
EVEN IF IT MEANS I'LL DIE, WE SHOULD BE HEADED TO RESCUE HIM.
GRRRR!
IT'S OKAY, FRAU.
LANCE IS CURRENTLY INFILTRATING THE MILITARY, AND HE SENT US A MESSAGE.
MMF!
SH
FWU
AYANAMI REALIZED THAT...
...KILLING TEITO WON'T HELP HIM OPEN PANDORA'S BOX.
INSTEAD, HE PLANS TO USE THE BRAIN-WASHING SYSTEM OF THE ROYAL FAMILY RESEARCH LABORATORY...
...TO MAKE TEITO OPEN PANDORA'S BOX HIMSELF.

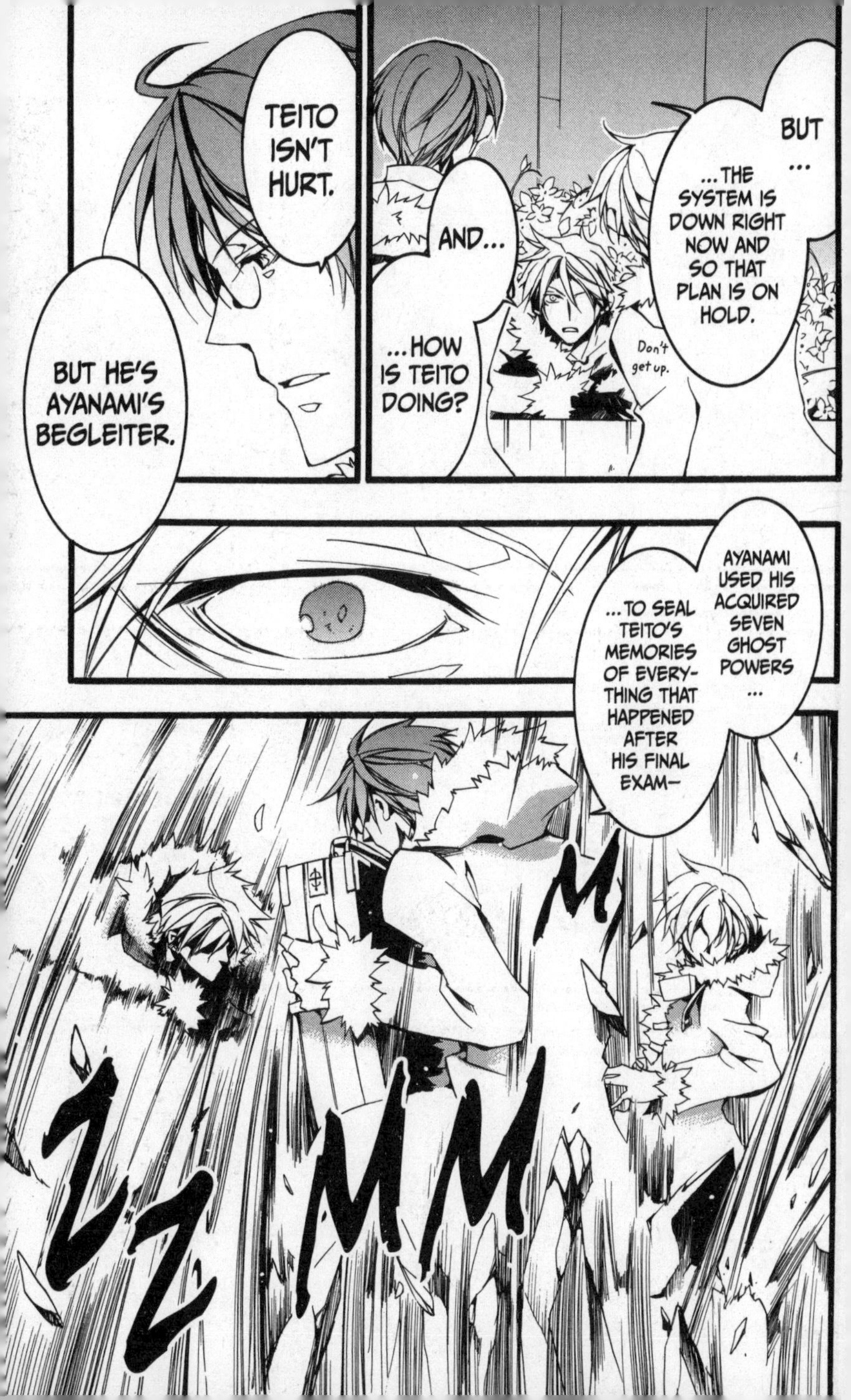
BUT ...
...THE SYSTEM IS DOWN RIGHT NOW AND SO THAT PLAN IS ON HOLD.
Don't get up.
AND...
...HOW IS TEITO DOING?
TEITO ISN'T HURT.
BUT HE'S AYANAMI'S BEGLEITER.
AYANAMI USED HIS ACQUIRED SEVEN GHOST POWERS ...
...TO SEAL TEITO'S MEMORIES OF EVERY-THING THAT HAPPENED AFTER HIS FINAL EXAM–
ZZMMM

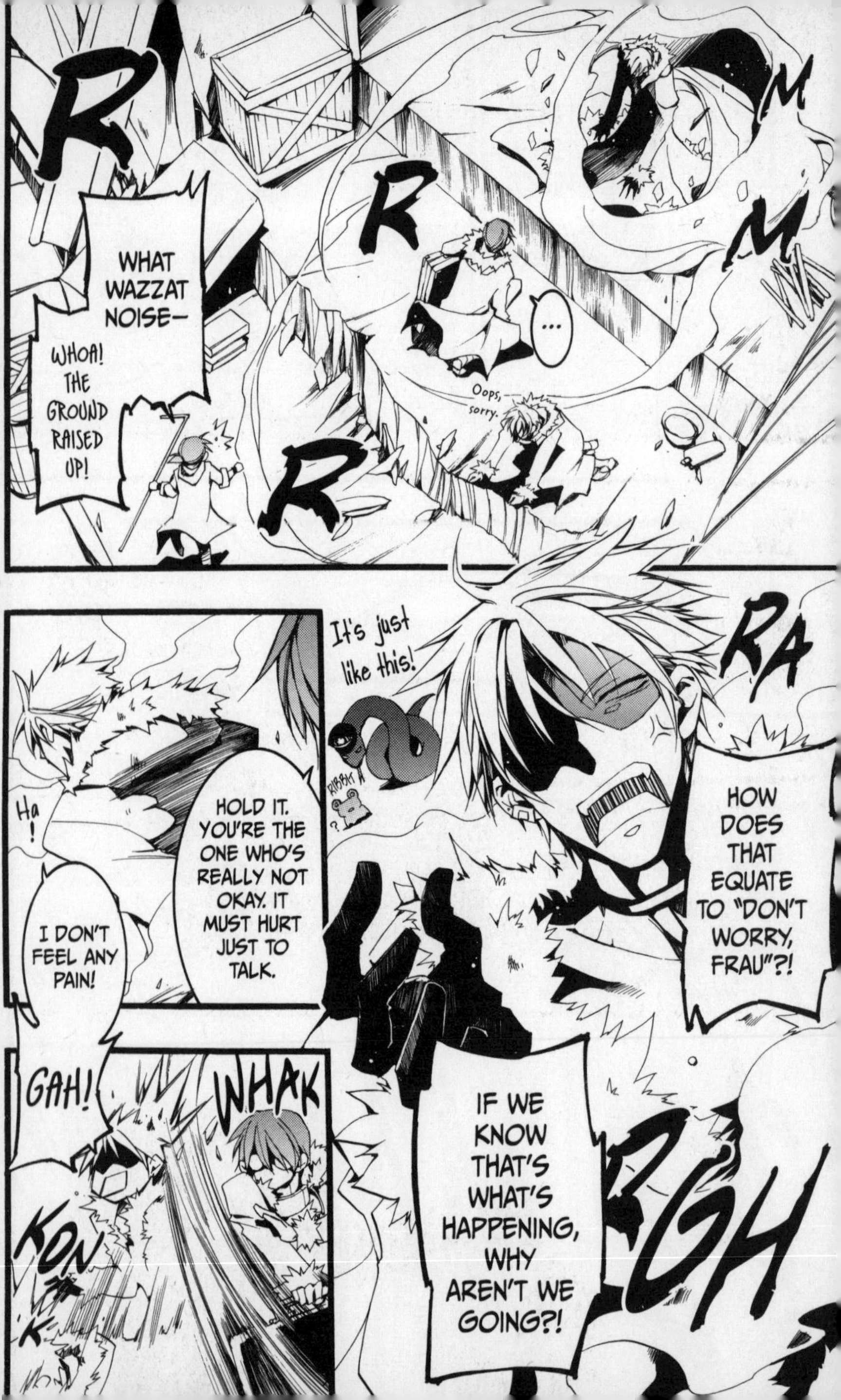
M
M
R
R
R
...
Oops, sorry.
WHAT WAZZAT NOISE—
WHOA! THE GROUND RAISED UP!
RA
HOW DOES THAT EQUATE TO "DON'T WORRY, FRAU"?!
It's just like this!
RIBBIT
?
HOLD IT. YOU'RE THE ONE WHO'S REALLY NOT OKAY. IT MUST HURT JUST TO TALK.
Ha!
I DON'T FEEL ANY PAIN!
IF WE KNOW THAT'S WHAT'S HAPPENING, WHY AREN'T WE GOING?!
RGH
WHAK
GAH!
KONK

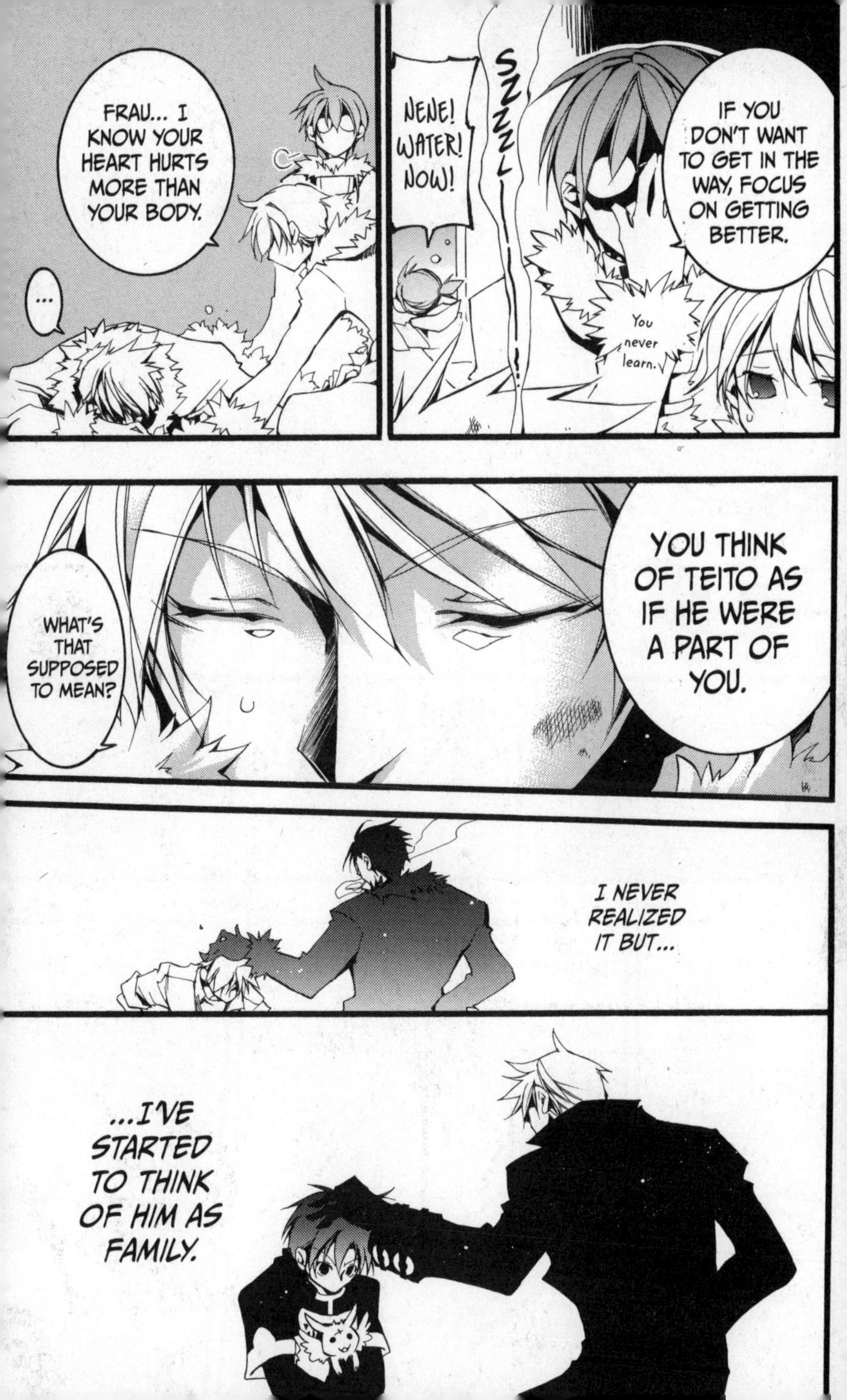
IF YOU DON'T WANT TO GET IN THE WAY, FOCUS ON GETTING BETTER.
You never learn.
SZZZZ
NENE! WATER! NOW!
FRAU... I KNOW YOUR HEART HURTS MORE THAN YOUR BODY.
...
YOU THINK OF TEITO AS IF HE WERE A PART OF YOU.
WHAT'S THAT SUPPOSED TO MEAN?
I NEVER REALIZED IT BUT...
...I'VE STARTED TO THINK OF HIM AS FAMILY.

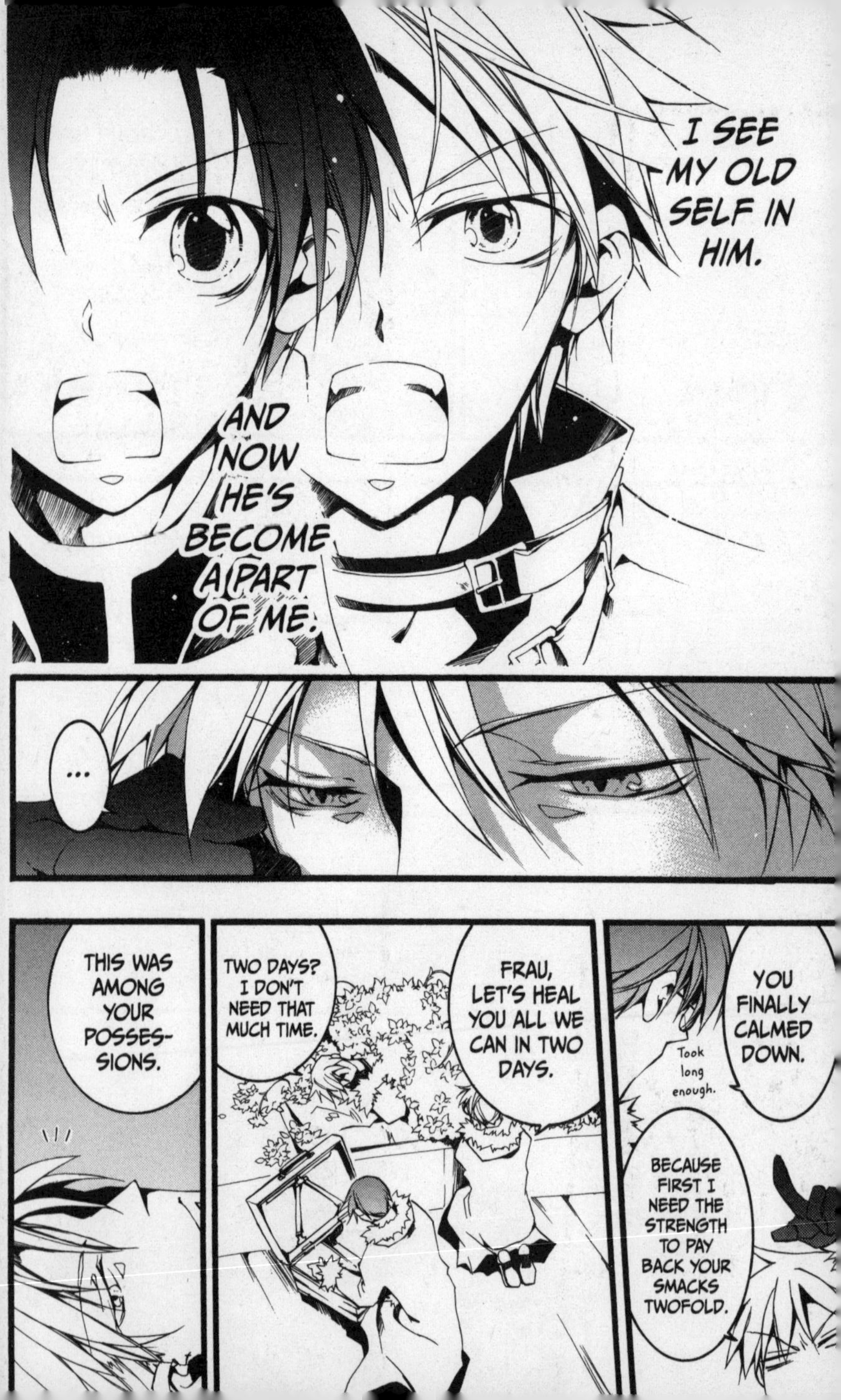
I SEE MY OLD SELF IN HIM.
AND NOW HE'S BECOME A PART OF ME.
...
YOU FINALLY CALMED DOWN.
Took long enough.
BECAUSE FIRST I NEED THE STRENGTH TO PAY BACK YOUR SMACKS TWOFOLD.
FRAU, LET'S HEAL YOU ALL WE CAN IN TWO DAYS.
TWO DAYS? I DON'T NEED THAT MUCH TIME.
THIS WAS AMONG YOUR POSSESSIONS.

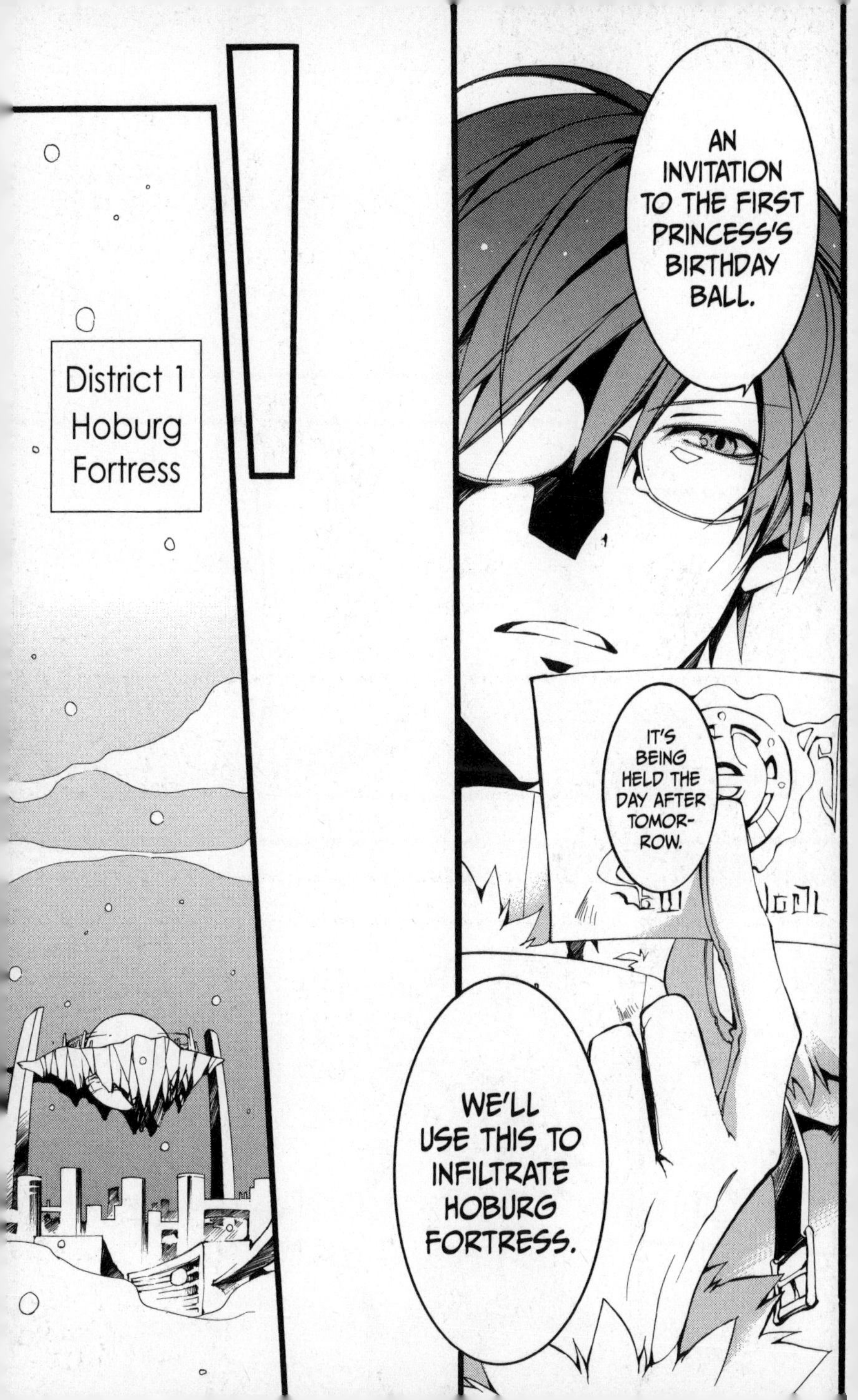
AN INVITATION TO THE FIRST PRINCESS'S BIRTHDAY BALL.
IT'S BEING HELD THE DAY AFTER TOMOR-ROW.
WE'LL USE THIS TO INFILTRATE HOBURG FORTRESS.
District 1 Hoburg Fortress

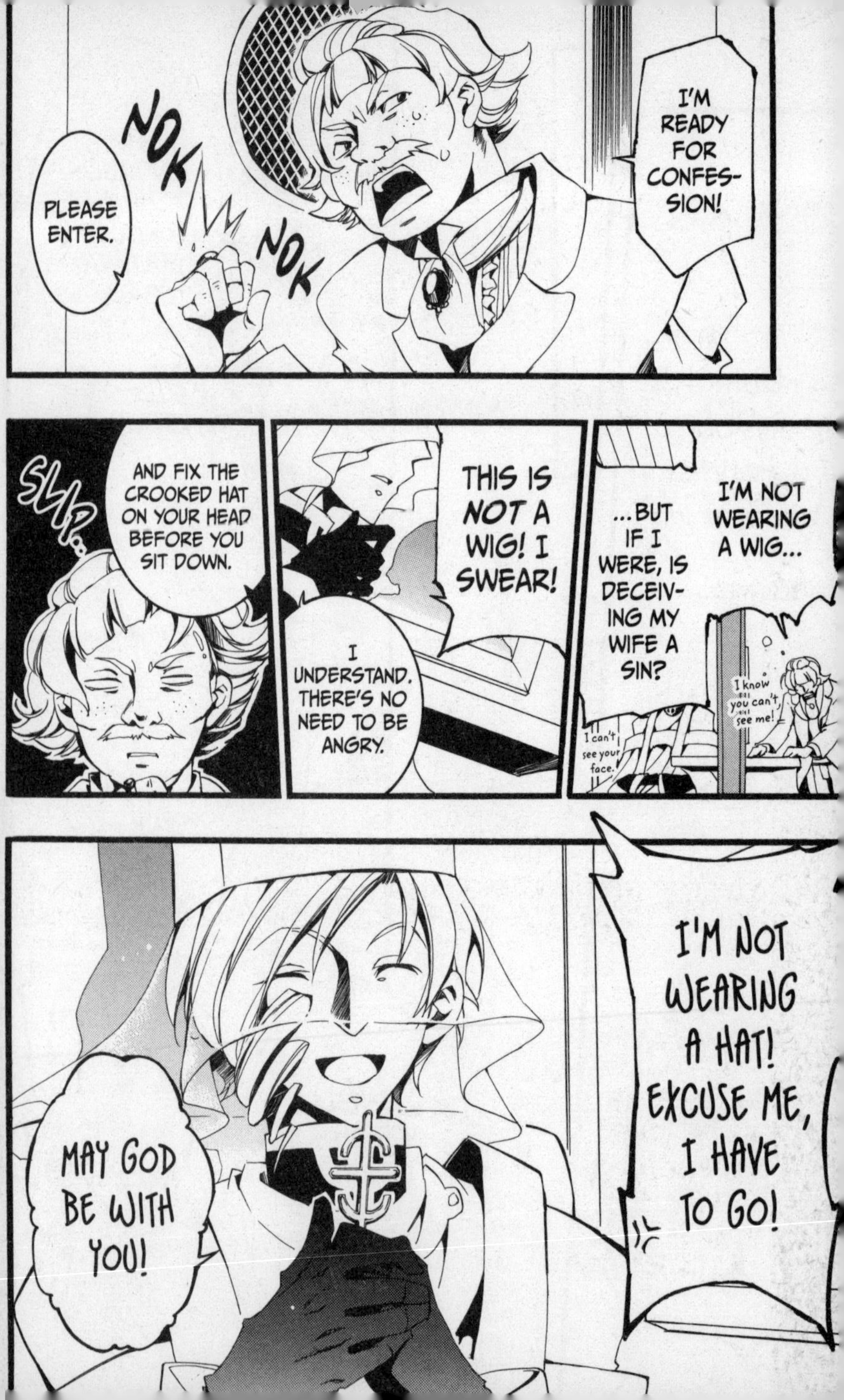
I'M READY FOR CONFESSION!
NOK NOK
PLEASE ENTER.
I'M NOT WEARING A WIG...
...BUT IF I WERE, IS DECEIVING MY WIFE A SIN?
I know you can't see me!
I can't see your face.
THIS IS *NOT* A WIG! I SWEAR!
I UNDERSTAND. THERE'S NO NEED TO BE ANGRY.
AND FIX THE CROOKED HAT ON YOUR HEAD BEFORE YOU SIT DOWN.
SLIP
I'M NOT WEARING A HAT! EXCUSE ME, I HAVE TO GO!
MAY GOD BE WITH YOU!

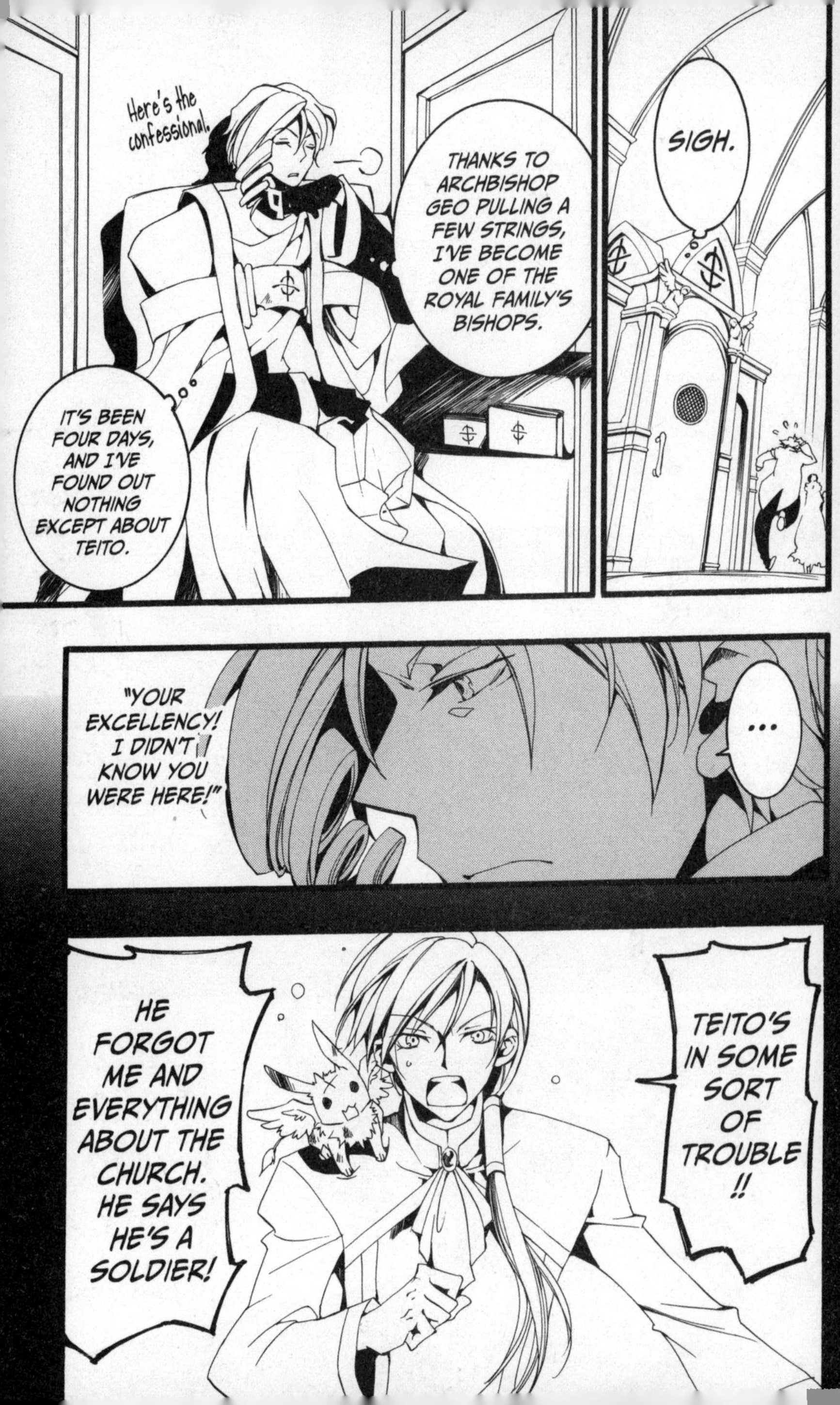
SIGH.
THANKS TO ARCHBISHOP GEO PULLING A FEW STRINGS, I'VE BECOME ONE OF THE ROYAL FAMILY'S BISHOPS.
Here's the confessional.
IT'S BEEN FOUR DAYS, AND I'VE FOUND OUT NOTHING EXCEPT ABOUT TEITO.
...
"YOUR EXCELLENCY! I DIDN'T KNOW YOU WERE HERE!"
TEITO'S IN SOME SORT OF TROUBLE!!
HE FORGOT ME AND EVERYTHING ABOUT THE CHURCH. HE SAYS HE'S A SOLDIER!

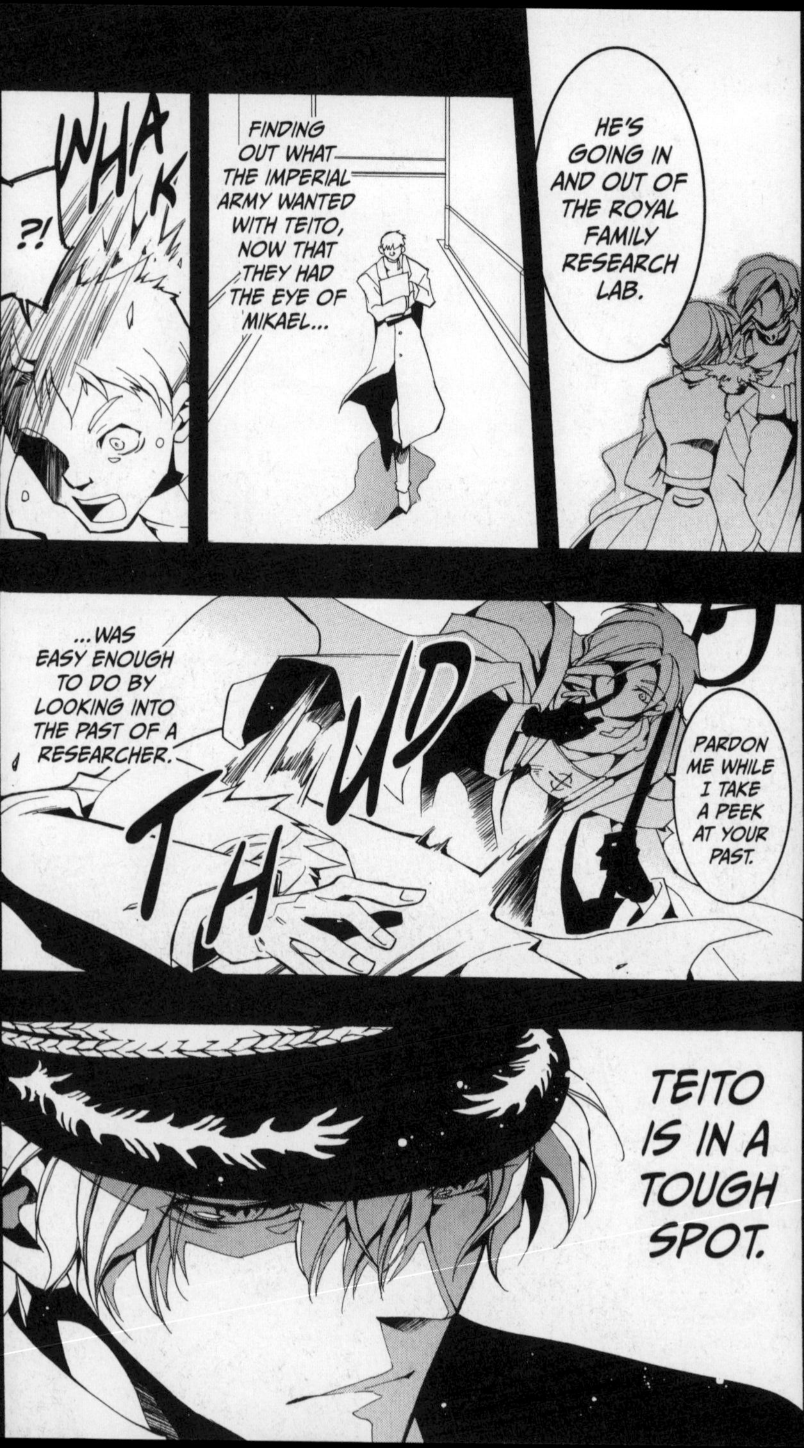
HE'S GOING IN AND OUT OF THE ROYAL FAMILY RESEARCH LAB.
FINDING OUT WHAT THE IMPERIAL ARMY WANTED WITH TEITO, NOW THAT THEY HAD THE EYE OF MIKAEL...
WHAK
?!
PARDON ME WHILE I TAKE A PEEK AT YOUR PAST.
...WAS EASY ENOUGH TO DO BY LOOKING INTO THE PAST OF A RESEARCHER.
THUD
TEITO IS IN A TOUGH SPOT.

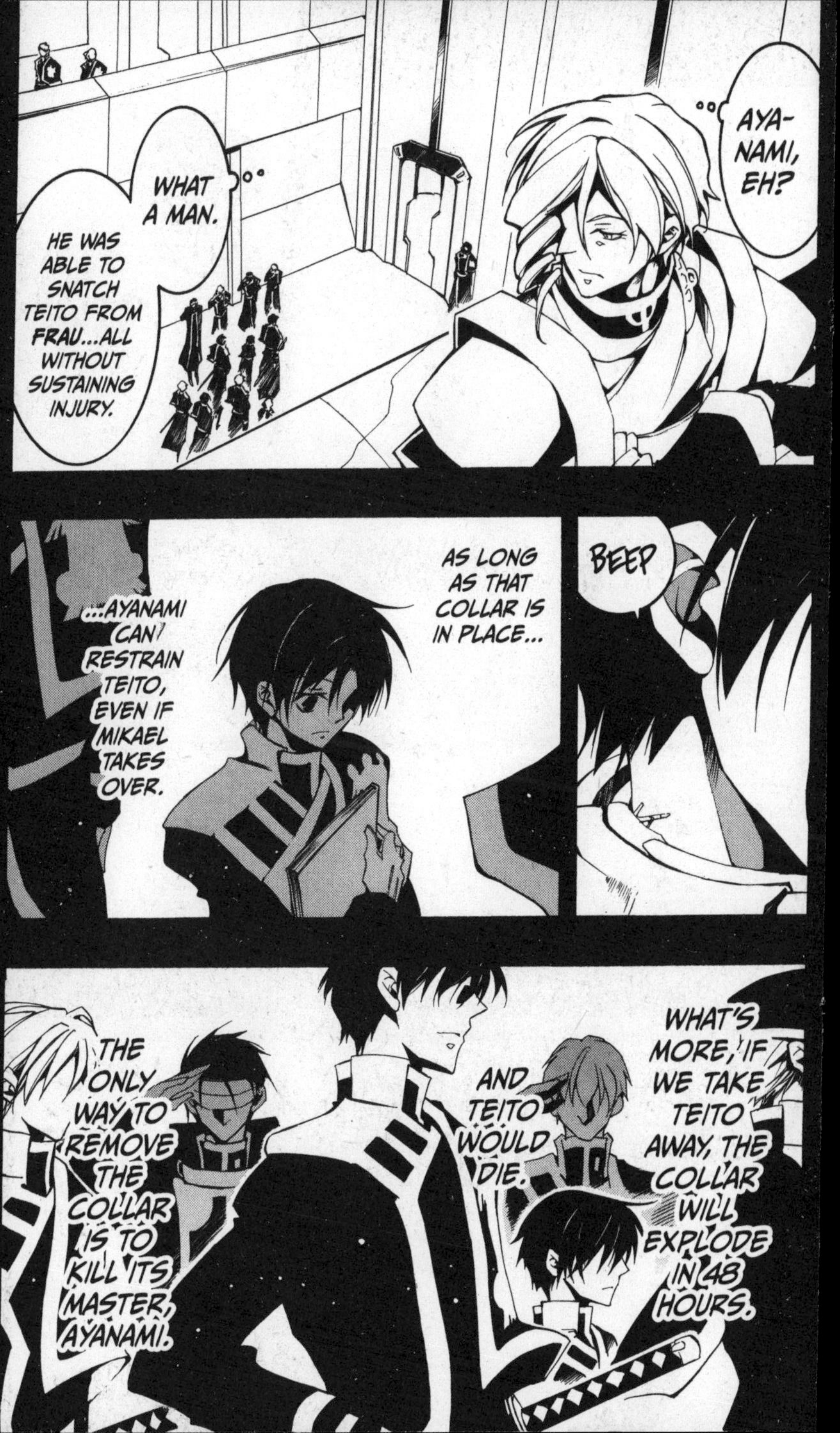
AYA-NAMI, EH?
WHAT A MAN.
HE WAS ABLE TO SNATCH TEITO FROM FRAU...ALL WITHOUT SUSTAINING INJURY.
BEEP
AS LONG AS THAT COLLAR IS IN PLACE...
...AYANAMI CAN RESTRAIN TEITO, EVEN IF MIKAEL TAKES OVER.
WHAT'S MORE, IF WE TAKE TEITO AWAY, THE COLLAR WILL EXPLODE IN 48 HOURS.
AND TEITO WOULD DIE.
THE ONLY WAY TO REMOVE THE COLLAR IS TO KILL ITS MASTER, AYANAMI.

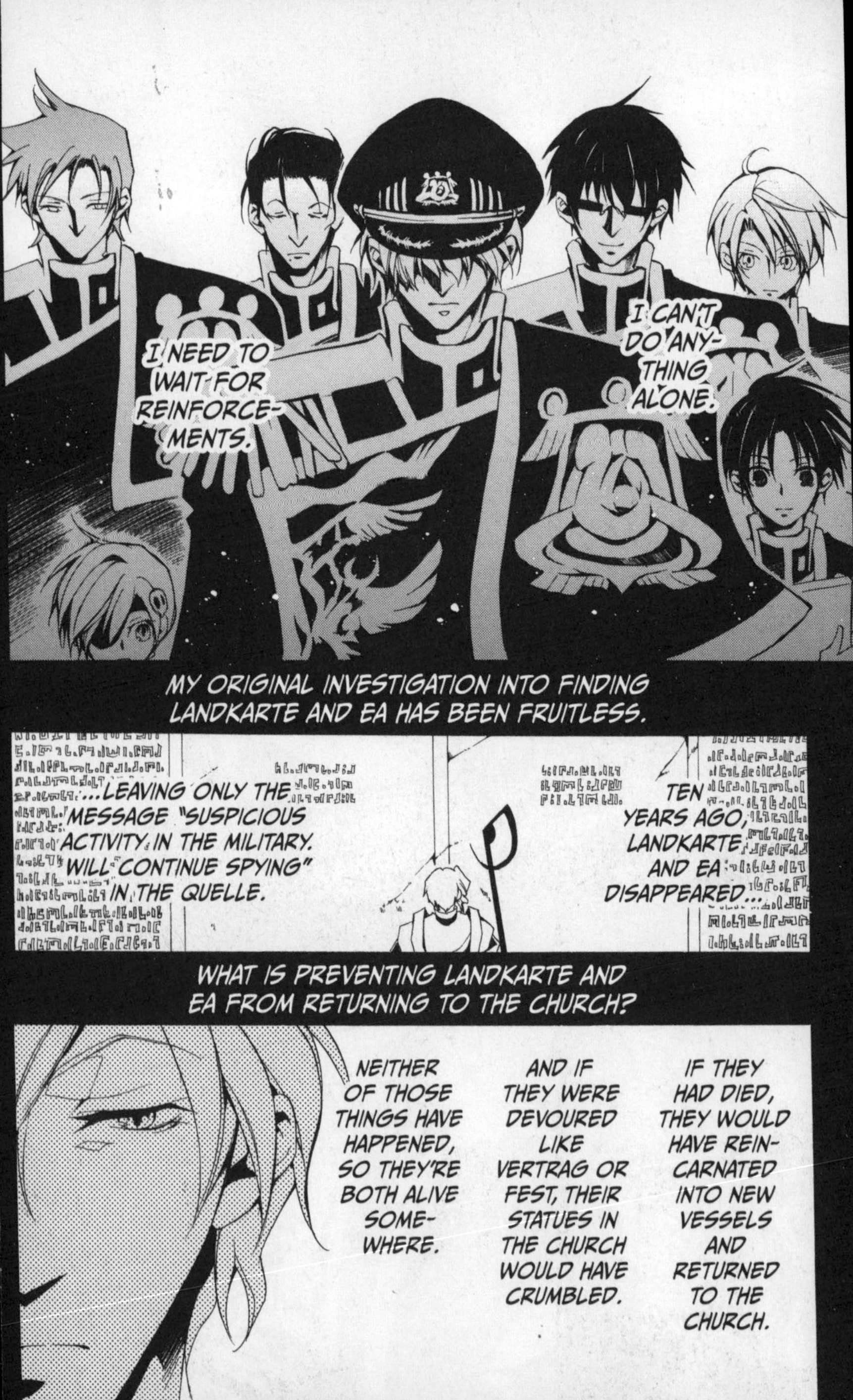
I CAN'T DO ANYTHING ALONE.
I NEED TO WAIT FOR REINFORCEMENTS.
MY ORIGINAL INVESTIGATION INTO FINDING LANDKARTE AND EA HAS BEEN FRUITLESS.
TEN YEARS AGO, LANDKARTE AND EA DISAPPEARED...
...LEAVING ONLY THE MESSAGE "SUSPICIOUS ACTIVITY IN THE MILITARY. WILL CONTINUE SPYING" IN THE QUELLE.
WHAT IS PREVENTING LANDKARTE AND EA FROM RETURNING TO THE CHURCH?
IF THEY HAD DIED, THEY WOULD HAVE REINCARNATED INTO NEW VESSELS AND RETURNED TO THE CHURCH.
AND IF THEY WERE DEVOURED LIKE VERTRAG OR FEST, THEIR STATUES IN THE CHURCH WOULD HAVE CRUMBLED.
NEITHER OF THOSE THINGS HAVE HAPPENED, SO THEY'RE BOTH ALIVE SOMEWHERE.

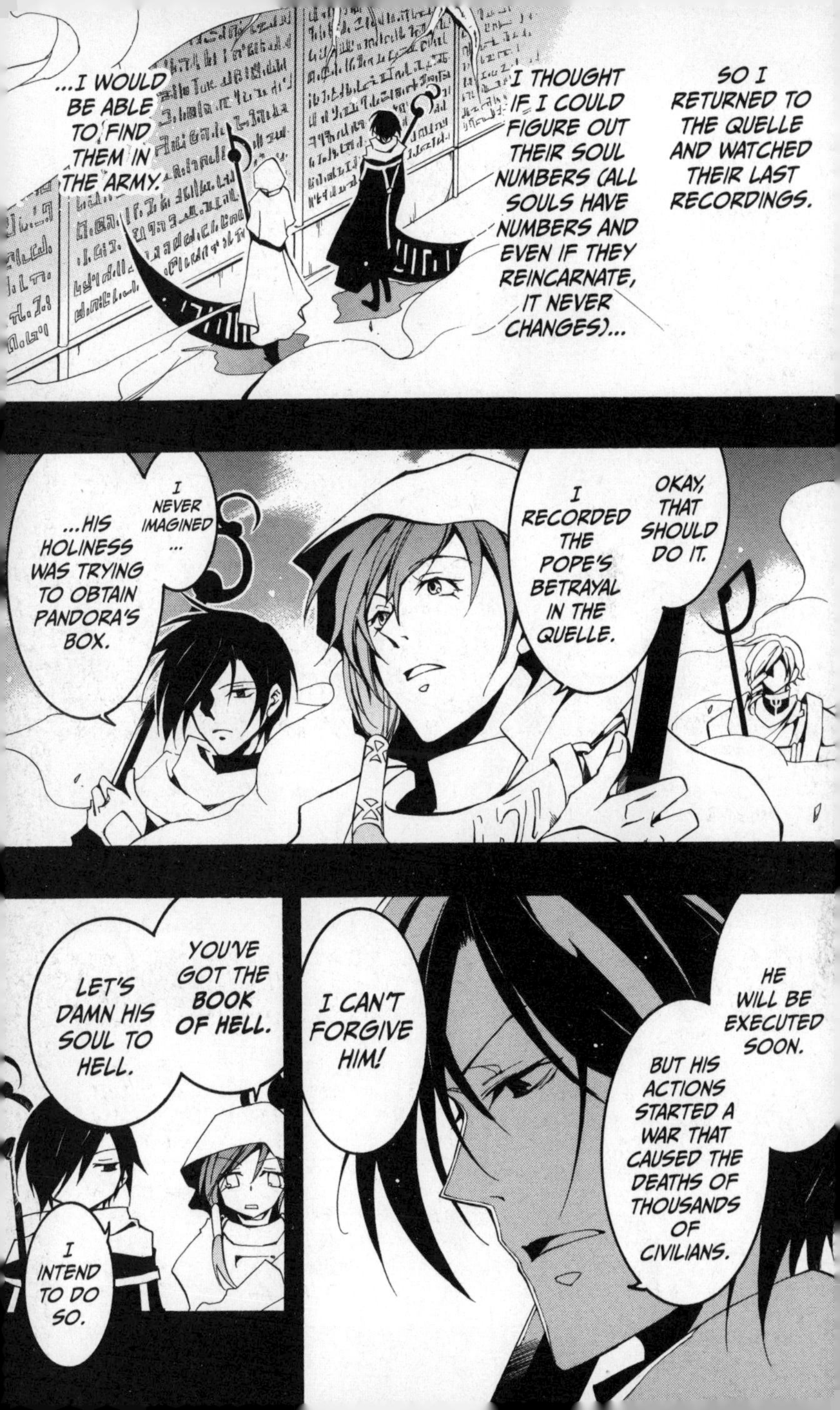
SO I RETURNED TO THE QUELLE AND WATCHED THEIR LAST RECORDINGS.
I THOUGHT IF I COULD FIGURE OUT THEIR SOUL NUMBERS (ALL SOULS HAVE NUMBERS AND EVEN IF THEY REINCARNATE, IT NEVER CHANGES)...
...I WOULD BE ABLE TO FIND THEM IN THE ARMY.
OKAY, THAT SHOULD DO IT.
I RECORDED THE POPE'S BETRAYAL IN THE QUELLE.
I NEVER IMAGINED...
...HIS HOLINESS WAS TRYING TO OBTAIN PANDORA'S BOX.
HE WILL BE EXECUTED SOON.
BUT HIS ACTIONS STARTED A WAR THAT CAUSED THE DEATHS OF THOUSANDS OF CIVILIANS.
I CAN'T FORGIVE HIM!
YOU'VE GOT THE BOOK OF HELL.
LET'S DAMN HIS SOUL TO HELL.
I INTEND TO DO SO.

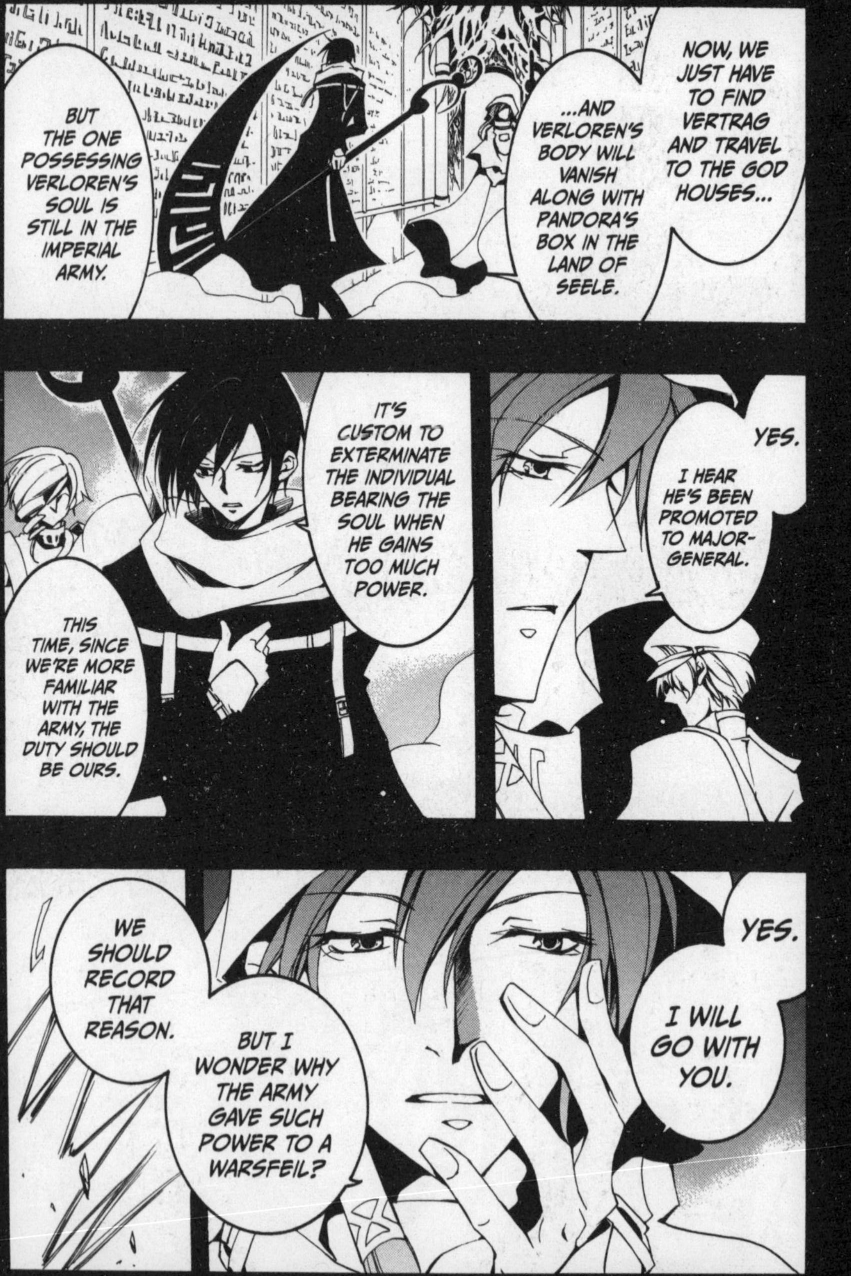
NOW, WE JUST HAVE TO FIND VERTRAG AND TRAVEL TO THE GOD HOUSES...
...AND VERLOREN'S BODY WILL VANISH ALONG WITH PANDORA'S BOX IN THE LAND OF SEELE.
BUT THE ONE POSSESSING VERLOREN'S SOUL IS STILL IN THE IMPERIAL ARMY.
YES.
I HEAR HE'S BEEN PROMOTED TO MAJOR-GENERAL.
IT'S CUSTOM TO EXTERMINATE THE INDIVIDUAL BEARING THE SOUL WHEN HE GAINS TOO MUCH POWER.
THIS TIME, SINCE WE'RE MORE FAMILIAR WITH THE ARMY, THE DUTY SHOULD BE OURS.
YES.
I WILL GO WITH YOU.
WE SHOULD RECORD THAT REASON.
BUT I WONDER WHY THE ARMY GAVE SUCH POWER TO A WARSFEIL?

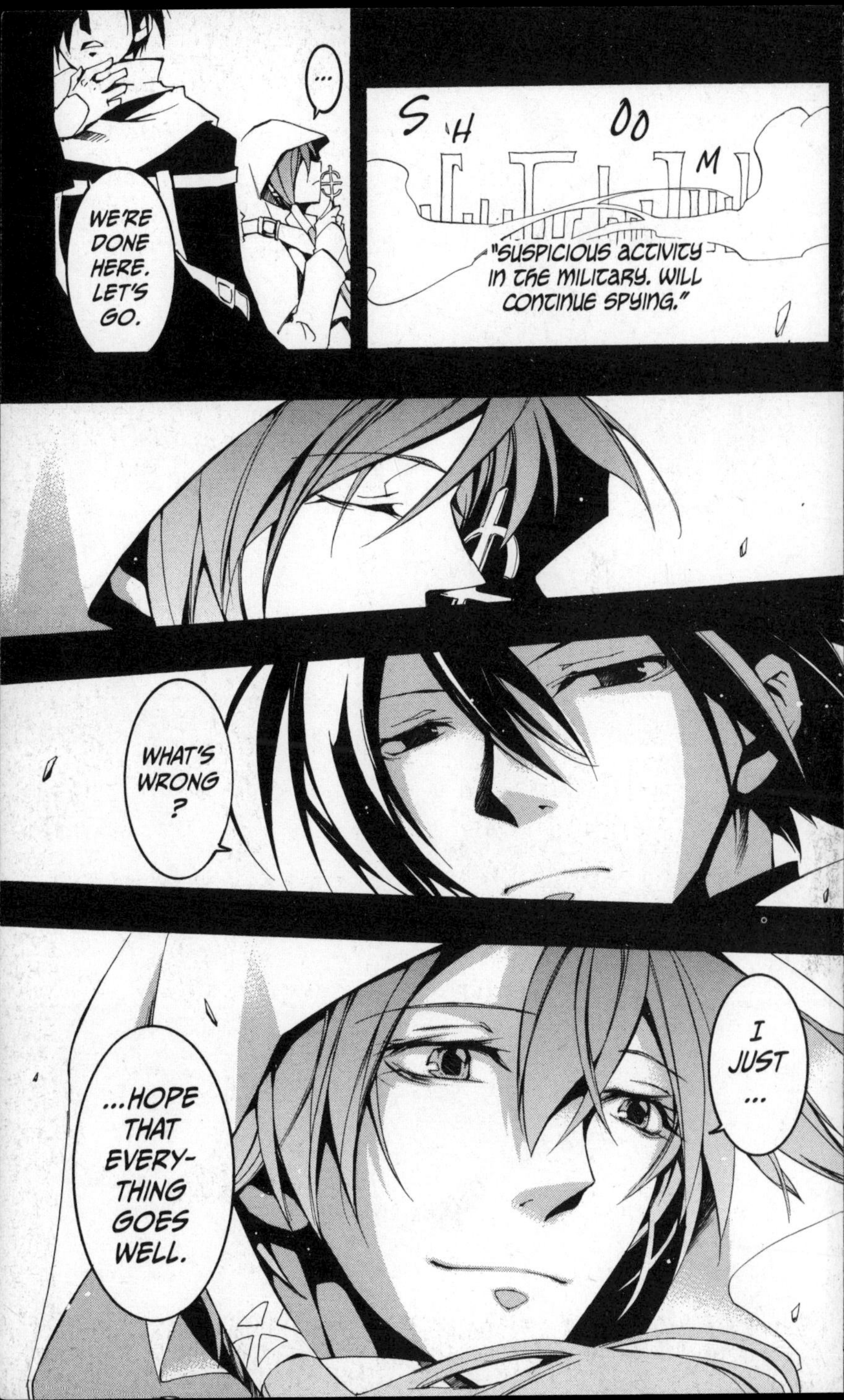
SHOOM
"SUSPICIOUS ACTIVITY IN THE MILITARY. WILL CONTINUE SPYING."
...
WE'RE DONE HERE. LET'S GO.
WHAT'S WRONG?
I JUST...
...HOPE THAT EVERY-THING GOES WELL.

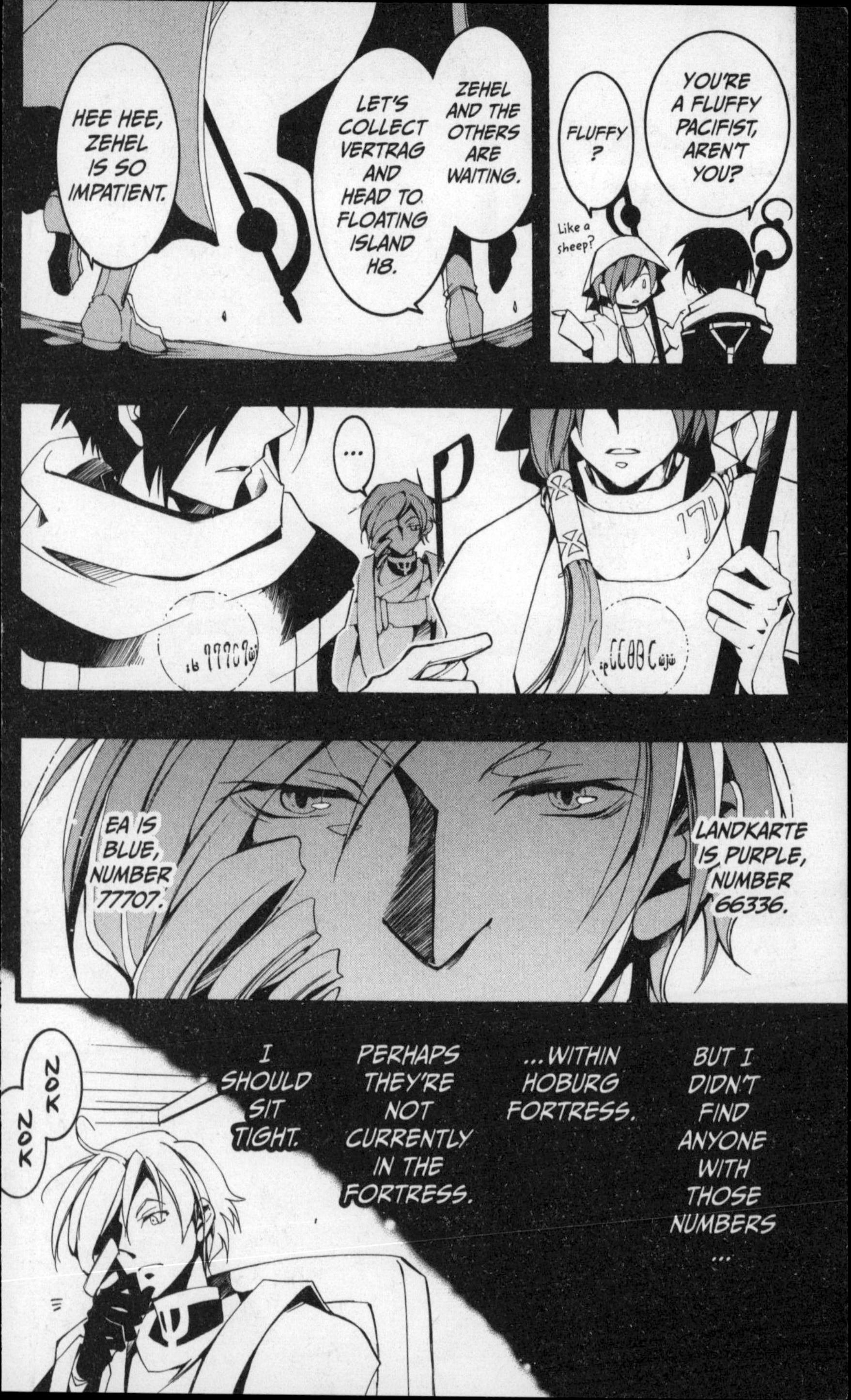
YOU'RE A FLUFFY PACIFIST, AREN'T YOU?
FLUFFY?
Like a sheep?
ZEHEL AND THE OTHERS ARE WAITING.
LET'S COLLECT VERTRAG AND HEAD TO FLOATING ISLAND H8.
HEE HEE, ZEHEL IS SO IMPATIENT.
...
LANDKARTE IS PURPLE, NUMBER 66336.
EA IS BLUE, NUMBER 77707.
BUT I DIDN'T FIND ANYONE WITH THOSE NUMBERS...
...WITHIN HOBURG FORTRESS.
PERHAPS THEY'RE NOT CURRENTLY IN THE FORTRESS.
I SHOULD SIT TIGHT.
NOK NOK
NOK

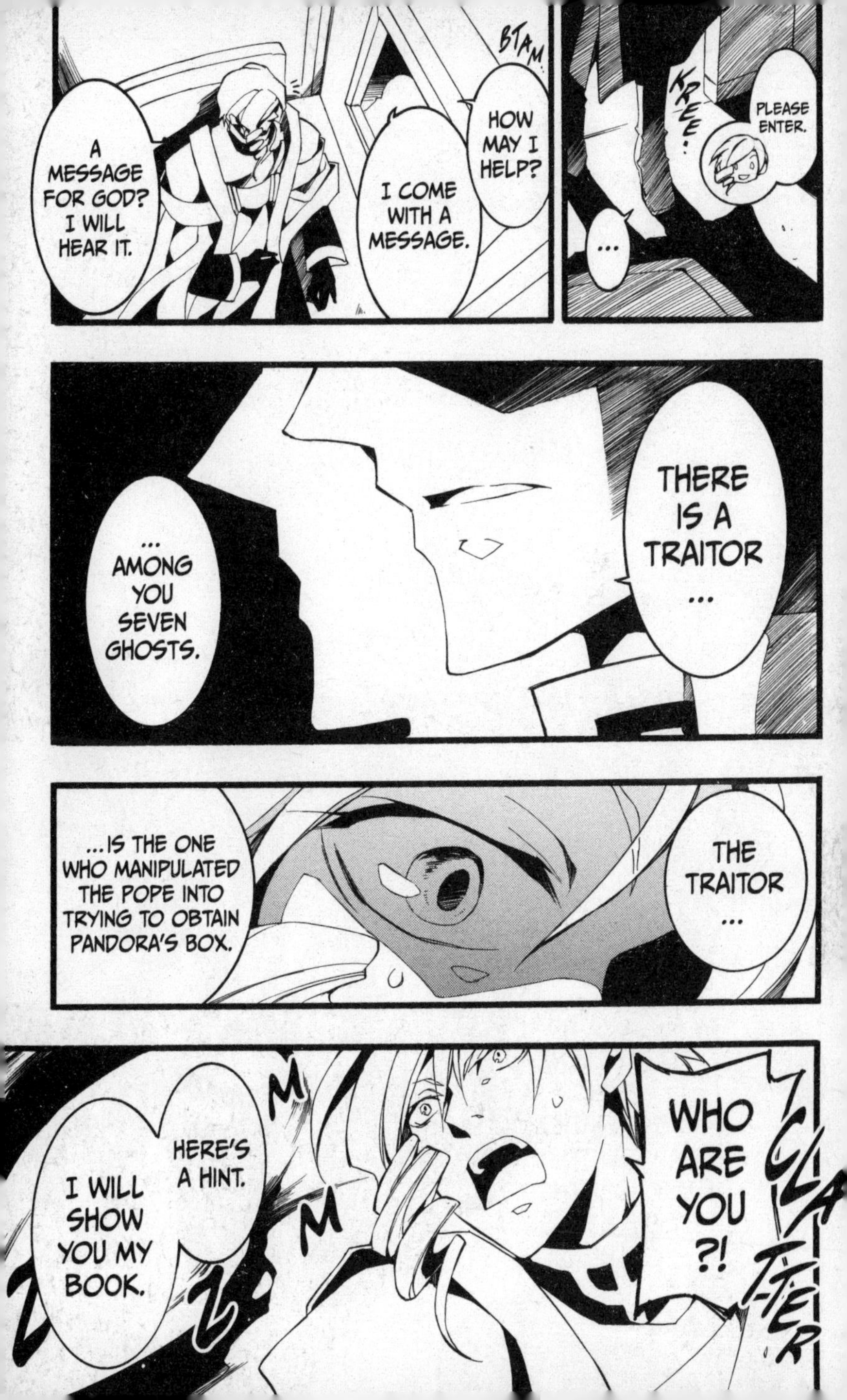
KREE...
PLEASE ENTER.
...
BTAM!
HOW MAY I HELP?
I COME WITH A MESSAGE.
A MESSAGE FOR GOD? I WILL HEAR IT.
THERE IS A TRAITOR ...
... AMONG YOU SEVEN GHOSTS.
THE TRAITOR ...
...IS THE ONE WHO MANIPULATED THE POPE INTO TRYING TO OBTAIN PANDORA'S BOX.
CLATTER
WHO ARE YOU ?!
HERE'S A HINT.
I WILL SHOW YOU MY BOOK.

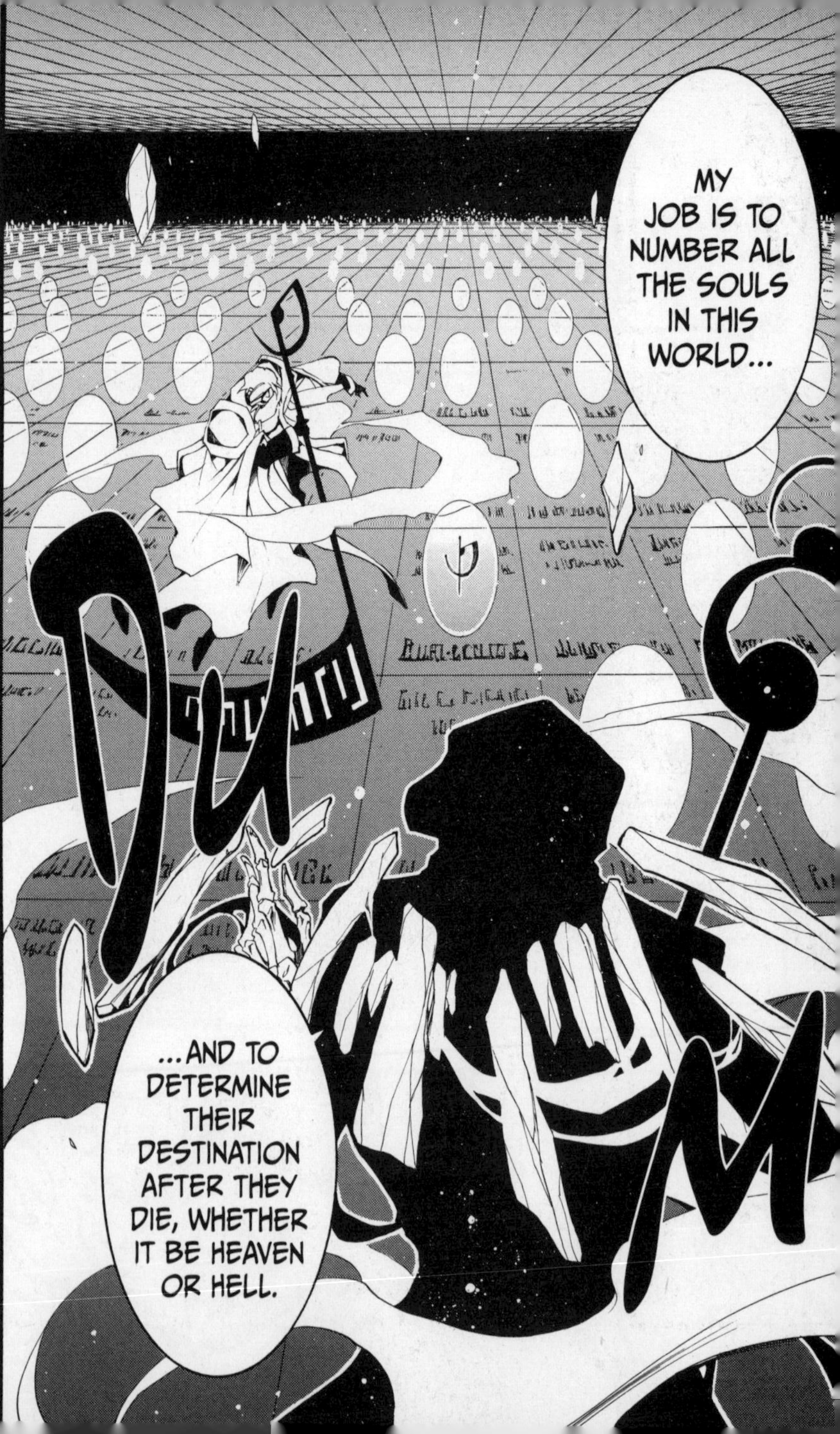
MY JOB IS TO NUMBER ALL THE SOULS IN THIS WORLD...
...AND TO DETERMINE THEIR DESTINATION AFTER THEY DIE, WHETHER IT BE HEAVEN OR HELL.

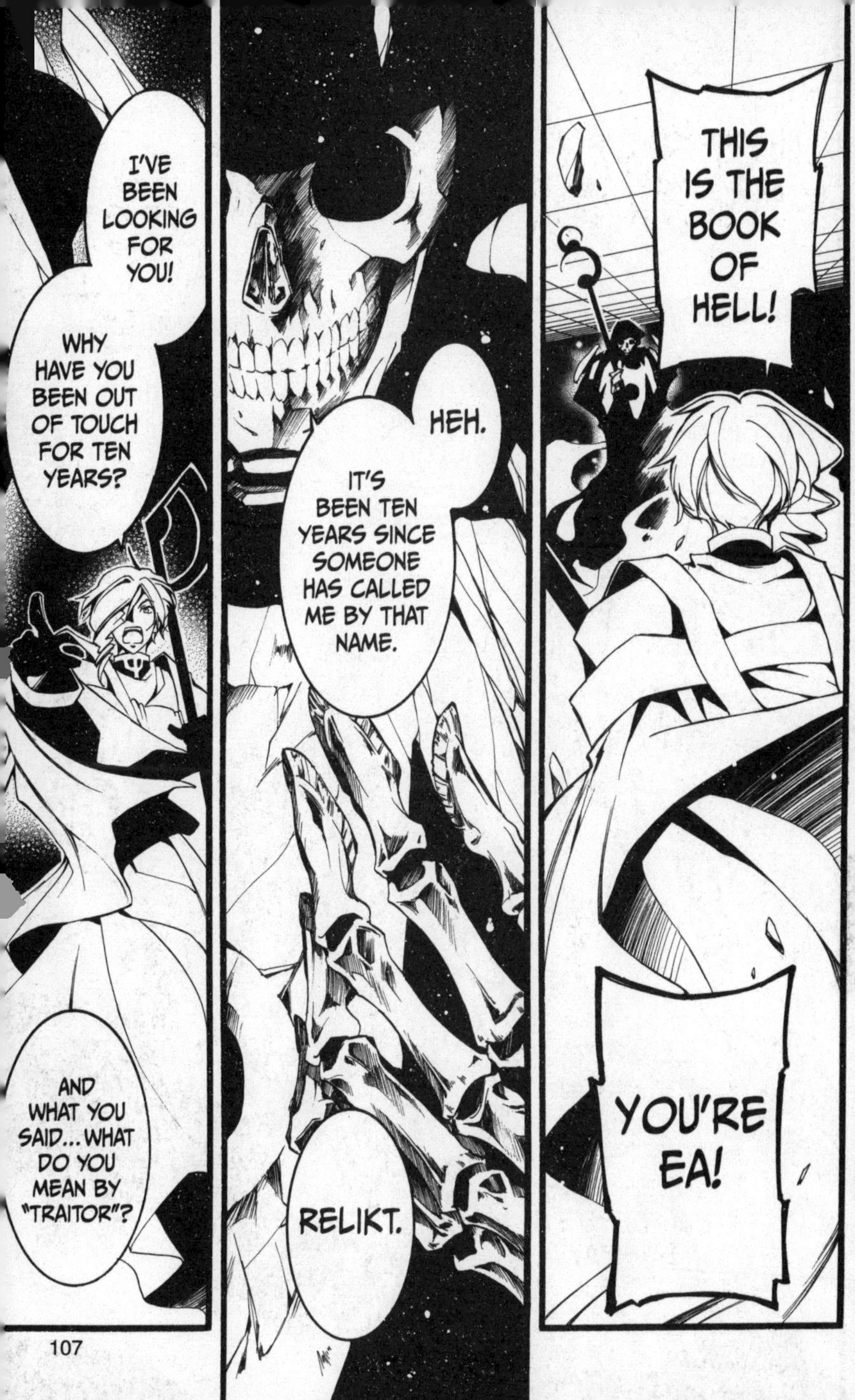
THIS IS THE BOOK OF HELL!
YOU'RE EA!
HEH.
IT'S BEEN TEN YEARS SINCE SOMEONE HAS CALLED ME BY THAT NAME.
RELIKT.
I'VE BEEN LOOKING FOR YOU!
WHY HAVE YOU BEEN OUT OF TOUCH FOR TEN YEARS?
AND WHAT YOU SAID... WHAT DO YOU MEAN BY "TRAITOR"?

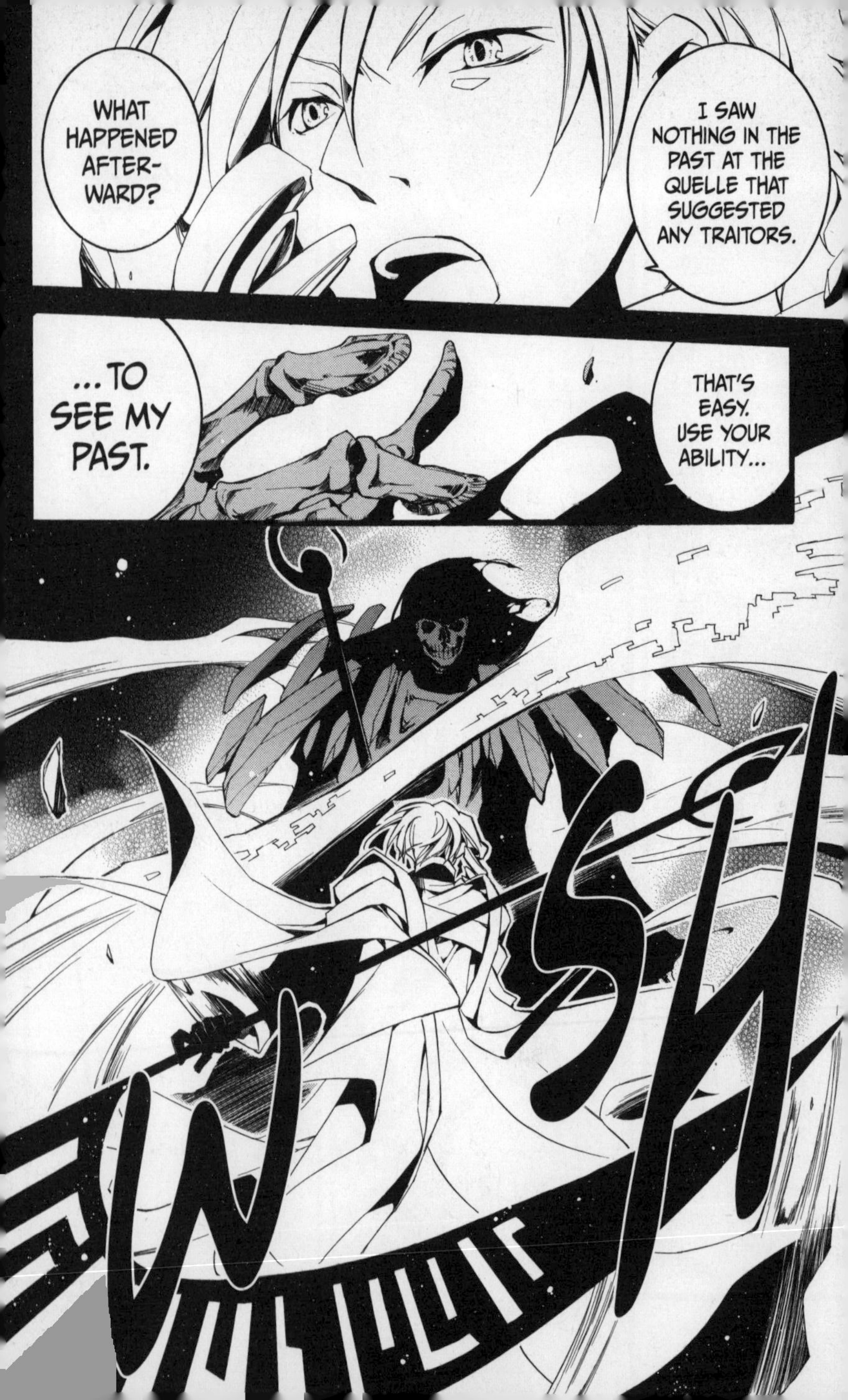
I SAW NOTHING IN THE PAST AT THE QUELLE THAT SUGGESTED ANY TRAITORS.
WHAT HAPPENED AFTER-WARD?
THAT'S EASY. USE YOUR ABILITY...
...TO SEE MY PAST.

Kapitel.77 "Black Gem"

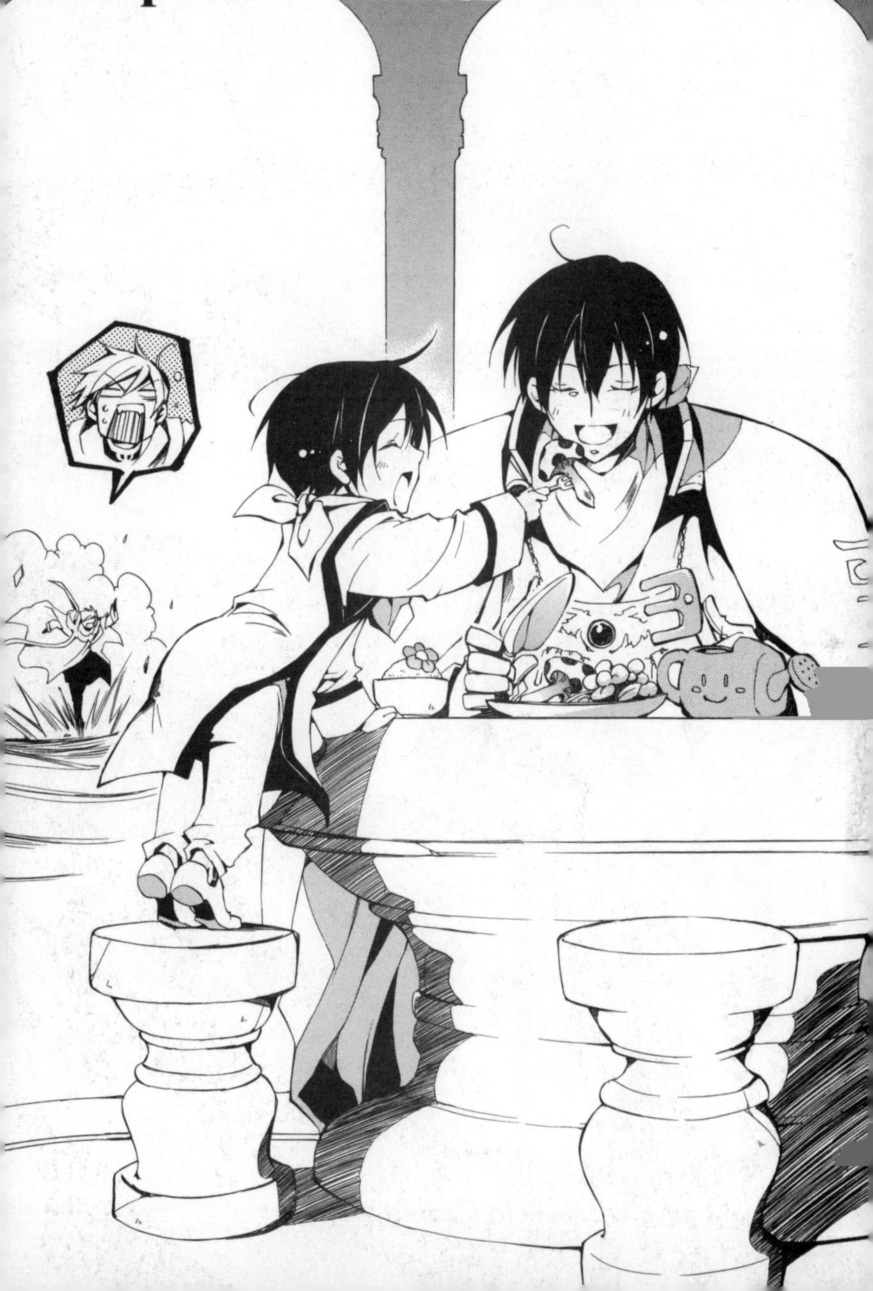

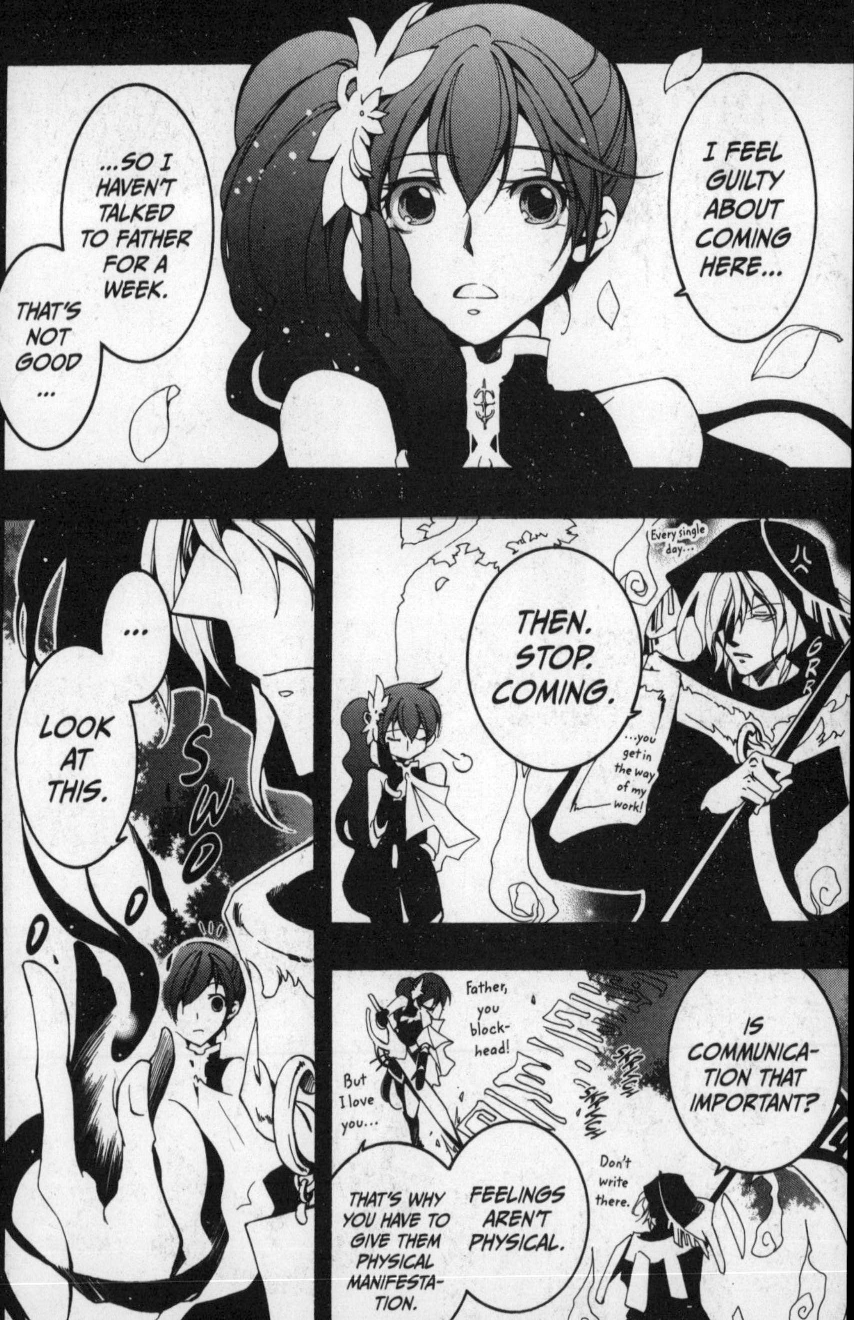
I FEEL GUILTY ABOUT COMING HERE...
...SO I HAVEN'T TALKED TO FATHER FOR A WEEK.
THAT'S NOT GOOD ...
Every single day...
THEN. STOP. COMING.
...you get in the way of my work!
GRR
IS COMMUNICATION THAT IMPORTANT?
Don't write there.
SKRITCH SKRITCH SKRITCH
Father, you blockhead!
But I love you...
FEELINGS AREN'T PHYSICAL.
THAT'S WHY YOU HAVE TO GIVE THEM PHYSICAL MANIFESTATION.
...
LOOK AT THIS.
SWOOOO

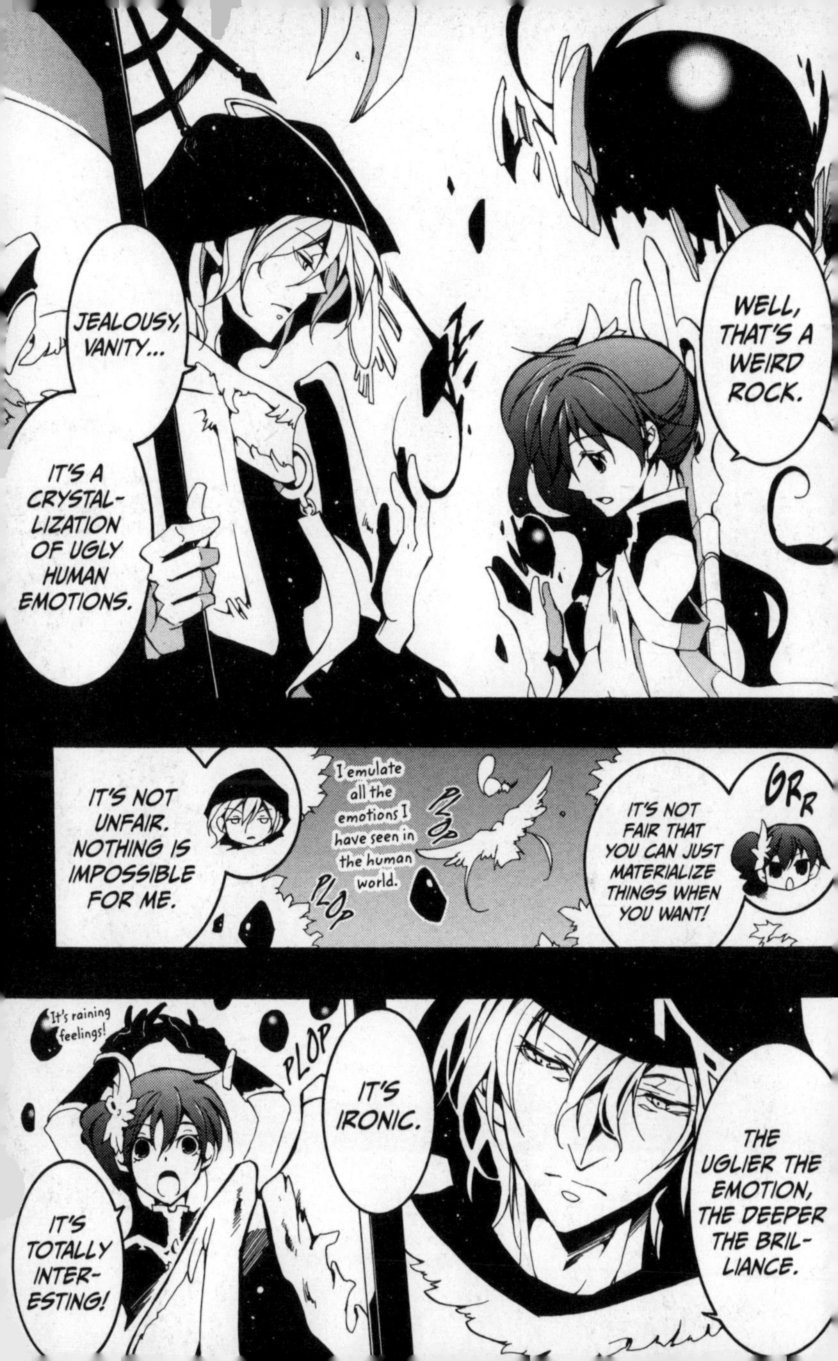
WELL, THAT'S A WEIRD ROCK.
JEALOUSY, VANITY...
IT'S A CRYSTALLIZATION OF UGLY HUMAN EMOTIONS.
GRR
IT'S NOT FAIR THAT YOU CAN JUST MATERIALIZE THINGS WHEN YOU WANT!
PLOP
I emulate all the emotions I have seen in the human world.
PLOP
IT'S NOT UNFAIR. NOTHING IS IMPOSSIBLE FOR ME.
THE UGLIER THE EMOTION, THE DEEPER THE BRILLIANCE.
IT'S IRONIC.
PLOP
It's raining feelings!
IT'S TOTALLY INTERESTING!

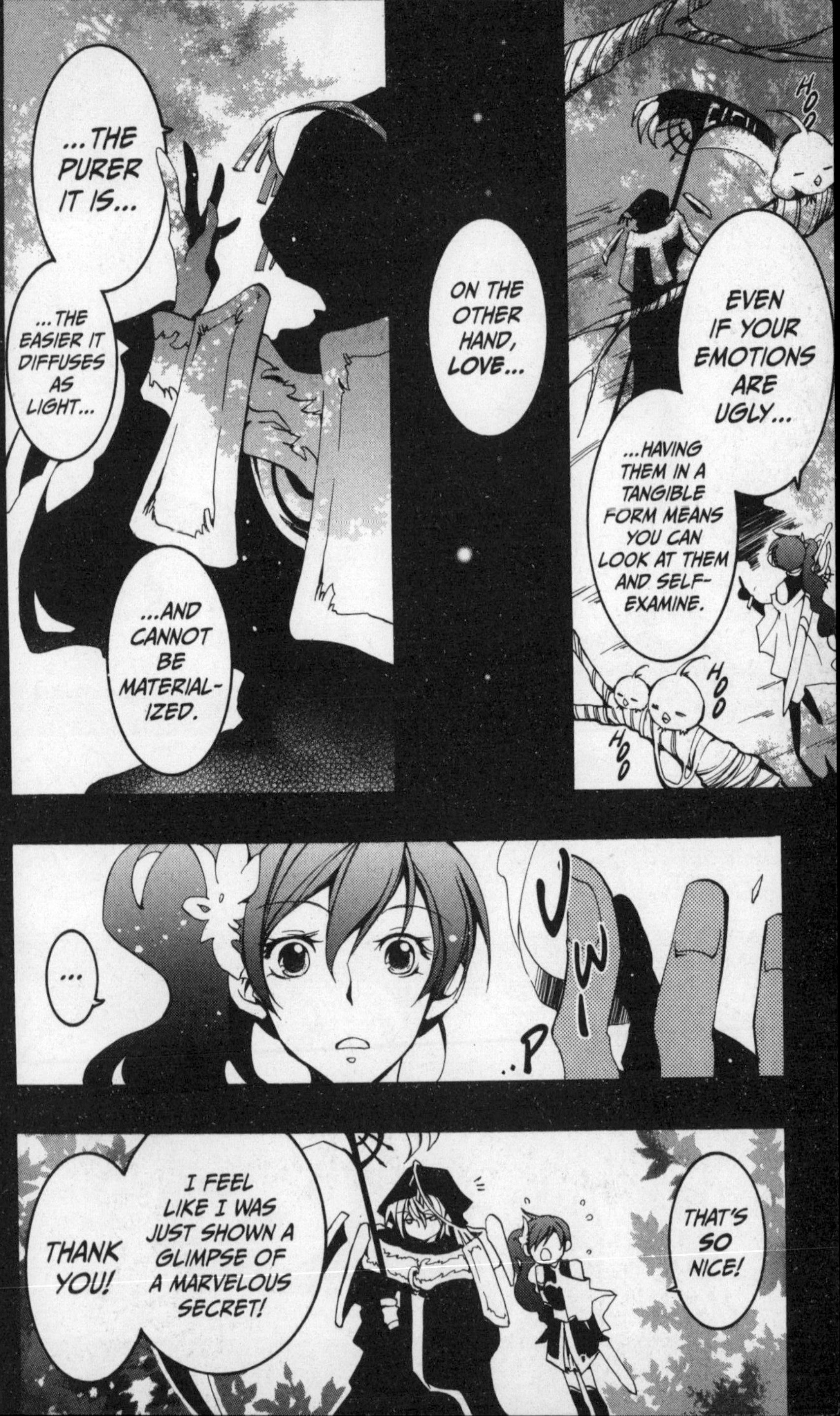
HOO
EVEN IF YOUR EMOTIONS ARE UGLY...
...HAVING THEM IN A TANGIBLE FORM MEANS YOU CAN LOOK AT THEM AND SELF-EXAMINE.
HOO
HOO
ON THE OTHER HAND, LOVE...
...THE PURER IT IS...
...THE EASIER IT DIFFUSES AS LIGHT...
...AND CANNOT BE MATERIALIZED.
...
THAT'S SO NICE!
I FEEL LIKE I WAS JUST SHOWN A GLIMPSE OF A MARVELOUS SECRET!
THANK YOU!

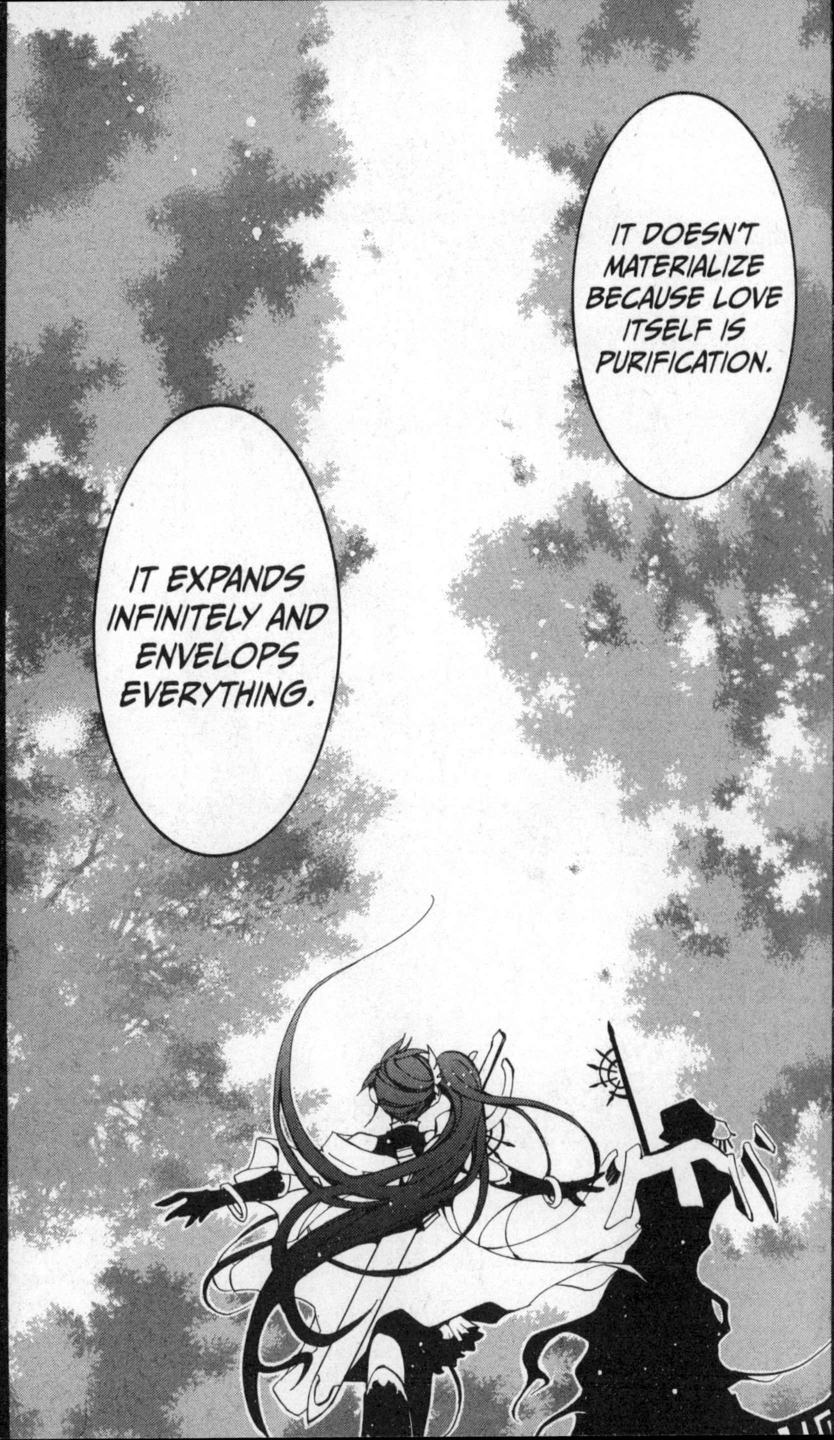
IT DOESN'T MATERIALIZE BECAUSE LOVE ITSELF IS PURIFICATION.
IT EXPANDS INFINITELY AND ENVELOPS EVERYTHING.

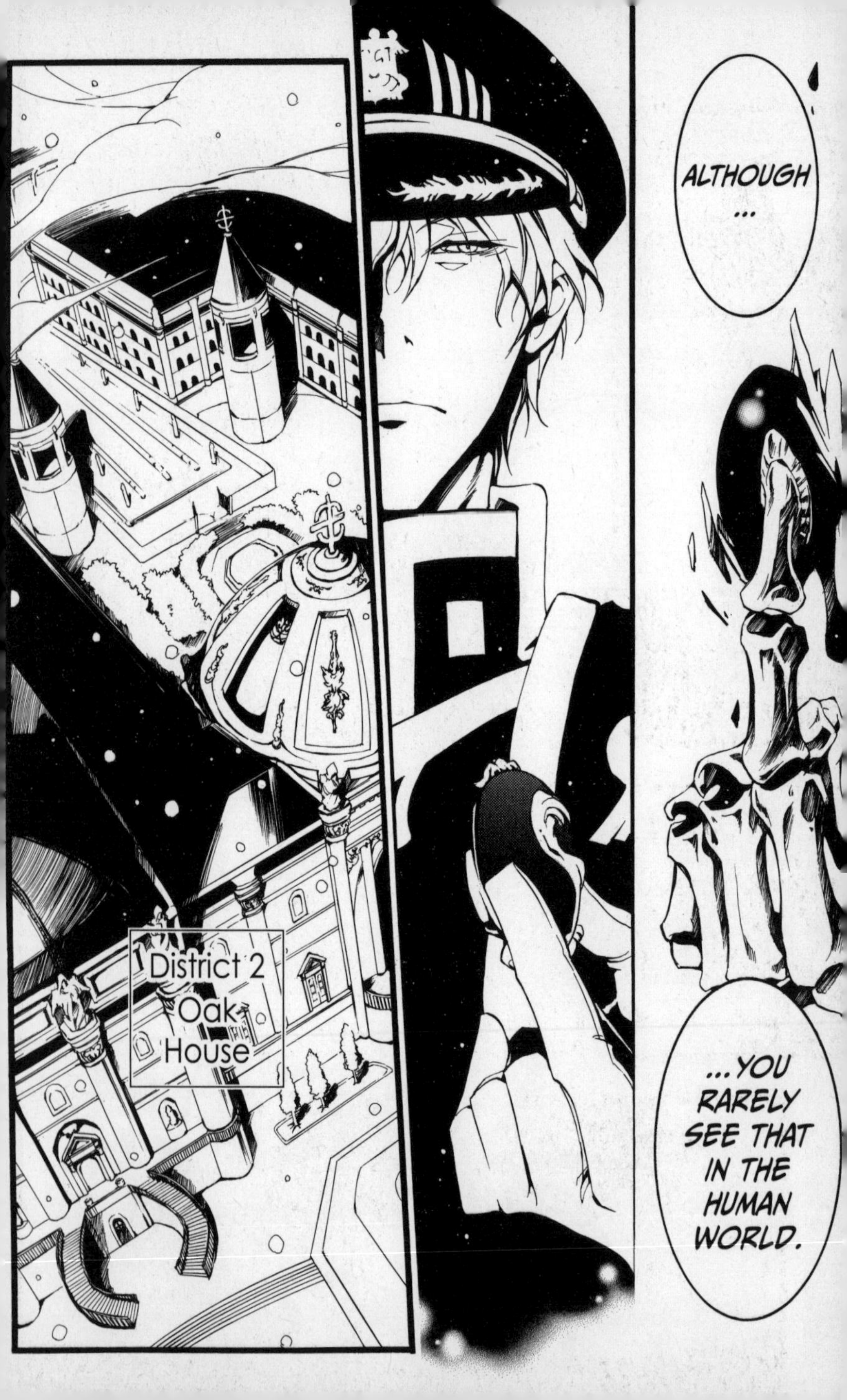
ALTHOUGH ...
...YOU RARELY SEE THAT IN THE HUMAN WORLD.
District 2 Oak House

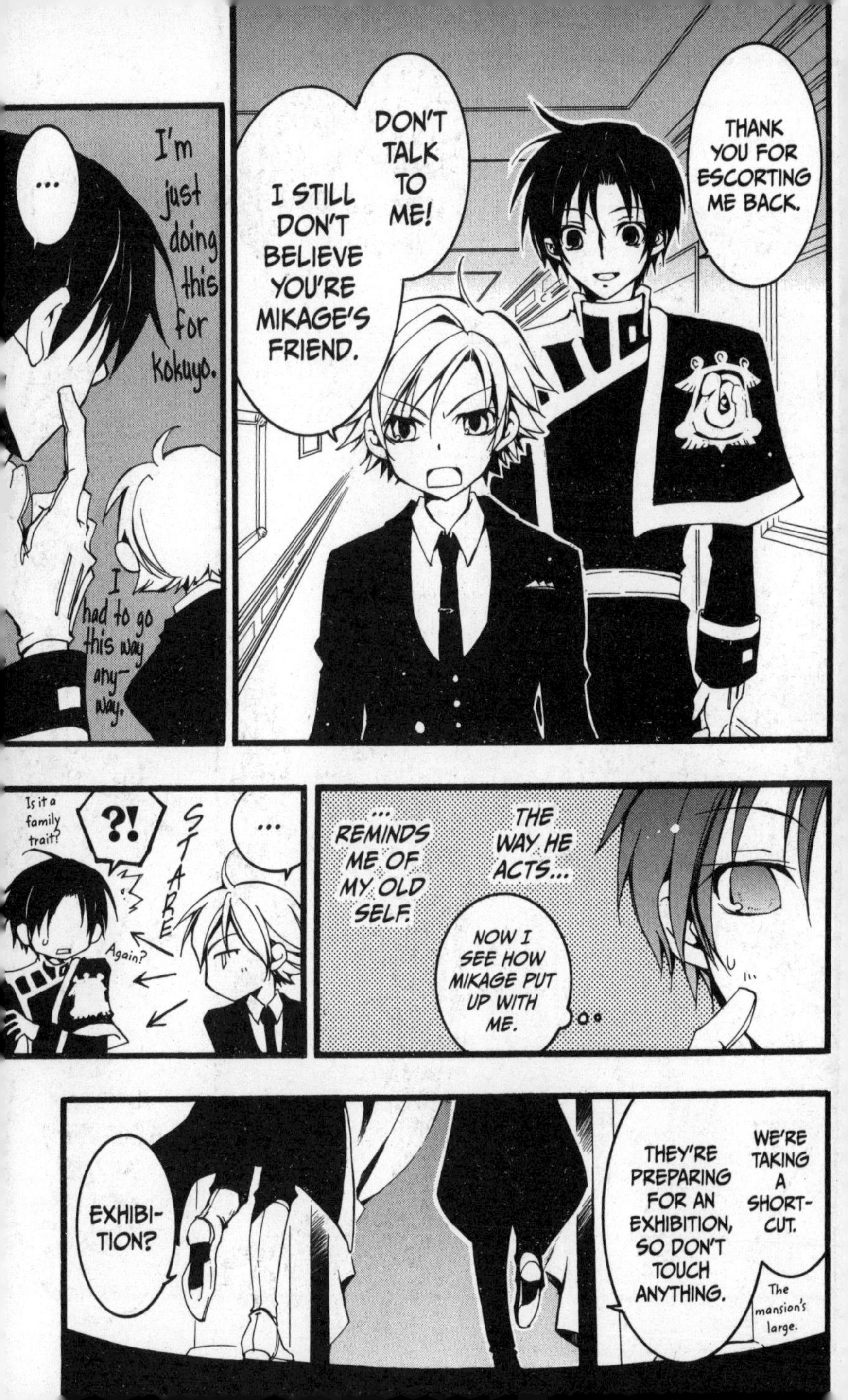
THANK YOU FOR ESCORTING ME BACK.
DON'T TALK TO ME!
I STILL DON'T BELIEVE YOU'RE MIKAGE'S FRIEND.
I'm just doing this for Kokuyo.
...
I had to go this way any-way.
THE WAY HE ACTS...
...REMINDS ME OF MY OLD SELF.
NOW I SEE HOW MIKAGE PUT UP WITH ME.
...
STARE
?!
Is it a family trait?
Again?
WE'RE TAKING A SHORT-CUT.
The mansion's large.
THEY'RE PREPARING FOR AN EXHIBITION, SO DON'T TOUCH ANYTHING.
EXHIBI-TION?

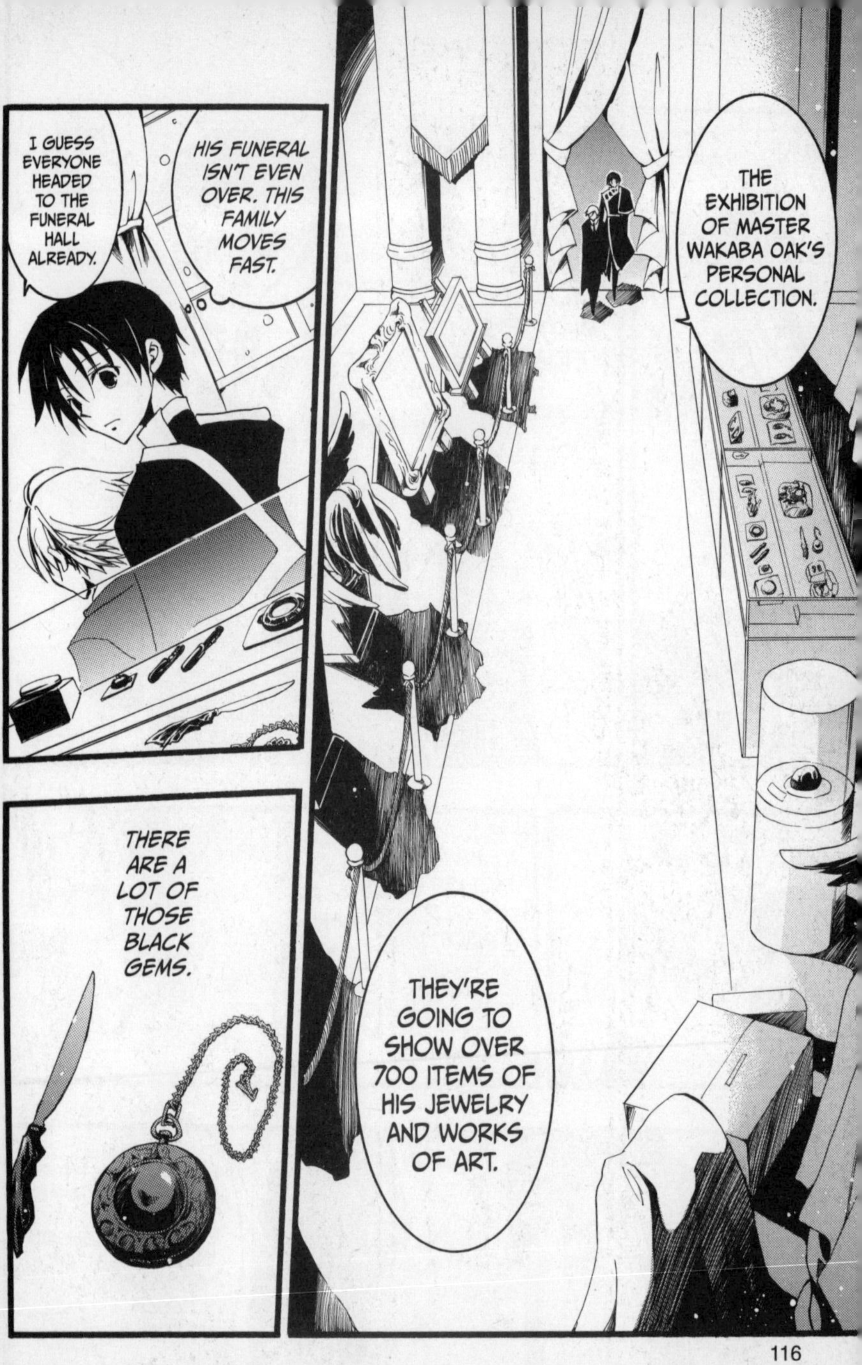
THE EXHIBITION OF MASTER WAKABA OAK'S PERSONAL COLLECTION.
THEY'RE GOING TO SHOW OVER 700 ITEMS OF HIS JEWELRY AND WORKS OF ART.
HIS FUNERAL ISN'T EVEN OVER. THIS FAMILY MOVES FAST.
I GUESS EVERYONE HEADED TO THE FUNERAL HALL ALREADY.
THERE ARE A LOT OF THOSE BLACK GEMS.

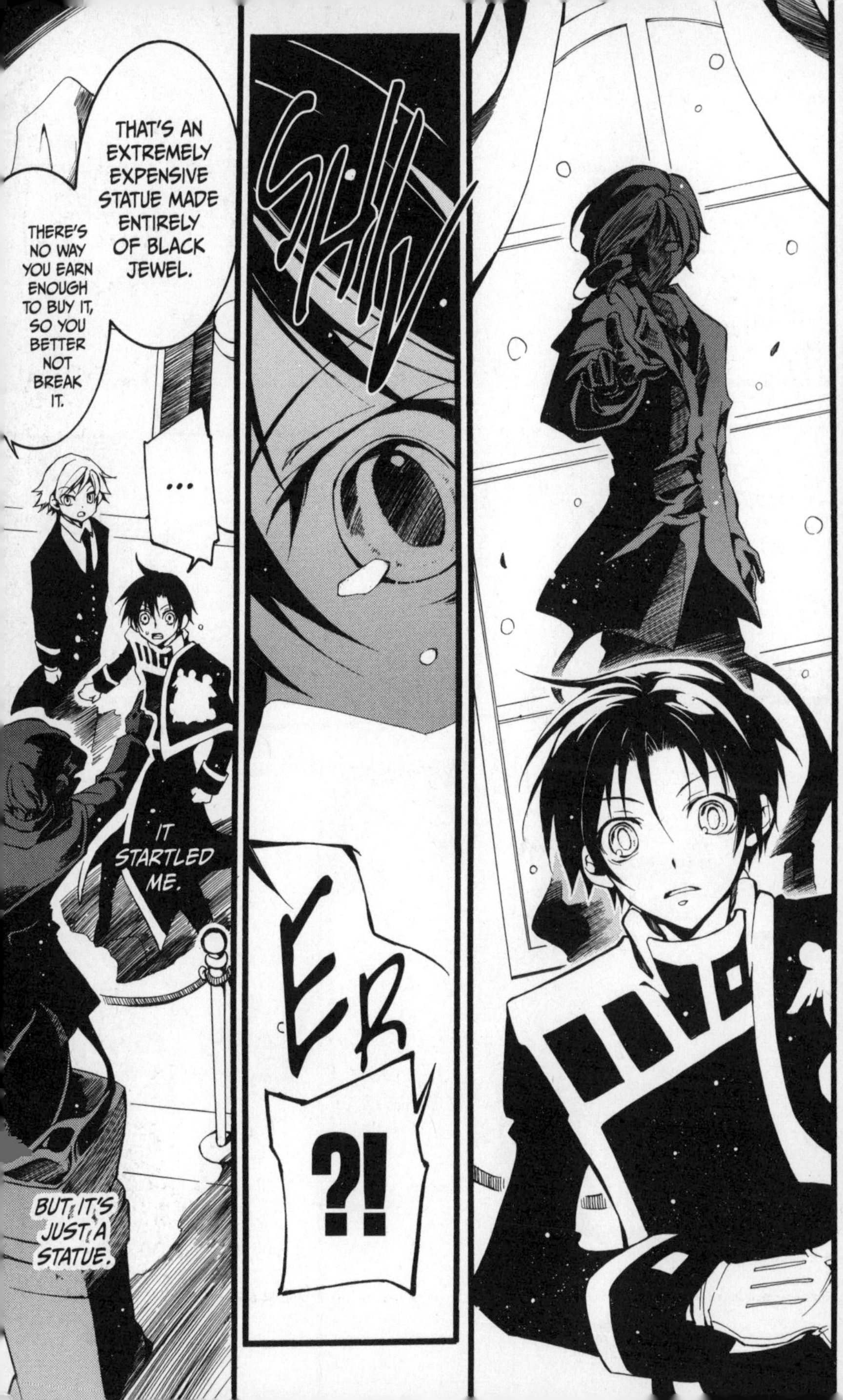
ER
?!
THAT'S AN EXTREMELY EXPENSIVE STATUE MADE ENTIRELY OF BLACK JEWEL.
THERE'S NO WAY YOU EARN ENOUGH TO BUY IT, SO YOU BETTER NOT BREAK IT.
...
IT STARTLED ME.
BUT IT'S JUST A STATUE.

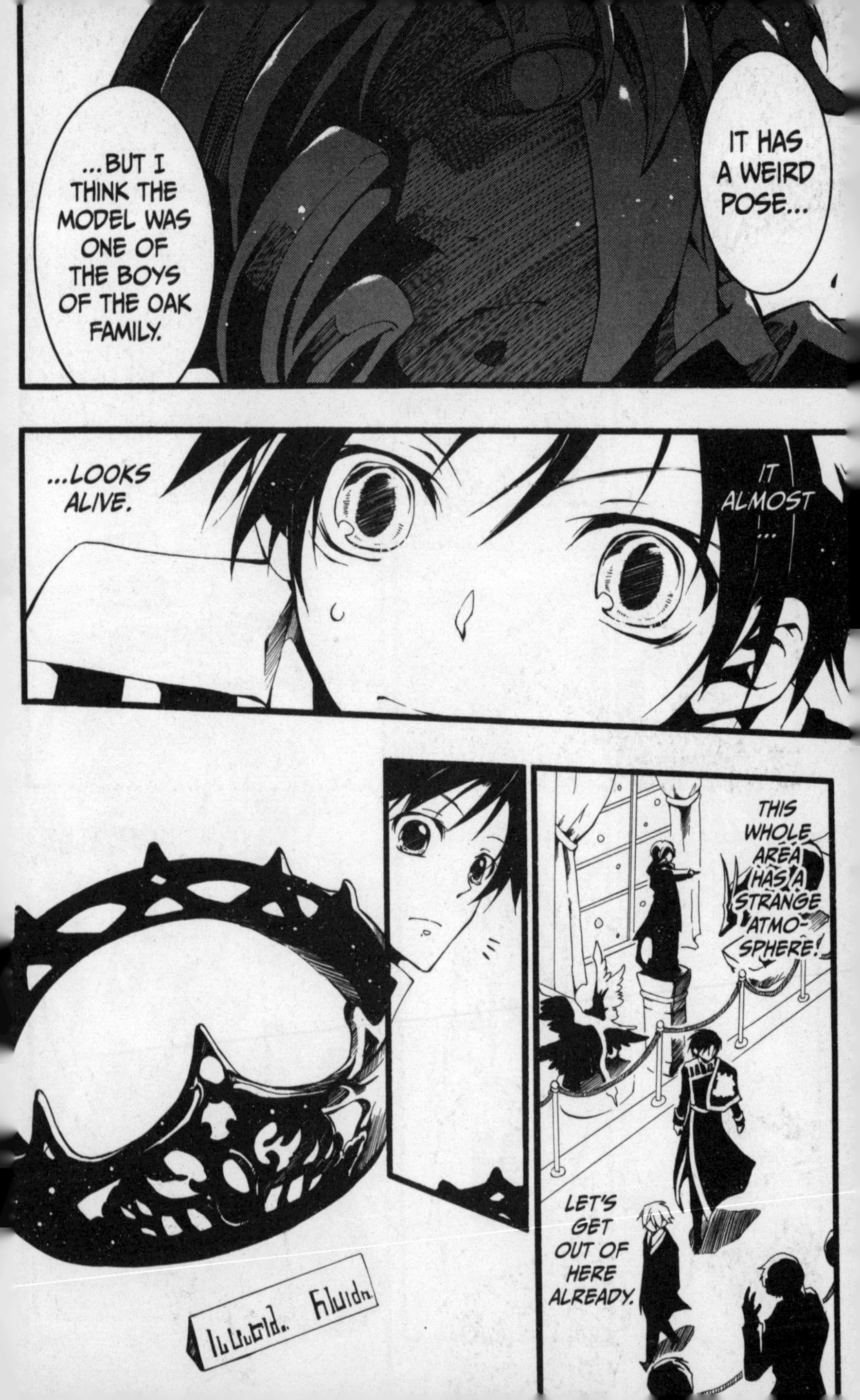
IT HAS A WEIRD POSE...
...BUT I THINK THE MODEL WAS ONE OF THE BOYS OF THE OAK FAMILY.
IT ALMOST...
...LOOKS ALIVE.
THIS WHOLE AREA HAS A STRANGE ATMOSPHERE!
LET'S GET OUT OF HERE ALREADY.

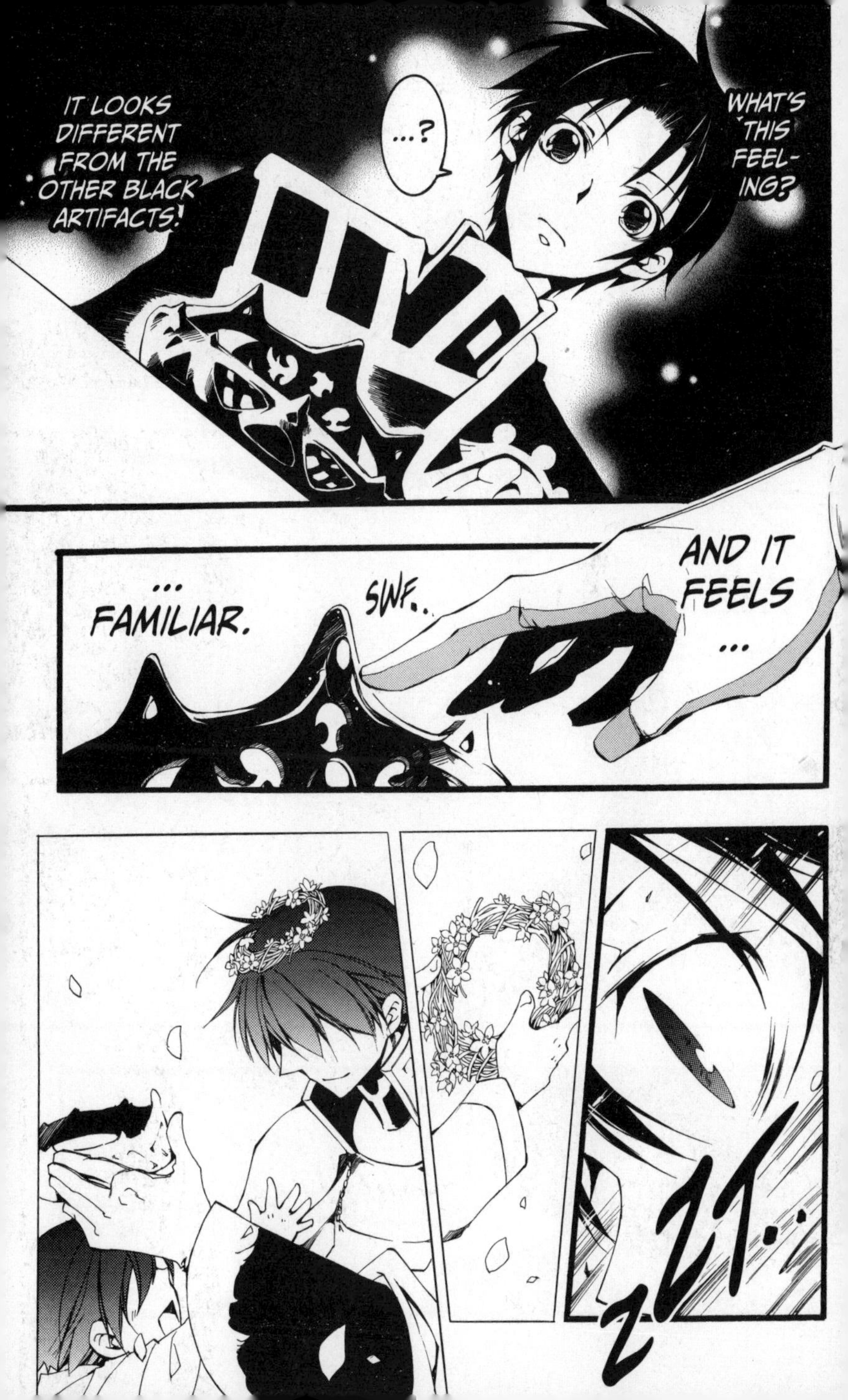
WHAT'S THIS FEEL-ING?
...?
IT LOOKS DIFFERENT FROM THE OTHER BLACK ARTIFACTS!
AND IT FEELS ...
SWF...
... FAMILIAR.
ZZT..

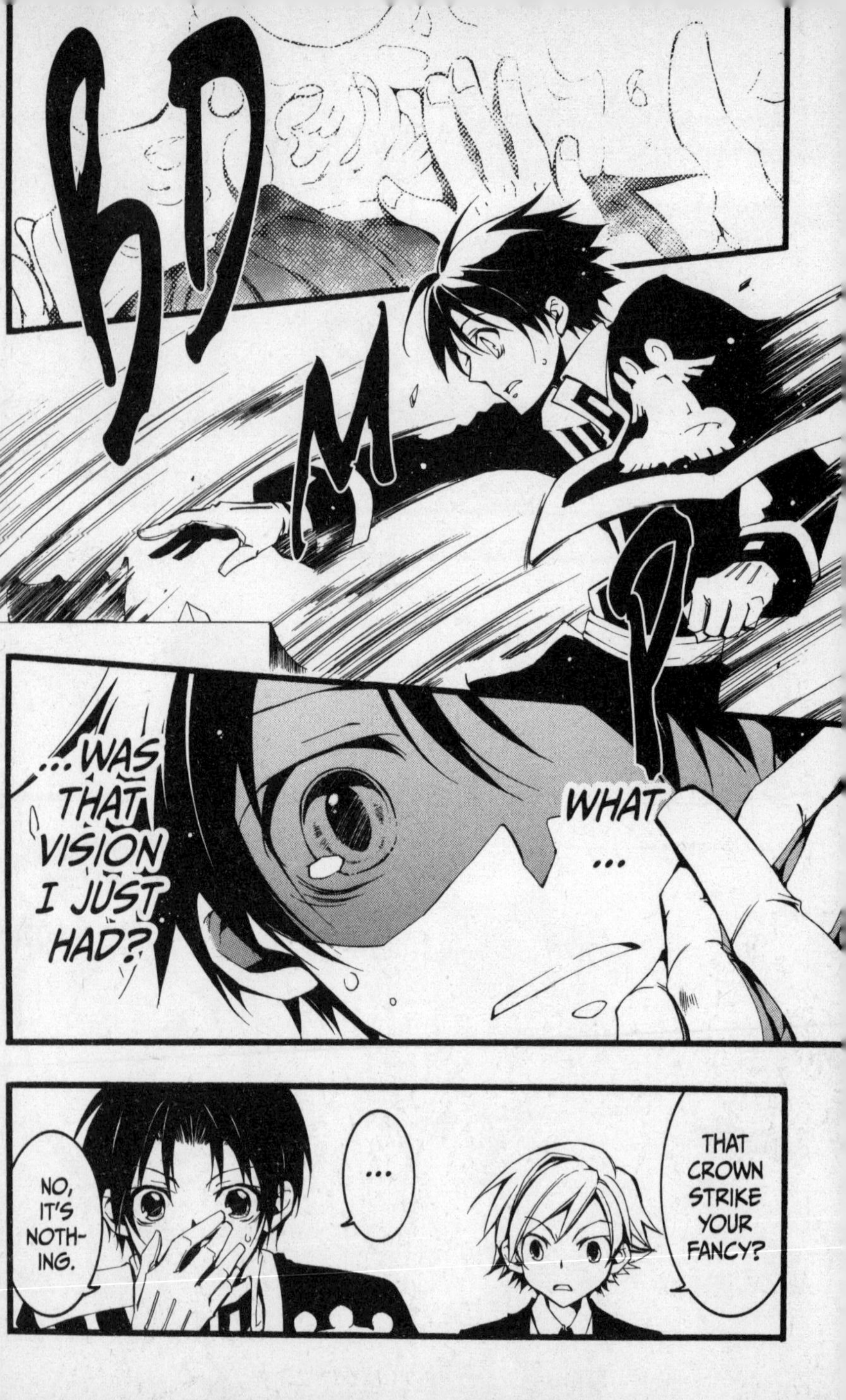
WHAT...
...WAS THAT VISION I JUST HAD?
THAT CROWN STRIKE YOUR FANCY?
...
NO, IT'S NOTH-ING.

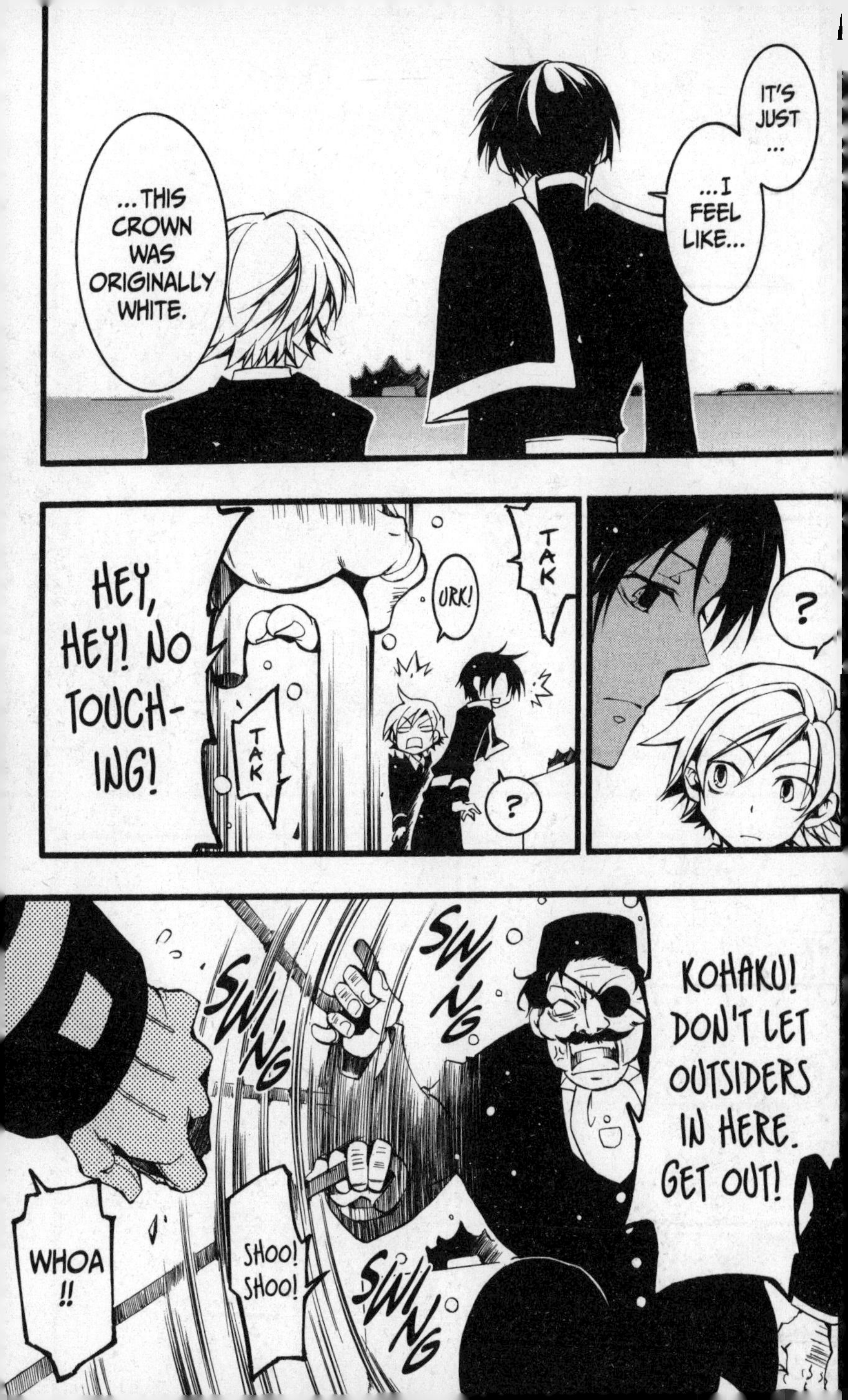
IT'S JUST ...
...I FEEL LIKE...
...THIS CROWN WAS ORIGINALLY WHITE.
?
TAK
URK!
HEY, HEY! NO TOUCHING!
TAK
?
KOHAKU! DON'T LET OUTSIDERS IN HERE. GET OUT!
SWING
SWING
SHOO! SHOO!
SWING
WHOA !!

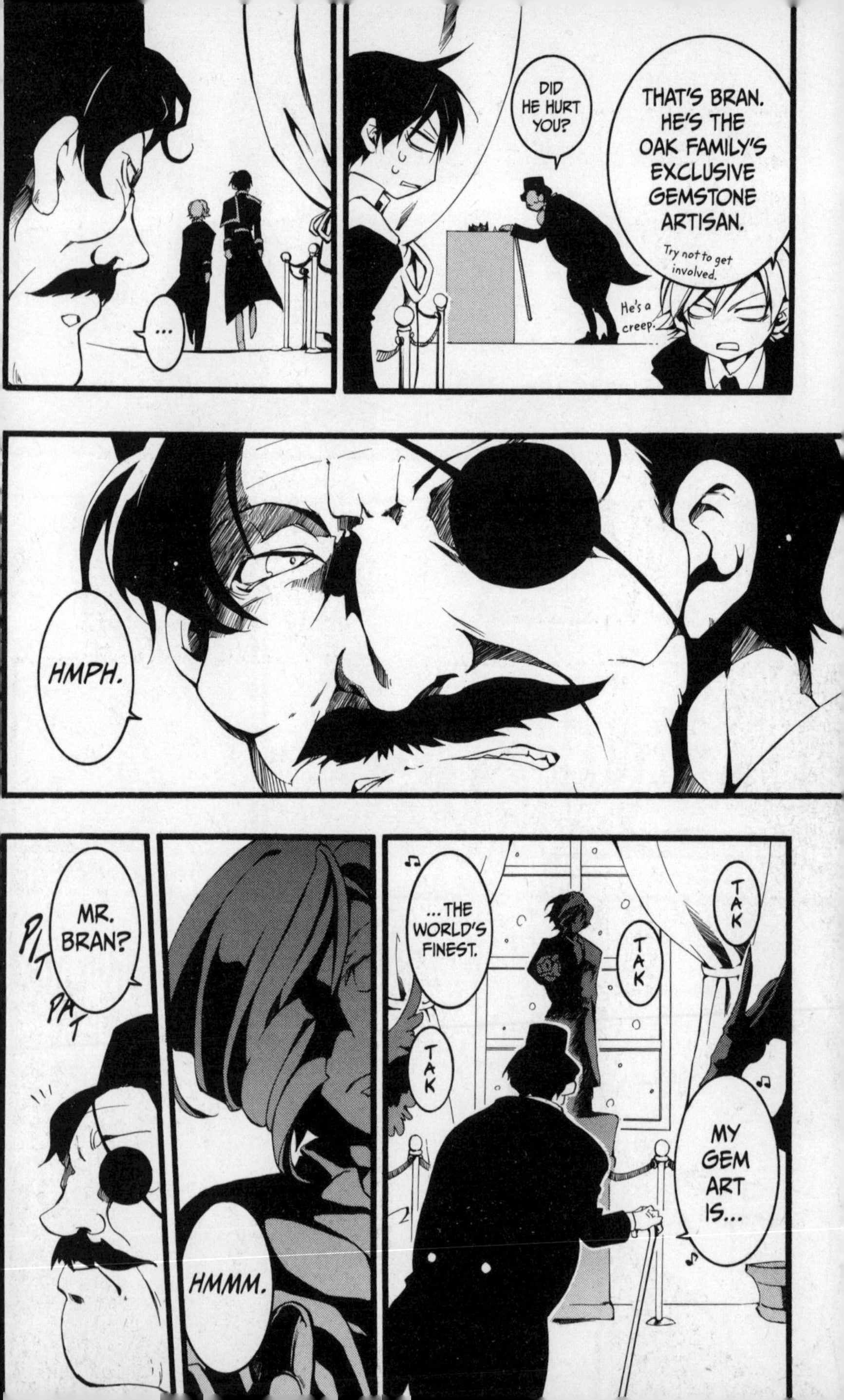
THAT'S BRAN. HE'S THE OAK FAMILY'S EXCLUSIVE GEMSTONE ARTISAN.
Try not to get involved.
He's a creep.
DID HE HURT YOU?
...
HMPH.
TAK
TAK
MY GEM ART IS...
...THE WORLD'S FINEST.
TAK
HMMM.
MR. BRAN?
PIT PAT

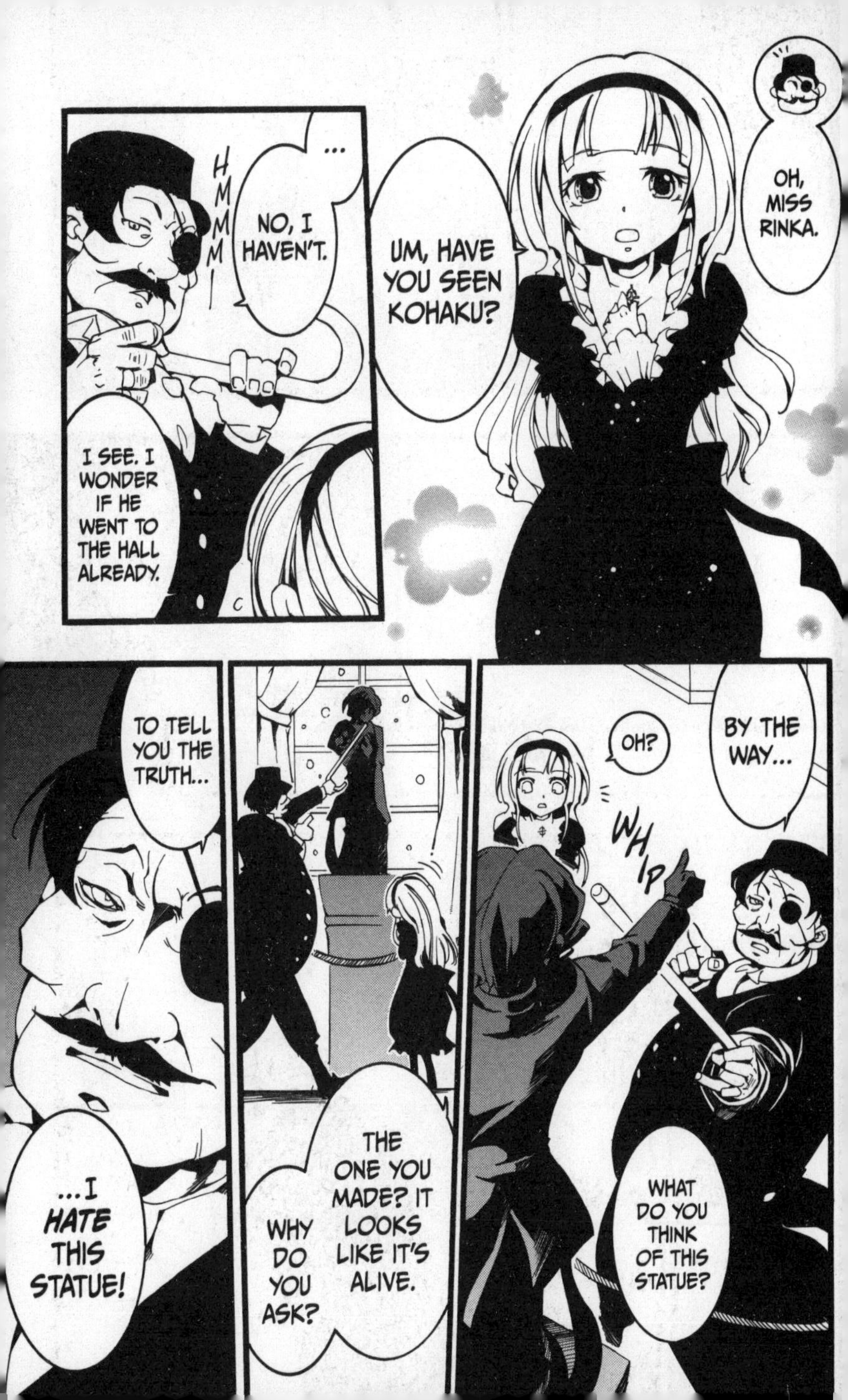
OH, MISS RINKA.
UM, HAVE YOU SEEN KOHAKU?
...
NO, I HAVEN'T.
HMMM
I SEE. I WONDER IF HE WENT TO THE HALL ALREADY.
BY THE WAY...
OH?
WHIP
WHAT DO YOU THINK OF THIS STATUE?
THE ONE YOU MADE? IT LOOKS LIKE IT'S ALIVE.
WHY DO YOU ASK?
TO TELL YOU THE TRUTH...
...I *HATE* THIS STATUE!

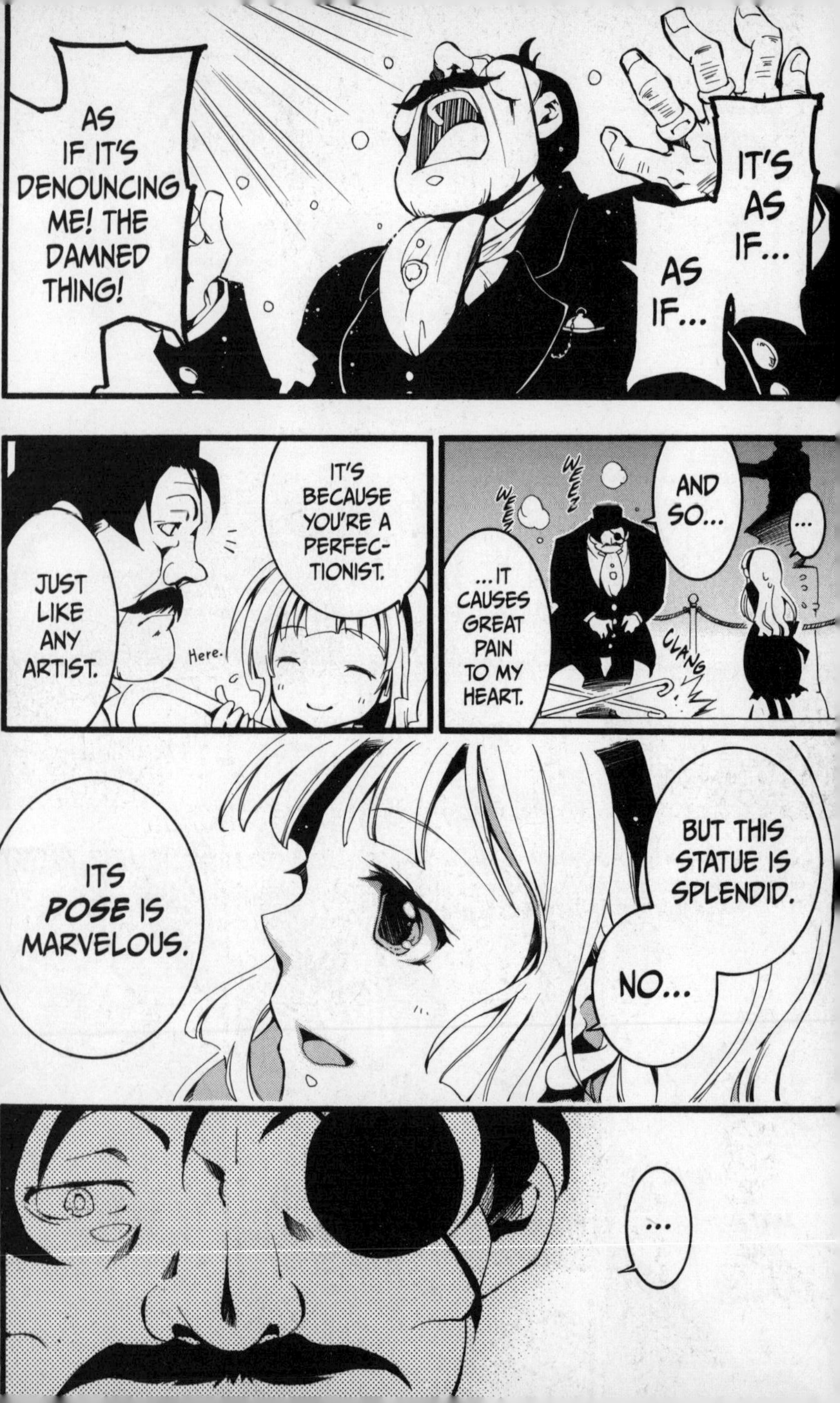
IT'S AS IF...
AS IF...
AS IF IT'S DENOUNCING ME! THE DAMNED THING!
AND SO...
...
WEEZ WEEZ
...IT CAUSES GREAT PAIN TO MY HEART.
CLANG
IT'S BECAUSE YOU'RE A PERFECTIONIST.
JUST LIKE ANY ARTIST.
Here.
BUT THIS STATUE IS SPLENDID.
NO...
ITS *POSE* IS MARVELOUS.
...

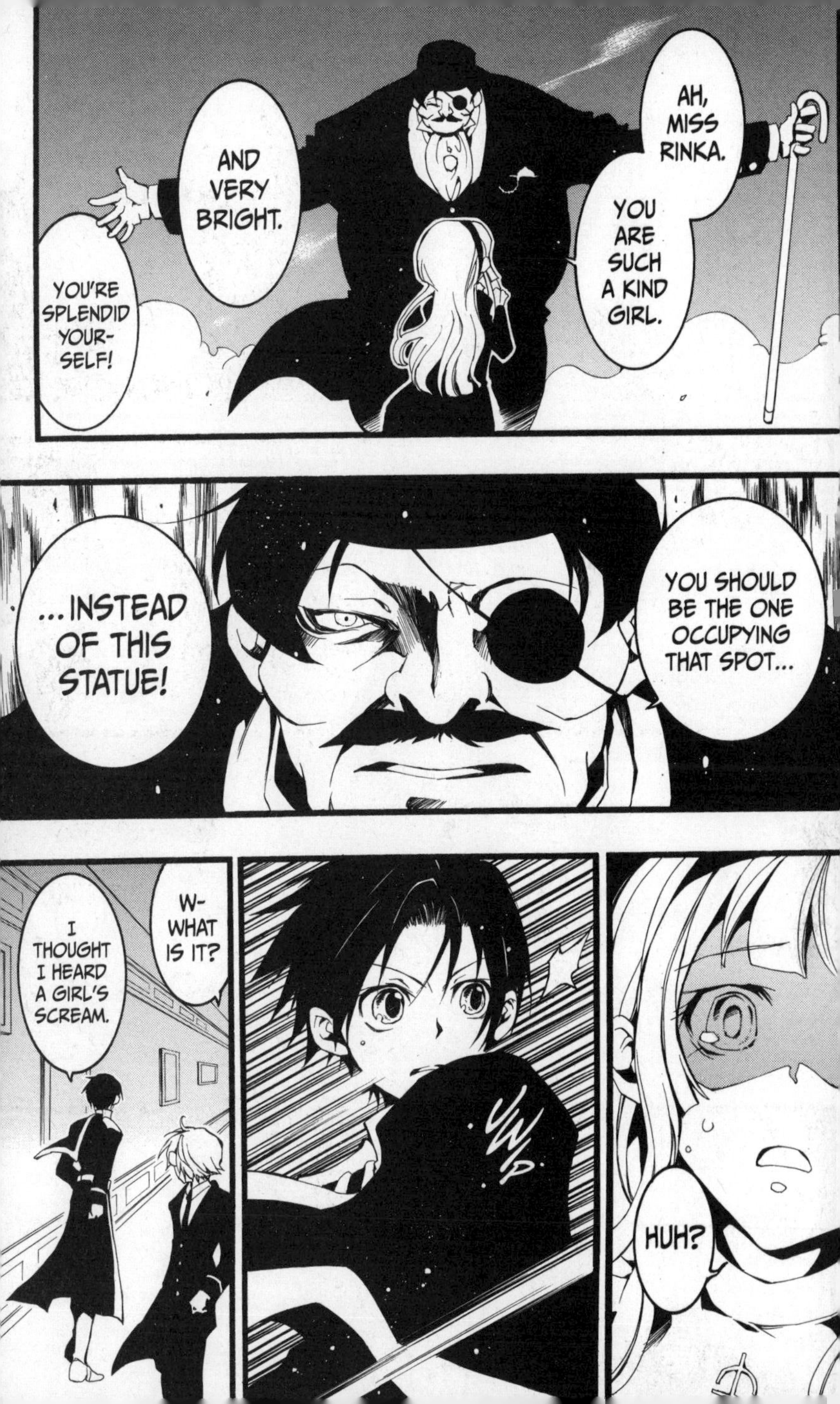
AH, MISS RINKA.
YOU ARE SUCH A KIND GIRL.
AND VERY BRIGHT.
YOU'RE SPLENDID YOUR-SELF!
YOU SHOULD BE THE ONE OCCUPYING THAT SPOT...
...INSTEAD OF THIS STATUE!
HUH?
WHIP
W- WHAT IS IT?
I THOUGHT I HEARD A GIRL'S SCREAM.

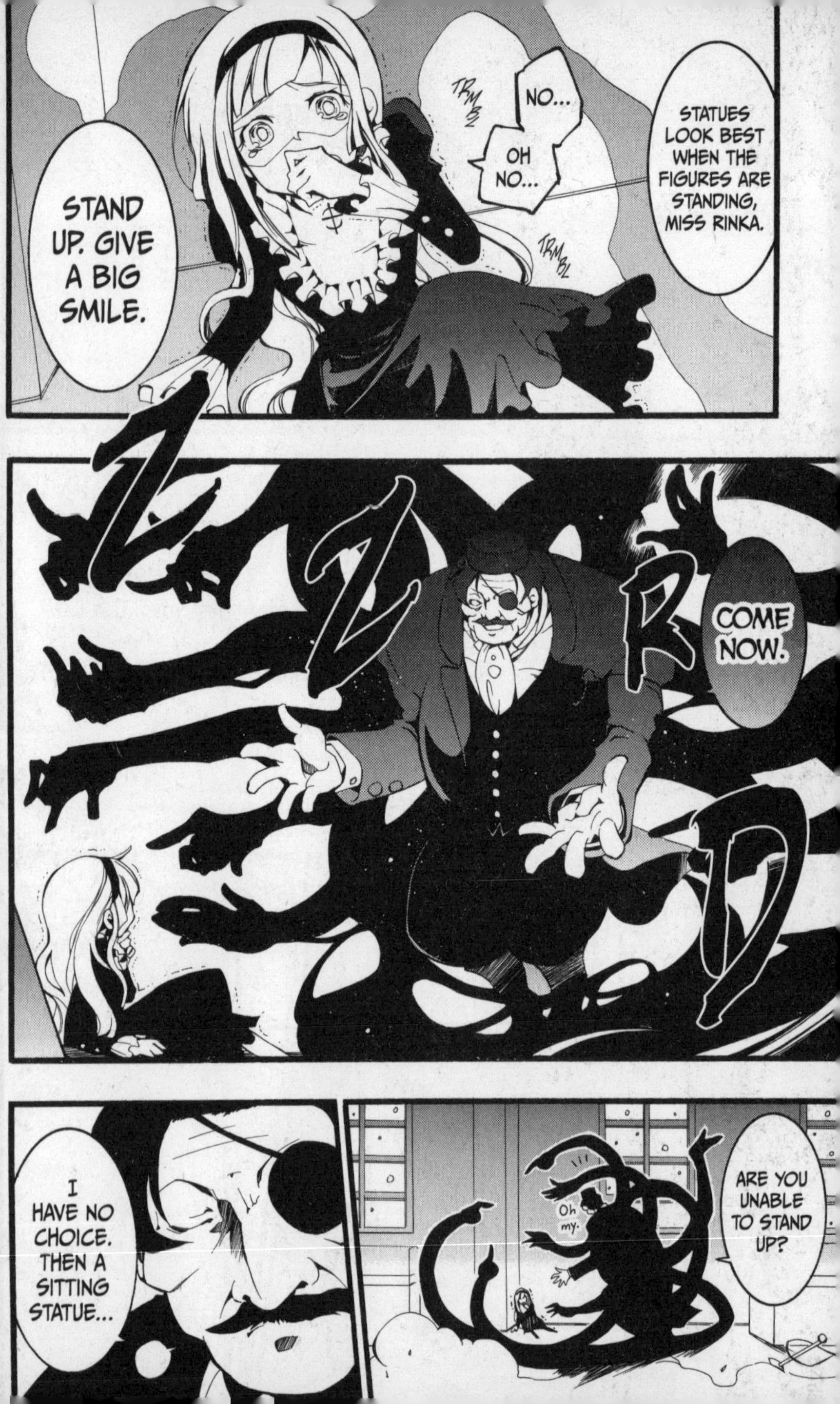
STATUES LOOK BEST WHEN THE FIGURES ARE STANDING, MISS RINKA.
TRMBL
NO...
OH NO...
TRMBL
STAND UP. GIVE A BIG SMILE.
COME NOW.
ZZRD
ARE YOU UNABLE TO STAND UP?
Oh my.
I HAVE NO CHOICE. THEN A SITTING STATUE...

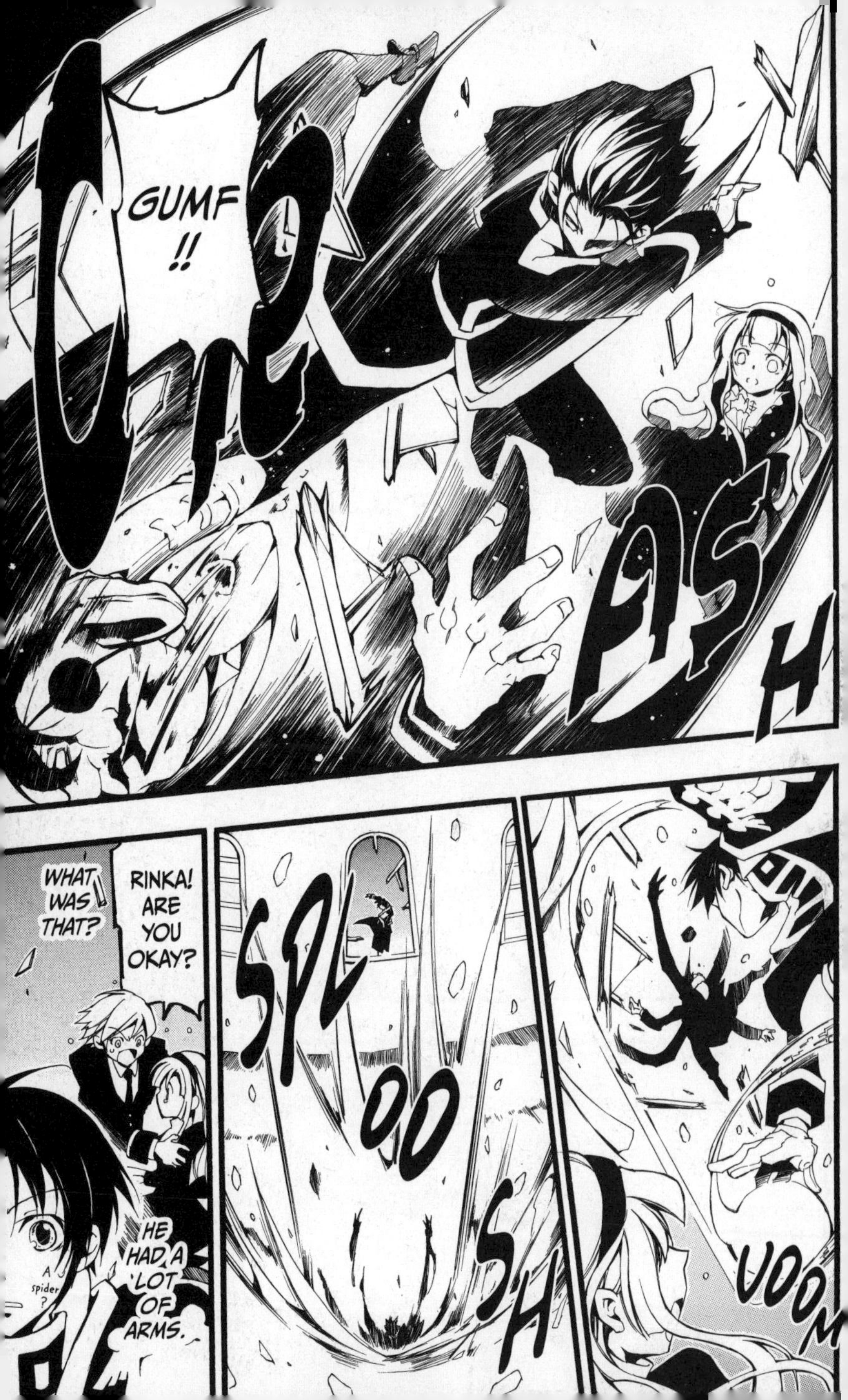
GUMF !!
VOOM
SPLOOSH
RINKA! ARE YOU OKAY?
WHAT WAS THAT?
HE HAD A LOT OF ARMS.
A spider?

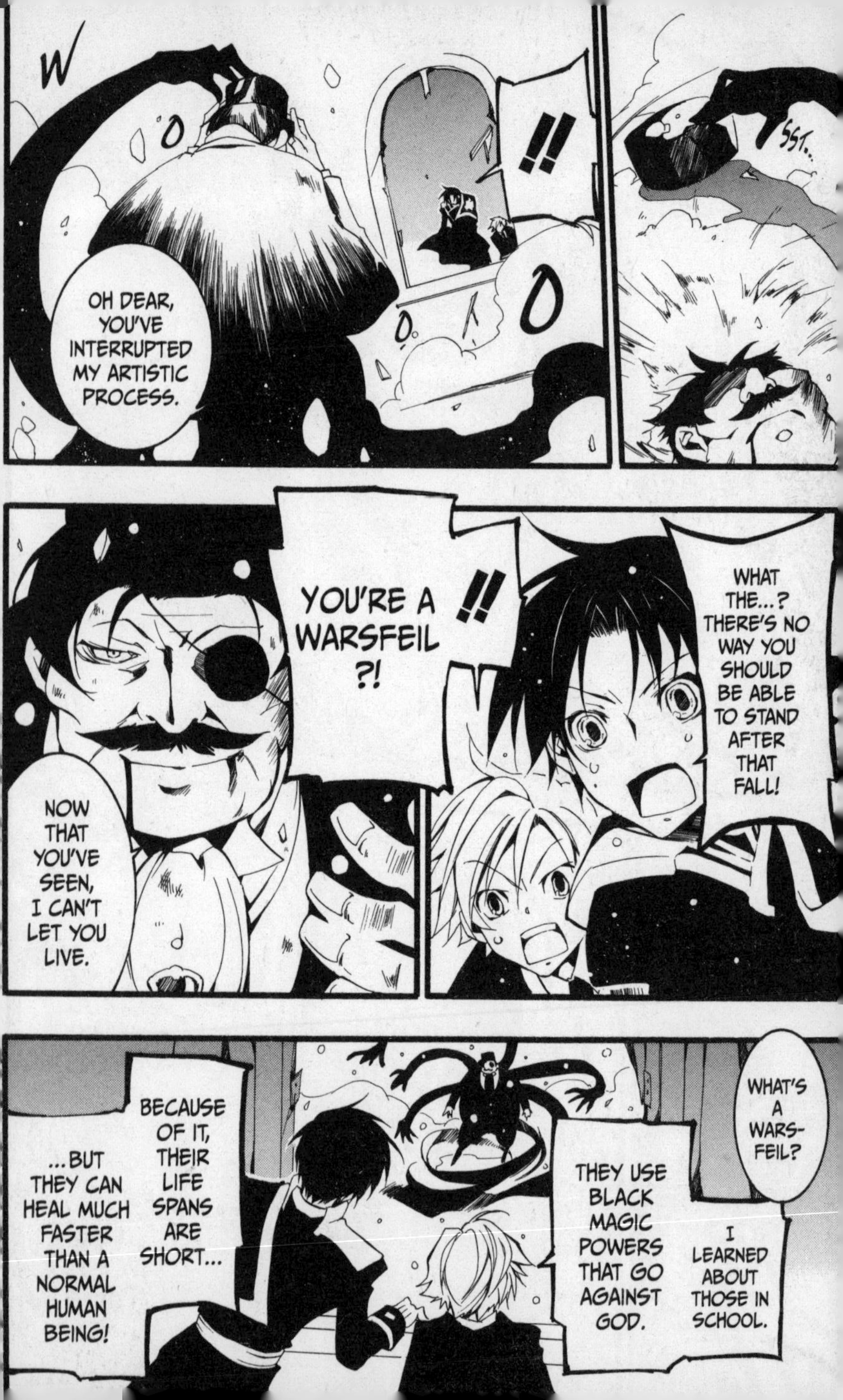
SST...
!!
O
W
O
O
OH DEAR, YOU'VE INTERRUPTED MY ARTISTIC PROCESS.
WHAT THE...? THERE'S NO WAY YOU SHOULD BE ABLE TO STAND AFTER THAT FALL!
!!
YOU'RE A WARSFEIL?!
NOW THAT YOU'VE SEEN, I CAN'T LET YOU LIVE.
WHAT'S A WARS-FEIL?
I LEARNED ABOUT THOSE IN SCHOOL.
THEY USE BLACK MAGIC POWERS THAT GO AGAINST GOD.
BECAUSE OF IT, THEIR LIFE SPANS ARE SHORT...
...BUT THEY CAN HEAL MUCH FASTER THAN A NORMAL HUMAN BEING!

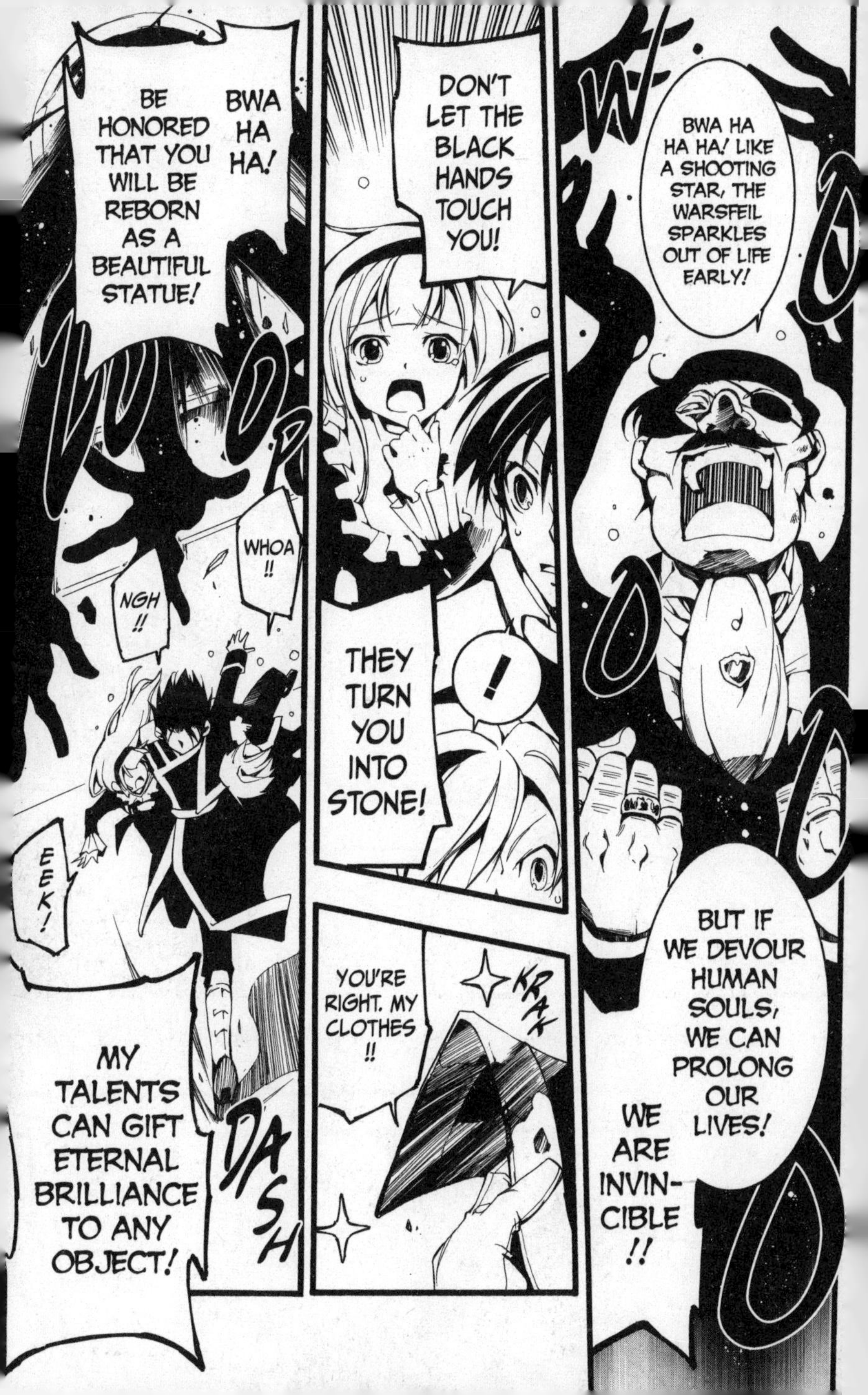
BWA HA HA HA! LIKE A SHOOTING STAR, THE WARSFEIL SPARKLES OUT OF LIFE EARLY!
BUT IF WE DEVOUR HUMAN SOULS, WE CAN PROLONG OUR LIVES!
WE ARE INVINCIBLE!!
DON'T LET THE BLACK HANDS TOUCH YOU!
!
THEY TURN YOU INTO STONE!
KRAK
YOU'RE RIGHT. MY CLOTHES!!
BWA HA HA!
BE HONORED THAT YOU WILL BE REBORN AS A BEAUTIFUL STATUE!
WHOA!!
NGH!!
EEK!
DASH
MY TALENTS CAN GIFT ETERNAL BRILLIANCE TO ANY OBJECT!

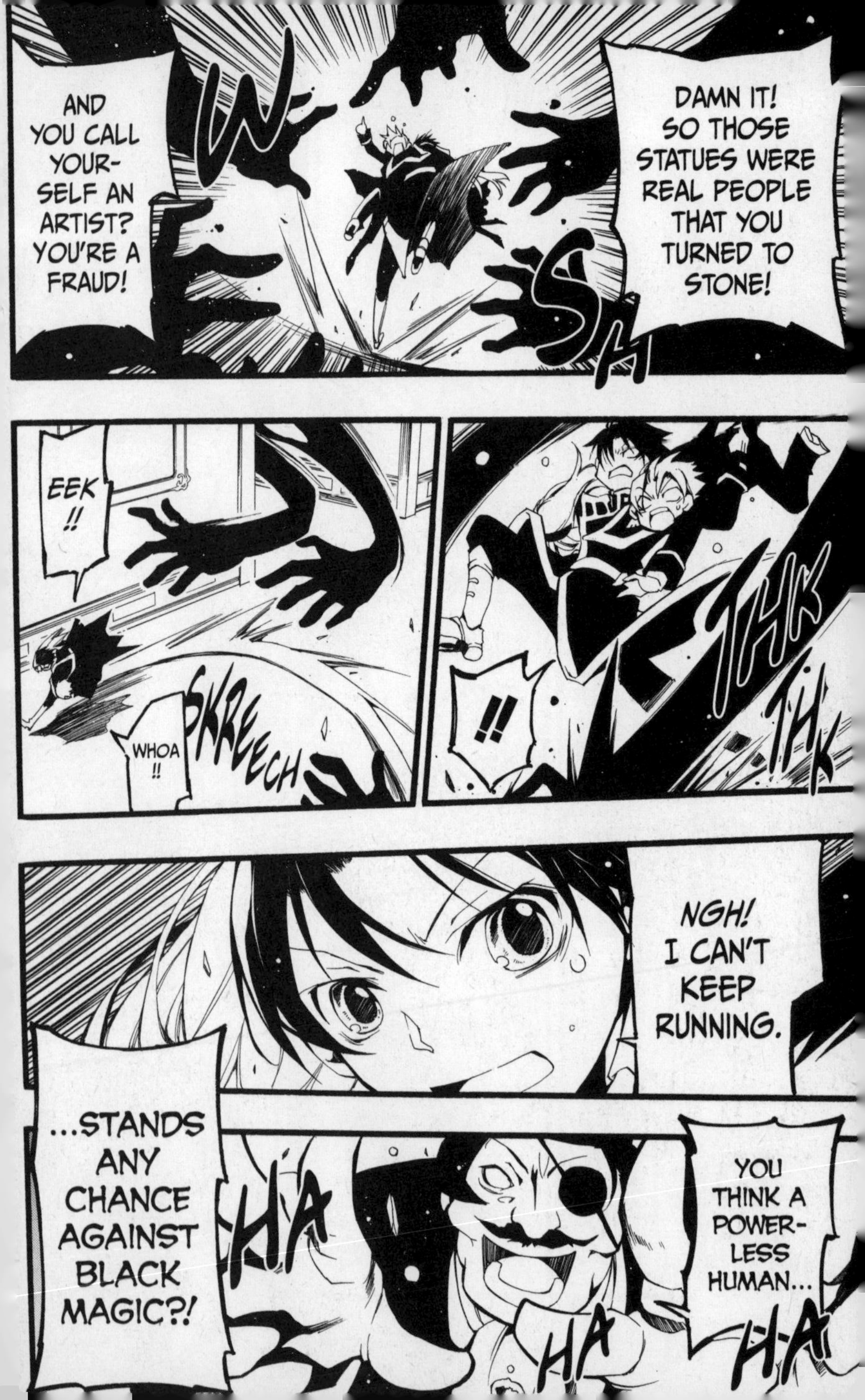
DAMN IT! SO THOSE STATUES WERE REAL PEOPLE THAT YOU TURNED TO STONE!
W
SH
AND YOU CALL YOUR-SELF AN ARTIST? YOU'RE A FRAUD!
THK
THK
!!
EEK!!
SKREECH
WHOA!!
NGH! I CAN'T KEEP RUNNING.
YOU THINK A POWER-LESS HUMAN...
HA
HA
HA
HA
...STANDS ANY CHANCE AGAINST BLACK MAGIC?!

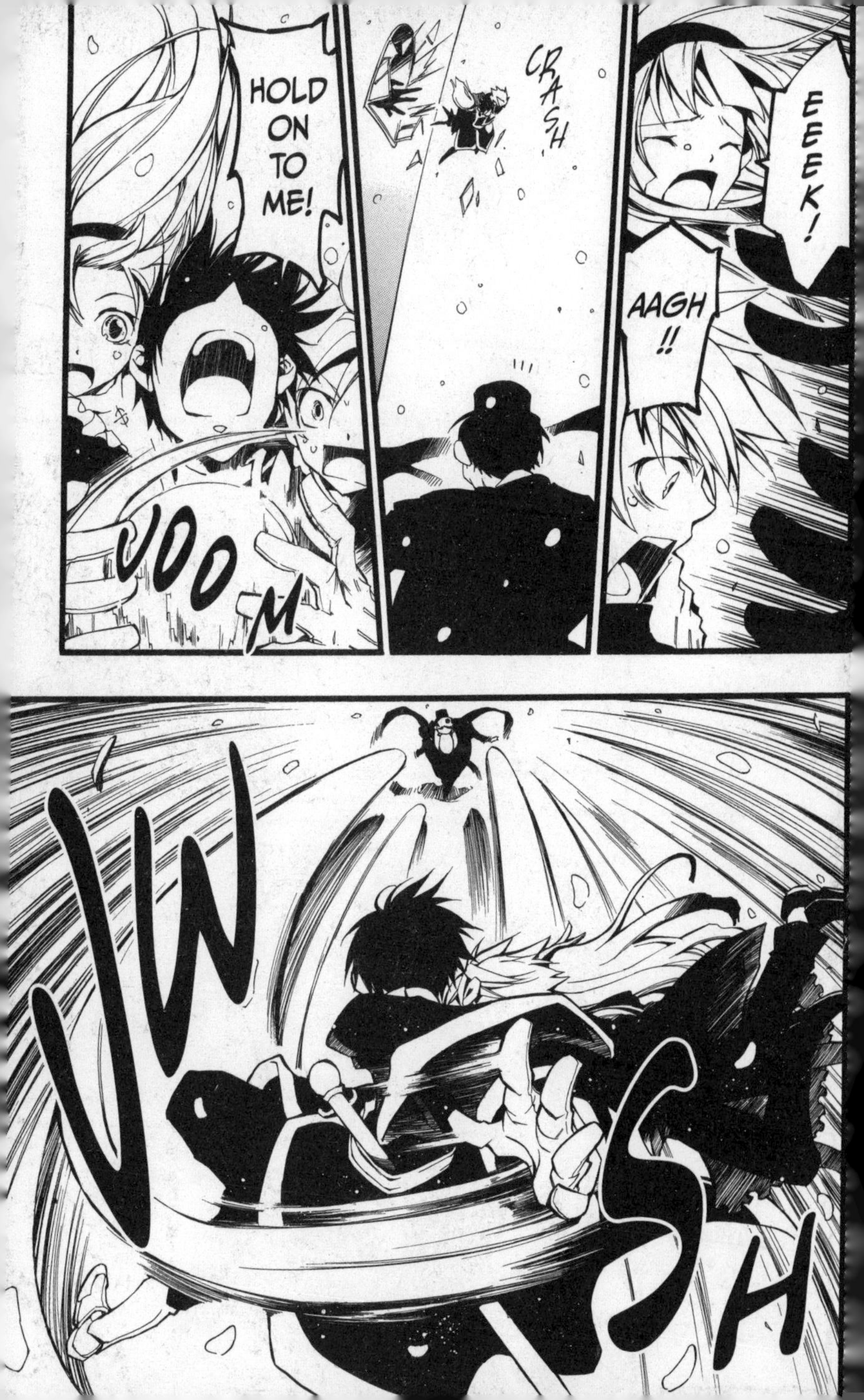
EEEK!
AAGH!!
CRASH
HOLD ON TO ME!
VOOM
WSH

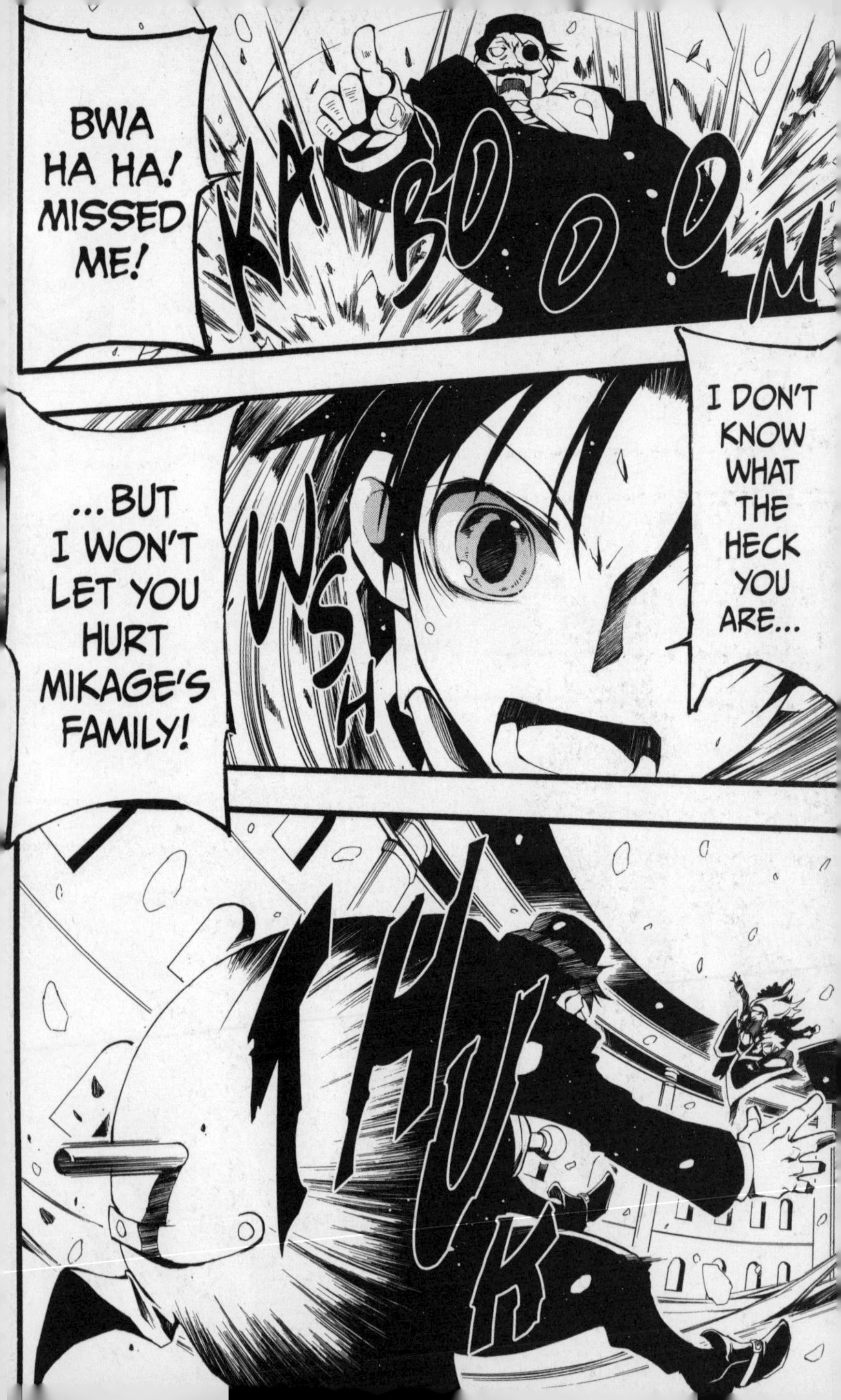
BWA HA HA! MISSED ME!
KABOOOM
I DON'T KNOW WHAT THE HECK YOU ARE...
WSH
...BUT I WON'T LET YOU HURT MIKAGE'S FAMILY!

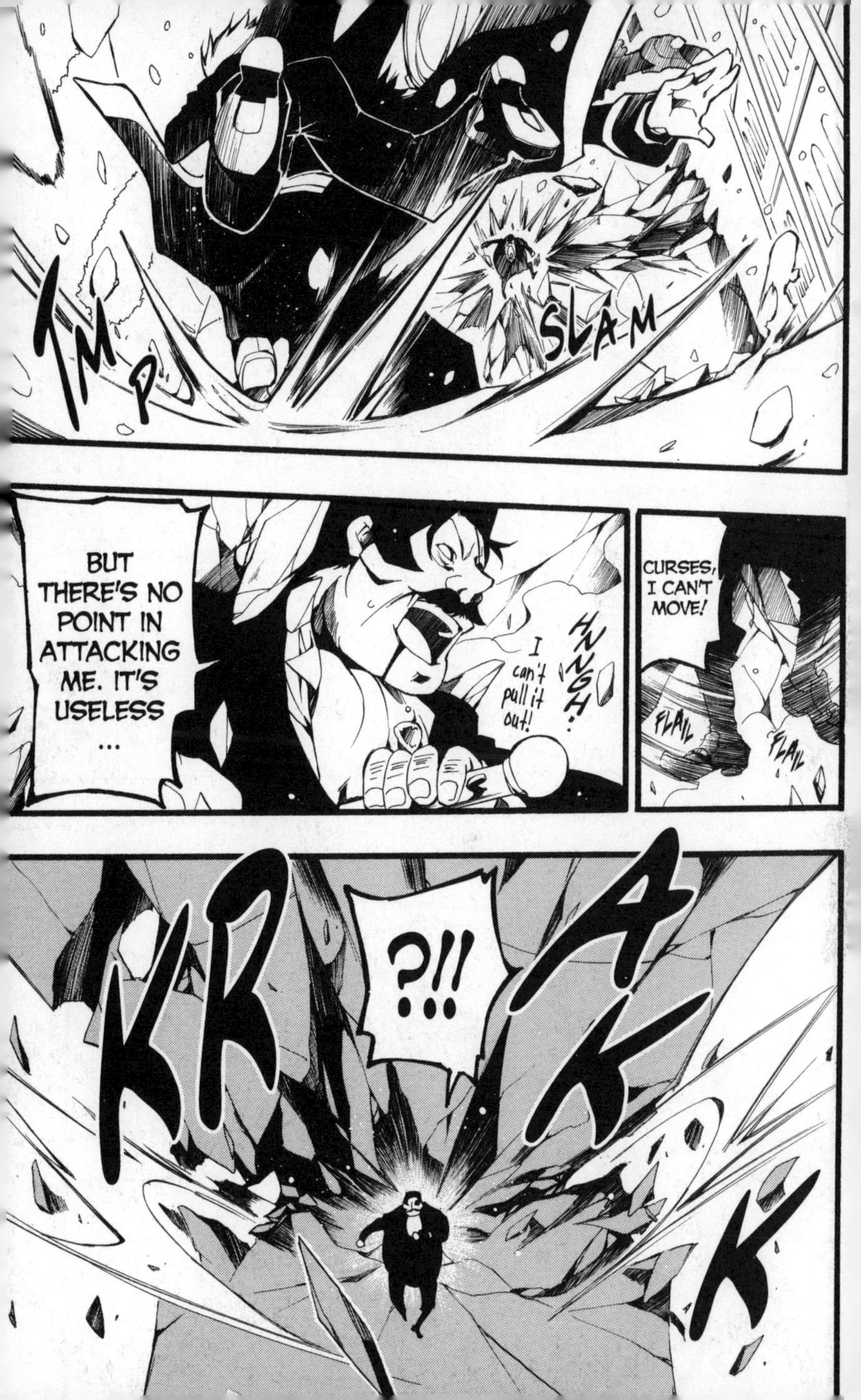
SLAM
TMP
CURSES, I CAN'T MOVE!
FLAIL
FLAIL
BUT THERE'S NO POINT IN ATTACKING ME. IT'S USELESS ...
HNNGH..
I can't pull it out!
KRAKK
?!!

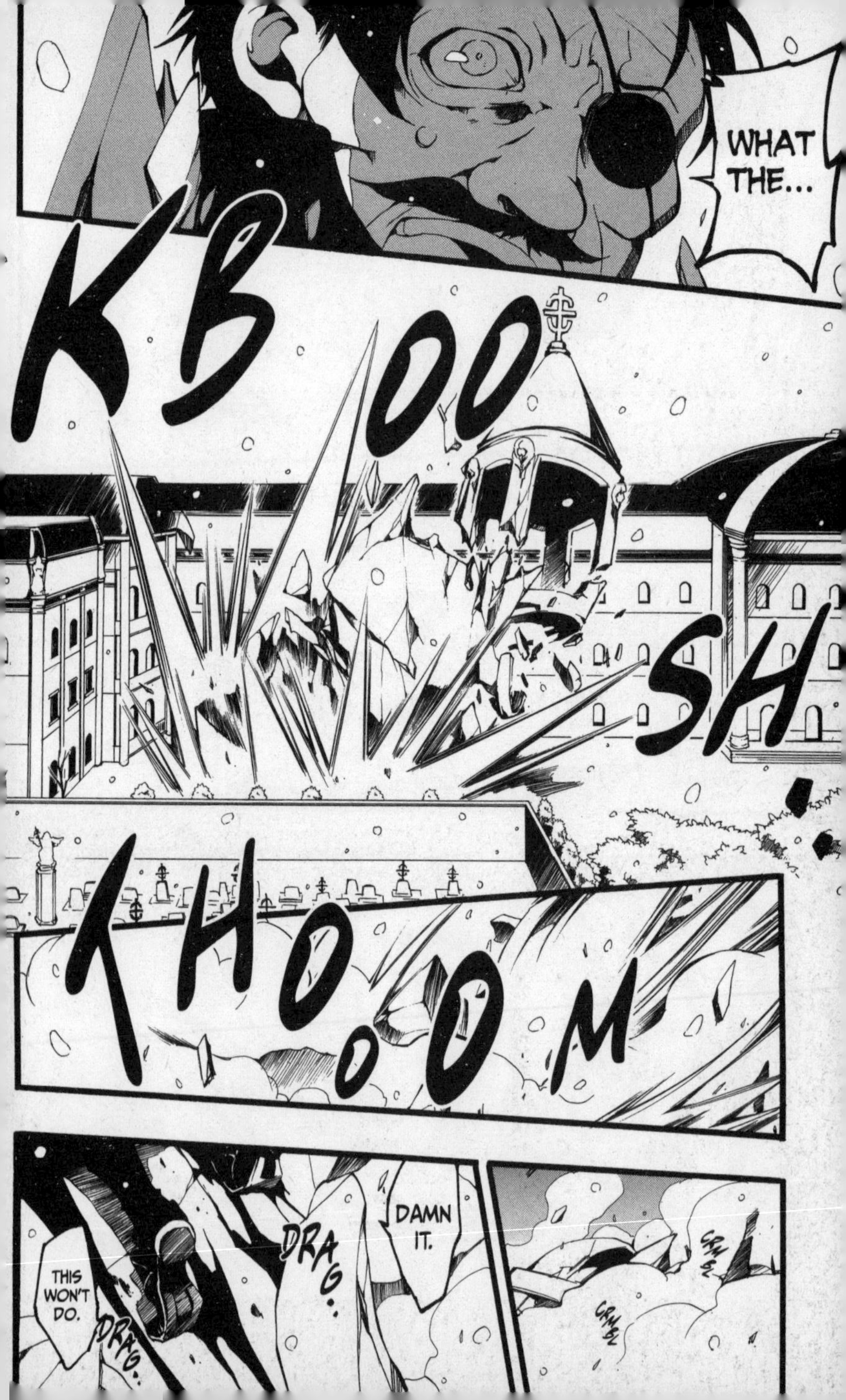
WHAT THE...
KBOOSH
KHOOOM
GRMBL
GRMBL
DAMN IT.
DRAG..
THIS WON'T DO.
DRAG..

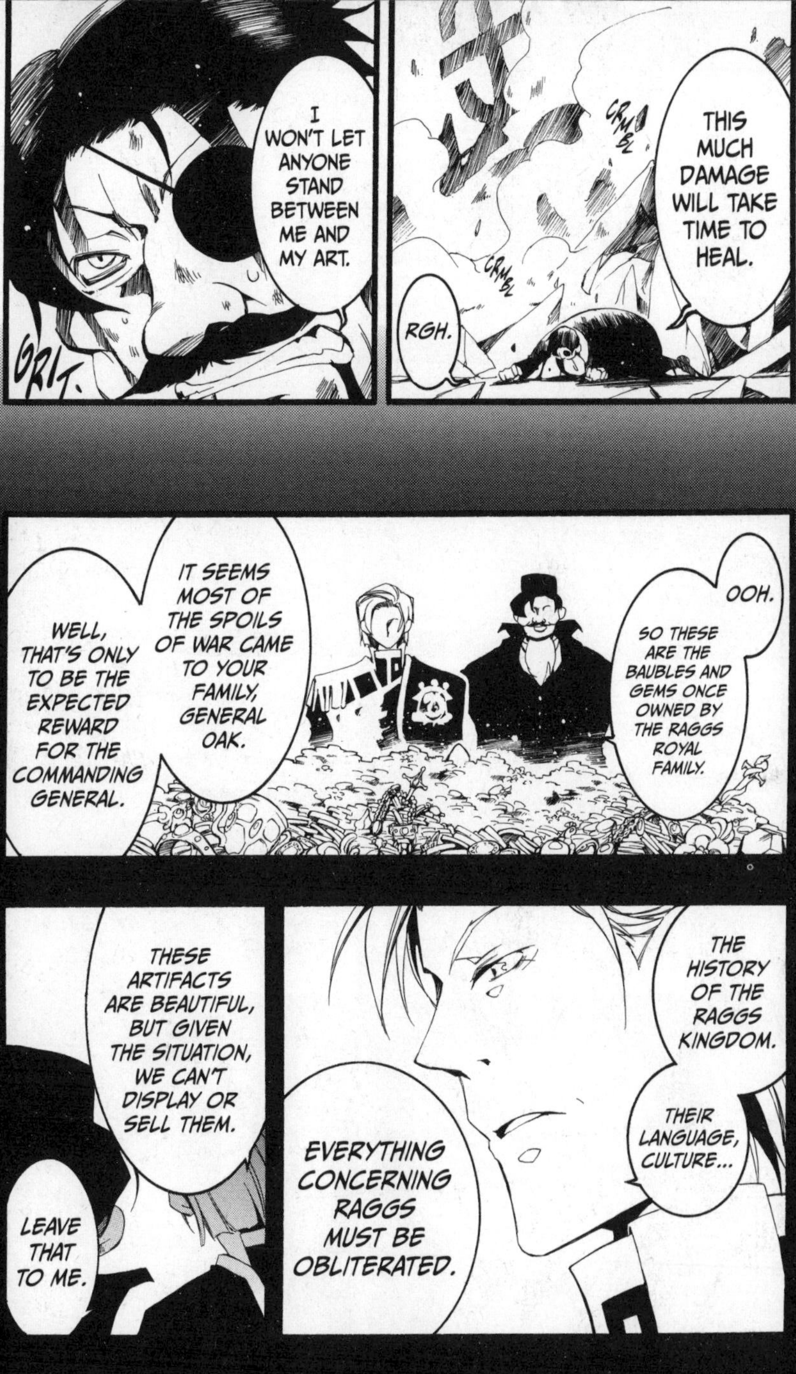
THIS MUCH DAMAGE WILL TAKE TIME TO HEAL.
CRMBL
CRMBL
RGH.
I WON'T LET ANYONE STAND BETWEEN ME AND MY ART.
GRIT
OOH.
SO THESE ARE THE BAUBLES AND GEMS ONCE OWNED BY THE RAGGS ROYAL FAMILY.
IT SEEMS MOST OF THE SPOILS OF WAR CAME TO YOUR FAMILY, GENERAL OAK.
WELL, THAT'S ONLY TO BE THE EXPECTED REWARD FOR THE COMMANDING GENERAL.
THE HISTORY OF THE RAGGS KINGDOM.
THEIR LANGUAGE, CULTURE...
EVERYTHING CONCERNING RAGGS MUST BE OBLITERATED.
THESE ARTIFACTS ARE BEAUTIFUL, BUT GIVEN THE SITUATION, WE CAN'T DISPLAY OR SELL THEM.
LEAVE THAT TO ME.

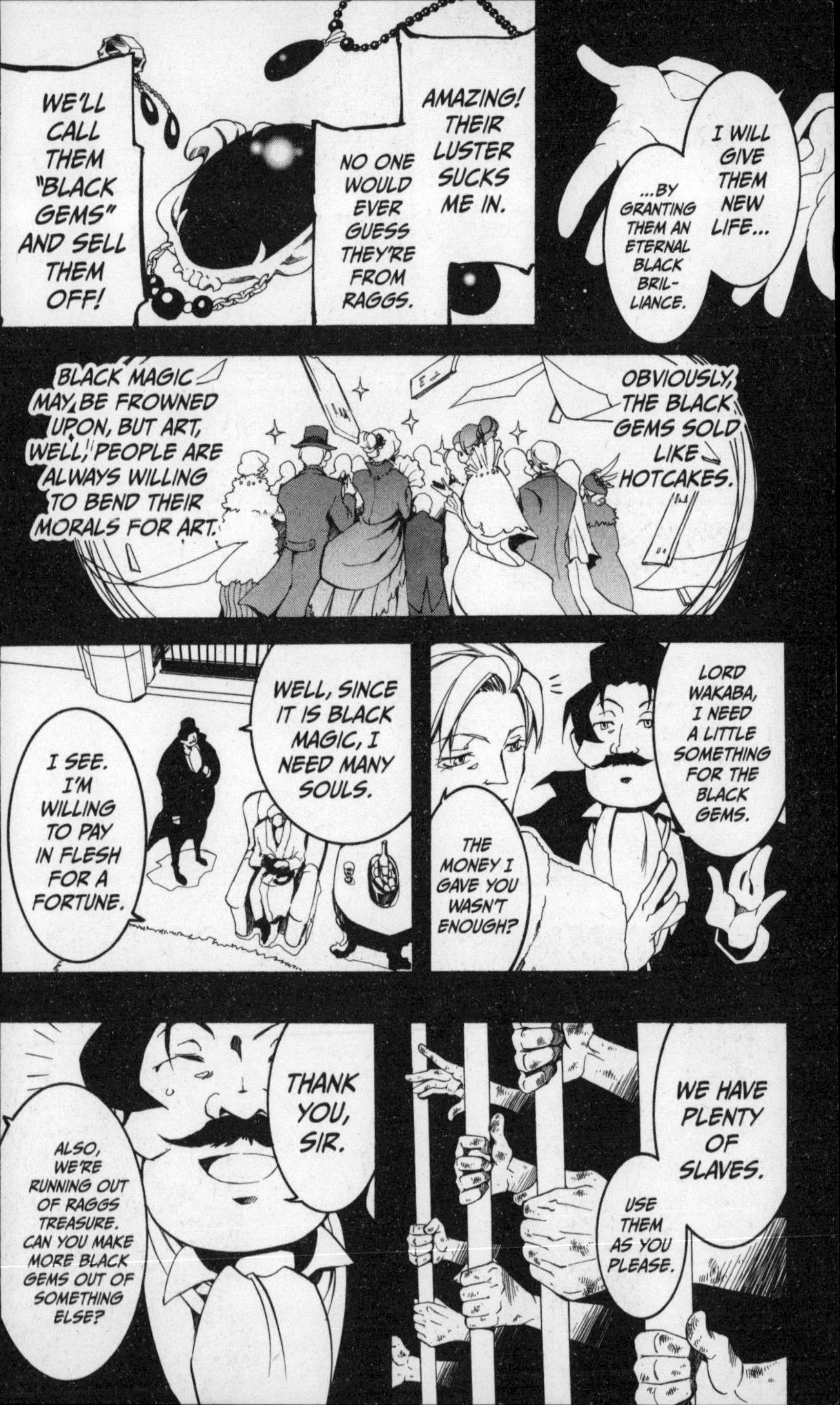
I WILL GIVE THEM NEW LIFE...
...BY GRANTING THEM AN ETERNAL BLACK BRILLIANCE.
AMAZING! THEIR LUSTER SUCKS ME IN.
NO ONE WOULD EVER GUESS THEY'RE FROM RAGGS.
WE'LL CALL THEM "BLACK GEMS" AND SELL THEM OFF!
OBVIOUSLY, THE BLACK GEMS SOLD LIKE HOTCAKES.
BLACK MAGIC MAY BE FROWNED UPON, BUT ART, WELL, PEOPLE ARE ALWAYS WILLING TO BEND THEIR MORALS FOR ART.
LORD WAKABA, I NEED A LITTLE SOMETHING FOR THE BLACK GEMS.
THE MONEY I GAVE YOU WASN'T ENOUGH?
WELL, SINCE IT IS BLACK MAGIC, I NEED MANY SOULS.
I SEE. I'M WILLING TO PAY IN FLESH FOR A FORTUNE.
WE HAVE PLENTY OF SLAVES.
USE THEM AS YOU PLEASE.
THANK YOU, SIR.
ALSO, WE'RE RUNNING OUT OF RAGGS TREASURE. CAN YOU MAKE MORE BLACK GEMS OUT OF SOMETHING ELSE?

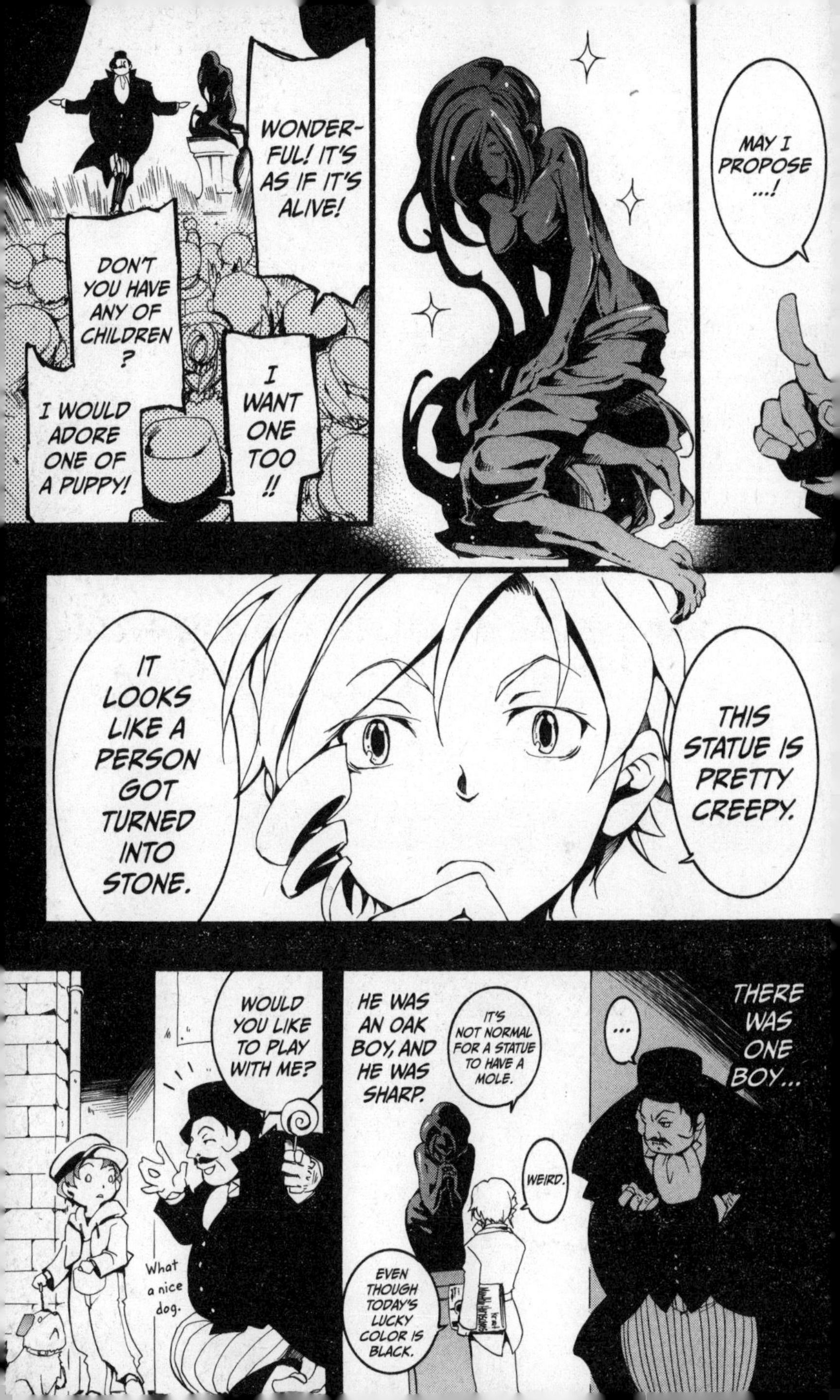
MAY I PROPOSE ...!
WONDER-FUL! IT'S AS IF IT'S ALIVE!
DON'T YOU HAVE ANY OF CHILDREN?
I WANT ONE TOO!!
I WOULD ADORE ONE OF A PUPPY!
THIS STATUE IS PRETTY CREEPY.
IT LOOKS LIKE A PERSON GOT TURNED INTO STONE.
THERE WAS ONE BOY...
...
HE WAS AN OAK BOY, AND HE WAS SHARP.
IT'S NOT NORMAL FOR A STATUE TO HAVE A MOLE.
WEIRD.
EVEN THOUGH TODAY'S LUCKY COLOR IS BLACK.
WOULD YOU LIKE TO PLAY WITH ME?
What a nice dog.

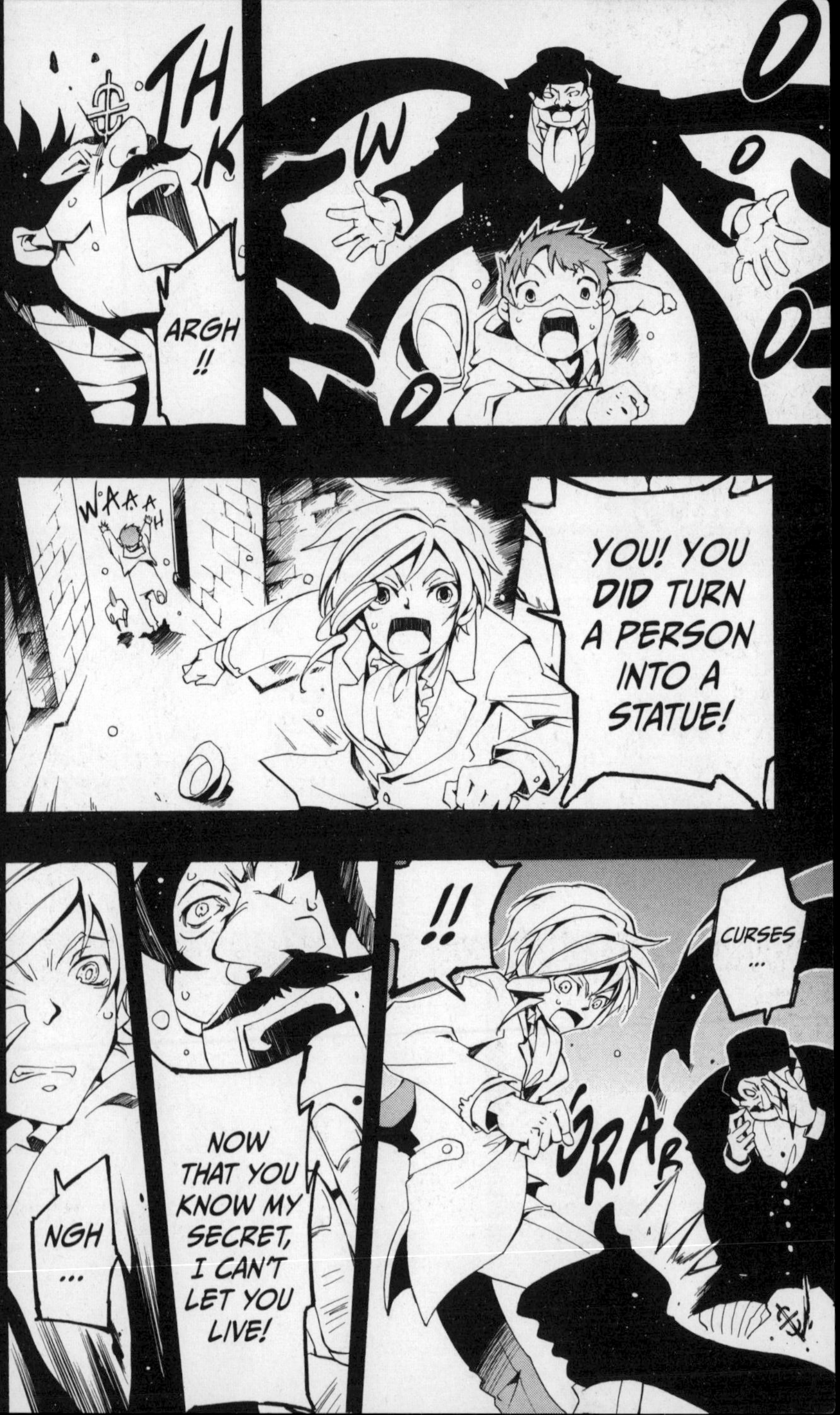
WOOOOO
THK
ARGH !!
YOU! YOU DID TURN A PERSON INTO A STATUE!
WAAAH
CURSES ...
GRAB
!!
NOW THAT YOU KNOW MY SECRET, I CAN'T LET YOU LIVE!
NGH ...

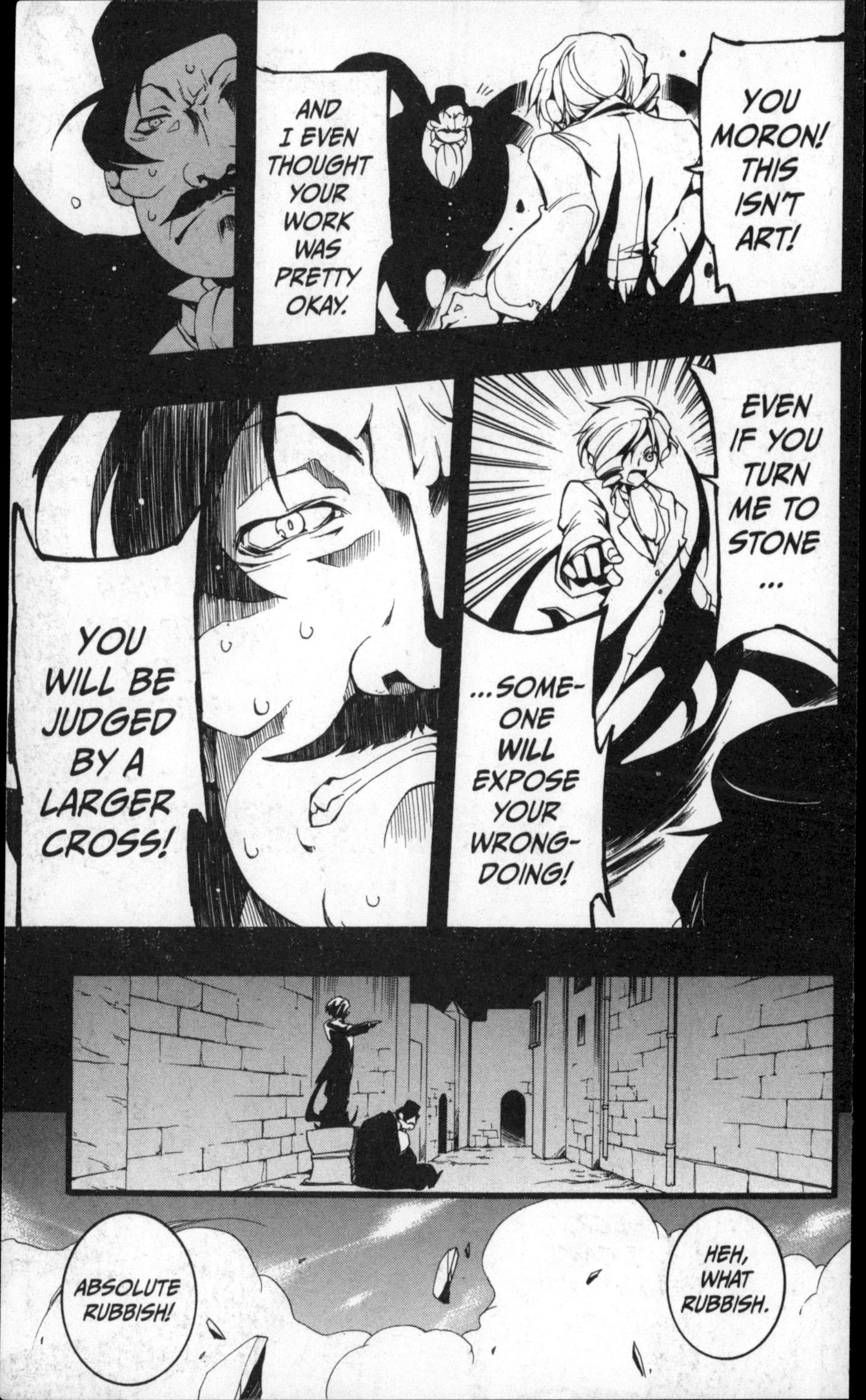
YOU MORON! THIS ISN'T ART!
AND I EVEN THOUGHT YOUR WORK WAS PRETTY OKAY.
EVEN IF YOU TURN ME TO STONE ...
...SOME-ONE WILL EXPOSE YOUR WRONG-DOING!
YOU WILL BE JUDGED BY A LARGER CROSS!
HEH, WHAT RUBBISH.
ABSOLUTE RUBBISH!

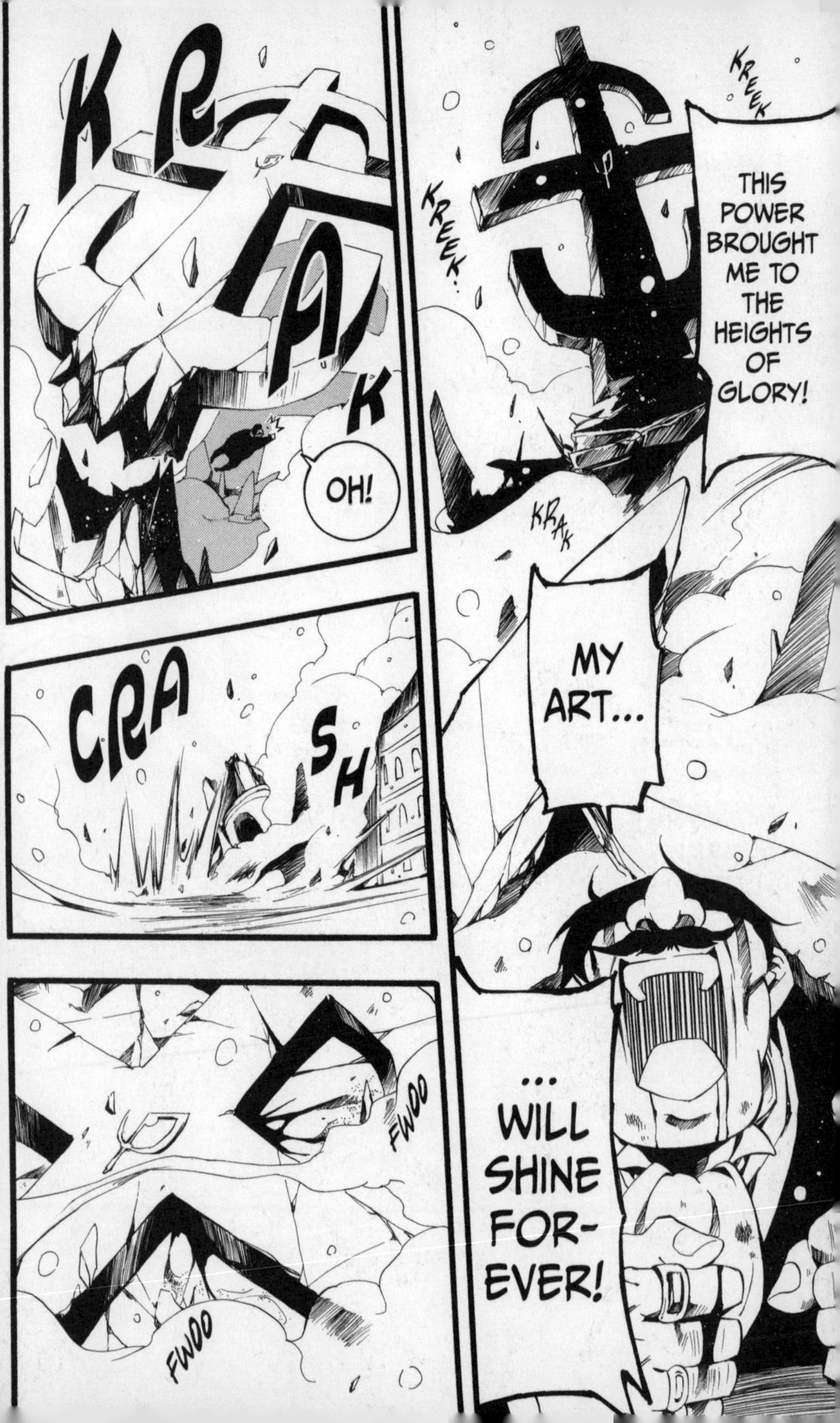
KREEK
KREEK
THIS POWER BROUGHT ME TO THE HEIGHTS OF GLORY!
KRAK
MY ART...
... WILL SHINE FOR-EVER!
KRAK
OH!
CRASH
FWOO
FWOO

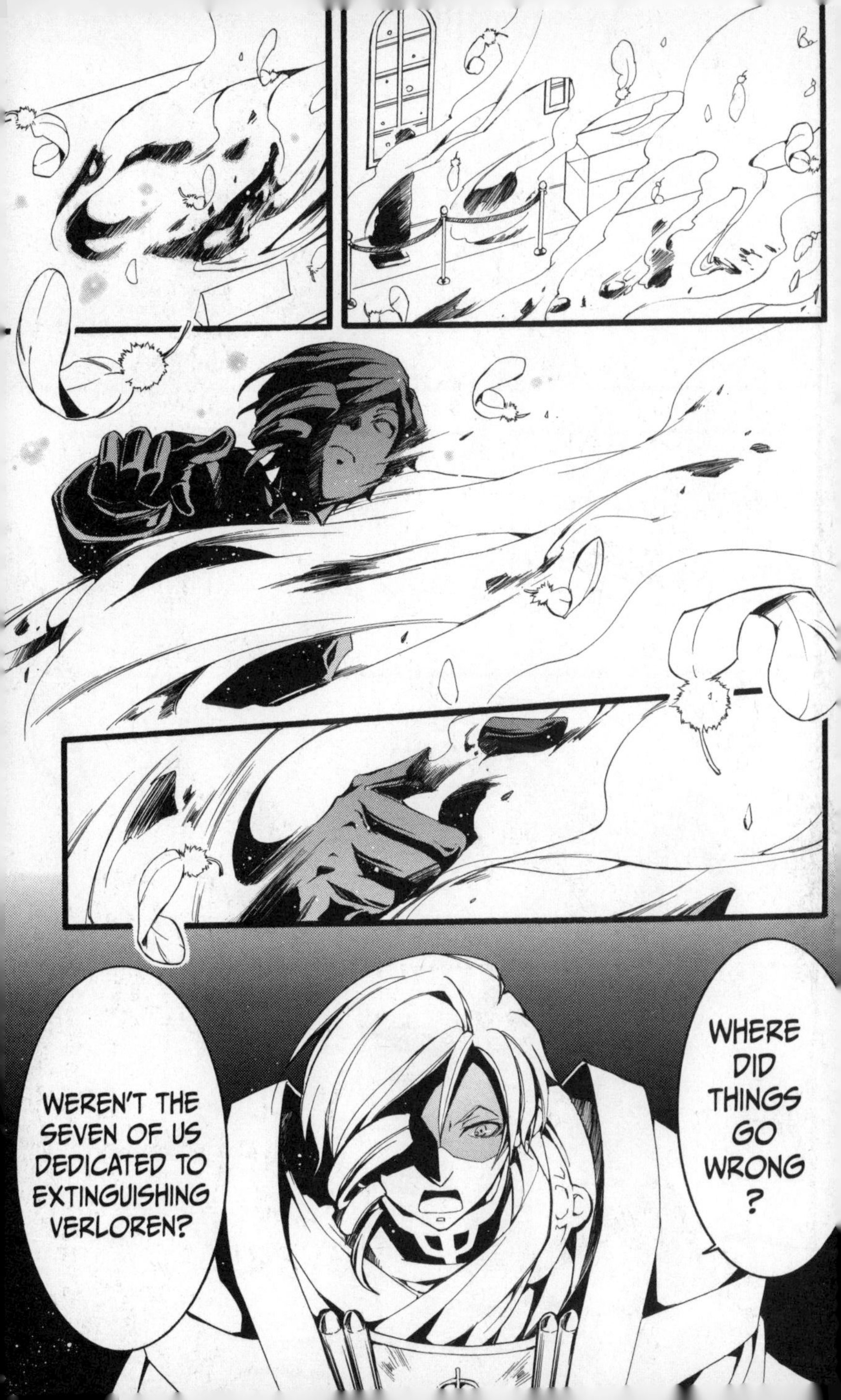
WHERE DID THINGS GO WRONG?
WEREN'T THE SEVEN OF US DEDICATED TO EXTINGUISHING VERLOREN?

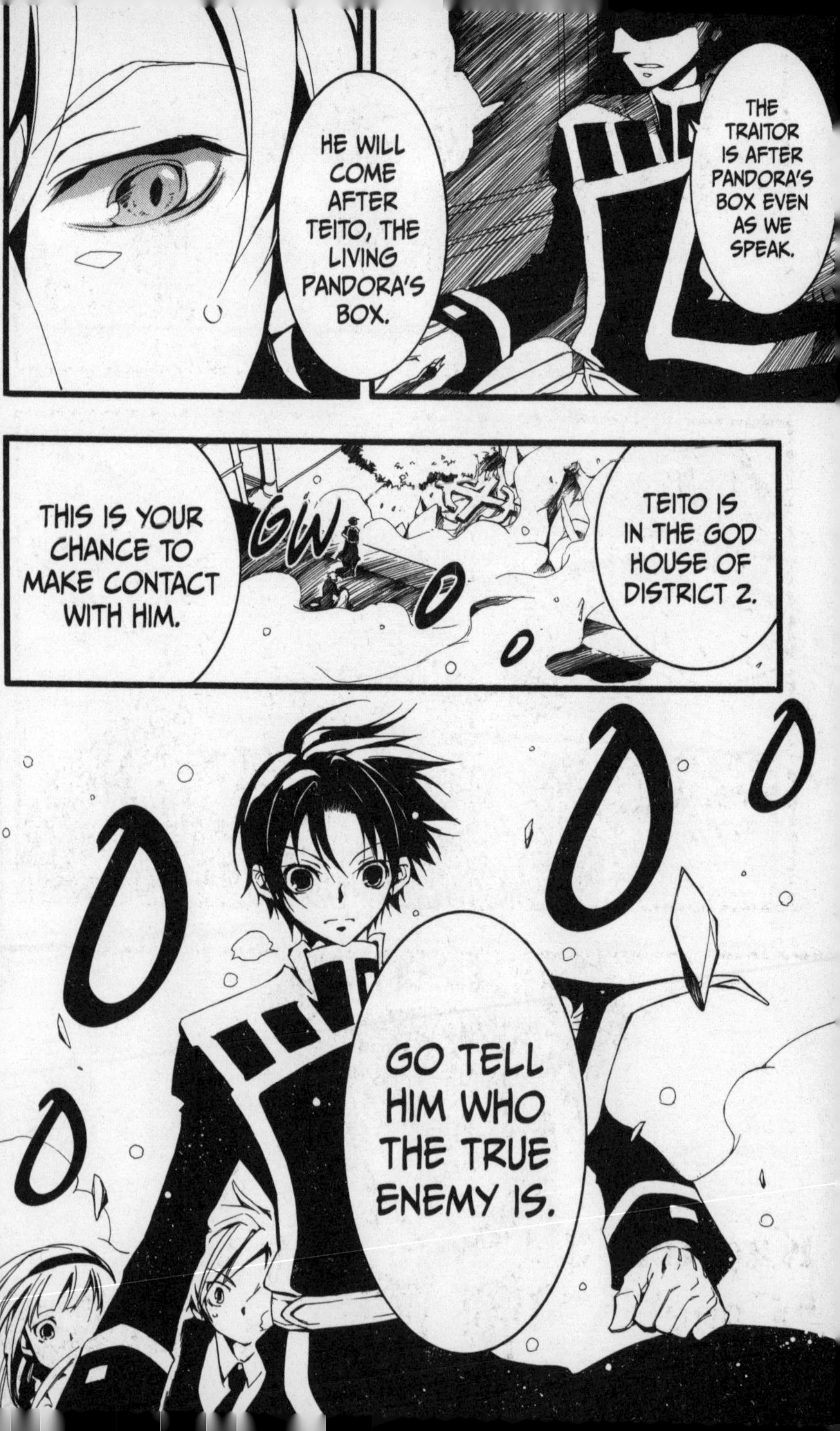
THE TRAITOR IS AFTER PANDORA'S BOX EVEN AS WE SPEAK.
HE WILL COME AFTER TEITO, THE LIVING PANDORA'S BOX.
TEITO IS IN THE GOD HOUSE OF DISTRICT 2.
GW
THIS IS YOUR CHANCE TO MAKE CONTACT WITH HIM.
GO TELL HIM WHO THE TRUE ENEMY IS.

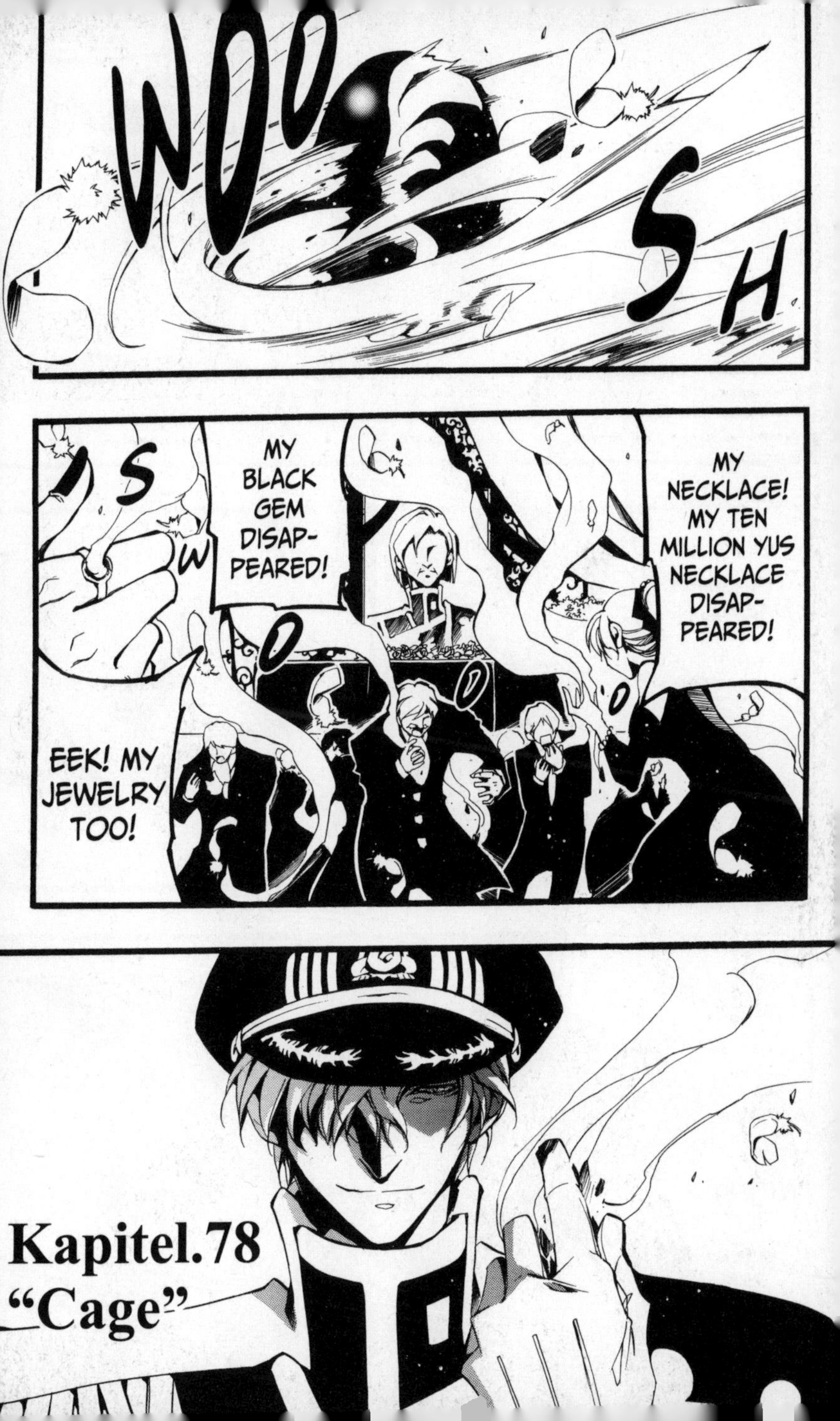
WOOOSH
MY NECKLACE! MY TEN MILLION YUS NECKLACE DISAP-PEARED!
MY BLACK GEM DISAP-PEARED!
SWOOOO
EEK! MY JEWELRY TOO!
Kapitel.78
"Cage"

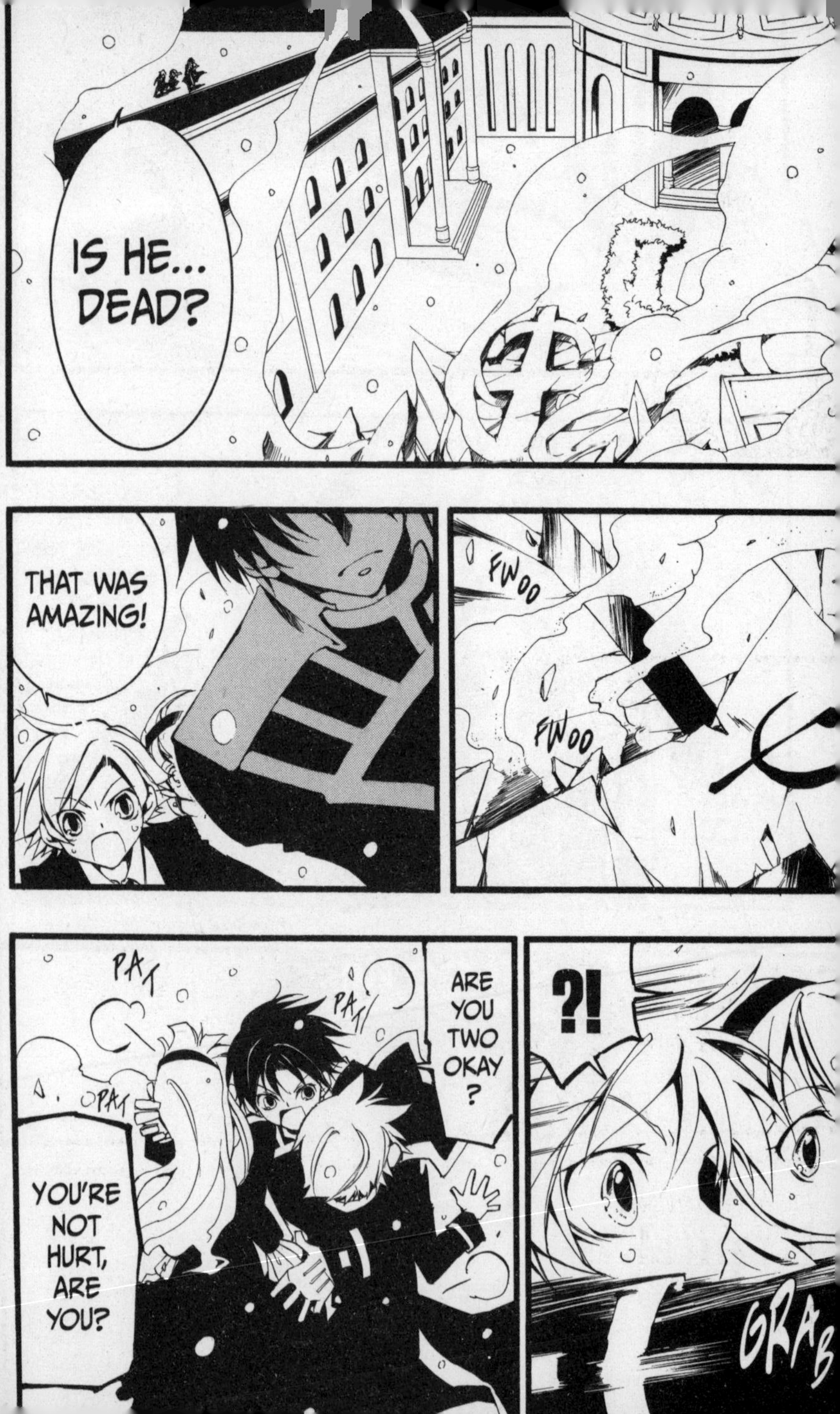
IS HE... DEAD?
FWOO
FWOO
THAT WAS AMAZING!
?!
GRAB
ARE YOU TWO OKAY?
PAT
PAT
PAT
YOU'RE NOT HURT, ARE YOU?

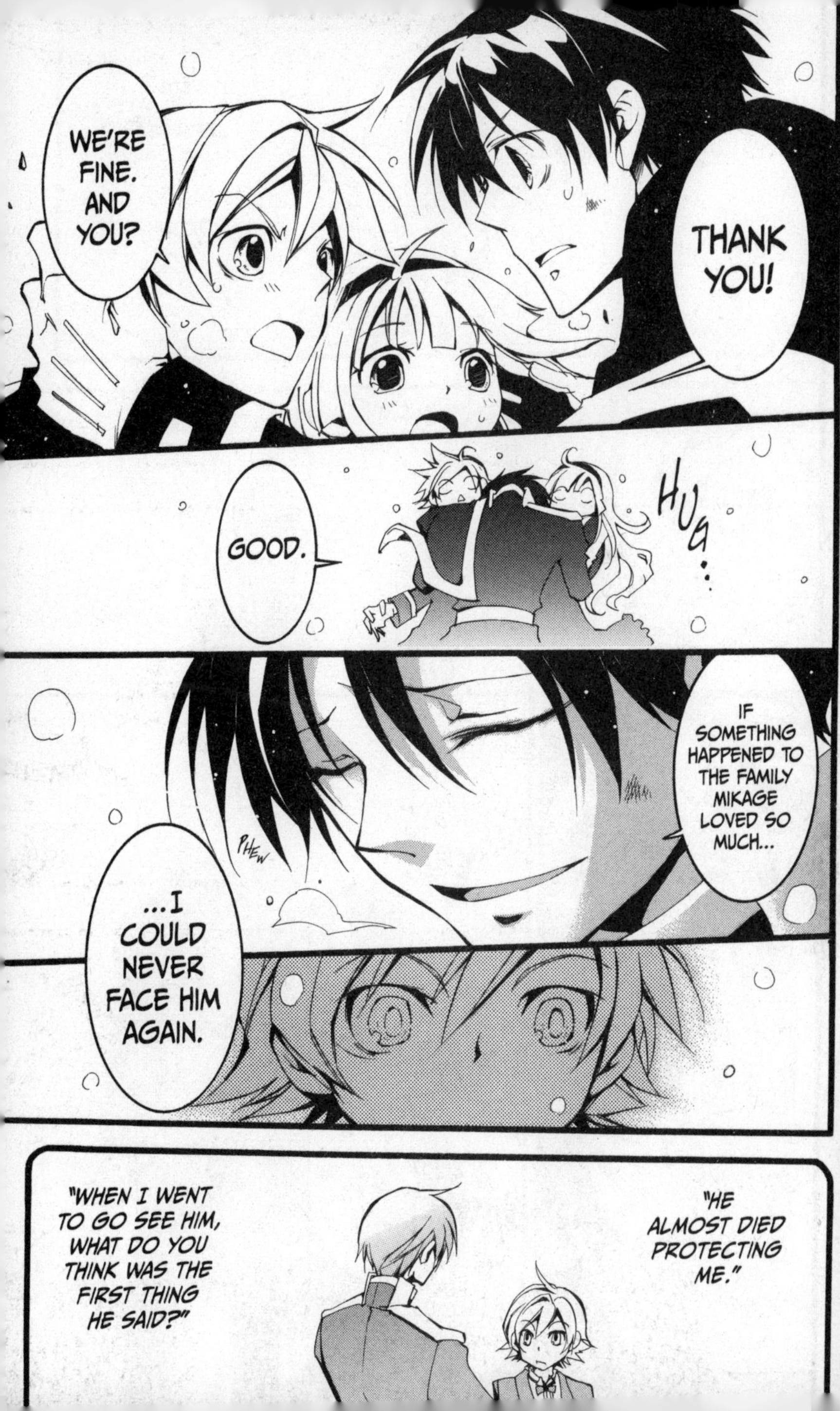
THANK YOU!
WE'RE FINE. AND YOU?
HUG...
GOOD.
IF SOMETHING HAPPENED TO THE FAMILY MIKAGE LOVED SO MUCH...
PHEW
...I COULD NEVER FACE HIM AGAIN.
"HE ALMOST DIED PROTECTING ME."
"WHEN I WENT TO GO SEE HIM, WHAT DO YOU THINK WAS THE FIRST THING HE SAID?"

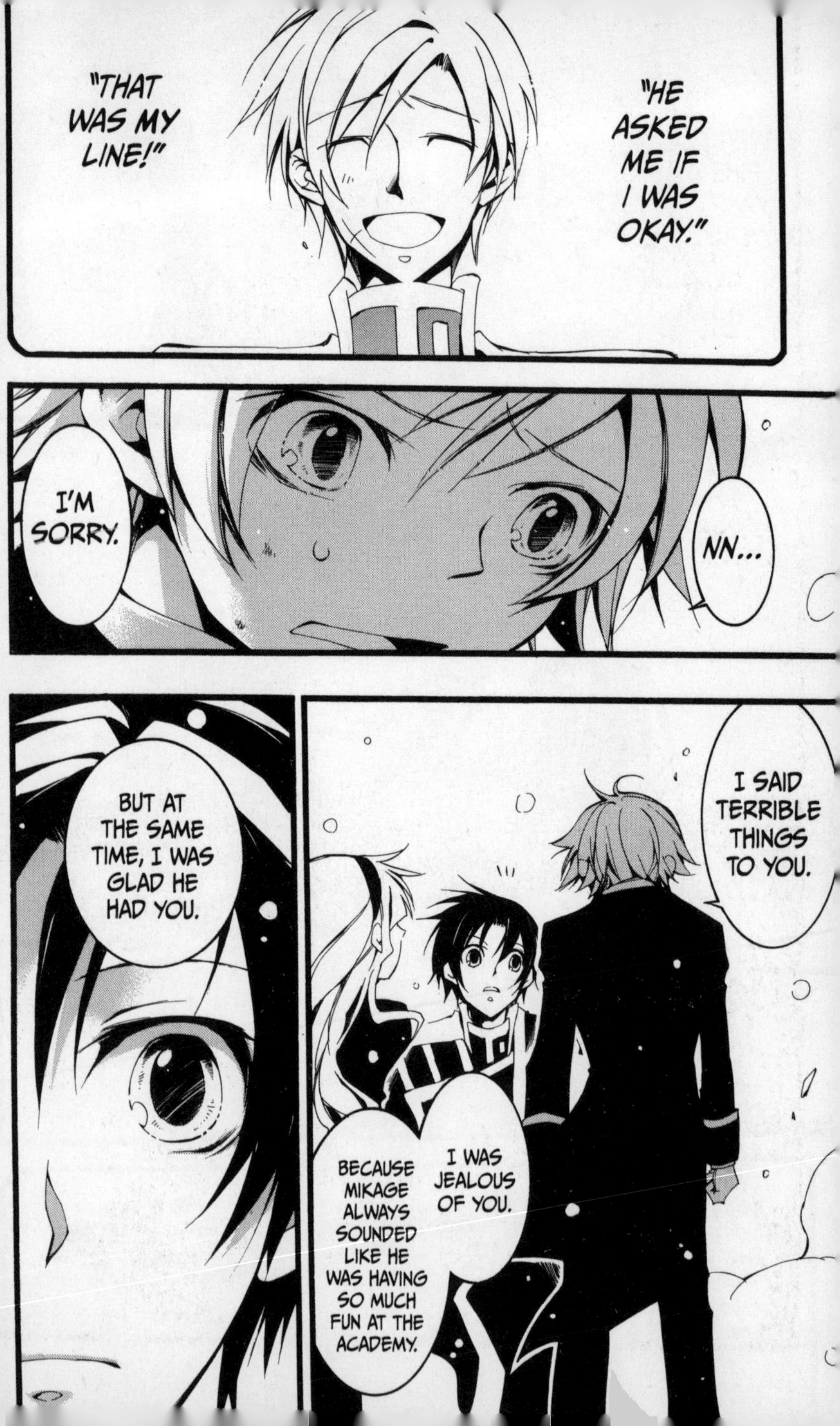
"HE ASKED ME IF I WAS OKAY."
"THAT WAS MY LINE!"
NN...
I'M SORRY.
I SAID TERRIBLE THINGS TO YOU.
I WAS JEALOUS OF YOU.
BECAUSE MIKAGE ALWAYS SOUNDED LIKE HE WAS HAVING SO MUCH FUN AT THE ACADEMY.
BUT AT THE SAME TIME, I WAS GLAD HE HAD YOU.

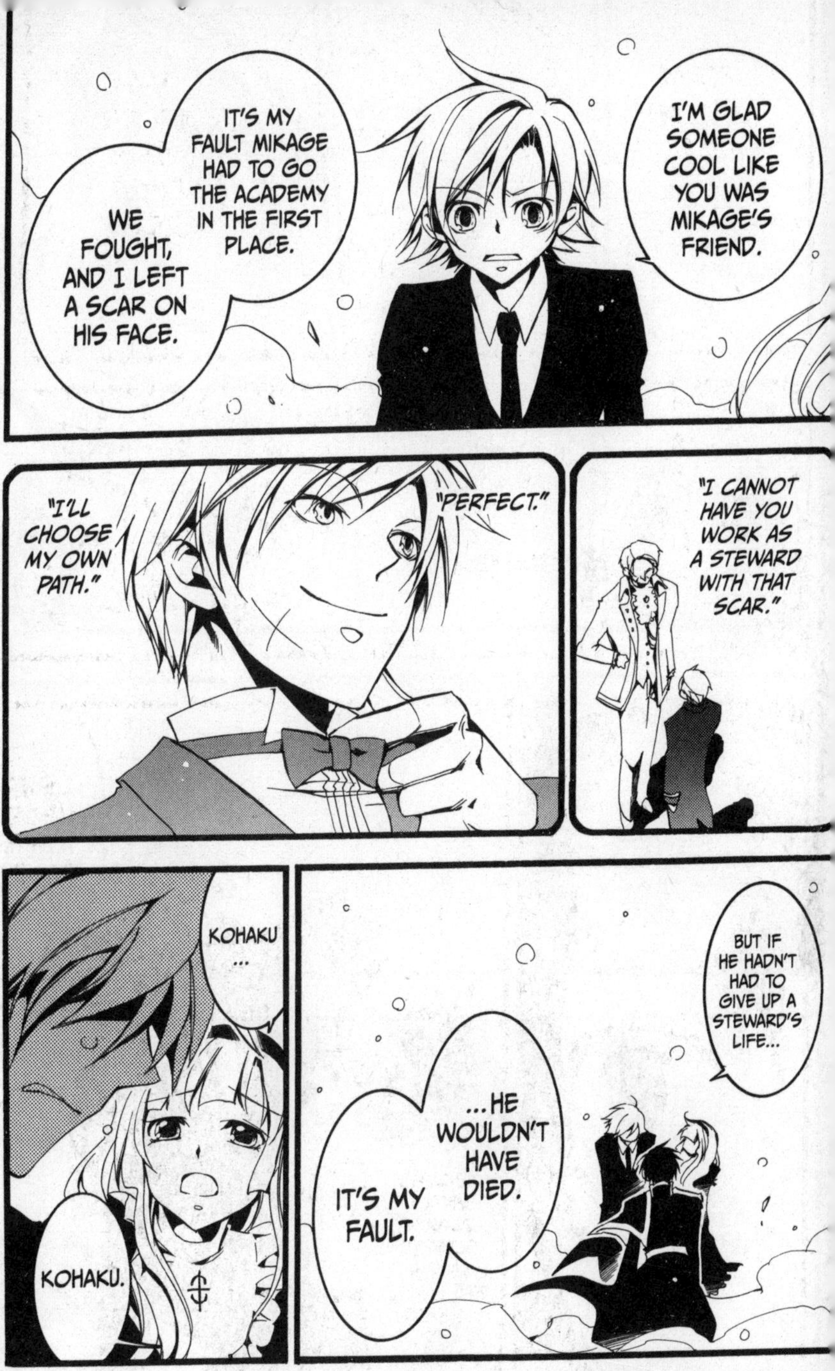
I'M GLAD SOMEONE COOL LIKE YOU WAS MIKAGE'S FRIEND.
IT'S MY FAULT MIKAGE HAD TO GO THE ACADEMY IN THE FIRST PLACE.
WE FOUGHT, AND I LEFT A SCAR ON HIS FACE.
"I CANNOT HAVE YOU WORK AS A STEWARD WITH THAT SCAR."
"PERFECT."
"I'LL CHOOSE MY OWN PATH."
BUT IF HE HADN'T HAD TO GIVE UP A STEWARD'S LIFE...
...HE WOULDN'T HAVE DIED.
IT'S MY FAULT.
KOHAKU...
KOHAKU.

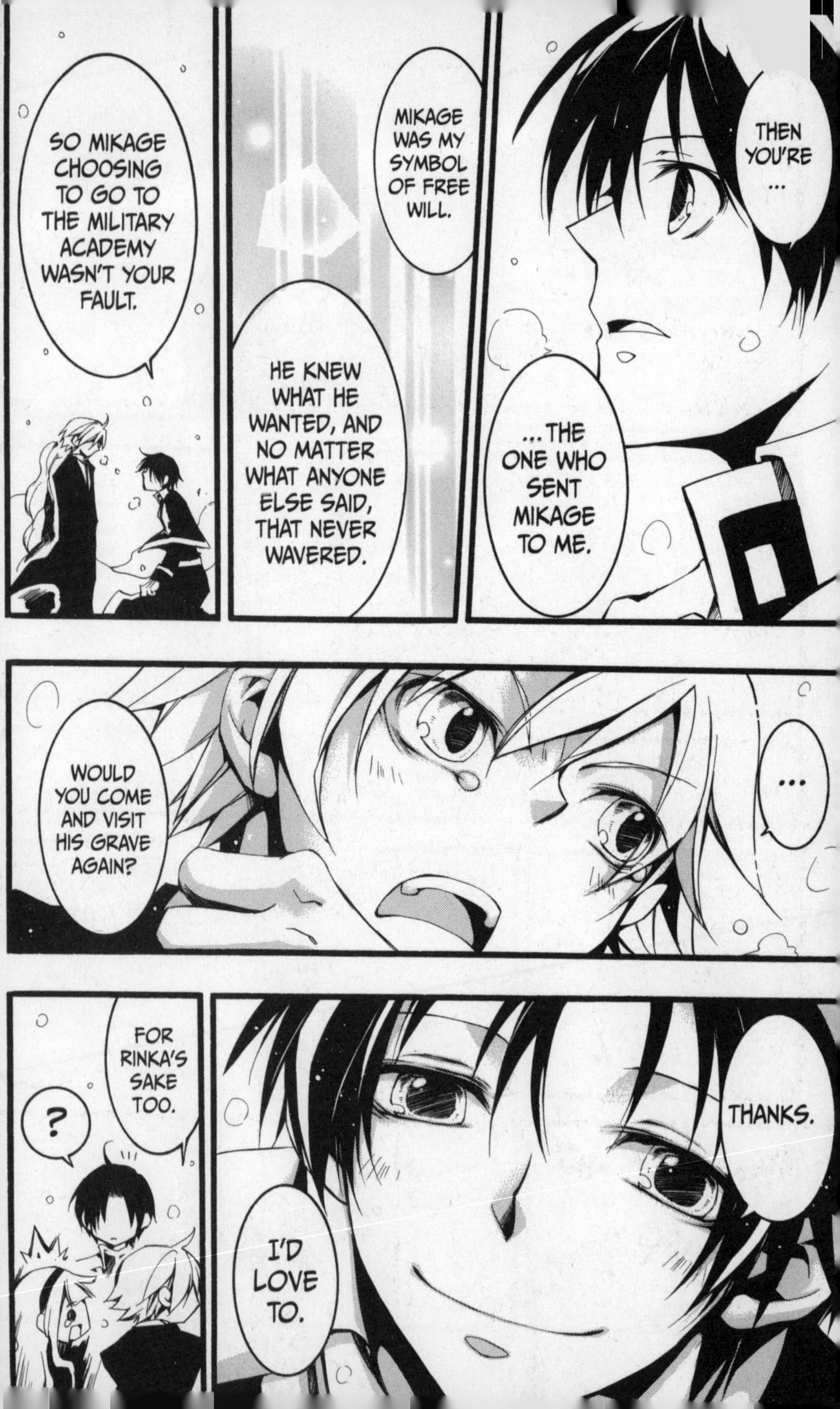
THEN YOU'RE ...
...THE ONE WHO SENT MIKAGE TO ME.
MIKAGE WAS MY SYMBOL OF FREE WILL.
HE KNEW WHAT HE WANTED, AND NO MATTER WHAT ANYONE ELSE SAID, THAT NEVER WAVERED.
SO MIKAGE CHOOSING TO GO TO THE MILITARY ACADEMY WASN'T YOUR FAULT.
...
WOULD YOU COME AND VISIT HIS GRAVE AGAIN?
THANKS.
I'D LOVE TO.
FOR RINKA'S SAKE TOO.
?

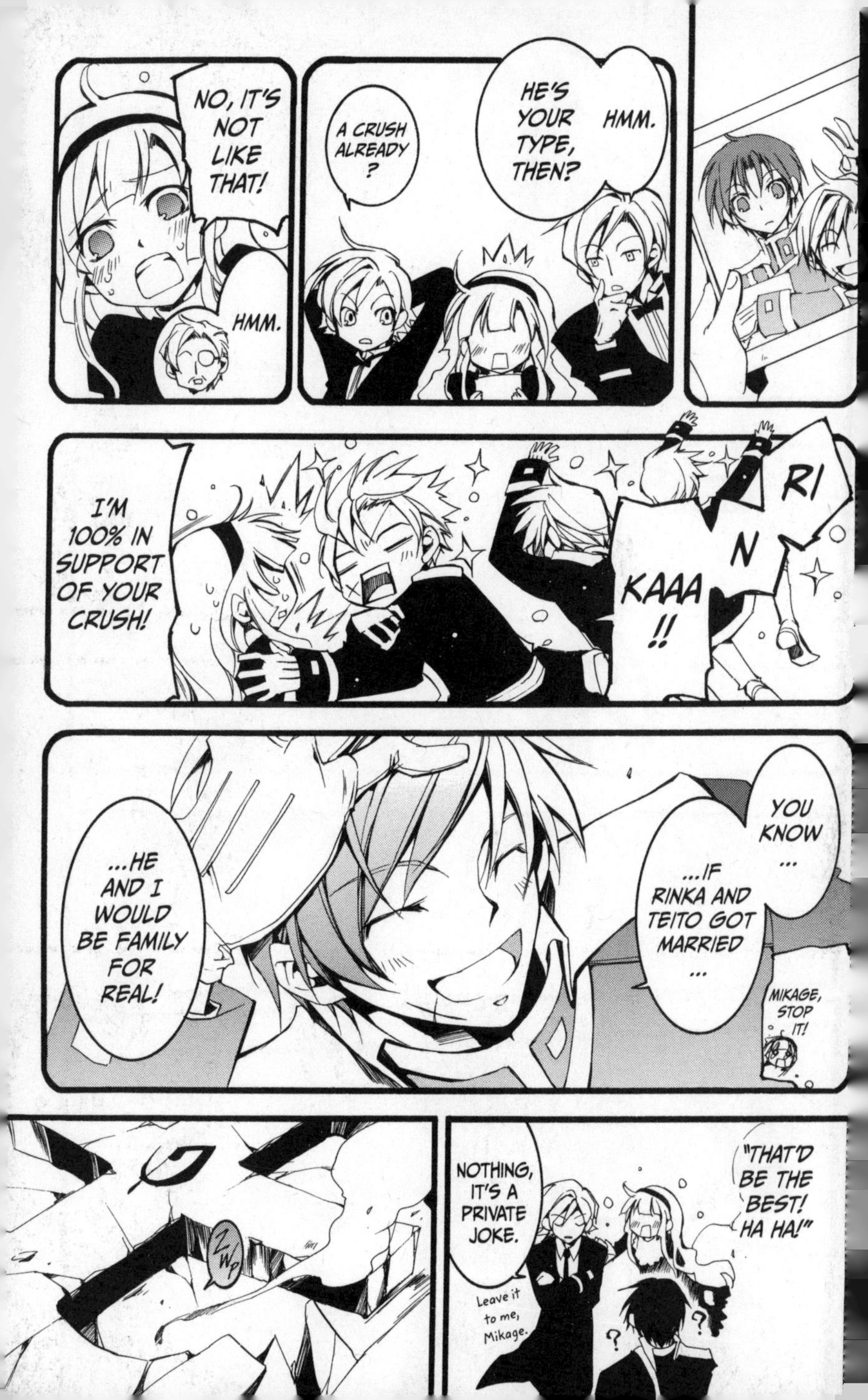
HMM.
HE'S YOUR TYPE, THEN?
A CRUSH ALREADY?
NO, IT'S NOT LIKE THAT!
HMM.
RINKAAA!!
I'M 100% IN SUPPORT OF YOUR CRUSH!
YOU KNOW...
...IF RINKA AND TEITO GOT MARRIED...
MIKAGE, STOP IT!
...HE AND I WOULD BE FAMILY FOR REAL!
"THAT'D BE THE BEST! HA HA!"
NOTHING, IT'S A PRIVATE JOKE.
Leave it to me, Mikage.
?
?
ZWP

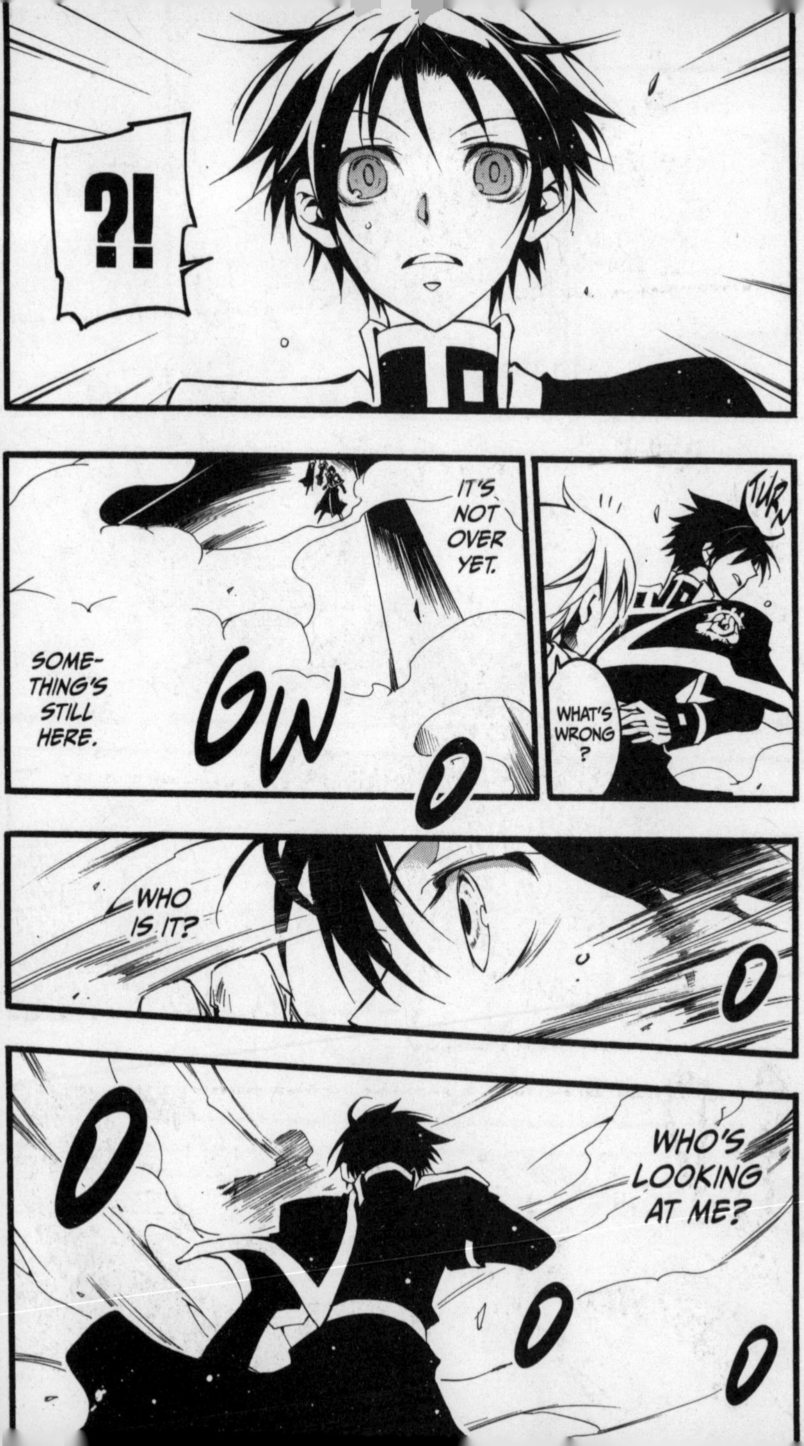
?!
TURN
WHAT'S WRONG?
IT'S NOT OVER YET.
SOME-THING'S STILL HERE.
GW
WHO IS IT?
WHO'S LOOKING AT ME?

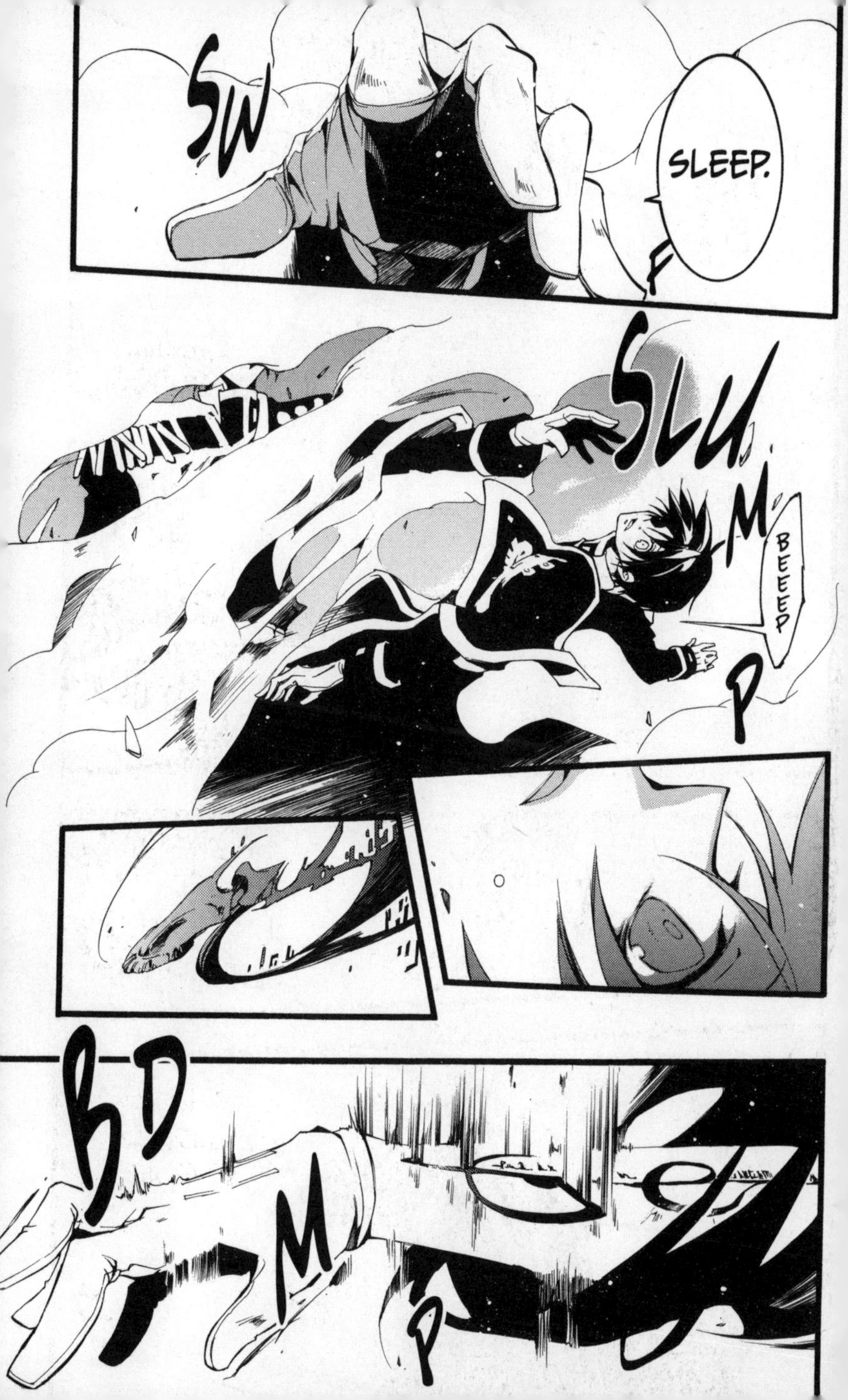
SLEEP.
F
SW
SLUMP
BEEEEP
BDMP

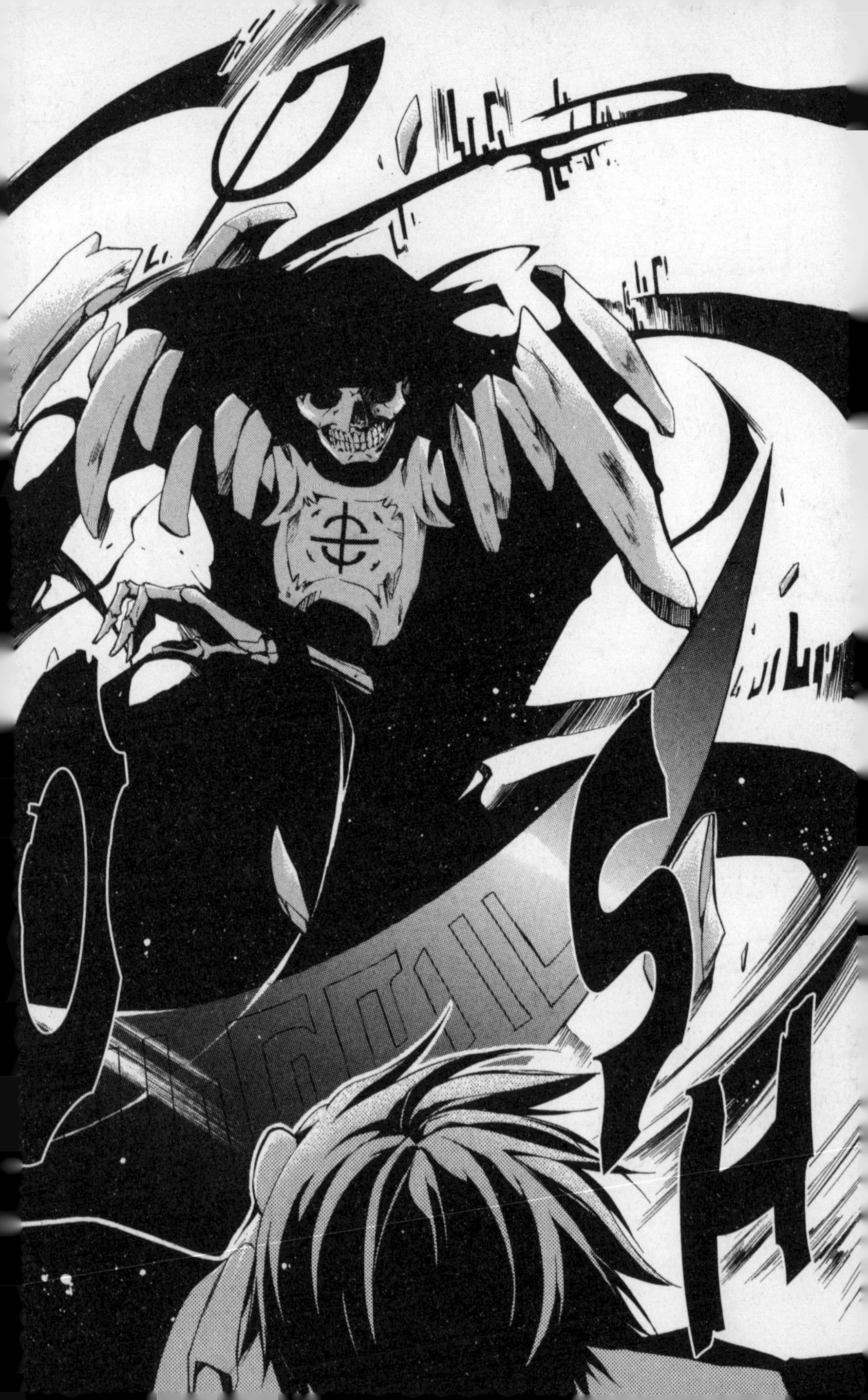

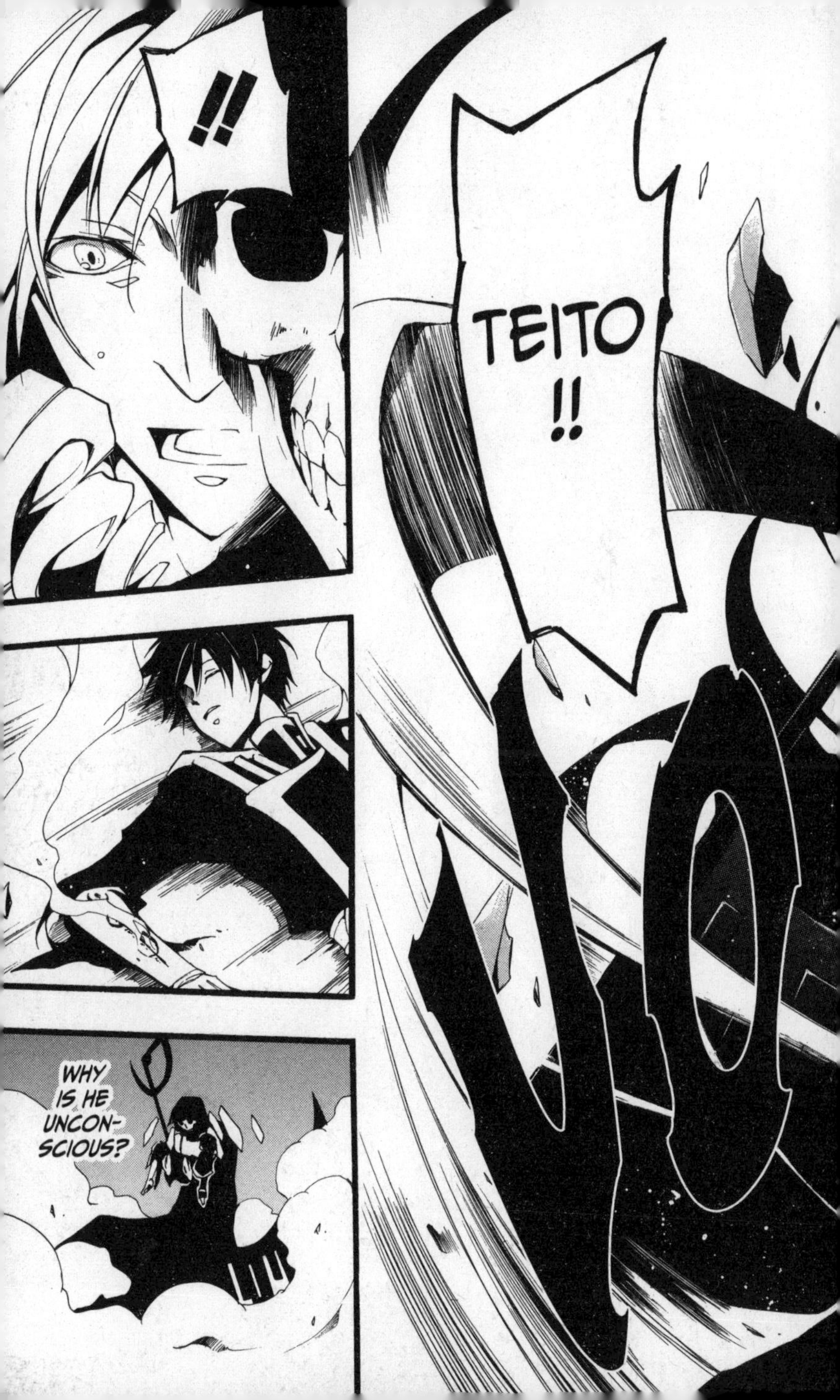
TEITO !!
!!
WHY IS HE UNCON-SCIOUS?

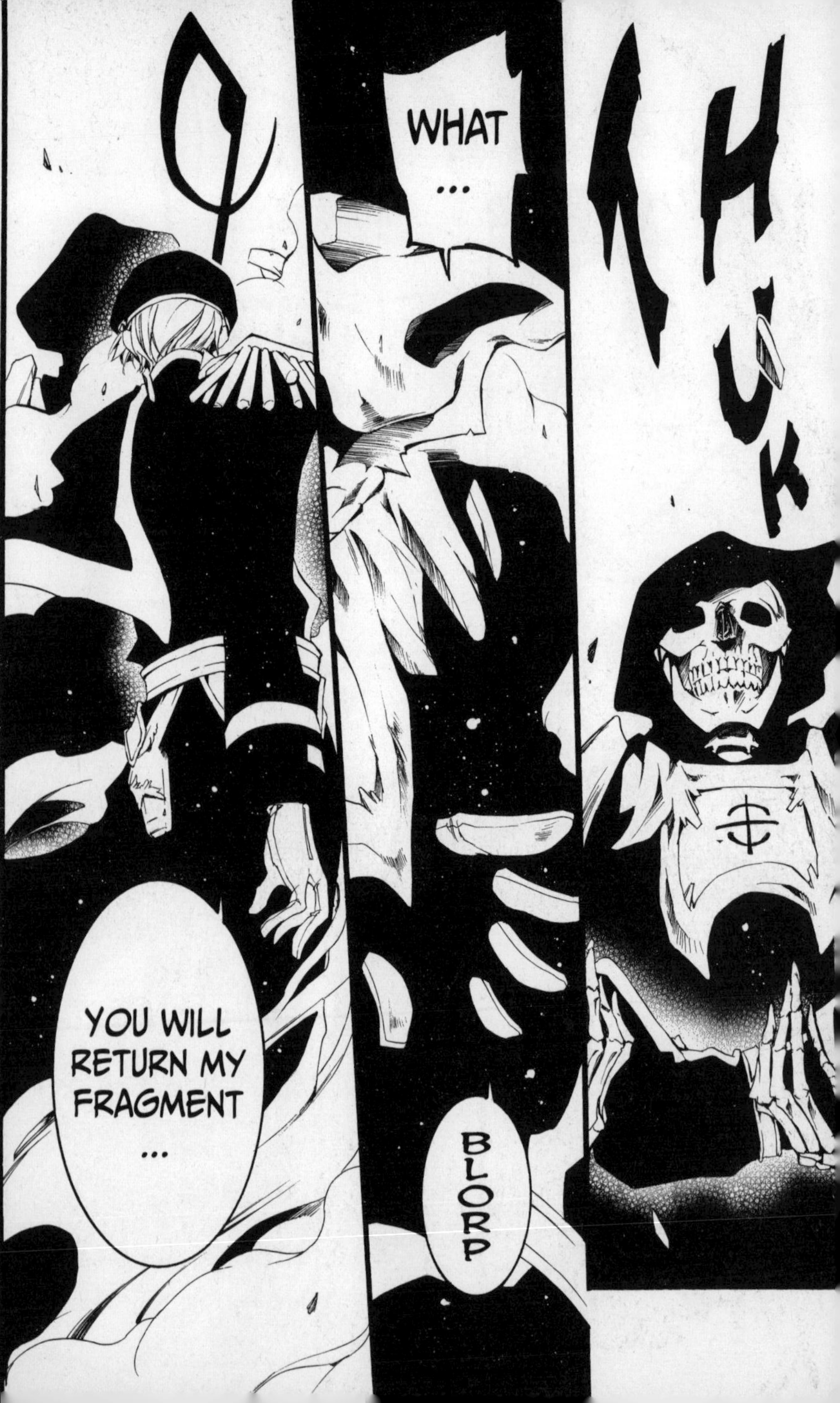
HUK
WHAT ...
BLORP
YOU WILL RETURN MY FRAGMENT ...

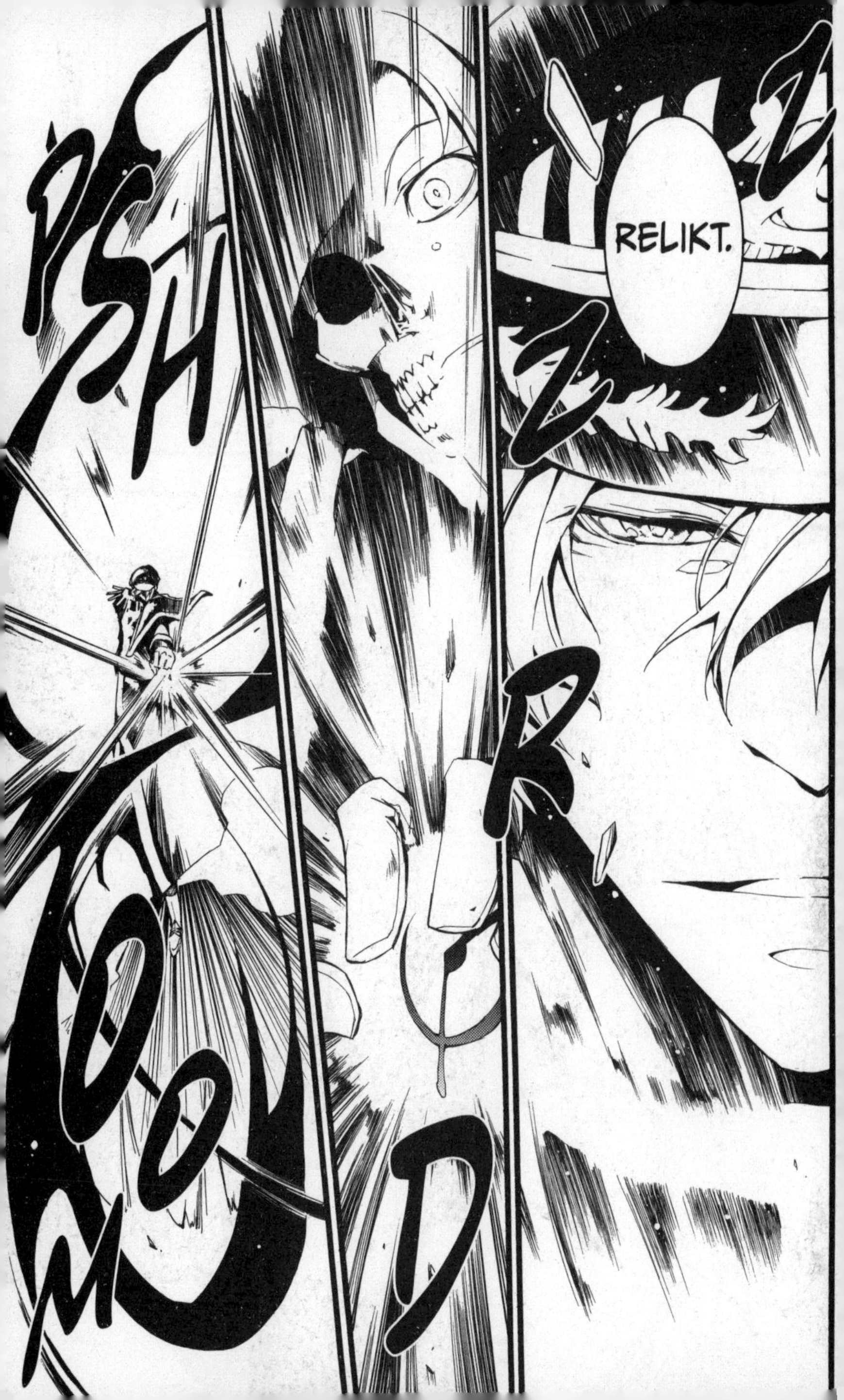
RELIKT.
PSH

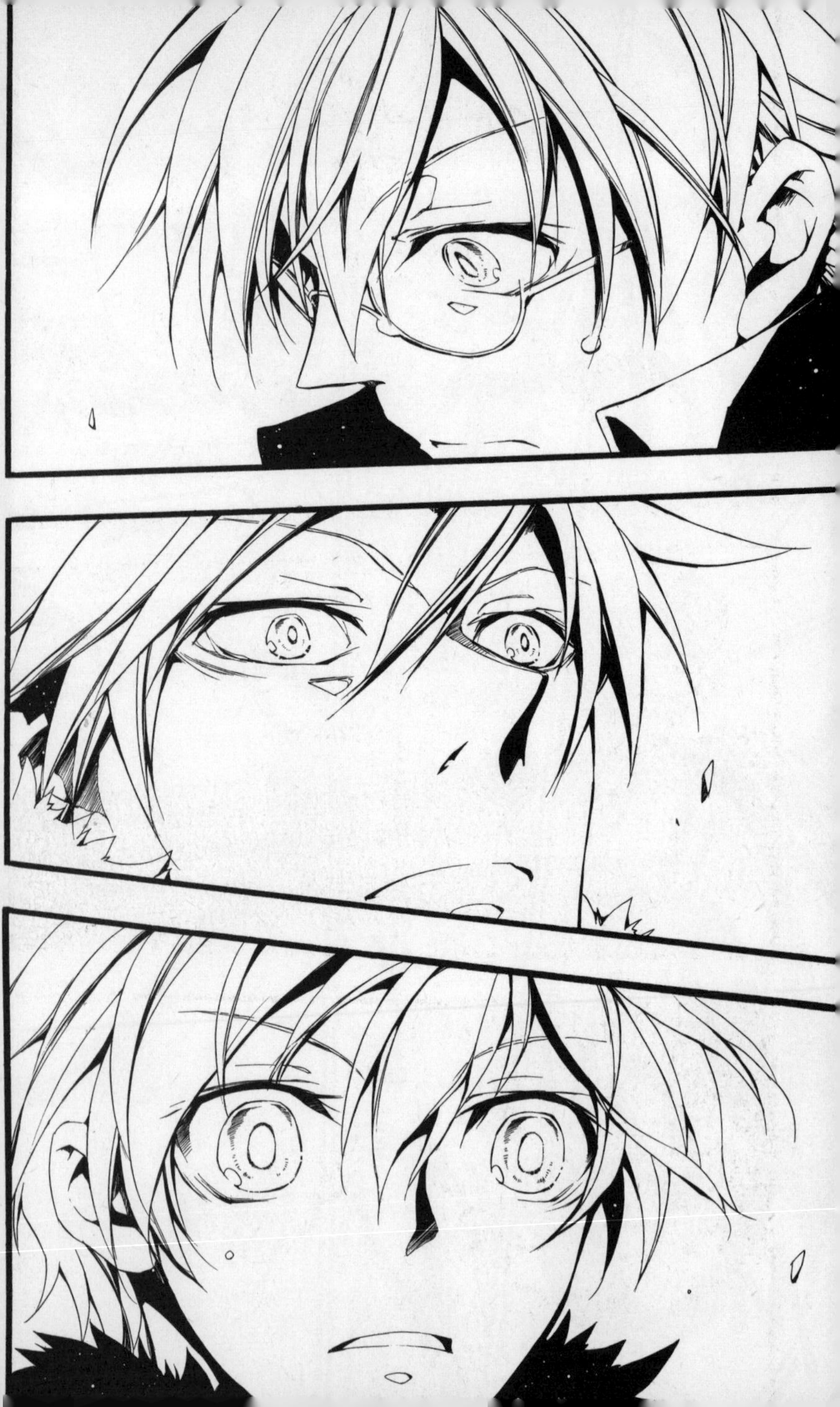

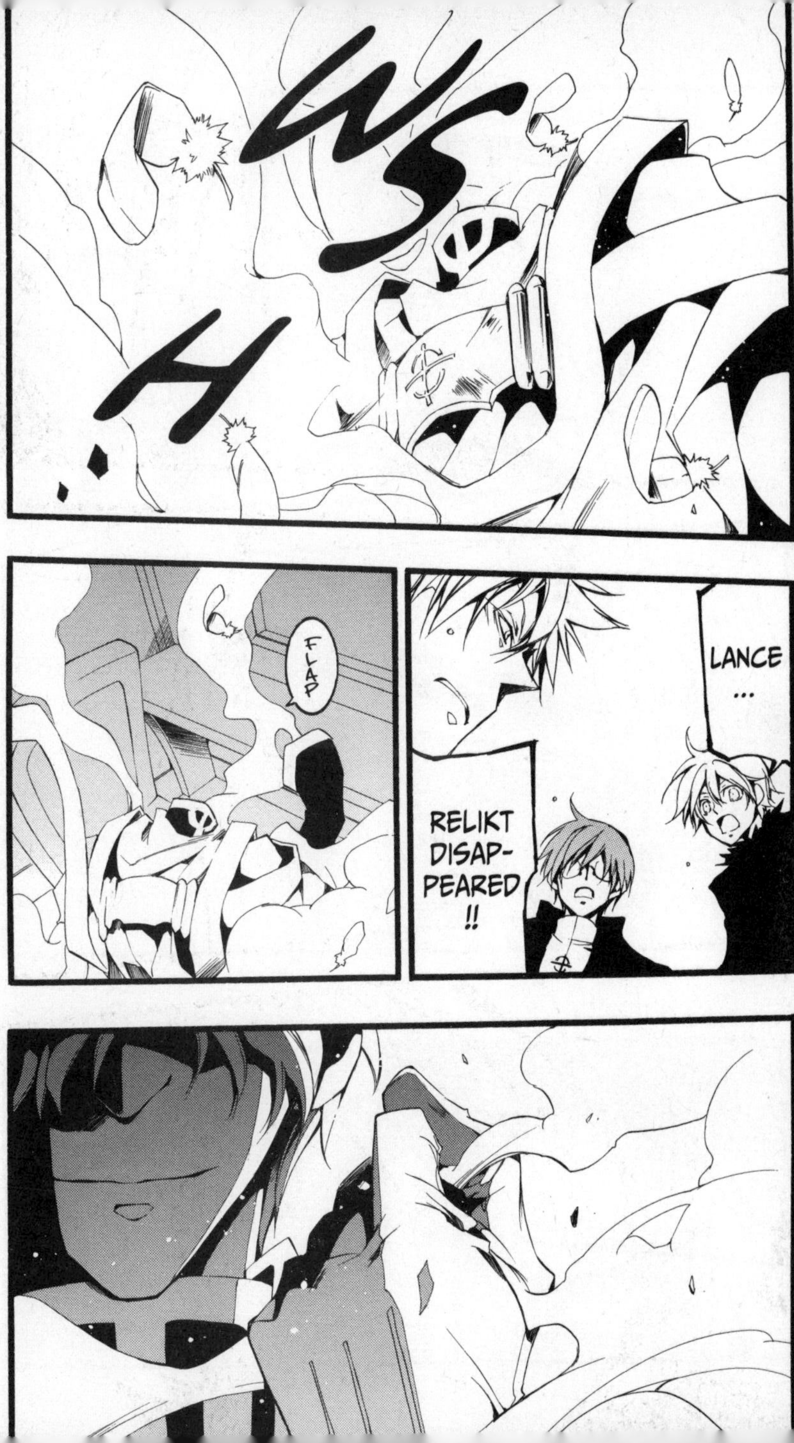
WSH
LANCE ...
RELIKT DISAP-PEARED !!
FLAP

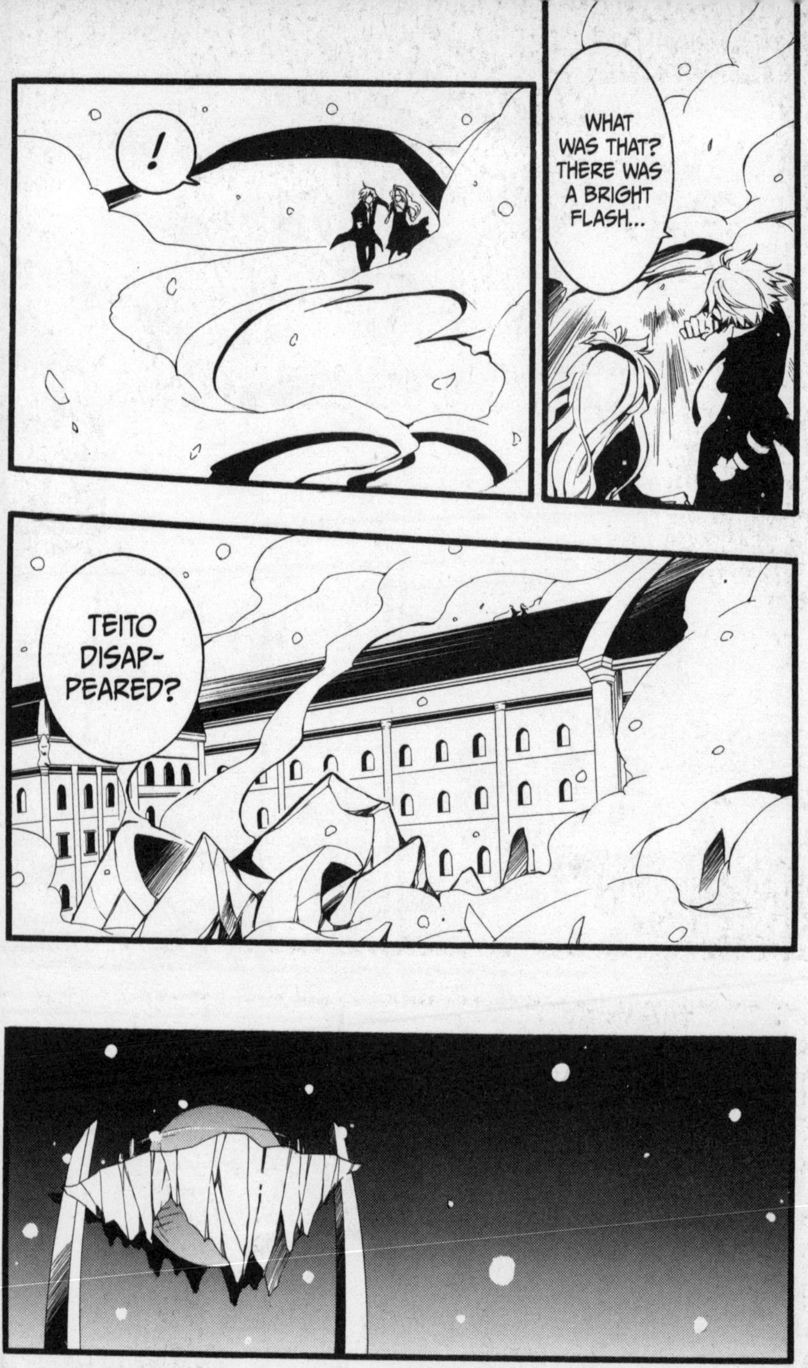
WHAT WAS THAT? THERE WAS A BRIGHT FLASH...
!
TEITO DISAP-PEARED?

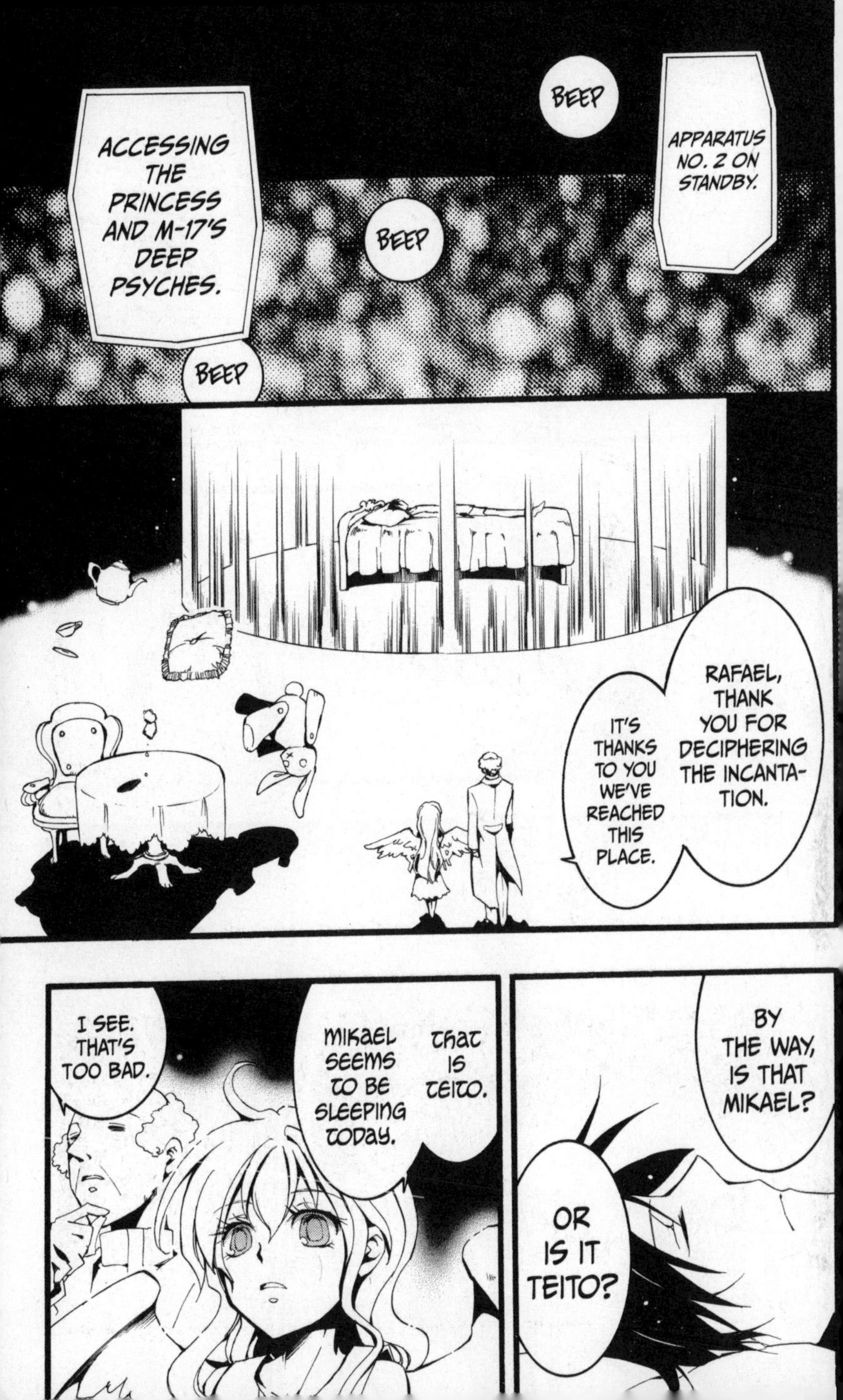
BEEP
APPARATUS NO. 2 ON STANDBY.
BEEP
ACCESSING THE PRINCESS AND M-17'S DEEP PSYCHES.
BEEP
RAFAEL, THANK YOU FOR DECIPHERING THE INCANTATION.
IT'S THANKS TO YOU WE'VE REACHED THIS PLACE.
BY THE WAY, IS THAT MIKAEL?
OR IS IT TEITO?
that is teito.
mikael seems to be sleeping today.
I SEE. THAT'S TOO BAD.

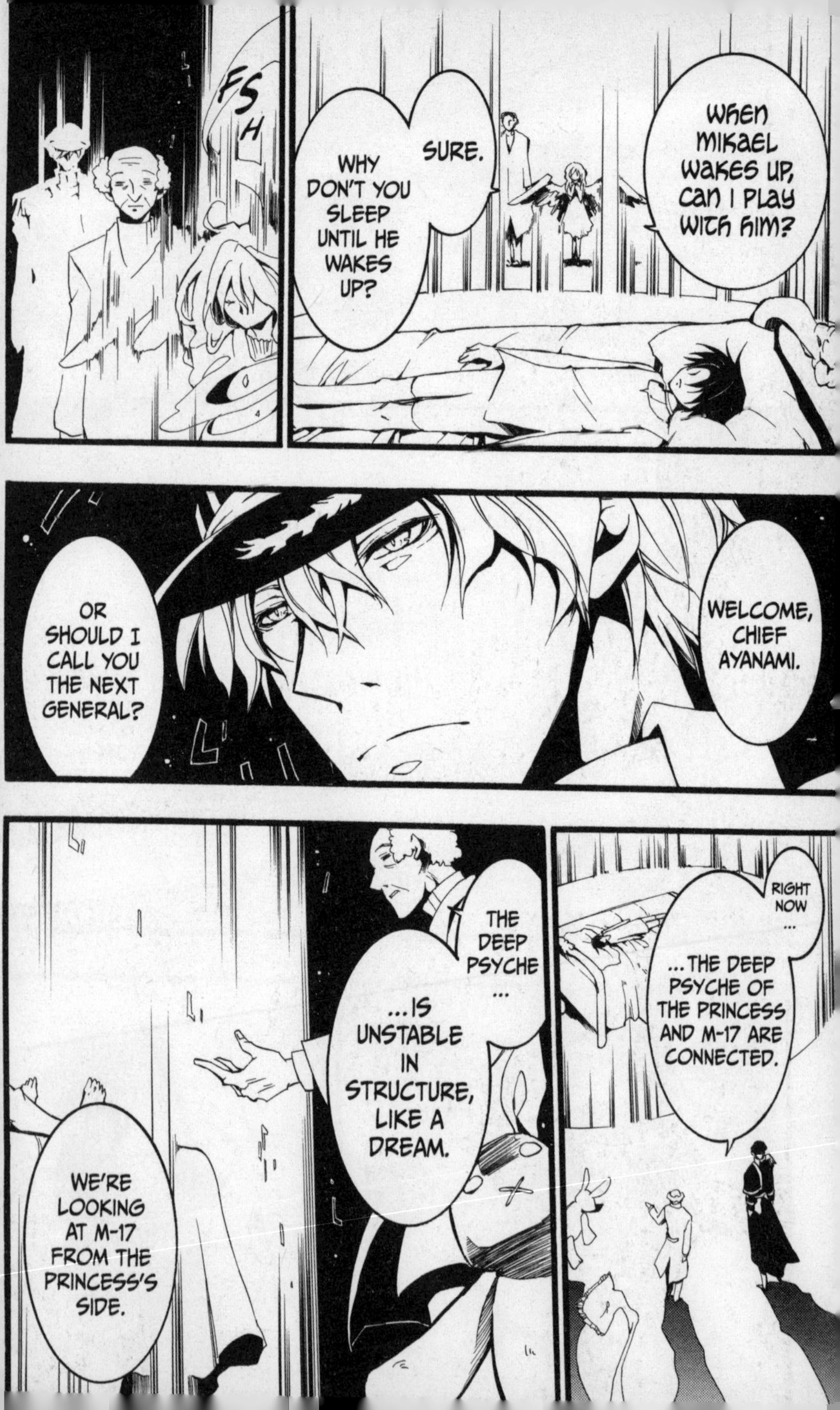
WHEN MIKAEL WAKES UP, CAN I PLAY WITH HIM?
SURE.
WHY DON'T YOU SLEEP UNTIL HE WAKES UP?
FSH
WELCOME, CHIEF AYANAMI.
OR SHOULD I CALL YOU THE NEXT GENERAL?
RIGHT NOW...
...THE DEEP PSYCHE OF THE PRINCESS AND M-17 ARE CONNECTED.
THE DEEP PSYCHE...
...IS UNSTABLE IN STRUCTURE, LIKE A DREAM.
WE'RE LOOKING AT M-17 FROM THE PRINCESS'S SIDE.

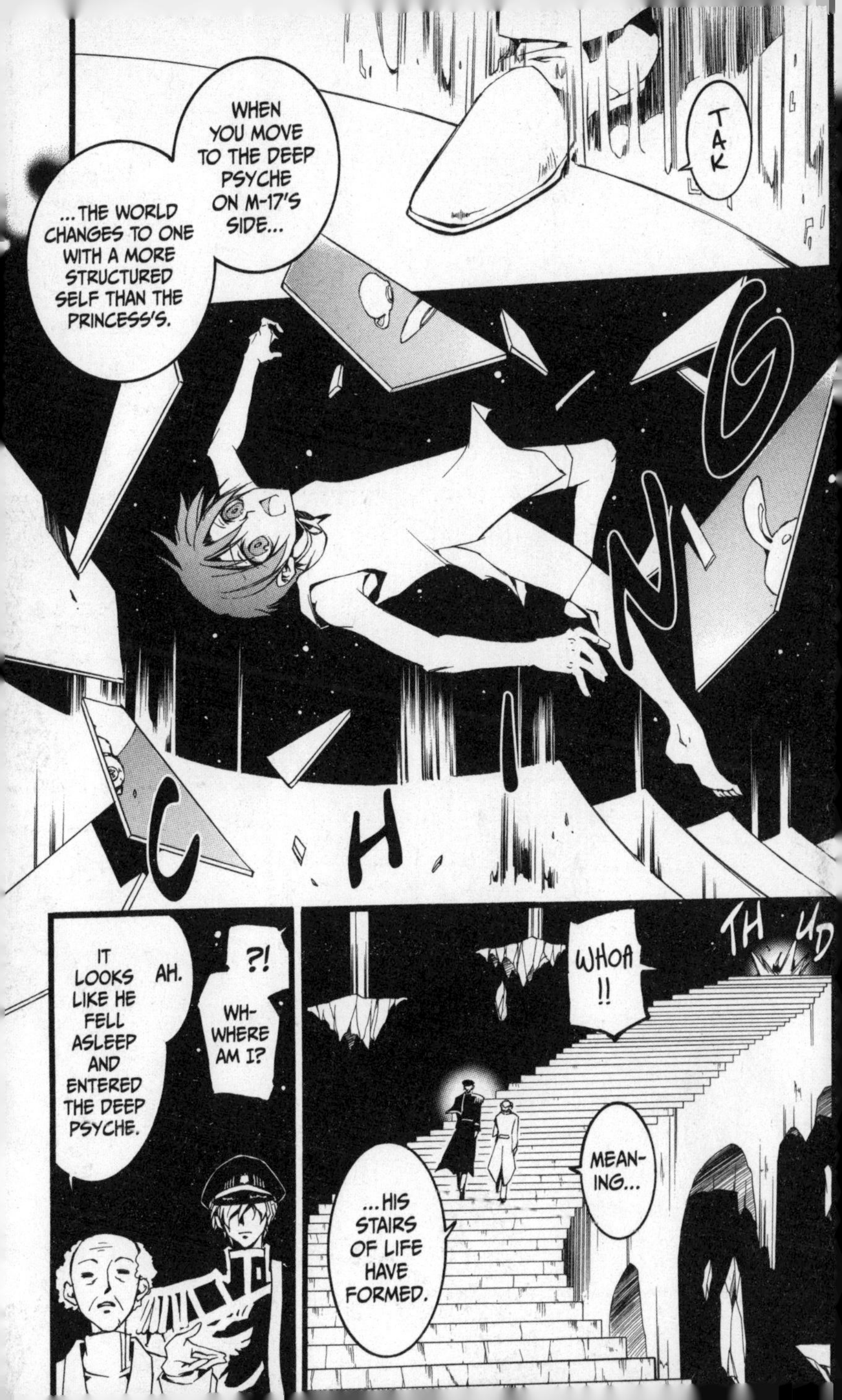

TAK
WHEN YOU MOVE TO THE DEEP PSYCHE ON M-17'S SIDE...
...THE WORLD CHANGES TO ONE WITH A MORE STRUCTURED SELF THAN THE PRINCESS'S.
CHING
THUD
WHOA !!
MEANING...
...HIS STAIRS OF LIFE HAVE FORMED.
?!
WH- WHERE AM I?
AH.
IT LOOKS LIKE HE FELL ASLEEP AND ENTERED THE DEEP PSYCHE.

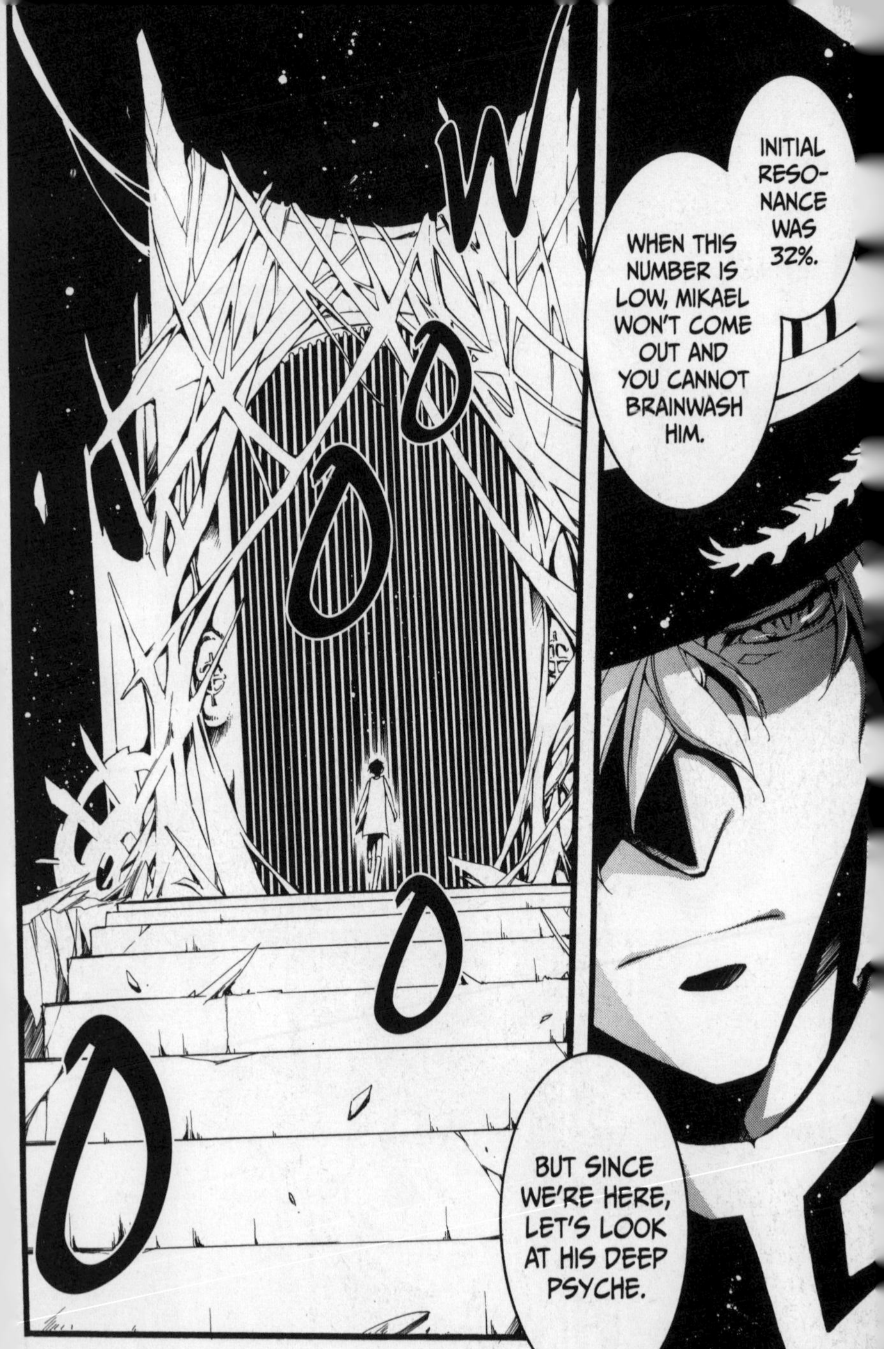
INITIAL RESO-NANCE WAS 32%.
WHEN THIS NUMBER IS LOW, MIKAEL WON'T COME OUT AND YOU CANNOT BRAINWASH HIM.
BUT SINCE WE'RE HERE, LET'S LOOK AT HIS DEEP PSYCHE.

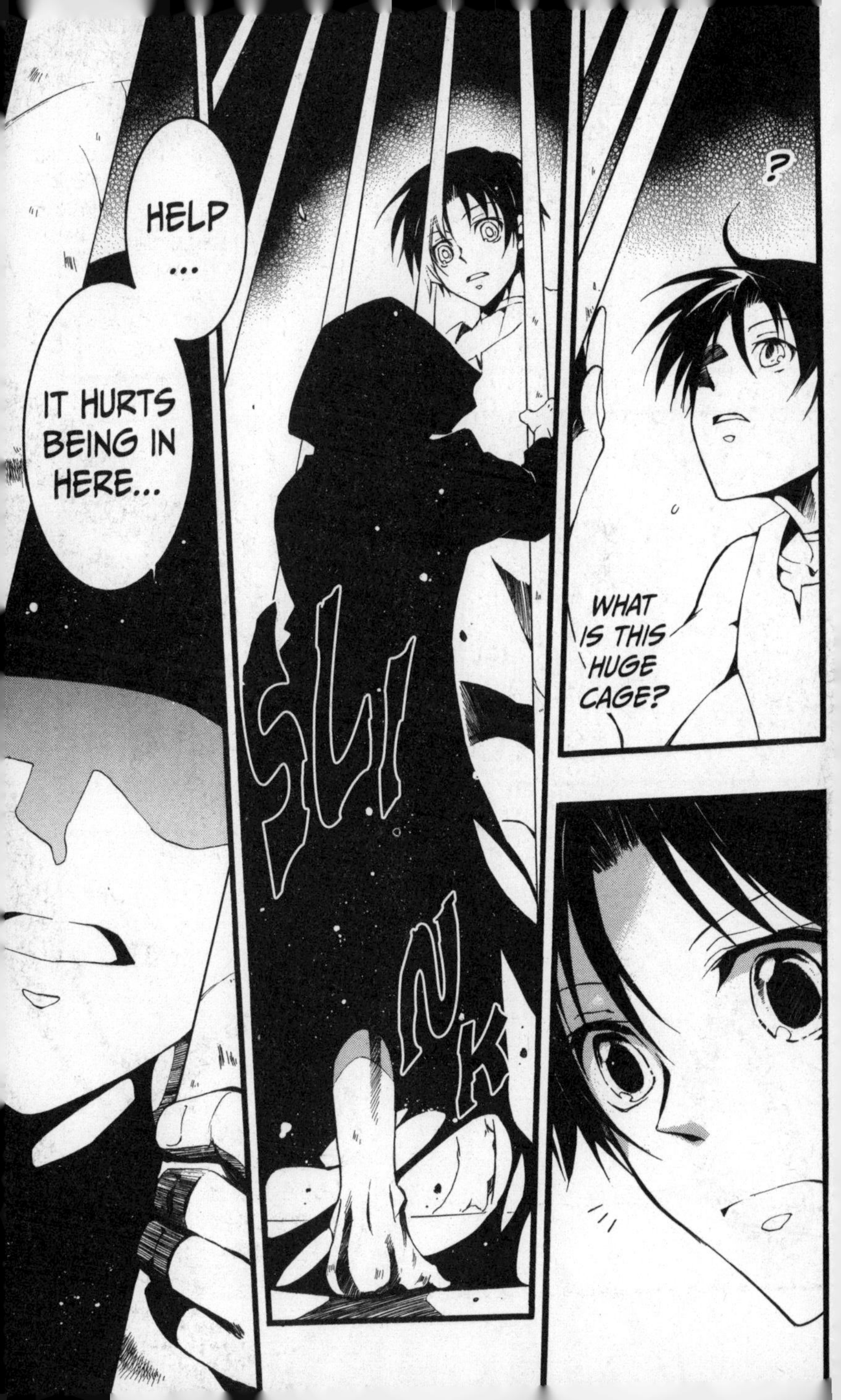
?
WHAT IS THIS HUGE CAGE?
SLINK
HELP...
IT HURTS BEING IN HERE...

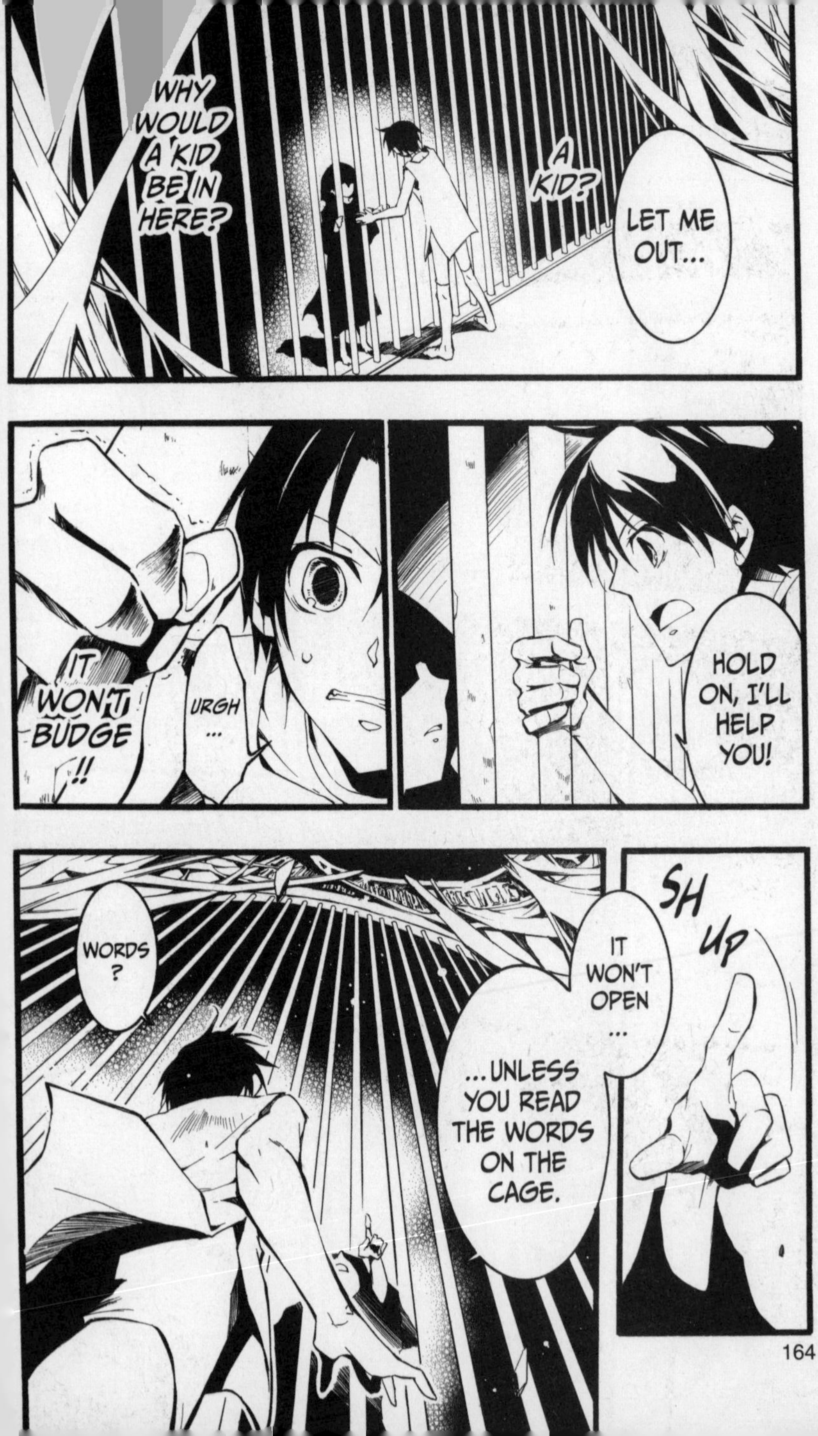
LET ME OUT...
A KID?
WHY WOULD A KID BE IN HERE?
HOLD ON, I'LL HELP YOU!
URGH ...
IT WON'T BUDGE!!
SH UP
IT WON'T OPEN ...
...UNLESS YOU READ THE WORDS ON THE CAGE.
WORDS ?

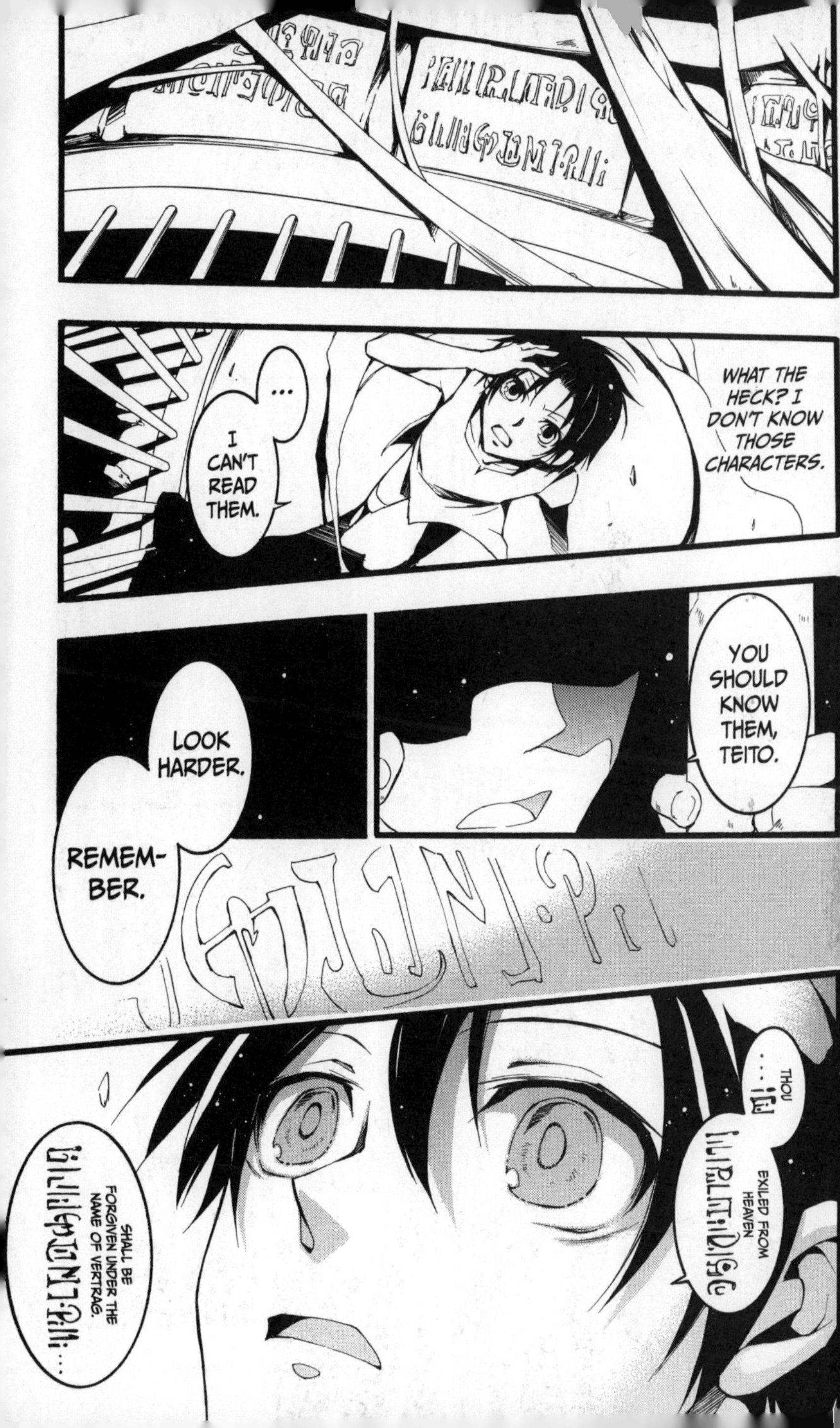
WHAT THE HECK? I DON'T KNOW THOSE CHARACTERS.
... I CAN'T READ THEM.
YOU SHOULD KNOW THEM, TEITO.
LOOK HARDER.
REMEMBER.
...THOU EXILED FROM HEAVEN
SHALL BE FORGIVEN UNDER THE NAME OF VERTRAG.

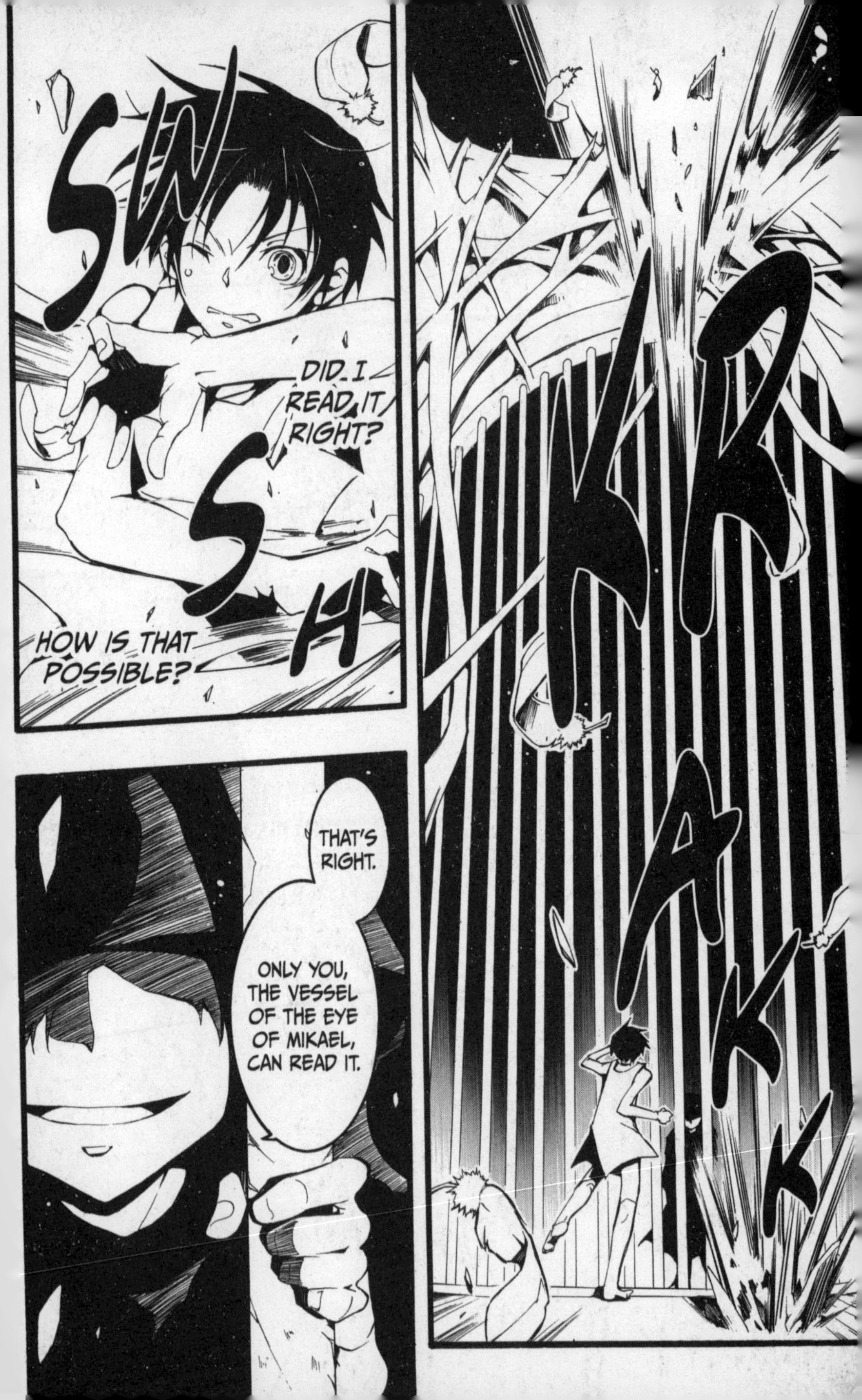
KRAKK
DID I READ IT RIGHT?
HOW IS THAT POSSIBLE?
THAT'S RIGHT.
ONLY YOU, THE VESSEL OF THE EYE OF MIKAEL, CAN READ IT.

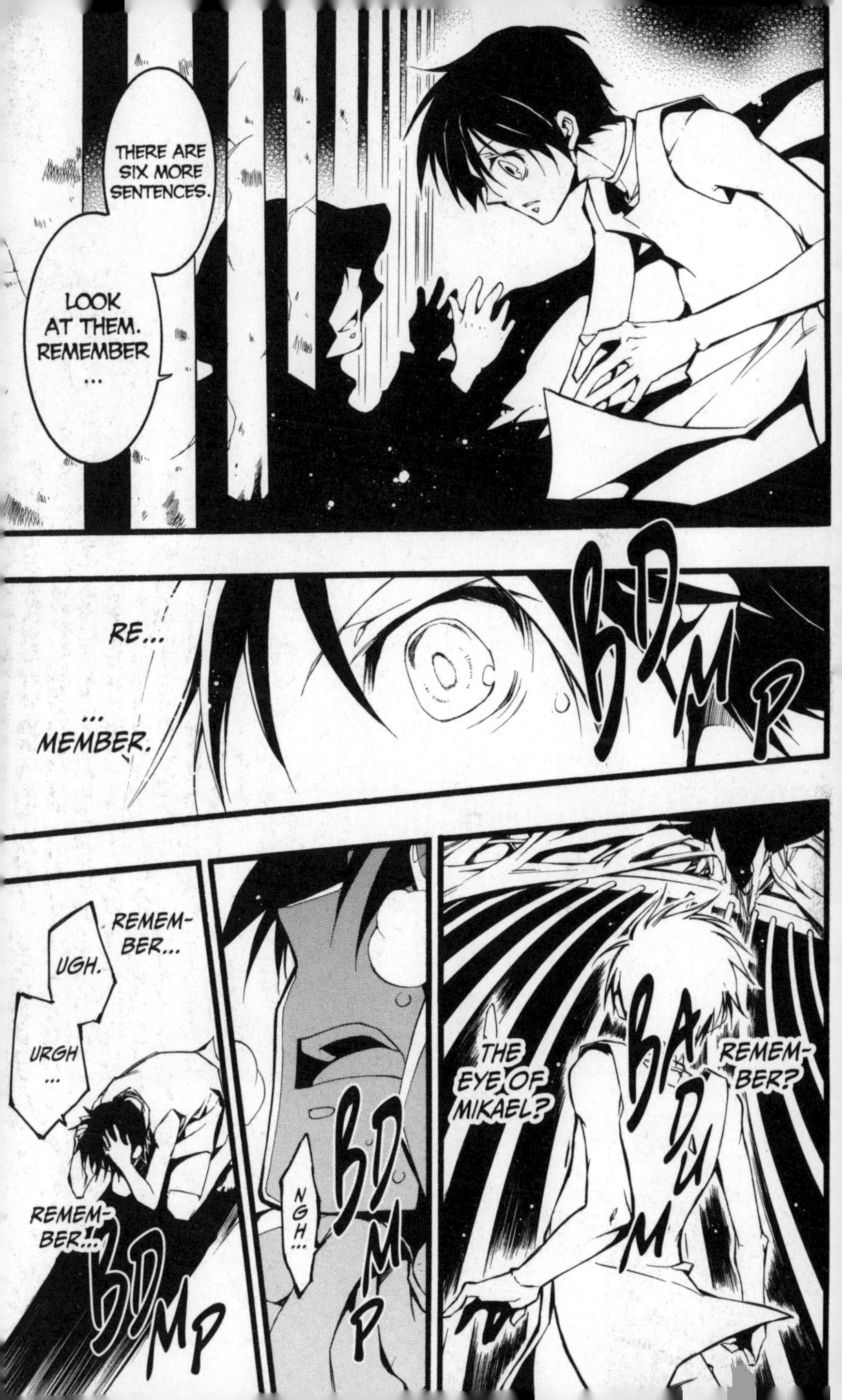

THERE ARE SIX MORE SENTENCES.
LOOK AT THEM. REMEMBER ...
BDMP
RE...
... MEMBER.
REMEM-BER?
BADUM
THE EYE OF MIKAEL?
BDMP
NGH...
REMEM-BER...
UGH.
URGH ...
REMEM-BER...
BDMP

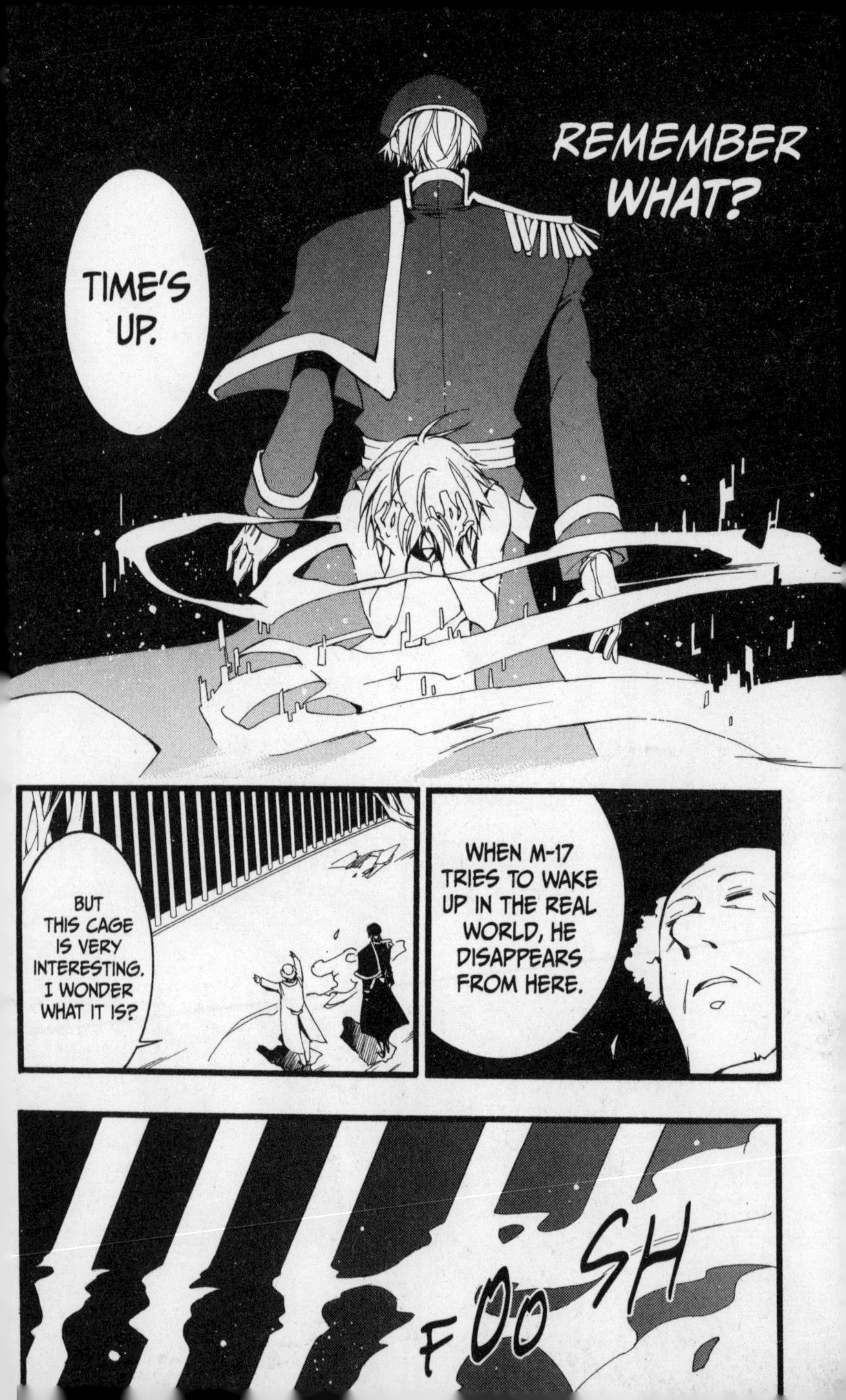
REMEMBER WHAT?
TIME'S UP.
WHEN M-17 TRIES TO WAKE UP IN THE REAL WORLD, HE DISAPPEARS FROM HERE.
BUT THIS CAGE IS VERY INTERESTING. I WONDER WHAT IT IS?
F OO SH

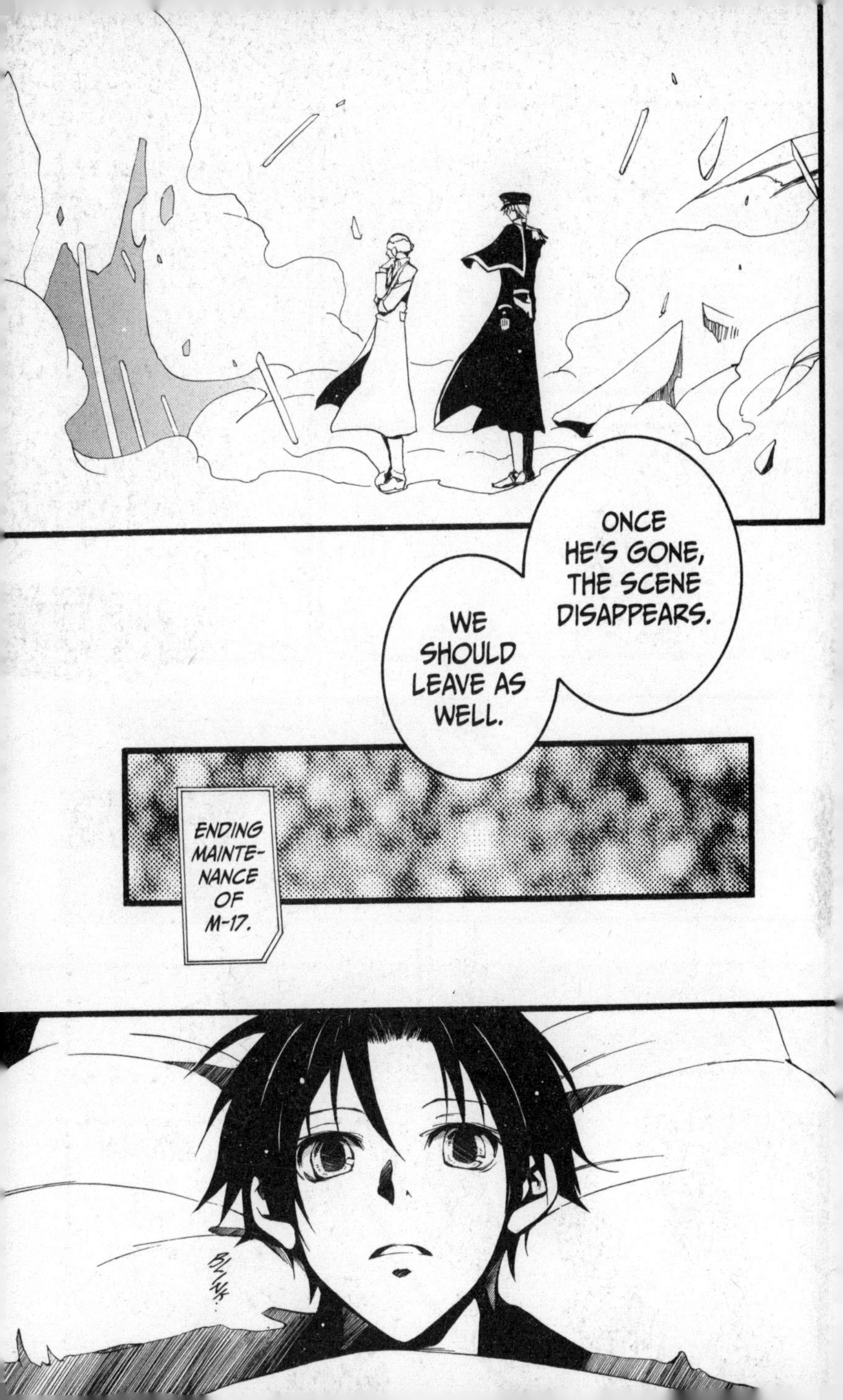
ONCE HE'S GONE, THE SCENE DISAPPEARS.
WE SHOULD LEAVE AS WELL.
ENDING MAINTE-NANCE OF M-17.
BLINK.

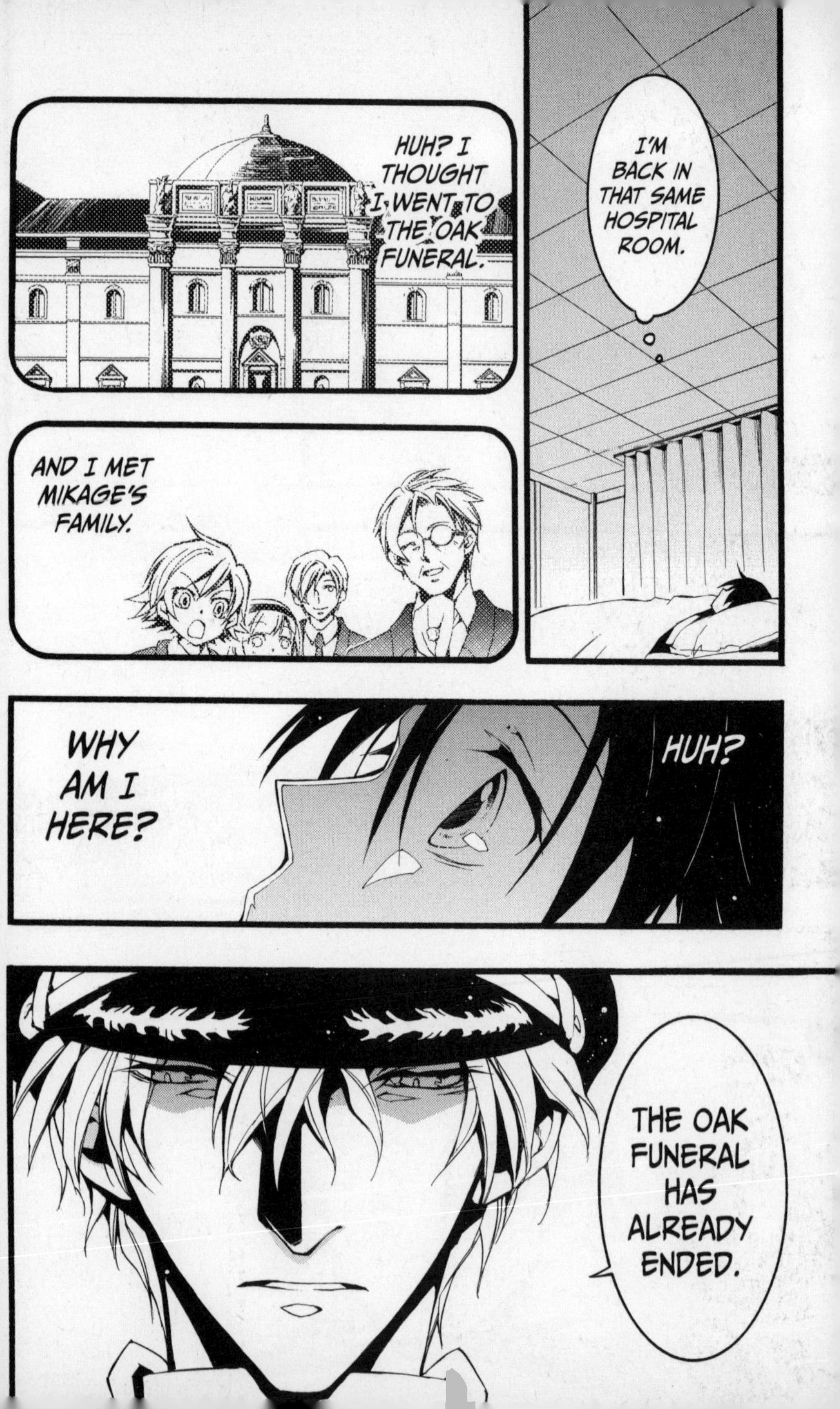
I'M BACK IN THAT SAME HOSPITAL ROOM.
HUH? I THOUGHT I WENT TO THE OAK FUNERAL.
AND I MET MIKAGE'S FAMILY.
HUH?
WHY AM I HERE?
THE OAK FUNERAL HAS ALREADY ENDED.

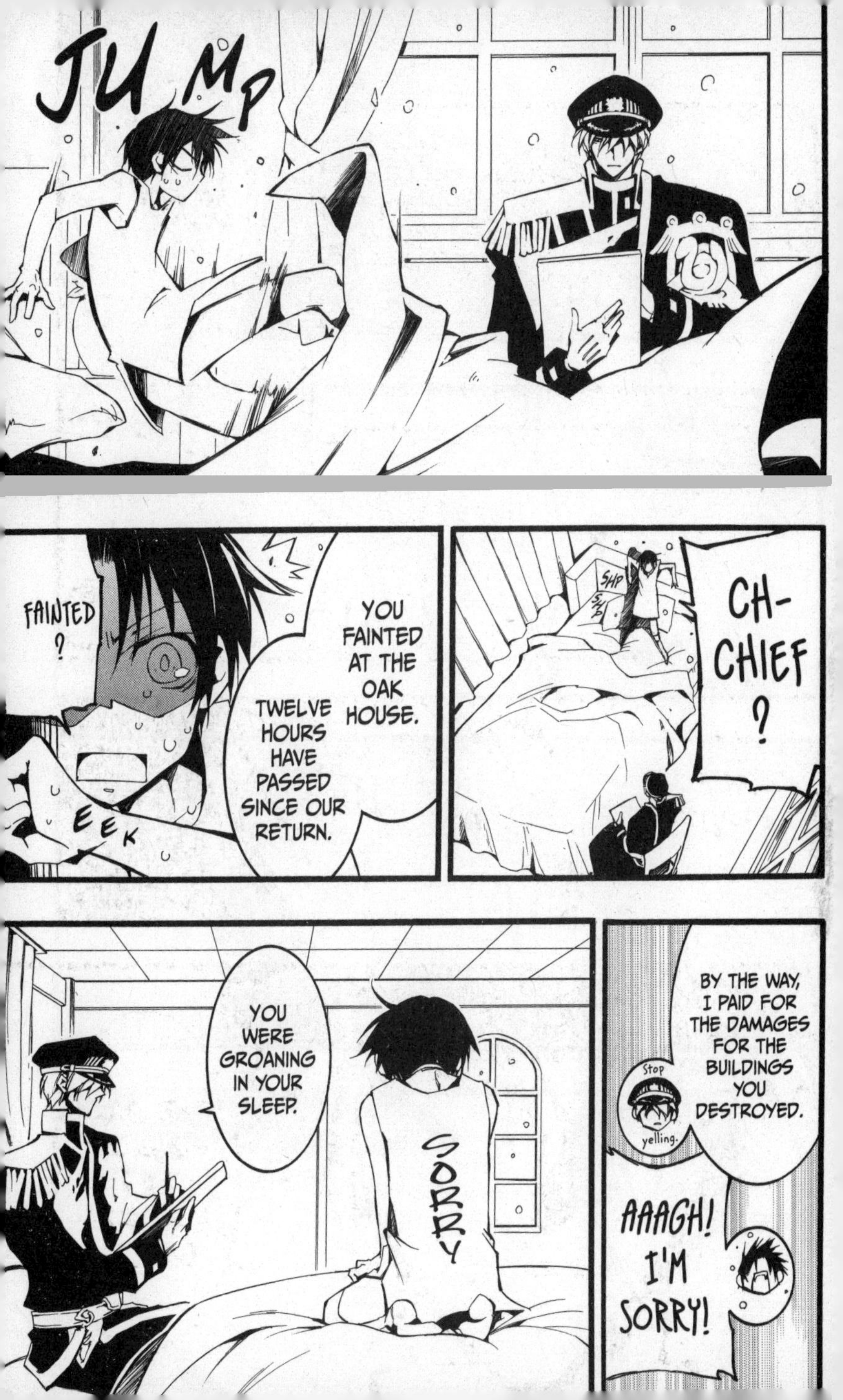

JUMP
SHP
SHP
CH-CHIEF?
YOU FAINTED AT THE OAK HOUSE.
TWELVE HOURS HAVE PASSED SINCE OUR RETURN.
FAINTED?
EEK
BY THE WAY, I PAID FOR THE DAMAGES FOR THE BUILDINGS YOU DESTROYED.
Stop yelling.
AAAGH! I'M SORRY!
YOU WERE GROANING IN YOUR SLEEP.
SORRY

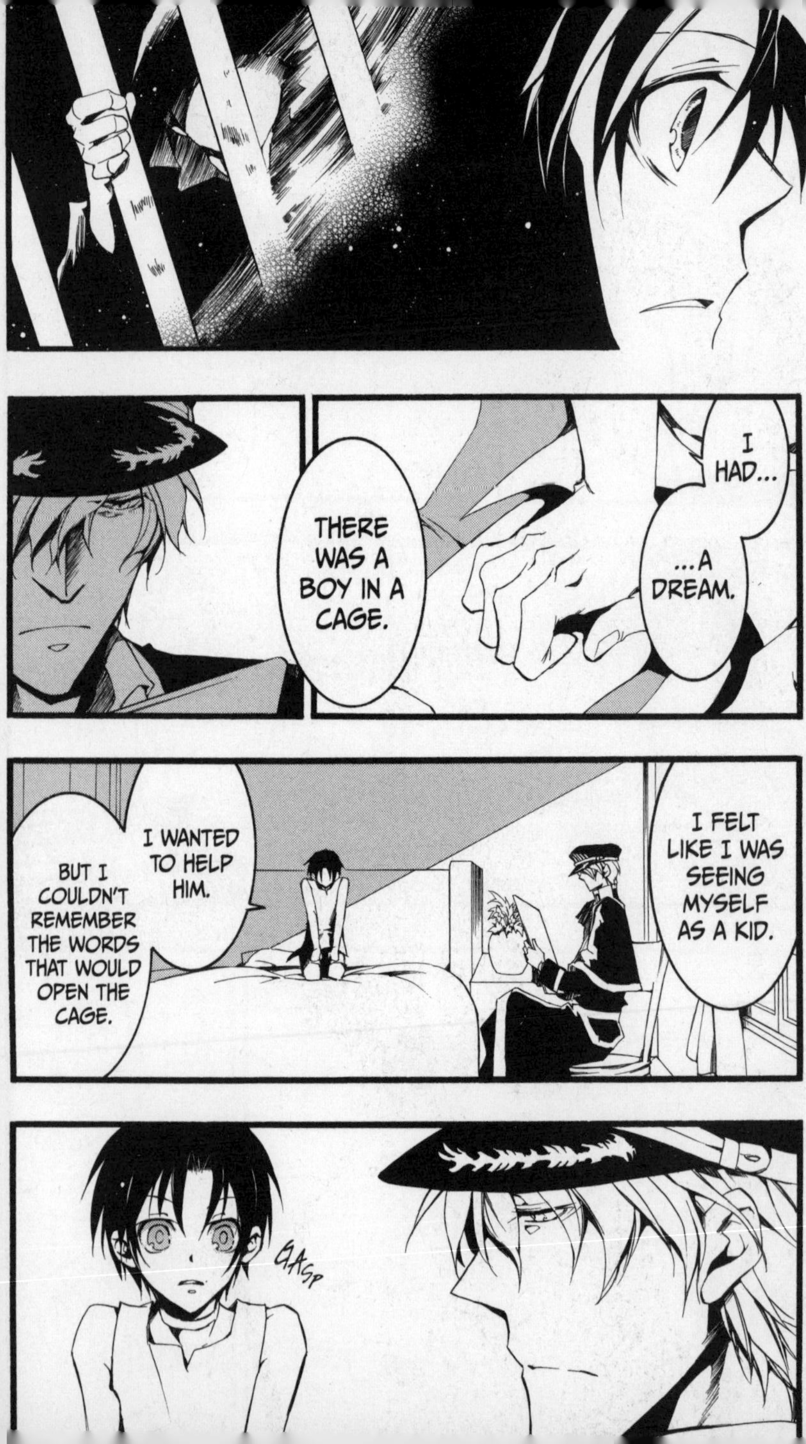
I HAD...
...A DREAM.
THERE WAS A BOY IN A CAGE.
I FELT LIKE I WAS SEEING MYSELF AS A KID.
I WANTED TO HELP HIM.
BUT I COULDN'T REMEMBER THE WORDS THAT WOULD OPEN THE CAGE.
GASP

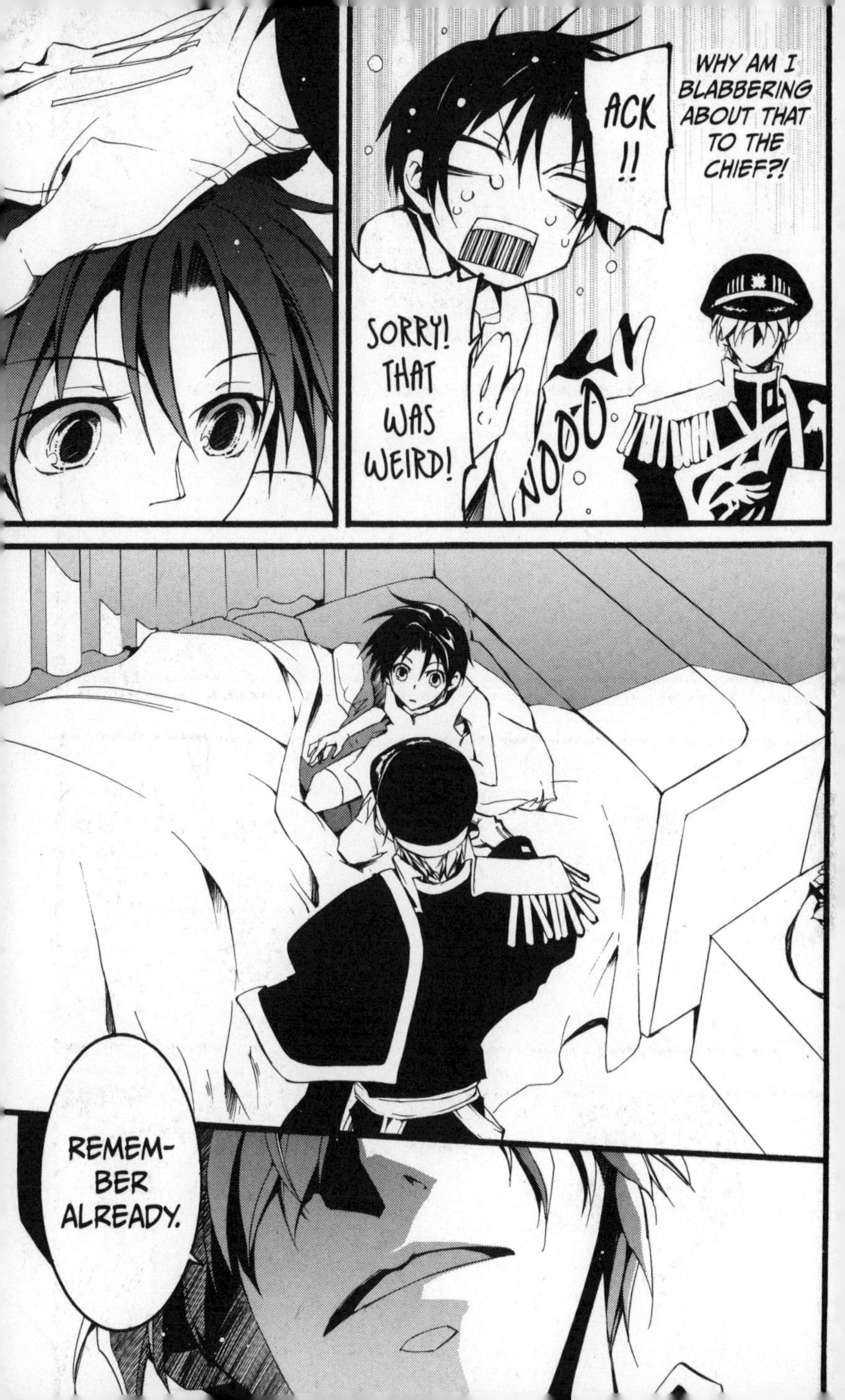
WHY AM I BLABBERING ABOUT THAT TO THE CHIEF?!
ACK !!
SORRY! THAT WAS WEIRD!
NOOO
REMEM-BER ALREADY.

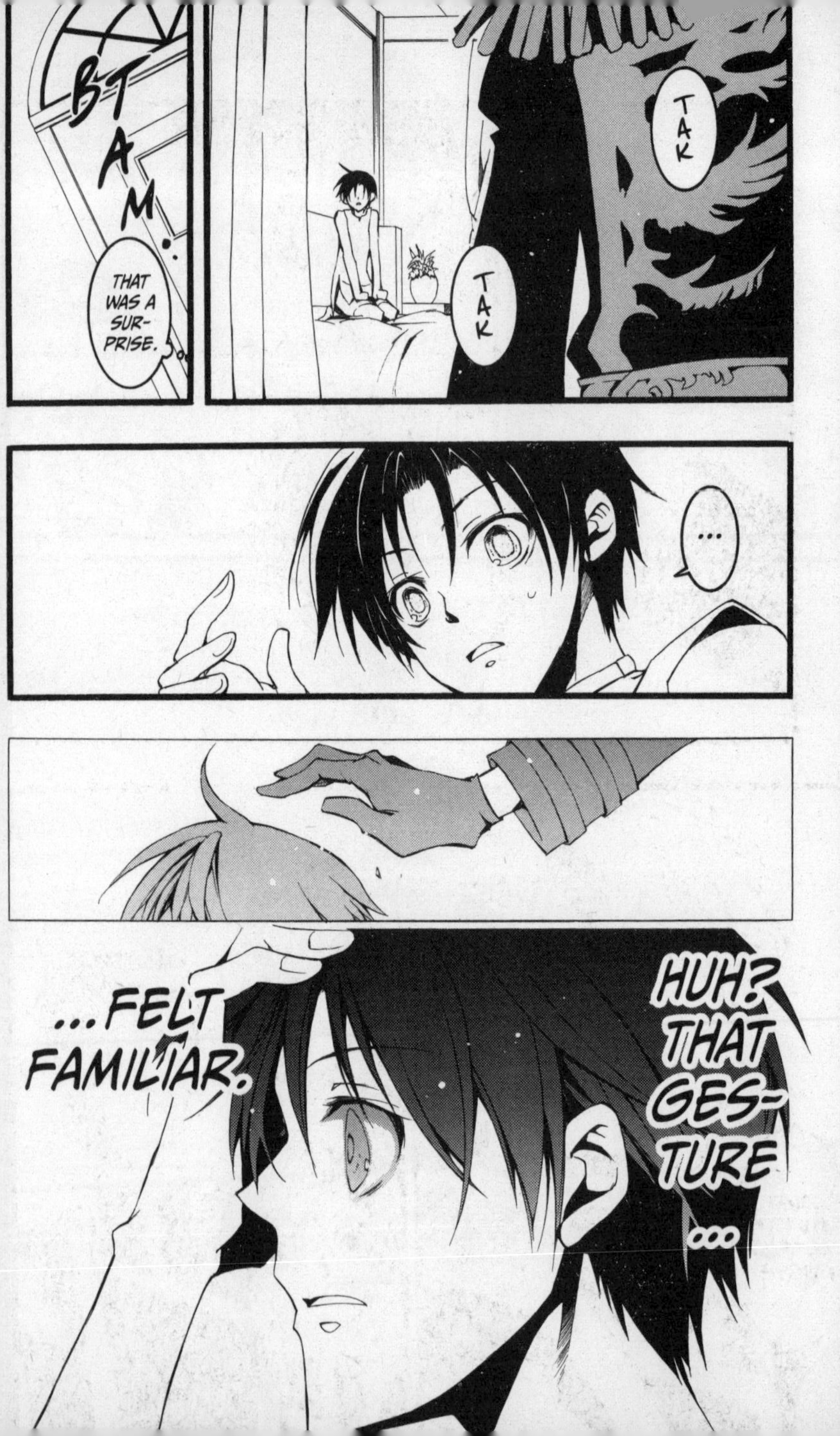
TAK
TAK
BTAM
THAT WAS A SUR-PRISE.
...
HUH? THAT GES-TURE...
...FELT FAMILIAR.

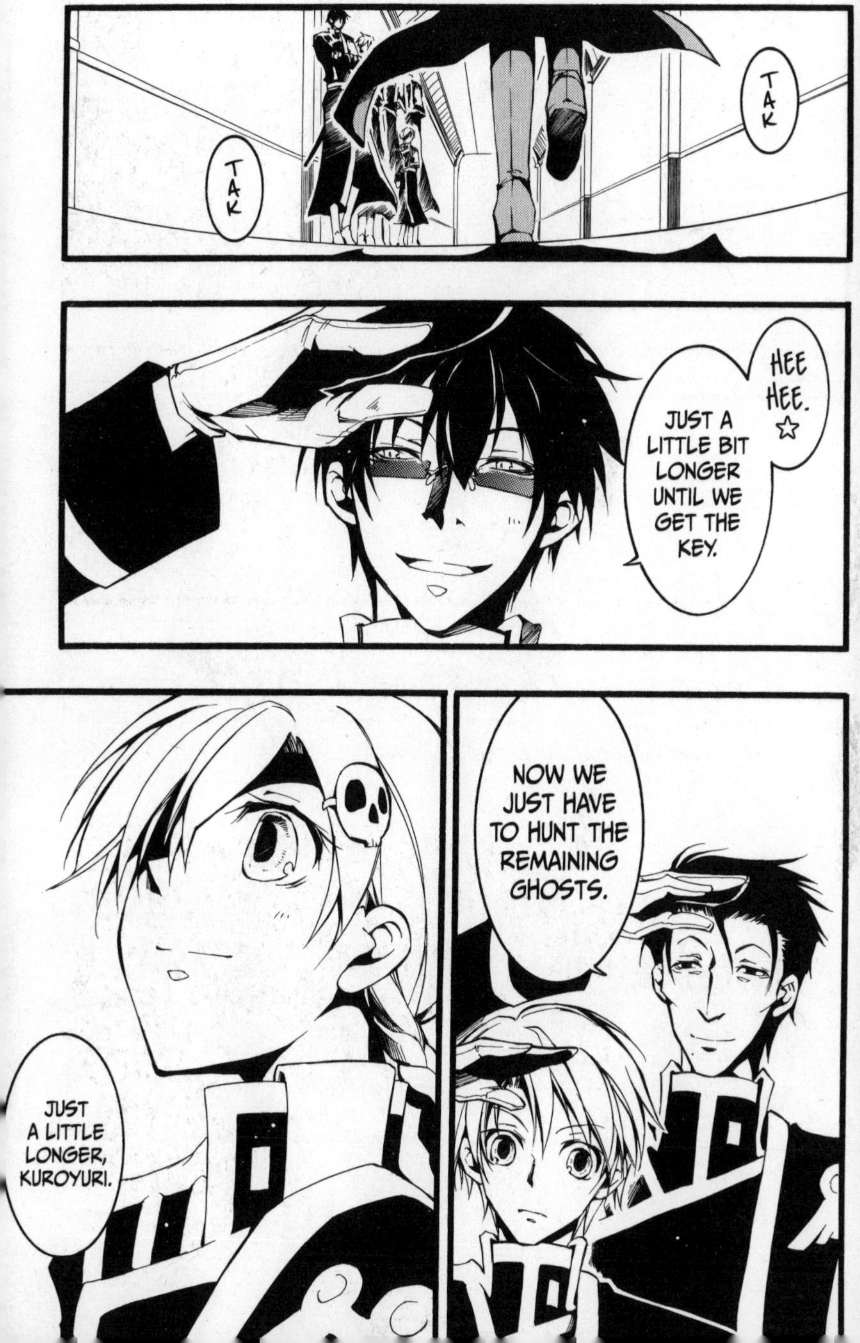
TAK
TAK
HEE HEE. ☆
JUST A LITTLE BIT LONGER UNTIL WE GET THE KEY.
NOW WE JUST HAVE TO HUNT THE REMAINING GHOSTS.
JUST A LITTLE LONGER, KUROYURI.

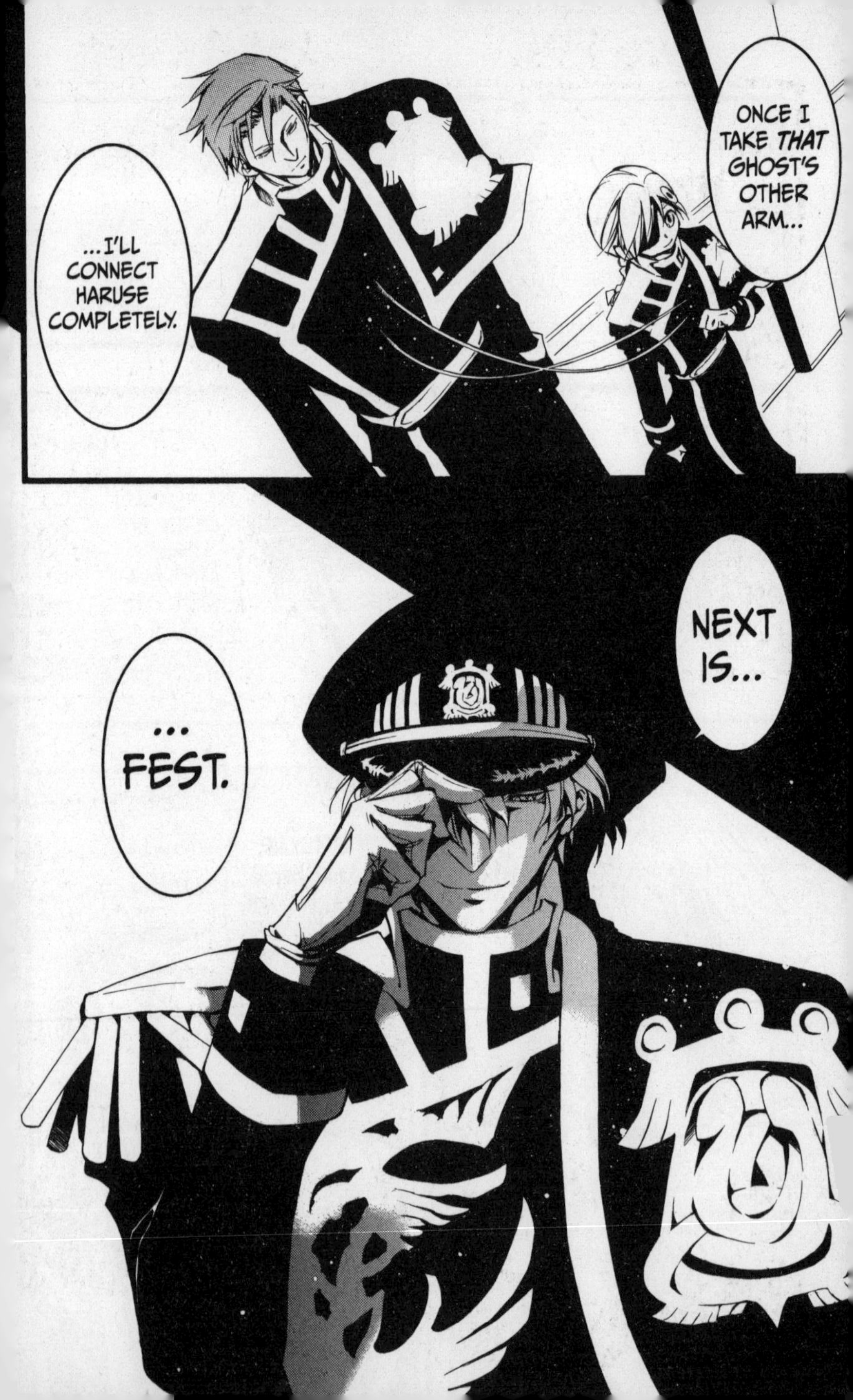
ONCE I TAKE *THAT* GHOST'S OTHER ARM...
...I'LL CONNECT HARUSE COMPLETELY.
NEXT IS...
... FEST.

Anti Sweets

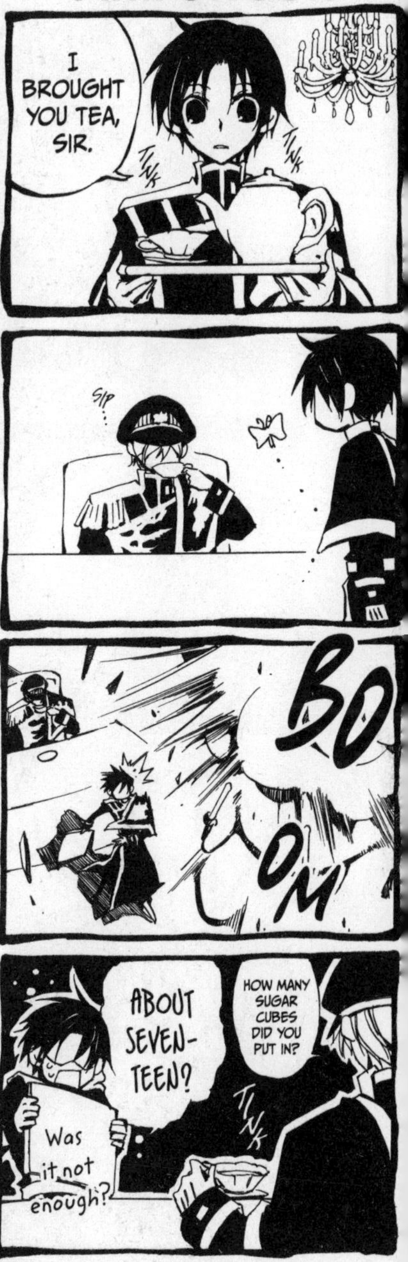
I BROUGHT YOU TEA, SIR.
TINK
TINK
SIP
BOOM
HOW MANY SUGAR CUBES DID YOU PUT IN?
ABOUT SEVEN-TEEN?
Was it not enough?
TINK

Buildings at Oak House + chandelier
Total = 34,000,000 yus

Two Hits!

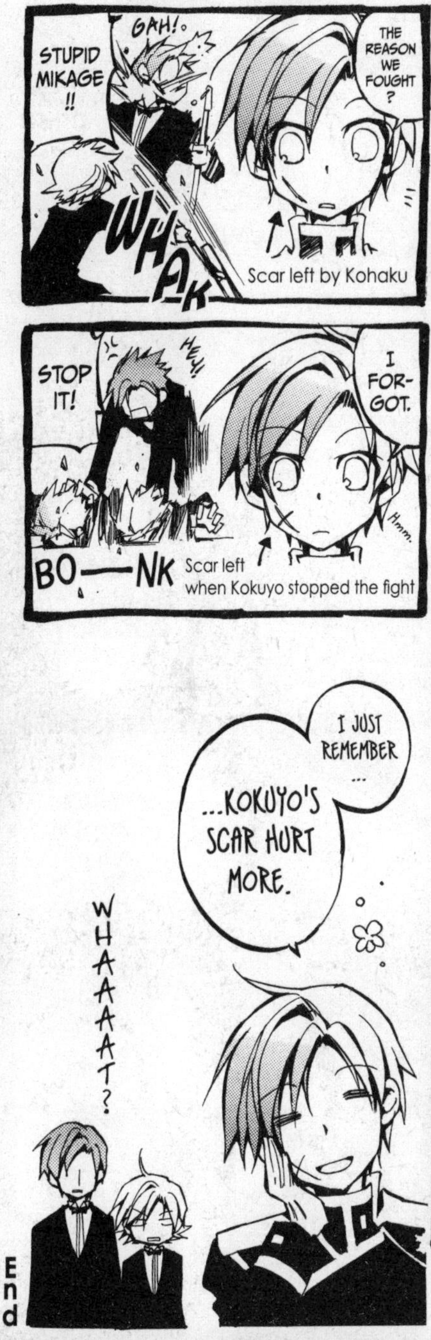
THE REASON WE FOUGHT?
GAH!
STUPID MIKAGE !!
WHAK
Scar left by Kohaku
I FOR-GOT.
HEY!
STOP IT!
Hmm.
BO—NK
Scar left when Kokuyo stopped the fight
I JUST REMEMBER ...
...KOKUYO'S SCAR HURT MORE.
WHAAAAAT?
End

07-Ghost 13 is on sale!

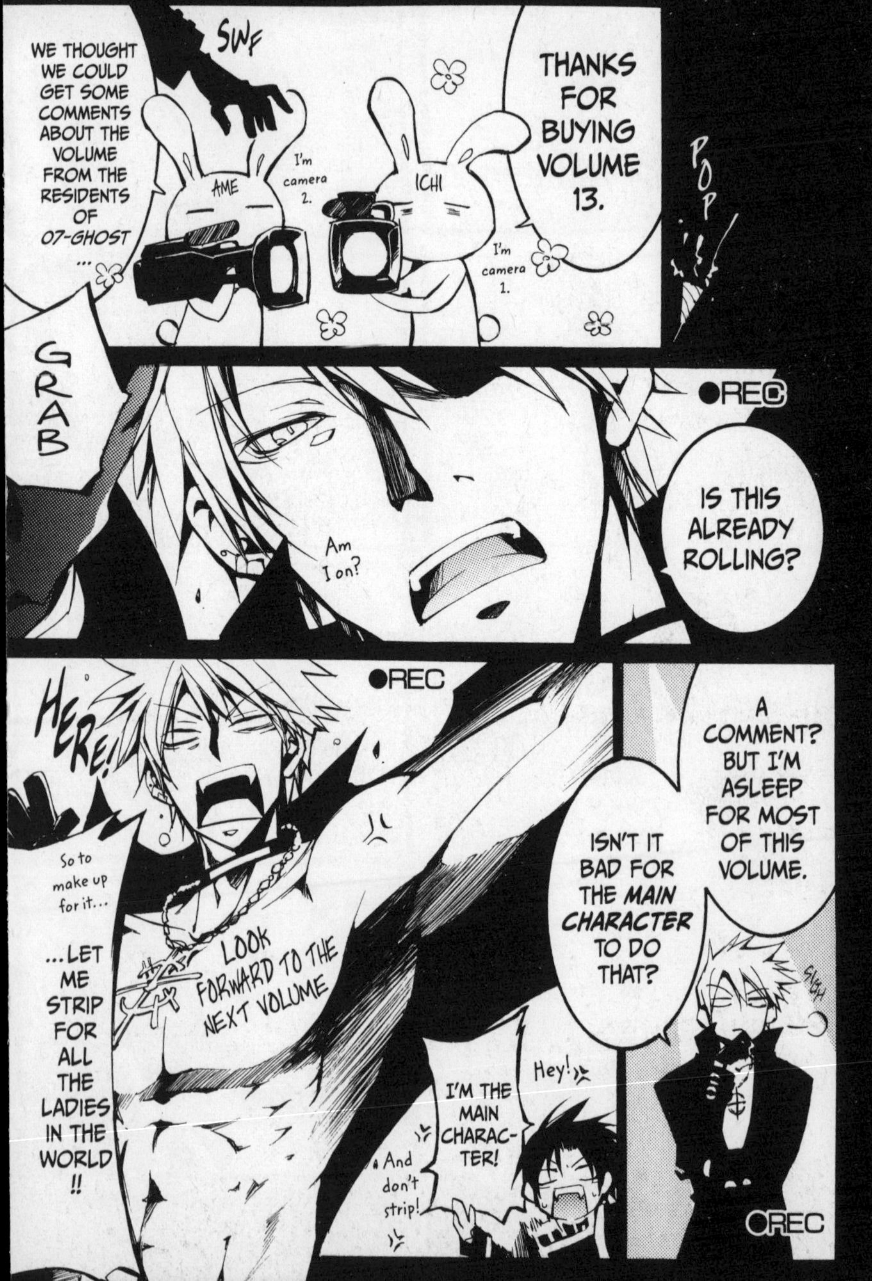

POP
THANKS FOR BUYING VOLUME 13.
I'm camera 1.
I'm camera 2.
SWF
WE THOUGHT WE COULD GET SOME COMMENTS ABOUT THE VOLUME FROM THE RESIDENTS OF 07-GHOST ...
AME
ICHI
●REC
IS THIS ALREADY ROLLING?
Am I on?
GRAB
A COMMENT? BUT I'M ASLEEP FOR MOST OF THIS VOLUME.
ISN'T IT BAD FOR THE *MAIN CHARACTER* TO DO THAT?
SIGH
●REC
HERE!
So to make up for it...
LOOK FORWARD TO THE NEXT VOLUME
...LET ME STRIP FOR ALL THE LADIES IN THE WORLD!!
Hey!
I'M THE MAIN CHARACTER!
And don't strip!
●REC

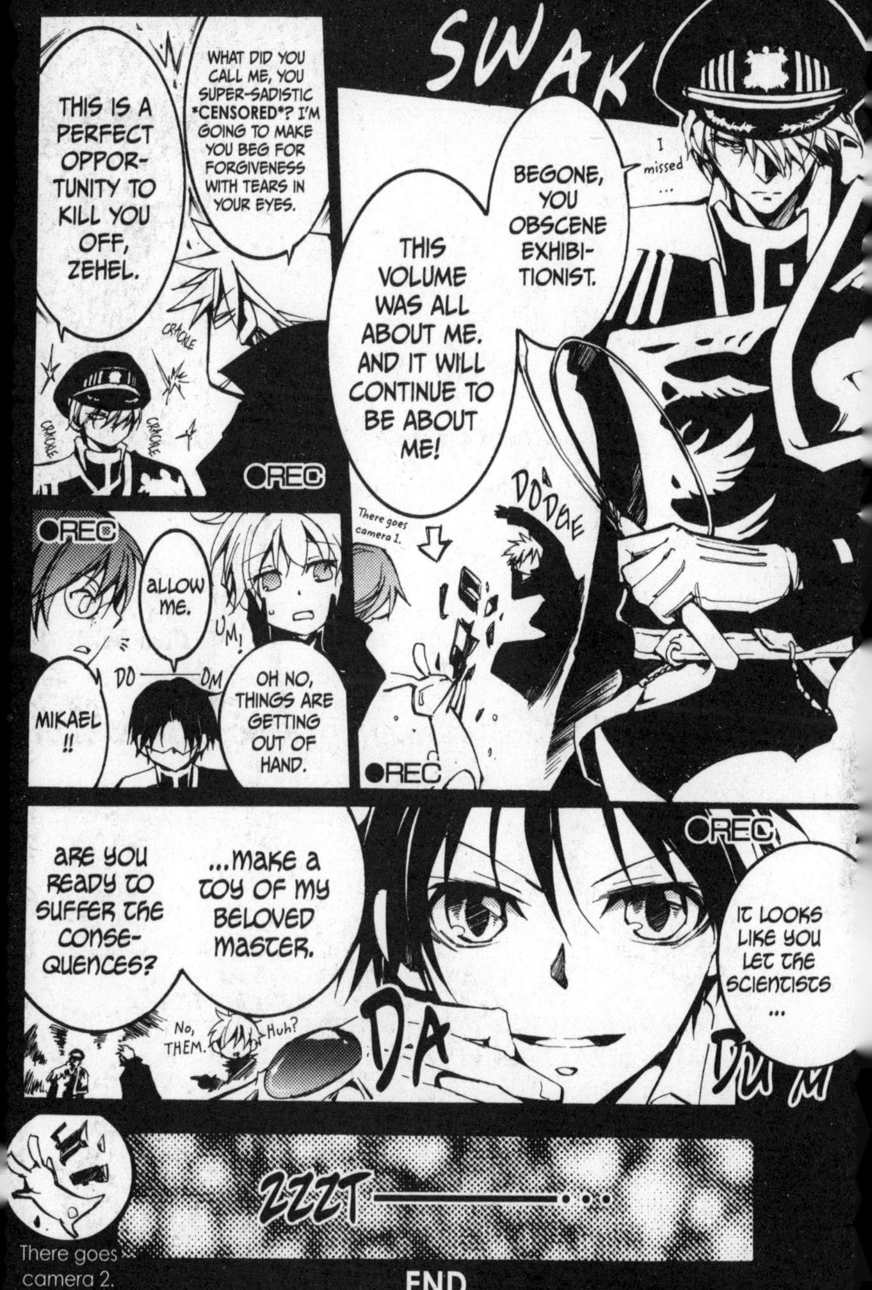
SWAK
I missed...
BEGONE, YOU OBSCENE EXHIBITIONIST.
THIS VOLUME WAS ALL ABOUT ME. AND IT WILL CONTINUE TO BE ABOUT ME!
DODGE
There goes camera 1.
REC
WHAT DID YOU CALL ME, YOU SUPER-SADISTIC *CENSORED*? I'M GOING TO MAKE YOU BEG FOR FORGIVENESS WITH TEARS IN YOUR EYES.
THIS IS A PERFECT OPPORTUNITY TO KILL YOU OFF, ZEHEL.
CRACKLE
CRACKLE
CRACKLE
REC
OH NO, THINGS ARE GETTING OUT OF HAND.
UM!
allow me.
DO—DOM
MIKAEL!!
REC
REC
IT LOOKS LIKE YOU LET THE SCIENTISTS...
...make a toy of my beloved master.
are you ready to suffer the consequences?
DA
DUM
Huh?
No, THEM.
ZZZT—...
There goes camera 2.
END

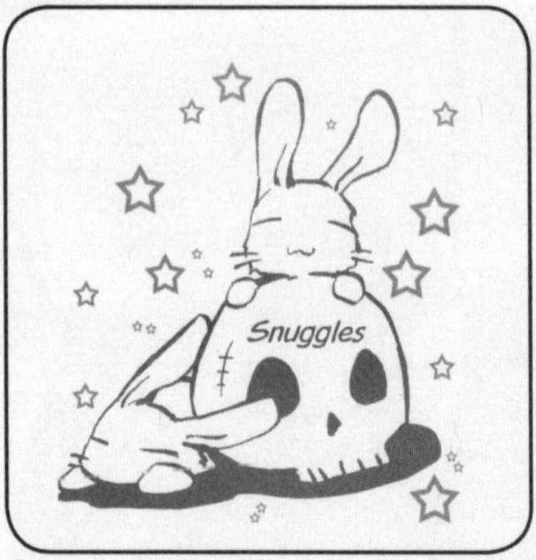
Snuggles

Sometimes we get an urge to make jam and then find ourselves simmering fruit in the middle of the night. Making pectin is a fun challenge, and as long as you have sugar and lemon, you can make jam from almost any fruit. Creating manga takes a long time, so it's nice to feel a sense of accomplishment from smaller projects every now and then.

—Yuki Amemiya & Yukino Ichihara, 2012

Yuki Amemiya was born in Miyagi, Japan, on March 25. Yukino Ichihara was born in Fukushima, Japan, on November 24. Together they write and illustrate *07-Ghost*, the duo's first series. Since its debut in 2005, *07-Ghost* has been translated into a dozen languages, and in 2009 it was adapted into a TV anime series.

07-GHOST

Volume 13

STORY AND ART BY
YUKI AMEMIYA and
YUKINO ICHIHARA

Translation/Satsuki Yamashita
Touch-up Art & Lettering/Vanessa Satone
Design/Yukiko Whitley
Editor/Hope Donovan

07-GHOST © 2011
by Yuki Amemiya/Yukino Ichihara
All rights reserved.
Original Japanese edition published by
ICHIJINSHA, INC., Tokyo.
English translation rights arranged with
ICHIJINSHA, INC.

Printed in Canada

Published by VIZ Media, LLC
P.O. Box 77010
San Francisco, CA 94107

10 9 8 7 6 5 4 3 2 1
First printing, November 2014

PARENTAL ADVISORY
07-GHOST is rated T for Teen and is
recommended for ages 13 and up. This
volume contains realistic and fantasy violence.
ratings.viz.com

www.viz.com

Hey! You're Reading in the Wrong Direction!

This is the end of this graphic novel!

To properly enjoy this VIZ graphic novel, please turn it around and begin reading from right to left. Unlike English, Japanese is read right to left, so Japanese comics are read in reverse order from the way English comics are typically read.

This book has been printed in the original Japanese format in order to preserve the orientation of the original artwork. Have fun with it!

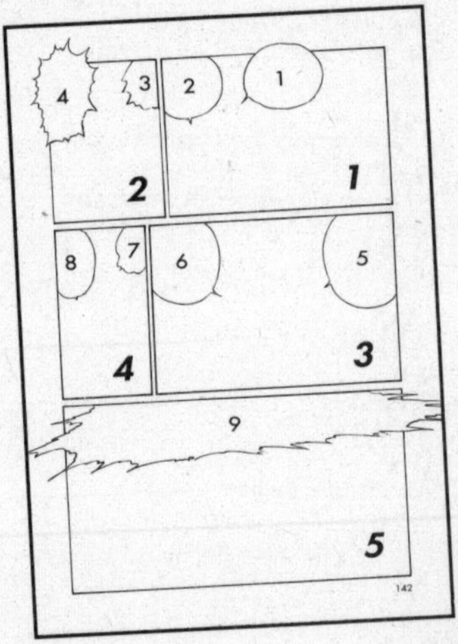
1
2
1
3
4
2
5
6
3
7
8
4
9
5
142

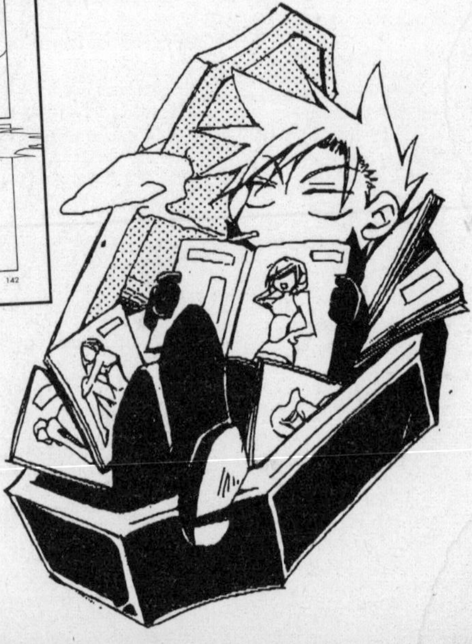

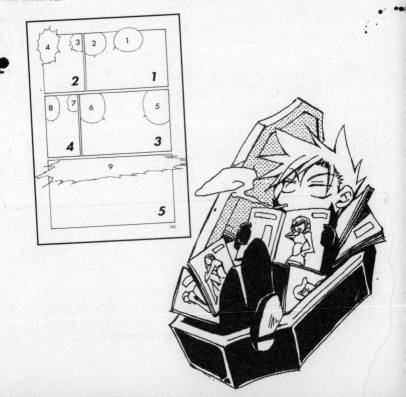